W9-AOD-205

DRAMATIZED FOLK TALES
OF THE WORLD

Dramatized Folk Tales of the World

A collection of 50 one-act plays—royalty-free adaptations of stories from many lands

Edited by

SYLVIA E. KAMERMAN

Publishers   PLAYS, INC.   *Boston*

Contents

DRAMATIZED FOLK TALES
OF THE WORLD

African Trio

Three folk tales from Africa

by Barbara Winther

I. The Fierce Creature

Characters

THREE STORYTELLERS	LEOPARD
STAGEHAND	RHINOCEROS
CATERPILLAR	ELEPHANT
HARE	FROG

BEFORE RISE: THREE STORYTELLERS *enter before curtain and sit on three stools at left.* 2ND STORYTELLER *beats African drum during opening lines.*

1ST STORYTELLER: Listen!

3RD STORYTELLER: Listen!

2ND STORYTELLER: Listen to a continent!

1ST STORYTELLER: Listen!

1ST *and* 2ND STORYTELLERS: Listen!

ALL: Listen to the rhythm. Boom, boom, boom, boom. Boomity boom, boom, boom.

2ND STORYTELLER: African beat! (1ST *and* 3RD STORY-

3

TELLERS *slap thighs.*) Up through your feet! (*All stamp feet.*)

1ST *and* 3RD STORYTELLERS: Telling the folk tales . . .

2ND STORYTELLER: Native, tribal folk tales . . .

ALL: Of—(*They pause, then shout*) Africa! (2ND STORY-TELLER *stops beating drum.*)

1ST STORYTELLER (*Rising*): The story I shall tell you is from Eastern Africa. It is told by the tall Masai who live in the high country of Kenya. It is the story of "The Fierce Creature." (*Curtain opens.*)

* * *

SETTING: *The stage is bare. A slide of East Africa is projected on the screen which serves as a backdrop.*

AT RISE: STAGEHAND *carries in a large cut-out of a Masai house, then exits.*

1ST STORYTELLER: A caterpillar came crawling along, looking for a place to rest. He entered the house of the hare. (*As he speaks,* CATERPILLAR *crawls onstage and enters house.*) When the hare came home he noticed strange marks on the ground in front of his house. (HARE *enters and inspects ground in front of house.*)

HARE (*Shouting*): Who is in my house?

1ST STORYTELLER: The caterpillar did not want to be eaten by the hare, so he answered in a fierce voice.

CATERPILLAR (*From inside house*): I am the terrible warrior, deadlier than the leopard. I crush the rhinoceros to earth and trample the mighty elephant.

1ST STORYTELLER: The hare was most frightened. (HARE *hops about and trembles.*) He didn't know what to do, so when the Leopard came padding by, searching for meat, the hare stopped her. (LEOPARD *roars off left, then enters stealthily, sniffing wind.*)

HARE: There is a fierce creature in my house, leopard. (LEOPARD *crosses to house, sniffing stage.*)

LEOPARD (*Loudly*): Who is in the hare's house?

CATERPILLAR (*Fiercely*): I am the terrible warrior, deadlier than the leopard. I crush the rhinoceros to earth and trample the mighty elephant. (LEOPARD *yelps in fear and hides behind* HARE.)

1ST STORYTELLER: Soon a rhinoceros came charging by on his way to the water hole. (RHINOCEROS *snorts off left, and enters, charging, with his horn lowered.*)

HARE: Can you help me, rhinoceros? There is a fierce creature in my house. (RHINOCEROS *snorts, then charges to* HARE'S *house.*)

RHINOCEROS (*Loudly*): Who is in the hare's house?

CATERPILLAR (*Fiercely*): I am the terrible warrior, deadlier than the leopard. I crush the rhinoceros to earth and trample the mighty elephant. (RHINOCEROS *snorts in fear and hides behind* LEOPARD.)

1ST STORYTELLER: Soon an elephant came lumbering by, looking for bananas. (ELEPHANT *trumpets off left, then lumbers in, pretending to look in trees.*)

HARE: Can you help us, elephant? There is a fierce creature in my house. (ELEPHANT *lumbers to house.*)

ELEPHANT (*Loudly*): Who is in the hare's house?

CATERPILLAR (*Fiercely*): I am the terrible warrior, deadlier than the leopard. I crush the rhinoceros to earth, and trample the mighty elephant. (ELEPHANT *trumpets in fear and hides behind* RHINOCEROS.)

1ST STORYTELLER: Finally, a clever frog came hopping by on his way to catch bugs. (FROG *croaks and enters, hopping.*)

HARE: Frog, can you help me? There is a fierce creature in my house. (FROG *hops to house.*)

FROG: Who is in the hare's house?

CATERPILLAR: I am the terrible warrior, deadlier than the

leopard. I crush the rhinoceros to earth and trample the mighty elephant.

FROG (*Shouting*): I, the hideous leaper, have come. I am slimy, green, and full of great big warts. (CATERPILLAR *squeaks in fear and crawls out of* HARE's *house and off right.*)

CATERPILLAR (*Exiting*): Help! Help! (*Animals watch him go, then fall down laughing.*)

FROG (*Bowing*): Kindly excuse me. I believe I just saw a fierce creature come crawling out of the hare's house. I, the terrible warrior, will pursue him, for my dinner is long past due. (FROG *exits right, hopping.* 1ST STORYTELLER *sits. Curtain.*)

*　　*　　*

II. When the Hare Brought the Sun

Characters

THREE STORYTELLERS	SUN GIRL
HEADMAN	MOON GIRL
STAGEHAND	HARE
CHIEF	PURSUERS

BEFORE RISE: THREE STORYTELLERS *remain seated.* 2ND STORYTELLER *begins to beat drum.*

1ST STORYTELLER: Listen!

3RD STORYTELLER: Listen!

2ND STORYTELLER: Listen to a continent.

1ST STORYTELLER: Listen!

1ST *and* 3RD STORYTELLER: Listen!

ALL: Listen to the rhythm. Boom, boom, boom, boom. Boomity boom, boom, boom.

2ND STORYTELLER: African beat! African beat! (1ST *and*
3RD STORYTELLERS *slap thighs.*) Up through your feet!
(*All stamp feet.*)

1ST *and* 3RD STORYTELLERS: Telling the folk tales . . .

2ND STORYTELLER: Native, tribal folk tales . . .

ALL: Of—(*Pause, then shout*) Africa! (*Drum stops.*)

2ND STORYTELLER (*Rising*): I shall tell another story of the
hare. It is told among the tribes who live on the flat
grasslands of the veld in Southern Africa. It is called,
"When the Hare Brought the Sun." (*Curtain opens.*)

*   *   *

SETTING: *Bare stage. A view of South Africa is projected
on the screen.*

AT RISE: 2ND STORYTELLER *begins narration.*

2ND STORYTELLER: In the early days when the earth had
no sun or moon, the hare took his musical instrument,
called the mbira, and climbed up a giant spider web
to visit the great country which was up there. (HARE
*enters, playing mbira, or another simple stringed instru-
ment.*) He came to the village, seeking shelter. (STAGE-
HAND *carries on cutout of veld house, then exits.*)

HARE (*Looking at house, then calling loudly*): Where is
the chief?

HEADMAN (*Entering right*): I am the headman of this
village. Why do you wish to see the chief?

HARE: I will play my instrument for him if he gives me
shelter.

HEADMAN (*Calling off right*): Great chief, there is a hare
who comes to our village playing the mbira. He seeks
shelter.

CHIEF (*Entering right; to HARE*): Play for me. (HARE *plays instrument and dances.*) You play well. I shall give you lodging in this house. (CHIEF *points to house.*)

HARE: Thank you. I have had a tiring journey. It will be good to rest. (CHIEF *and* HEADMAN *exit.* HARE *enters house.*)

2ND STORYTELLER: That evening the hare looked out of his door and saw a girl sitting in front of two large pots. (MOON GIRL *enters right with a large red pot and a large yellow pot. She sits, and places pots before her.* HARE *peers out of door and watches. Suddenly,* SUN GIRL *enters, running, carrying a large red disc.*)

SUN GIRL: I bring the sun back from our sky. (*Puts disc into red pot.*)

MOON GIRL: Then it is time for me to hang out the moon. (*Takes yellow disc from yellow pot and exits.*)

SUN GIRL: It is time for me to go to bed. (*Yawns and exits.*)

HARE (*Creeping out of house*): It would be a fine thing for my world below to have some of that sun. (*He takes red disc from red pot and tears off a piece of it.*) I'll climb back down the spider web to earth. (*Runs off right*)

2ND STORYTELLER: The next morning the two girls returned.

MOON GIRL (*Entering left with yellow disc*): It is time for me to rest. (*Puts yellow disc into yellow pot*)

SUN GIRL (*Entering*): It is time for me to hang out the sun. (*Reaches into red pot*) Something is wrong with the sun! (*Pulls out torn disc*) Look! Part of it is missing. Someone has stolen part of the sun! (HEADMAN *and* CHIEF *rush on from right.*)

CHIEF: How dare anybody do such a thing?

HEADMAN (*Looking at ground and pointing*): It must have been the hare. These are his footprints.

CHIEF: We shall follow him. (CHIEF *and* HEADMAN *exit*

left, running. SUN GIRL *and* MOON GIRL *follow, carrying pots. House is removed.*)

2ND STORYTELLER: The chief and his headman climbed down the great spider web to earth, and called together the animals to pursue the hare. (HARE *enters left and runs across stage in "slow motion."* CHIEF, HEADMAN *and* PURSUERS—*animals from first play—enter left in single file and move after* HARE, *also in "slow motion."*) As the pursuers drew closer, the hare threw the three-spiked devil thorns across his trail. (HARE *pantomimes throwing thorns.* CHIEF, HEADMAN *and* PURSUERS *cry out in pain as they step on "thorns," rub feet or paws, and continue to track* HARE.) The hare pulled down huge vines to block his path. (HARE *pantomimes pulling down vines, and others pantomime fighting through them.*) The hare caused a great rain to wash away his footprints. (HARE *points to sky and others cover heads with hands, peering closer to ground.*) The hare came to a stream. He lay down and turned into a log. (HARE *lies down and remains motionless.*)

CHIEF (*Stopping and looking around*): I don't see the hare's footprints anymore.

HEADMAN: Neither do I.

1ST PURSUER (*Sniffing*): We don't smell him, either.

CHIEF: I guess we've lost him. Come on, let's go home. (*In single file,* CHIEF, HEADMAN *and* PURSUERS *pretend to walk across "log" and exit.* HARE *jumps up and leaps for joy.*)

2ND STORYTELLER: So the hare gave the sun to the earth, and we have had it ever since that day. (HARE *waves "sun" as curtains close.*)

*   *   *

III. The Princess Who Was
Hidden from the World

Characters

THREE STORYTELLERS	SERVANT GIRL
OLD CHIEF	EMISSARY
PRINCESS	PROPERTY GIRL
YOUNG CHIEF	

BEFORE RISE: 2ND STORYTELLER *beats drum.*

1ST STORYTELLER: Listen!

3RD STORYTELLER: Listen!

2ND STORYTELLER: Listen to a continent.

1ST STORYTELLER: Listen!

1ST *and* 3RD STORYTELLERS: Listen!

ALL: Listen to the rhythm. Boom, boom, boom, boom. Boomity boom, boom, boom.

2ND STORYTELLER: African beat! African beat! (1ST *and* 3RD STORYTELLERS *slap thighs.*) Up through your feet! (*All stamp feet.*)

1ST *and* 3RD STORYTELLERS: Telling the folk tales . . .

2ND STORYTELLER: Native, tribal folk tales . . .

ALL: Of—(*Pause, then shout*) Africa! (*Drum stops.*)

3RD STORYTELLER (*Standing*): The story I shall tell you is from Western Africa. It is told by the Vai tribe in the rain forests of Liberia. The name of the story is "The Princess Who Was Hidden from the World." (*Curtains open.*)

*   *   *

SETTING: *Slide of Liberia is projected on screen. Liberian house is at right.*

AT RISE: OLD CHIEF *enters.*

3RD STORYTELLER: There was an old chief who was very good but not very wise. He had a beautiful daughter. (PRINCESS *enters and stands by* OLD CHIEF.) Although she was well trained in being a princess (PRINCESS *poses gracefully.*), she was kept hidden away from the world. (OLD CHIEF *puts his hand over his daughter's eyes and peers about suspiciously.*) The young chief of another tribe heard about this lovely girl. (YOUNG CHIEF *and* EMISSARY *enter at left.*) He sent an emissary with gifts and an offer of marriage. (YOUNG CHIEF *pantomimes handing gifts to* EMISSARY, *who staggers under their weight, then crosses to* OLD CHIEF.) The old chief agreed to the marriage. (OLD CHIEF *nods happily as he examines gifts.* EMISSARY *exits left.*) He called for a servant girl to take his daughter to marry the young tribal chief. (OLD CHIEF *beckons off right.* SERVANT GIRL *enters and takes* PRINCESS's *hand.* OLD CHIEF *smiles happily and exits.*) The servant girl and the princess traveled through the rain forest. (PRINCESS *follows* SERVANT GIRL *offstage.* PROPERTY GIRL *enters, carrying long blue streamers, and stands at center.*)

PRINCESS (*Entering and seeing waterfall*): Look! The water is flowing down over the rocks. What is this?

SERVANT (*Following her*): It is a waterfall.

PRINCESS: Tell me about it.

SERVANT (*Sadly*): I can only tell you the story for a price. If I told you the story for nothing you would become terribly ill.

PRINCESS: What is the price?

SERVANT: Your sandals.

PRINCESS (*Taking off sandals*): Take them. (*They exchange sandals.*)

3RD STORYTELLER: Then the servant girl told the story of how the waterfall flowed down to join a big river, and how the river flowed out to join the big ocean. The princess was amazed, and she walked on through the rain forest, thinking of all she had heard. (PRINCESS *and* SERVANT GIRL *exit, followed by* PROPERTY GIRL, *who re-enters with cutout of a palm tree.*)

PRINCESS (*Re-entering; seeing tree*): What is this?

SERVANT (*Following*): It is a palm tree.

PRINCESS: Tell me about it.

SERVANT: I can only tell you the story for a price.

PRINCESS: What is the price?

SERVANT: Your headdress.

PRINCESS: Here. (*Gives headdress to* SERVANT *to wear.*)

3RD STORYTELLER: Then the servant girl told the story of palm trees and many other trees, and how some bore delicious fruit and others gave their wood. The princess was amazed, and she walked on through the rain forest, thinking of all she had heard. (PRINCESS *and* SERVANT GIRL *exit, followed by* PROPERTY GIRL, *who re-enters with model of a peacock.*)

PRINCESS (*Re-entering*): What is this beautiful creature?

SERVANT (*Following her*): It is a peacock.

PRINCESS: Tell me about it.

SERVANT (*Sadly*): I can only tell you the story for a price.

PRINCESS: What is the price?

SERVANT: Your royal cloak and jewels.

PRINCESS: Take them. (*Hands cloak and jewels to* SERVANT GIRL, *who puts them on.*)

3RD STORYTELLER: The servant girl told the princess all about peacocks and other animals, those that flew, those that swam, those that crawled, and those that ran. The princess was amazed, and she walked on through the rain forest, thinking of all she had heard. (PRINCESS *exits, followed by* SERVANT GIRL *and* PROPERTY GIRL, *who re-enters with cutout of a rainbow.*)

PRINCESS (*Re-entering, followed by* SERVANT GIRL): What is that beautiful sight in the sky?

SERVANT GIRL: It is a rainbow.

PRINCESS: Tell me about it.

SERVANT: This is the greatest secret of all, so the price is the most.

PRINCESS: What is the price?

SERVANT: You must promise never to tell that you are a princess and I am a servant girl.

PRINCESS: I agree.

3RD STORYTELLER: Then the servant girl told the story of the sun shining through the water in the sky. She told about the clouds and the storms and the white, cold powder that fell on the high mountains far to the east. The princess was amazed, and she walked on to the village, thinking of all she had heard. (PRINCESS *and* SERVANT GIRL *exit, followed by* PROPERTY GIRL, *who re-enters with Liberian house and stands it at left.* YOUNG CHIEF *enters left and stands by house.*) When the princess and the servant girl came to the village, the young chief mistook the servant girl for the princess, and he married her. (PRINCESS *and* SERVANT GIRL *enter right and cross to* YOUNG CHIEF, *who beckons to* SERVANT GIRL *to follow. They exit into house.*) Even though the real princess was treated as a servant and had to crush casava roots and rice all day long, she was so kind and good that everybody loved her. (PRINCESS *pantomimes pounding roots.*) But the servant girl acted as she thought a princess should. She was selfish and cruel, and everybody disliked her. (SERVANT GIRL *struts out of house, pretends to kick* PRINCESS, *and struts around with her nose in the air.* PRINCESS *exits.*) Several years later, the father of the real princess came to the village to visit his daughter. (OLD CHIEF *enters.* SERVANT GIRL *sees him and runs to hide in house.* YOUNG CHIEF *enters and shakes hands with* OLD CHIEF.)

OLD CHIEF: Where is my daughter?

Young Chief (*Pointing to house*): In there, and I would be most happy if you would take her away.

Old Chief (*Peering into house*): That is not my daughter!

Young Chief: That is not your daughter? (Princess *enters. Seeing* Old Chief, *she kneels at his feet.*)

Old Chief: This is my daughter!

Young Chief: That is your daughter? I've been deceived. (*He pulls* Servant Girl *out of house and shoos her off left. To* Princess) You shall be my wife. (*He enters house and* Princess *follows him.*)

Old Chief: Now I realize that I should have taught my daughter more about the world! I'm a wiser man than I was when I left my village. (*Taps head and exits. Curtains close.* Storytellers *exit, dancing and beating drum.*)

THE END

The Secret of the Wishing Well

An Austrian folk tale

by Eleanor D. Leuser

Characters

ELF	FAT WOMAN
SUSAN	MISER
TOMMY	KING
ELSA	TWO COURTIERS
HANS	WISE MAN
RICHARD	CHILD
JON	TWO GIRLS
RITA	BALLET DANCERS
CARL	MUSICIAN

TIME: *Long ago in Austria.*

SETTING: *A roadside.*

AT RISE: ELF *is standing beside the wishing well talking to* TOMMY *and* SUSAN. SUSAN *is carrying a doll, and* TOMMY *a hammer.*

SUSAN (*To* ELF): This must be a very curious kind of well.

TOMMY (*Tapping it with his hammer*): It looks pretty old. If it needs fixing, maybe I could do it.

ELF (*Quickly*): Oh, no, don't touch it. As I told you before, it's a Wishing Well, and it works just once a year

15

—tonight on Magic Eve. Take a leaf from that tree, say a wish over it, throw it into the well, and there you are. Sometime in the future your wish will come true.

SUSAN: But you said we must wish only for something that we think will make us happy.

TOMMY: Yes, how do we know what will make us happy when we're grown up? That's a long way off.

SUSAN: Something that seems good now might be pretty silly, then.

ELF: There's a secret to making the right kind of wish. If you catch on to the secret, your wish will be pretty sure to make you happy.

TOMMY: But how will we find out the secret? How do other people know what to wish?

ELF: That's the trouble. Lots of times people don't know the right wish to bring them happiness, and then they're never satisfied.

SUSAN: I wish we could hear other people's wishes before we had to wish. We might get some ideas from them.

TOMMY: Yes, then maybe we wouldn't make a mistake.

ELF: I'll tell you what I'll do. You're pretty smart children. Why don't you hide behind this tree and listen to the next people who come along? You might catch on to the secret of making the right kind of wish. Anyway, you can see what *not* to do. (*Looks off*) Somebody's coming now. Run, hide! (*He pushes them behind tree, as* HANS *enters, followed by* ELSA, *who is eating a large cake.* ELF *approaches them.*)

ELF: It's Magic Eve, good folk. Stop at our Wishing Well and throw in some wishes for the future.

HANS (*Laughing*): Sounds like a good idea, my friend. How do we do it?

ELF: Think hard of what will bring you happiness in the future. (*He hands each of them a leaf.*) Take this leaf, wish on it, then throw it into the well. Because it's Magic Eve your wishes will come true.

HANS: Go first, Elsa. What do you wish?

ELSA (*Eating her cake as she steps up to well*): I know exactly what I want. Lots and lots of cream cakes to eat every single day. That is my wish. (*She throws leaf into well and steps to one side.*)

HANS (*Stepping up*): It's easy for me to wish, too. Look, Elf (*Turns out his pockets*) —not a cent in my pockets, not even to buy a cream cake for myself. (*Slowly*) I wish for money—lots of money—so much money that I never can count it all. (*He throws leaf into well.*)

ELF: All right. Now just wait twenty years or so. Your wishes will come true.

HANS (*Laughing as he and* ELSA *go left*): See that they do, Elf. Lots of good things to eat for Elsa, and plenty of money for me. Don't forget. (*They go off.* TOMMY *and* SUSAN *come out from behind tree.*)

ELF: They don't believe their wishes will come true.

TOMMY: And will they?

ELF: They really will! (*Looks off*) Here comes someone else. Hide! (TOMMY *and* SUSAN *jump back behind tree, as* JON *and* RICHARD *enter.* JON *carries a large pile of books. They are quarreling.*)

JON: I tell you, I don't want to go with you, Richard. Let me alone. I just want peace and quiet to read my books.

RICHARD (*Pulling at* JON): Don't be stupid. If you do what I tell you, we can get others to follow us and we will have the biggest and best gang around. We'll be the leaders.

JON (*Pulling away*): But I don't want to be the leader of a gang. I just want to read my books.

ELF (*Stepping toward them*): Pardon me. Perhaps I can

help you. Each of you wants something and with a little wishing, you can have it.

RICHARD (*Suspiciously*): How could you help us?

ELF (*Handing each of them a leaf*): This is Magic Eve. If you take a leaf, wish on it and throw it into the Magic Well here (*Pointing*), your wishes will come true—some time in the future.

RICHARD (*Taking leaf, gruffly*): Probably a lot of foolishness, but I'll try it. (*Holds leaf over well*) I wish everybody to obey my commands at once. (*Throws leaf into well*) Now, we'll see if I get my wish, Elf, or—if your magic is just a piece of rubbish. (*He exits.*)

JON (*Coming forward timidly*): I just want to know everything that's in books, sir.

ELF (*Curiously*): What will you do with all that knowledge?

JON: Do I have to do anything with it? I'll be happy just to know about everything.

ELF: A kind of walking encyclopedia, eh? Well, go ahead and wish.

JON (*Holding leaf over well*): I wish I could know everything in these books. (JON *drops leaf into well, goes off.* TOMMY *and* SUSAN *come out from behind tree.*)

ELF: You see how many different things people wish for?

SUSAN: Will all their wishes come true?

ELF: They will. Now you two must think of some good wishes for yourselves. (*Looking off*) Wait a minute— here come some others you can watch. Hide quickly. (TOMMY *and* SUSAN *run behind tree, as* RITA *and* CARL *enter.* CARL *is playing a mouth organ, and* RITA *is dancing to the music. They stop in front of* ELF.)

RITA: Who are you, funny little man?

CARL: Don't you know, silly? He's the Elf of the Wishing Well. You can see him only on Magic Eve, when you can make a wish for the future.

ELF (*Bowing*): That's right. Just take one of these leaves, wish on it, throw it into the well, and your wish will come true. Now, little dancing lady and young sir, make a wish for your future happiness. (*Hands each of them a leaf*)

RITA (*Pirouetting and taking leaf*): Oh, what fun, Elf! I know exactly what I want. (*Holding leaf high over well*) I wish that I may be able to dance so well that everyone who sees my dancing will be happy.

CARL: Bravo, Rita, that is a good wish, and I have one to go with it. (*Looking at leaf and speaking earnestly*) I wish that someday I may be able to play such wonderful music that it will bring joy to the hearts of all who hear it. (*Throws leaf into well*) Come, Rita, let's start practicing for that great day, now. (*He starts playing a gay little tune, and* RITA *dances in time, as they go off.*)

ELF (*Beckoning to* TOMMY *and* SUSAN): You can come out now. I don't see anyone else coming. Are you ready to wish for yourselves? You must have heard enough to give you some ideas.

TOMMY (*Coming out with* SUSAN): We heard, all right. But most of them didn't act as if it were important.

SUSAN: Wishing for something to make you happy in the future is important. I wish I could see how their wishes turned out.

TOMMY: So do I.

ELF: Because it's Magic Eve, maybe I can do something about that. If you'll keep very quiet, I'll say some magic words and you can see these same people in the future after their wishes have come true.

SUSAN: Oh, how wonderful!

TOMMY: I'd like that.

ELF: Well, just watch quietly, then. There were six who wished, weren't there? Let's see if you can recognize them. (*Makes a sweeping motion with his hands*) Aldebaran, Aldebaray. Let us look forward many a day. (*Lights dim briefly, then spotlight shines on* FAT WOMAN.)

TOMMY (*To* SUSAN, *who is watching with him down front*): I'll bet that's the girl who liked cream cakes and wished for things to eat.

ELF: Hush, she's going to speak.

FAT WOMAN: More . . . Bring me more. I never get enough to eat. There should be more than three meals a day. I need more food. Bring me more to eat. I'm still hungry. (*Light dims,* FAT WOMAN *exits, music plays in background. Then spotlight shines on old* MISER, *who sits at table, counting piles of gold coins.*)

SUSAN (*Excitedly*): That's the boy who wanted money!

ELF: Listen!

MISER (*Counting money*): 1 . . . 2 . . . 3 . . . 4 . . . ah, where is that other piece of gold? There it is. See . . . lovely gold, beautiful gold! How can I add to my precious gold? Beautiful gold, I will keep you locked up where no one can see you but myself. (*He begins counting again, as the light slowly dims, and music comes up loud. Music fades and spotlight shines on* KING, *seated.* COURTIER *stands on each side.*)

KING (*To* COURTIERS): How many prisoners do we have now?

1ST COURTIER: One hundred, Sire, of the most noble blood.

2ND COURTIER: More are put in jail every day, Your Majesty. They say they would rather lose their heads than obey your orders to spy on their friends.

KING: Then execute them at once.

1ST COURTIER (*Anxiously*): But, Sire, if you keep on executing people, there will be no one left to obey you.

2ND COURTIER: The people are already muttering against your orders, and I fear there will be an uprising.

KING: Do what I say. Execute everybody who will not obey

my will. I will not stop till I have conquered the whole world even though I stand alone. (*Light dims. Music comes up, then fades. Lights come up again on empty stage.*)

TOMMY (*Slowly*): He was the boy who wanted power. He got it but he looks pretty unhappy. Everybody must hate him.

SUSAN: Oh, do you remember the boy with the books? Look, there he is now. (WISE MAN *enters, carrying many books. He sits down and puts his pile of books beside him. He is reading as* CHILD *enters with a flower.*)

CHILD: See this flower, Wise Man. Isn't it beautiful?

WISE MAN (*Impatiently*): Yes, yes, but do not bother me, child. Do you not see that I have much to read?

CHILD: But its perfume is so sweet. Here, smell it.

WISE MAN (*Pushing* CHILD *away*): No, no. Run away, child. I have much more important things to do than look at flowers. Go. (CHILD *runs out and* TWO GIRLS *enter.*)

1ST GIRL: The day is so lovely, Wise Man. Come with us and watch us dance and play.

WISE MAN (*Sadly*): I have no time for play. All these many years I have read and read, and yet I fear my life will not be long enough to finish all the books.

2ND GIRL: But life is passing you by while you read your books, old man. Come. We will show you the beautiful world.

WISE MAN: I cannot. Leave me to my books. I must finish them before it is too late. Go and enjoy yourselves. (*They exit, and he goes back to reading, as the spot dims and music changes to dance time. Spot now shines on ballet group dancing in. At the end of their dance, a* SOLO DANCER *dances in, and others form circle. They applaud as she finishes.*)

SUSAN: That's Rita, the little girl who danced. Isn't she lovely! Hear how they applaud.

TOMMY: She looks happy, too. I'll bet everyone likes her.

ELF: Look, here comes the boy who played the mouth organ. See what you think of him now. (*As the dancers move to one side,* CARL *enters. He is playing a violin or pretending to play it as the real music is played offstage. All join in applause, then spotlight fades, music stops. Lights go up on stage, which is empty except for* TOMMY, SUSAN, *and* ELF.)

SUSAN: Oh, that was wonderful! Do you know something? Carl and Rita were the only two who looked really happy with their wishes.

ELF: That's because only those who give happiness ever really find happiness for themselves. Do you know what to wish for now?

TOMMY (*Slowly*): Yes, I think I do. I want to make things with my hands—lots of things. I'll keep on learning as I grow older, for I want to be a builder. I want to be a good builder, so that other people will want to cross my bridges or use my roads or live in my houses. Then they will be happy.

SUSAN: I know how to wish, too. I want to take care of people as I take care of my doll or my kitty. If they're sick, I'll make them well. If they're sad I'll make them laugh. But I'll love them most of all. Will that do, Elf?

ELF: Indeed it will. You two have really learned the secret of right wishing. Come, take your leaves and make your wishes for the future. On Magic Eve much is possible. I will see that your wishes come true. I know that they will bring you happiness. (*Each takes a leaf and is holding it over the Wishing Well, saying his wish as the curtain falls.*)

THE END

Lady Moon and the Thief

A Chinese fantasy

by Claire Boiko

Characters

BOW-LOW, *the storyteller*
WONG ⎤
LING ⎬ *fishermen*
MING ⎦
NID-NOD, *the sage*
AH ME, *his servant*
CHOW, *the farmer*

LORD SUN
LADY MOON
CHANG, *the thief*
GONG HO, *the gong player*
DING, *the xylophonist*
VILLAGERS
TWO PROPERTY BOYS

TIME: *Long ago in China.*
SETTING: *Ting-a-ling, a village in ancient China.*
AT RISE: *At center on a platform there is a blue pagoda, on top of which stands* LORD SUN, *holding a golden shield downward.* VILLAGERS *are seated around the pagoda, holding fans. At left, sitting on a bridge over a pond, are* WONG, LING, *and* MING, *fishing with long poles. Up right,* CHOW *kneels at edge of rice paddy. There is a basket of rice shoots beside him. Down right, under a pine tree,* NID-NOD *sits at a low tea table, while* AH ME *holds a long-handled fan over him. At left,* GONG HO, *with his gong, sits crosslegged on a silk pillow, and* DING, *with his xylophone, sits on a pillow at right. At*

23

*the back, on each side of the pagoda are Day Screens
painted with trees, sky, birds, etc., and next to each
screen stands a* PROPERTY BOY. *All hold their poses.
Oriental music is heard as* BOW-LOW *enters, and bows
to audience. He carries a scroll from which he reads.*

BOW-LOW: Honorable ladies and gentlemen, please observe before your eyes the humble village of Ting-a-ling.
It is not Ting-a-ling now; it is Ting-a-ling of a thousand
years ago. Before electric light, before candlelight, before—yes, even before moonlight. Why did the lovely
moon decide to shine upon such a small, insignificant
place as Ting-a-ling? Please turn your ears to me, and I
will bring this picture to life, so you will know why the
moon came to Ting-a-ling. (GONG HO *rings the gong
once softly.*) Here, upon the topmost ridge of the blue
pagoda, is the ruler of the sky (*Gong sounds again.*),
Lord Sun. (LORD SUN *lifts his shield half-way up.*) It is
morning. Chow, the farmer, is planting shoots of rice.
(CHOW *begins to move, taking rice shoots from basket
and putting them in the ground.*) Nid-Nod, the resident
sage, has begun to think. (NID-NOD *smiles and nods
slowly.*) His servant, Ah Me, fans him. (AH ME *slowly
fans his master.*) The three fishermen, Wong, Ling, and
Ming, cast their lines for glittering carp. (*They bob
their poles up and down slowly.*) The villagers sit in the
shade of the blue pagoda and gossip.

VILLAGERS (*Fluttering fans slowly and chanting rhythmi-
cally in unison*): Chitter-chatter-talk-talk. Chitter-chatter-talk-talk. Talk-talk-chitter-chatter. Chitter-chatter-
talk-talk.

BOW-LOW (*Wiping his brow*): Whew, Lord Sun is strong
today. (LORD SUN *raises his shield above his head. All
wipe their brows.*)

ALL: Whew!

Bow-Low: But is this not excellent? A strong sun will make the rice grow faster. (Chow *plants faster*.) And the fish leap. (*Fishermen bob their poles more rapidly*.) And the sage think deeper. (Nid-Nod *nods quickly*.) And his servant earn his wages. (Ah Me *fans faster*.) And the villagers will have the most lively conversations in the shadow of the pagoda.

Villagers (*Fanning rapidly and chanting very fast*): Chitter-chatter-talk-talk. Chitter-chatter-talk-talk. Talk-talk. Chitter-chatter-talk-talk. Talk-talk-chitter-chatter. Chitter-chatter-talk-talk.

Bow-Low: Afternoon comes. Lord Sun grows weary. (Lord Sun *puts his shield down slowly. As he does so, all work slower and slower and finally stop*.) It is the time of the darkening of the sky. (Gong Ho *sounds his gong once.* Property Boys *take a dark cloak from behind screen and put it around* Lord Sun, *who puts his shield under the cloak*) It is the time of the going-down of Lord Sun. (Gong Ho *sounds his gong twice. All stand and bow toward* Lord Sun. Property Boys *assist him down from pagoda. He stands behind it.* Property Boys *slide the Day Screens off into the wings, revealing the Night Screens in place behind them.* Gong Ho *sounds his gong a third time*.) It is night. Deep, dark night. (*All face front again, sit, and put their hands to the side of their faces, closing their eyes. They hold the pose while slow oriental music is played. After a few bars,* Chang *peers from behind pagoda.* Gong Ho *beats gong softly and steadily like a warning.* Chang *sidles to center and looks about with satisfaction*.) Ah . . . who is this? Who is this who slithers and sidles and slinks in the darkness? (Bow-Low *stands down left*.)

Chang (*Bowing to audience*): I am Chang. Chang the dishonorable. Chang, the thief. Please to watch Chang's nimble fingers like darting minnows. (*He swiftly plucks*

the fans from the laps of the sleeping VILLAGERS.) Please
to notice Chang's fancy footwork, soft as kitten in the
snow. (CHANG *dances over to* CHOW *and takes his basket, slipping the fans in, then he runs to the bridge.*)
Please to enjoy Chang's artistic pole-snatching. (*He
takes the poles from the sleeping fishermen, then steals
the large fan from* AH ME *and the tea cups from* NID-
NOD. *He puts everything into basket, then goes down
center and bows.*) Was that not first-class thievery?
Please do not applaud. It might wake up the villagers.
Did you see how the darkness helped me? (*He bows to
Night Screens.*) Thank you, friend darkness, for making
me the shadow of a shadow. May you always keep midnight over the eyes of the people so that Chang may
become the number one thief of China. (*He looks left
and right, then darts to the pool, dips his hand in and
pulls out a large gold carp, putting it, too, into basket.
He then runs off right, as* PROPERTY BOYS *push in Day
Screens and* LORD SUN, *without cloak, his shield raised,
mounts to the top of the pagoda.* GONG HO *rings the
gong urgently. All except* NID-NOD, *who remains sound
asleep, rub their eyes and stretch, then discover their
losses.*)

ALL (*Waving hands in the air*): Help! Help! Help! A
thief! A thief!

WONG: Help! The fishing poles are gone!

LING: Quite gone.

MING: Help! The golden carp is gone!

LING: Quite gone.

ALL: Everything is gone! Quite gone!

CHOW: What shall we do?

ALL: What shall we do?

WONG: Ask Nid-Nod—

VILLAGERS: Yes, ask the sage.

ALL: Yes, ask Nid-Nod, the wise man. Help us, Nid-Nod. (NID-NOD *remains asleep.*)

AH ME: I am sorry. Nid-Nod cannot help you. Look for yourselves.

ALL (*Shading eyes and looking at* NID-NOD): Asleep!

CHOW: Asleep! In the middle of the day. Wake up, Nid-Nod.

AH ME: Nid-Nod is not here. He is enjoying a voyage to the back of his mind. He will return to the front of his mind when the leaves are falling.

ALL: Oh! Who will help us? Who?

AH ME: I will help you.

CHOW: You? Are you an ancient sage?

WONG: You? Are you a wise man?

AH ME: I am not ancient. I am not wise. But I have a head on my shoulders and it thinks sometimes. Listen—

ALL (*Putting hands to right ears*): We listen.

AH ME: This wicked thief who stole our treasures comes covered from head to toe in darkness. Therefore, we cannot see him. Therefore, we cannot catch him. Therefore—

ALL: Therefore—

AH ME: Therefore, we need a light. A light at night.

ALL: A light at night!

CHOW: A welcome sight.

LING: Where shall we find this light at night?

AH ME: The Lord Sun has light and light to spare. Ask him to send you a little globe of glow. A little ball of brightness. (*All turn to* LORD SUN *and chant.*)

ALL:

Great Lord Sun, burnished bright,
Send to us a light at night.

(GONG HO *strikes the gong softly.* PROPERTY BOYS *put the dark robe on* LORD SUN. *He covers his shield and goes behind the pagoda.* PROPERTY BOYS *remove Day Screens.*)

CHOW: Did he hear us?

MING: Did he listen?

VILLAGERS: Did he heed our plea?

AH ME: Look up. (*All look at pagoda.*) Look higher, higher. Look up. Look up and see. (DING *plays a gentle arpeggio on the xylophone, as* LADY MOON, *dressed in silver with two silver fans, appears on the top of the pagoda.*)

ALL (*Bowing*): Ah, how beautiful. A silver maiden.

LADY MOON (*Motioning with a fan*): Good evening.

CHOW (*In awe*): What shall we call you, silver lady of the sky?

LADY MOON: You may call me Lady Moon. I am the consort of the great Lord Sun. (*She bows and gestures with her fans*) I shine in his reflected glory. Great Lord Sun has heard your plea. He has sent me to watch over you, a light in the night. (*She puts her fans above her head.*)

ALL: Ah, how bright she is.

LADY MOON: I will not always be so bright. Listen, I must tell you something important about my light— (CHANG *enters right, from behind the pagoda, carrying a fishnet on a pole.*)

ALL (*Interrupting her*): Oh. Look there. A stranger. A sly, skulking stranger! (GONG Ho *plays the same insistent soft gong music as before.*)

CHANG (*To audience*): Chang has returned. Chang will steal the rest of the fish from the pool while the village sleeps. Perhaps Chang will even steal the blue pagoda! And then Chang will be the number one thief in China.

ALL (*Putting fingers to their lips*): Sh-h-h! We will watch this stranger. Sh-h-h! (*They shade their eyes and watch him.* CHANG *tiptoes over to the pool to dip the net in.* LADY MOON *points her fan at him.*)

LADY MOON: No, no, Chang. (CHANG *straightens up, startled, and looks around.*)

CHANG: Who said that? Who sees me in the dark?

LADY MOON: Lady Moon sees you, Chang. Up here. (CHANG *turns and looks up at her, astonished.*)

CHANG: Oh, there you are. In the sky, of all places. This is none of your business. (*He turns back to the pool and slides the fishnet into it again.*)

LADY MOON: Don't do that, Chang.

CHANG: Oh, bother. (*He waves her away.*) Go away. Stop watching me. (LADY MOON *turns slightly. The back of her kimono is black. She turns one fan so that its dark side is to the audience.*)

LADY MOON: Dishonorable Chang, I am not the only one who is watching you. Look around you.

CHANG: Ha! How can I look around me when the darkness covers me from tip to toe. (*He points his finger at his head and feet, and suddenly becomes aware that he can see his finger. He looks at it for a moment.*) Ho! What is this? I can see my finger, and my feet, and—and— (*He suddenly sees the others who are watching him*)—everybody. (*Bowing embarrassedly.*) Good evening, honorable everybody.

ALL (*Pointing at him*): Shame. Shame. Bad Chang. Bad Chang. (LADY MOON *turns so that half of her dark side shows.*)

CHANG (*To* LADY MOON): You, up there. You spy-in-the-sky. You have caused all my troubles. (*He raises the fishnet and begins to climb up the pagoda, left*) What a prize you are. A great silver prize. (*He is halfway up*) I will end my troubles and become number one thief in all the world. (*Just as he pretends to clap the net over* LADY MOON's *head, she turns dark side and dark fans to the audience. He does not catch her*) I will steal *you!*

ALL: Oh, wicked Chang!

CHOW: Lady Moon is gone! You have stolen her!

CHANG (*Climbing down and putting the fishnet under his cloak as he gloats*): Chang the Greatest has stolen Lady Moon. She is here. In my fishnet, under my cloak. (*To others*) I will not give her back unless you promise to let me go free and until you proclaim in a loud voice, "Chang is the number one thief in all the world."

ALL: Woe. Woe. Give us back our moon.

CHANG: Say it.

ALL (*Hanging their heads and repeating in subdued voices*): Chang is—Chang is— (LADY MOON *turns and reveals her silver side. She holds her fans high again. The xylophone ripples.*)

LADY MOON: Chang is a silly fool!

ALL: Lady Moon! (*They gaze up at her.*)

LADY MOON: I did not finish telling you. Once every moontime I must turn my dark side to your village. But I promise you I shall always return my light side for your protection and delight. (CHANG *takes out his fishnet and shakes it out.*)

CHANG (*Mournfully*): Empty.

LADY MOON: Empty as your head. And now, Chang, bring back all the things you have stolen. But before you do, you must proclaim in a loud voice, "Chang will steal no more."

CHANG: Oh, woe!

LADY MOON: Say it.

CHANG (*Sighing*): Chang will steal no more.

LADY MOON: Now—bring back the stolen goods. (CHANG *goes left, and gazes longingly into the pool. He turns his back to the pool and slyly slides his hand down into the water. All point at him and shout.*)

ALL: Chang will steal no more! (CHANG *takes his hand out and shakes the water off, then goes left behind the pagoda as* LADY MOON *steps down, and* LORD SUN *mounts the top ridge and holds up his shield.* PROPERTY BOYS *bring in Day Screens.* BOW-LOW *comes to center.* GONG HO *strikes gong three times.*)

BOW-LOW: It was so from that time until now. (CHANG *returns with the basket and fishing poles.*) Chang brought back the fans to the villagers, and they resumed their conversations. (*He gives the fans back.*)

VILLAGERS (*Fluttering fans*): Chitter-chatter-talk-talk. Chitter-chatter-talk-talk. Talk-talk-chitter-chatter. Chitter-chatter-talk-talk.

BOW-LOW: Wong, Ling, and Ming received their fishing poles and their beloved golden carp. (CHANG *returns the fishing poles and throws the carp into the pond.*) And as the sun rose higher (LORD SUN *raises shield above his head*), Ah Me fanned his sleeping master, Nid-Nod. (CHANG *returns fan to* AH ME, *and tea cups to table.*) And Chow, the farmer, began to plant rice shoots again from his rattan basket. (CHANG *returns basket to* CHOW. *The curtains slowly begin to close.*) It is all the same in the village of Ting-a-ling as it had been before, and as it will be tomorrow, except for Nid-Nod. When he wakens at the time of the falling of the leaves—will there not be a wonderful story to tell him about Lady Moon and the thief?

ALL (*Bowing low with* BOW-LOW): A wonderful story to tell! (NID-NOD *smiles gently and nods in his sleep. Curtain*)

THE END

The Tiger Catcher

A Chinese folk tale

Adapted by *Ethel McFarlan*

Characters

MAGISTRATE	WANG LEE, *a villager*
CONSTABLE	SHU LAI, *a village woman*
ELDERLY WIDOW	TIGER
LOO MING	VILLAGERS

TIME: *Long ago.*

SETTING: *An open space before the house of the Magistrate in a Chinese village. The stage is bare except for a gong at right, suspended from a support. A mallet is attached to the support.*

AT RISE: ELDERLY WIDOW, *walking with a staff, enters left, goes to gong, strikes it with mallet, stands leaning on her staff.* VILLAGERS, WANG LEE *and* SHU LAI *enter left, chattering excitedly. They sit on the ground at left.* CONSTABLE *enters right, followed by* LOO MING, *whose head is wrapped in a red cloth. He carries a small table which he places at center.* LOO MING *yawns and stretches.* CONSTABLE, *with gestures, tries to make him hurry.* LOO MING *shuffles off right and returns with a chair.* CONSTABLE *angrily snatches the cloth from* LOO MING'S *head, and spreads it on table.* LOO MING *places chair beside the table and sits down wearily.* CONSTABLE *tilts the chair, tumbling* LOO MING *to the ground, and places chair behind the table. The crowd laughs.*

SHU LAI: Look at lazy Loo Ming! He has no chair to sit on.

WANG LEE: Come, Loo Ming. Sit here on the ground with us. (LOO MING *gets up and sits at edge of crowd.*)

CONSTABLE: Order! The Magistrate's court is now in session. (*The* MAGISTRATE, *carrying a scroll, sweeps in right.* VILLAGERS *rise and bow.* LOO MING *rises and bows in wrong direction.* MAGISTRATE *sits in chair.* VILLAGERS *and* LOO MING *sit on ground.* LOO MING *nods sleepily as he tries to follow proceedings.*)

MAGISTRATE: The gong has been struck. Who wishes to be heard in this court?

WIDOW (*Crossing to table*): I do, Your Honor. I have come down from my little farm to seek justice. Until a few days ago, I lived there with my faithful ox. Now I am alone.

MAGISTRATE: Yes, go on.

WIDOW: Without the ox to plough my rice paddy, it is hard to live. Now he has been killed and I shall starve to death.

MAGISTRATE: Killed? Who did this thing? I promise you he shall pay for his wickedness.

WIDOW: A wicked, savage beast he is, not fit to live.

MAGISTRATE: Just tell me his name and I shall have him arrested and tried.

WIDOW: The tiger, that's who he is, the tiger that comes down from Head-in-Cloud Mountain.

MAGISTRATE: A tiger! Who can arrest a tiger?

WIDOW: You promised. Everyone here heard you promise. (VILLAGERS *nod.*)

MAGISTRATE: Very well. Constable, round up this tiger and bring him in. Go home now, old woman, and dry your tears. The case is in my hands. (CONSTABLE *whispers to* MAGISTRATE.) What?

WIDOW (*Pointing at* CONSTABLE): Sir, that man is shirking his duty. I heard what he said. He refuses to arrest the tiger.

MAGISTRATE: Not at all. My constable wisely suggested that a hunter can arrest this tiger better than a policeman.

WIDOW: What hunter? Where is this hunter?

MAGISTRATE: Old woman, please be quiet and let me settle this matter.

WIDOW: Honorable Magistrate, I put my trust in this court. Nevertheless, here I stay until you find the man to catch that demon tiger.

MAGISTRATE (*Exasperated, rising*): Who out there will volunteer to bring in this poor woman's tiger? (VILLAGERS *are silent.*) Quickly now. Someone must speak before I point my finger. All I am asking is, find the tiger and lead him to me. I shall do the rest. (CONSTABLE *whispers to* MAGISTRATE.) Who? Loo Ming? (MAGISTRATE *turns to look at* LOO MING, *who is asleep.*) Of course! (CONSTABLE *crosses to* LOO MING, *shakes him.*)

CONSTABLE: Wake up! The Magistrate is speaking to you. (LOO MING *stands, sleepily.*)

LOO MING (*Staggering up to table*): Your Honor?

MAGISTRATE: I have chosen you for special duty, Loo Ming. (CONSTABLE *runs off right and re-enters with rope.*)

LOO MING: Oh, thank you, honorable sir.

MAGISTRATE: Take this rope. (CONSTABLE *holds out rope.*)

LOO MING (*Fumbling for rope*): I have it, sir.

MAGISTRATE (*Taking scroll from pocket*): And this warrant, which gives you the authority (*Hands scroll to* LOO MING) to make the arrest for the killing of the widow's ox. Now on your way. Do you understand what you are to do?

Loo Ming: Very clearly, sir. Here is the warrant and here is the rope.

Magistrate: And don't come back without the tiger or you will be severely punished. Case dismissed. (Magistrate, *followed by* Constable, *goes out right.* Wang Lee *carries out table, chair and cloth. The others except* Loo Ming *go out left.*)

Loo Ming: The tiger! And don't come back without the *tiger!*

Constable (*Entering right*): Get moving, Loo Ming. You have a job to do.

Loo Ming: Constable, did I volunteer to catch a *tiger?* I didn't hear myself say that.

Constable: It doesn't matter. The Magistrate has given you the duty.

Loo Ming: But he doesn't understand. I think I should explain to him that a mistake has been made.

Constable: Go and explain if you wish a beating. Fifty lashes is the penalty for disobeying orders. You'd better hurry up that mountain trail and find that tiger. (*Goes out right*)

Loo Ming (*Holding conversation with himself*): Go on, Loo Ming. Don't be afraid. (*Pause*) I'm not afraid. I'm miserable! (*Pause*) Be a man, Loo Ming. The Magistrate thinks you're a big, strong man. (*Pause*) I don't want to be a man. I'd rather be something else, a fly or a tree or a rock, a quiet little rock just sitting there. (*Crouches, pretending to be a rock*) I'm a rock. Nobody can find Loo Ming. (Tiger *enters left, sits down beside* Loo Ming *and leans against him.* Loo Ming *jumps up and yells.* Tiger *puts a paw on his arm.*) Come on, eat me up, tiger. Get it over with. Hurry, eat me up. What are you waiting for? (Tiger *removes paw.*) Don't you want to eat Loo Ming? (Tiger *shakes head.*) But you did eat that great big ox, didn't you? (Tiger *nods.*) Aren't you ashamed of yourself? (TIGER *nods.*) You ought to be, you greedy thing! (TIGER *hangs his head.*) You know what they are going to do to you, don't you? (TIGER *shakes head.* LOO MING *shows him scroll.*) See this? It's a warrant for your arrest. I have orders to bring you in. Now don't make me use force. Will you go quietly? (TIGER *nods.*) All right then, hold still. I have to tie this rope around your neck. (LOO MING *ties rope around* TIGER'S *neck, leads him right and strikes gong.* VILLAGERS, *led by* SHU LAI, *enter and cheer.* WIDOW *enters and stands center.* CONSTABLE *enters, followed by* WANG LEE, *who carries table, chair and cloth, which he places center. Finally,* MAGISTRATE *enters and all bow.*)

MAGISTRATE: Well done, Loo Ming. Bring the prisoner here for questioning. (MAGISTRATE *sits down.* WANG LEE *and* VILLAGERS *sit on ground left.* LOO MING *leads* TIGER *to table.*) Prisoner, are you the same tiger that devoured this old widow's ox? (TIGER *nods.*) You are a very beautiful creature. It is hard to believe you have such a wicked heart.

WIDOW: Beautiful? He is an ugly, hateful tiger.

MAGISTRATE: Please do not interrupt. (*To* TIGER) You know, of course, that the penalty for your crime is death. (TIGER *hangs head sorrowfully.*) Then we shall have a dead ox and a dead tiger. Soon the old lady will die of starvation. What an unhappy ending! I don't like it. Tiger, did you know the ox you killed was the sole support of this old woman? (TIGER *shakes his head.*) No, you did not think of that. Selfishly, you thought only of yourself. Now I believe you are sorry. Isn't that true? (TIGER *nods.*) If I could only make you give back her ox. (MAGISTRATE *is quiet, pondering. Suddenly looks up as if a new idea occurs to him.*) Tiger, do you think you could learn to take the place of this woman's ox? (TIGER *nods vigorously.*) Work for her? Provide for her?

(TIGER *nods vigorously.*) If I let you go will you solemnly promise to be her faithful servant for the rest of her life? (TIGER *nods.*) Very well, then. See that you are. Sentence passed. (TIGER *dashes out left.*)

WIDOW: You have let him go! You have set him free!

MAGISTRATE: I have done the best I can for you, old woman. A dead tiger cannot bring back your ox, but a repentant tiger may be of help to you.

WIDOW: How? What good can he do me? I want him killed. I asked for justice. Is this justice? (TIGER *runs in left, drops a rabbit at* WIDOW's *feet and runs out.*) What's that?

MAGISTRATE: A rabbit. You see, he has brought you your dinner. You have someone to hunt game for you as long as you live. You will never be hungry again. Now do you understand why I let him go?

WIDOW: Yes, Your Honor.

MAGISTRATE (*Rising*):

This tiger now has changed his ways—

He'll serve you well through all your days.

(WIDOW *picks up rabbit and goes out left.* MAGISTRATE, *followed by* CONSTABLE, *goes out right.* VILLAGERS *rise and applaud* MAGISTRATE. LOO MING *takes a bow to the applause of* VILLAGERS *and goes out right.* VILLAGERS *also applaud* WANG LEE *as he carries off furniture. Then they straggle off, as the curtain falls.*)

THE END

Plum Blossom and the Dragon

A folk tale of ancient China

by Deborah Newman

Characters

PLUM BLOSSOM, *a Chinese girl*
MOTHER
CHORUS, *the person who tells the story*
LING PO, *the sleepy property man*
JADE PEARL ⎤
POPPY SEED ⎬ *proud sisters*
PEAR FLOWER ⎦
AH FANG, *the mean rich uncle*
BUTTERFLY FAIRY
DRAGON
EMPRESS
LADIES
MUSICIANS

TIME: *Long ago in China.*
SETTING: *The stage is bare except for a large red chest, upstage center, and some chairs down right.*
AT RISE: MUSICIANS *march onstage, playing various rhythm-band instruments. They go to chairs, down right, and stop playing. A cymbal player bangs cymbals twice, then all* MUSICIANS *bow and sit. The* CHORUS *enters, comes down front, and bows.*

CHORUS: Honorable Friends, I bid you welcome. Today we take you to the long-ago Flowery Kingdom of China. (*Points to box*) In this box, we have all of the properties we will need to tell you our story. Our Ancient and Honorable Property Man is in charge of them. (*Claps hands twice*) Property Man! Ling Po! We are ready to begin. Property Man! (*Bows to audience*) A thousand pardons, Honorable Friends. Our Property Man is old and often falls asleep. (*Motions to* MUSICIANS) Our Honorable Musicians will awaken him. (MUSICIANS *play*. LING PO *shuffles in and bows*. MUSICIANS *stop*.)

Ling Po, we are ready to begin our play. (LING PO *nods, shuffles over to chest, sits down, and falls asleep*. CHORUS *sighs*.) Do not worry, Honorable Friends. Ling Po has gone back to sleep again, but our Honorable Musicians will wake him up when we need him. I think you will agree that our Honorable Musicians could awaken anyone.

Our story takes place in the days of the Golden Emperor, during the month of the third moon. We are now outside the little hut where the lovely Plum Blossom lives with her mother. Here is Plum Blossom, coming from the hut with her mother. (CHORUS *sits by* MUSICIANS, *as* PLUM BLOSSOM *enters with* MOTHER.)

MOTHER (*Holding up an empty bowl*): Alas, my child, we have no food—and no money to buy more. I do not know what will become of us.

PLUM BLOSSOM (*Patting* MOTHER's *shoulder*): Do not worry, Honorable Mother. Today I will go to the house of our rich uncle in the city. He will help us.

MOTHER (*Anxiously*): Oh, my lovely Plum Blossom, the road that leads to the city is full of dangers.

PLUM BLOSSOM: I am not afraid, Honorable Mother. My journey will be swift, and I will return to you before the peonies bloom in the Garden of Sweet Blossoms.

MOTHER (*Putting her arm around* PLUM BLOSSOM): Then go, my child. But take care. Bid your Honorable Uncle health and happiness, and tell him of our many troubles. (MOTHER *waves goodbye and exits as* CHORUS *stands.*)

CHORUS: And so Plum Blossom sets out on the road to the city. She comes first to the garden of a wealthy family, where three girls are chasing a butterfly. (CHORUS *sits, as* JADE PEARL, POPPY SEED, *and* PEAR FLOWER *enter, fanning themselves with pretty paper fans.* PLUM BLOSSOM *takes a few steps toward them and watches them.*)

JADE PEARL (*Looking up and pointing*): Oh, see the beautiful yellow butterfly!

POPPY SEED (*Looking*): I don't see any butterfly.

PEAR FLOWER (*Angrily*): There isn't any butterfly! (*Points to* LING PO) *He* has fallen asleep again. (*To* MUSICIANS) Wake him up! (MUSICIANS *play.* PEAR FLOWER *raps* LING PO *with her fan.* MUSICIANS *stop playing.* LING PO *gets up, smiles sleepily, opens chest, and takes out a large paper fish, which he holds up.*)

JADE PEARL: No, no, no! The butterfly! We need the butterfly! (LING PO *shrugs, returns fish to chest, takes out large butterfly on a string, and then comes forward. He stands near girls with his eyes half-closed, waving butterfly back and forth.*)

POPPY SEED: What a beautiful butterfly! I want it for my very own.

JADE PEARL: I will catch it for you. (*She chases butterfly, but* LING PO *keeps it out of her reach.*)

PEAR FLOWER: I will get it. (*All three chase butterfly until* POPPY SEED *catches it.*)

POPPY SEED (*Holding up butterfly*): I have it!

PLUM BLOSSOM (*Running to* POPPY SEED): Oh, please, let the butterfly go. It will die.

POPPY SEED: The butterfly is in *my* garden, and I want it.

PLUM BLOSSOM: No, do not keep it. Let it go so that it may live. (*She takes butterfly away from* POPPY SEED *and gives it to* LING PO. LING PO *returns butterfly to chest, then goes back to sleep.*)

POPPY SEED (*Angrily*): Why did you do that, you horrible girl? How dare you come into our garden! Go away!

PLUM BLOSSOM: I have walked all day, and I am hungry. Please give me a bit of rice.

PEAR FLOWER: Be on your way! We do not give food to beggars.

PLUM BLOSSOM: I am not a beggar. I am on the way to the house of my uncle in the city.

JADE PEARL: You cannot go to the city. There is a horrible Golden Dragon who lives on the mountain near the city. If he sees you, he will eat you!

PLUM BLOSSOM (*Fearfully*): A dragon?

PEAR FLOWER (*Nodding*): A terrible dragon who breathes fire and smoke. He has just come to live in a cave by the road.

JADE PEARL: Go back to your home, girl. I would not go on the road to the city for all the gold in the world.

POPPY SEED: Come, sisters. It is tea time. Let us go into the Courtyard of Willows. (*She exits with* PEAR FLOWER *and* JADE PEARL. PLUM BLOSSOM *comes forward.*)

PLUM BLOSSOM: What shall I do? I cannot go home, for we have no money and no food. I *must* go to the city— but I am afraid of the dragon. (BUTTERFLY FAIRY *enters.* PLUM BLOSSOM *moves away from her.*)

BUTTERFLY FAIRY: Do not be afraid, little Plum Blossom. I am the Butterfly Fairy. You have just saved my life, and now I will help you.

PLUM BLOSSOM: Oh, Butterfly Fairy, I must go to my Honorable Uncle in the city. How can I get by the dragon who lives on the mountain?

BUTTERFLY FAIRY: It is true that the dragon is a dreadful

creature. But I have often flown above his cave, and I know a secret way to make him a friend. The dragon loves flowers, and none grow on the snowy mountainside near his cave. Take this branch of flowers with you. Give it to the dragon, and he will not harm you. (*She holds out her hand, and* LING PO *takes a flowering branch out of chest and gives it to her. She gives branch to* PLUM BLOSSOM.)

PLUM BLOSSOM: Why, thank you, Butterfly Fairy. I will do as you say. I will give the dragon these flowers.

BUTTERFLY FAIRY: Farewell, little Plum Blossom. Good fortune will be yours. (*She goes out.* LING PO *takes out a large, white cap and puts it on his head. He stands down center, and* PLUM BLOSSOM *walks around him, as* CHORUS *stands up and speaks.*)

CHORUS (*Pointing to* LING PO): There is the snow-capped mountain that Plum Blossom must cross on her way to the city. As she climbs over the rocks, she hears the roar of the dragon. (CHORUS *sits.* DRAGON *roars from offstage, then enters, and chases* PLUM BLOSSOM.)

PLUM BLOSSOM (*Holding out branch*): Stop! Honorable Dragon, stop! I bring you a gift. See—here are some flowers for you. (*She holds branch under the* DRAGON'S *nose. He sniffs, smiles, takes branch, and sits down happily, smelling flowers.* PLUM BLOSSOM *walks around* DRAGON, *looking at him.*)

You are such a beautiful dragon. (DRAGON *roars and nods head.*) Why do you always scare people? (DRAGON *hangs head and shrugs shoulders.*) It is not nice to scare people, you know. (DRAGON *shakes head.*) I want you to promise me that you will never scare anybody again for the rest of your life. Will you promise? (DRAGON *thinks, then shakes head and roars.*) Do you really like to scare people? (DRAGON *nods enthusiastically.* PLUM BLOSSOM *stamps her foot.*) Then I must be on my way.

I will not talk to you if you are going to be naughty. (DRAGON *hangs head, then puts his paws on* PLUM BLOSSOM's *shoulders.*) No! Let me go! (DRAGON *points to* PLUM BLOSSOM, *then to branch, then to himself, then to* PLUM BLOSSOM.)

Oh, I see. You want to give me a gift. (DRAGON *nods.*) I will wait here while you go to your cave. (DRAGON *goes up to* LING PO *and roars.* LING PO *hurries back to chest, takes out several necklaces and gives them to* DRAGON. *They return to* PLUM BLOSSOM. DRAGON *puts necklaces on* PLUM BLOSSOM.)

Thank you, my beautiful dragon. (DRAGON *acts embarrassed.*) I have never owned a necklace before, and these are so beautiful. (DRAGON *smiles and nods.*) Now I must be on my way. Goodbye, Dragon. (DRAGON *waves and goes out.* LING PO *goes back to chest, sits down, and falls asleep.* PLUM BLOSSOM *speaks to audience as she takes off the necklaces.*)

I do not want to hurt the dragon's feelings, but these necklaces are so heavy. I will take them off and keep them in my pockets. (*She puts necklaces into the pockets of her costume.* CHORUS *stands up and speaks.*)

CHORUS: In the city, Plum Blossom's rich uncle is very angry. His name is Ah Fang, and he thinks he is missing a gold piece. (AH FANG *enters, scowling. He is counting money, which he takes from a bag at his belt.*)

PLUM BLOSSOM (*Running to* AH FANG *and bowing*): A thousand greetings, Honorable Uncle. I bring you wishes for health and happiness from my Honorable Mother. May your happiness be as deep as the sea, your life as long as the golden streams.

AH FANG (*Scowling*): Who is it who calls me uncle? Get away, you little beggar!

PLUM BLOSSOM (*Surprised*): Honorable Uncle! I am Plum Blossom. I am the child of your dead brother. I have come to you because my mother and I have no food, and no money to buy more.

AH FANG (*Angrily*): Money! Everyone comes to me for money! Do you think I am made of money?

PLUM BLOSSOM: Oh, Honorable Uncle, our need is great, and I have traveled far to see you. I came over the snowy mountain, past the cave of the Golden Dragon. See what the Golden Dragon gave to me. (*She takes necklaces out of her pockets and shows them to* AH FANG, *who grabs them greedily.*)

AH FANG: What? The Golden Dragon gave you these? These are diamonds and rubies and emeralds, worth a fortune. Tell me how you got them. (PLUM BLOSSOM *whispers to* AH FANG, *who nods with delight, then takes flowering branch, as* CHORUS *speaks.*)

CHORUS: Plum Blossom tells her secret to Ah Fang. Ah Fang sets out for the dragon's cave at once, leaving Plum Blossom to rest at his home. (CHORUS *sits.* PLUM BLOSSOM *waves and goes out.* AH FANG *tucks branch into his belt and looks around.*)

AH FANG: Now, where is that mountain? (*Claps hands*) Mountain! I must have a mountain! (*To* MUSICIANS) Wake that lazy fellow up so that I may have a mountain. (MUSICIANS *play.* LING PO *gets up, sleepily;* MUSICIANS *stop;* AH FANG *shakes* LING PO *and pushes him forward, kicking him.*) Come on, you lazy fellow, do you think I have all day? I must climb the mountain. (AH FANG *marches around* LING PO. LING PO *shakes his fist at* AH FANG, *and sticks out his tongue. Then* LING PO *trips* AH FANG *as he walks around, and pulls flowering branch from* AH FANG'S *belt.* AH FANG *does not notice that branch is gone. The* DRAGON *enters, roaring horribly.* AH FANG *bows to* DRAGON.)

Ah, good day to you, Dragon. (DRAGON *roars.*) I understand you have some priceless jewels in your cave. I have brought you a gift, and you can go to your cave right now and get me some jewels. Go ahead. I have no time to waste. (DRAGON *roars*.) All right. I will give you your gift first. Here it is, a branch of flowers. (AH FANG *touches his belt, then looks around*.) Where is that branch? (LING PO *holds up flowering branch, but* AH FANG *does not see it; then* LING PO *winks, bows to audience, and hides branch behind him.* DRAGON *roars and crouches, about to spring on* AH FANG.) Just a minute, Dragon. I will find your flowers. (DRAGON *roars and chases* AH FANG *around stage.* AH FANG *tries to hide behind* LING PO, *but* LING PO *steps aside.* AH FANG *tries to hide behind* MUSICIANS, *who push him away. Finally,* DRAGON *chases* AH FANG *out—either down aisle or off-stage.* LING PO *bows, goes back to chest, takes off his white cap, and goes to sleep.*)

CHORUS (*Standing*): Honorable Friends, our Property Man is fast asleep again, but he has done well, and I think we should let him sleep. If you agree, clap your hands twice —thus! (*Claps hands twice, and motions to audience to clap also.*) Then it is agreed, Honorable Friends. I will tell you quickly about the happy ending of our story.

Plum Blossom gave the beautiful necklaces to the Empress of China, who asked the little girl and her mother to come to live at the royal court. (EMPRESS, LADIES, PLUM BLOSSOM *and* MOTHER *enter.* PLUM BLOS-SOM *bows to* EMPRESS *and gives her necklaces.* EMPRESS *puts necklaces on, and* LADIES *admire them.*)

Jade Pearl, Poppy Seed and Pear Flower came to Plum Blossom to ask her forgiveness and friendship. (JADE PEARL, POPPY SEED, *and* PEAR FLOWER *come in and bow to* PLUM BLOSSOM, *who returns bow.*)

The Golden Dragon still lives in his cave—but he is a peaceful dragon because the Butterfly Fairy drops sweet-smelling petals on him every day. (BUTTERFLY

FAIRY *enters, followed by* DRAGON, *who smiles as she drops petals on his head.*)

As for Ah Fang, he hardly dares to go outside the walls of his house. (AH FANG *enters.* DRAGON *roars at him.* AH FANG *runs to other side of stage, and* BUTTERFLY FAIRY *pats* DRAGON.) And so, Honorable Friends, this is our story. We bid you farewell, and much happiness. (*All bow.* LING PO *breaks through line of actors, smiling broadly. He holds up fish. They push him back. He returns with a large paper fan. They push him back again. Finally, he comes forward with a large scroll, which he unrolls and holds up. The scroll says in large letters:* THE END. *Curtain*)

THE END

Triumph for Two

A folk tale of old Czechoslovakia

by Hazel W. Corson

Characters

INTELLIGENCE	TWO GUARDS
LUCK	HERALD
VANEK	HEADSMAN
VANEK'S FATHER	HEAD GARDENER
KING	BORIS, *a royal gardener*
QUEEN	DOCTOR
PRINCESS	PRINCE RUDOLPH OF BAVARIA
COURT OFFICIAL	TWO WOMEN ⎫
TWO LADIES-IN-WAITING	MAN ⎭ *villagers*

SCENE 1

BEFORE RISE: INTELLIGENCE *enters right, in front of curtain. He is wearing a scholar's cap and gown, and carrying a book. He opens book and starts to read.* LUCK *enters left, wearing a top hat with a big four-leaf clover on it. He strolls over to* INTELLIGENCE *and tips his hat.*

LUCK (*Gaily*): Good morning, Mr. Intelligence. Make way for me!

INTELLIGENCE (*Reluctantly*): I don't know why I should, Mr. Luck. You are no better than I.

LUCK: Oh, I don't know about that, Mr. Intelligence.

INTELLIGENCE: You think luck is better than intelligence?

LUCK: The better man is the one who can do the most. Don't you agree?

INTELLIGENCE: Yes. But do you think that you can do more than I, Mr. Luck?

LUCK: Maybe, Mr. Intelligence.

INTELLIGENCE: And just how will you prove that, Mr. Luck? (VANEK *enters left. He plods across the stage, hands in pockets, head bowed, looking down. He does not notice* LUCK *and* INTELLIGENCE *and exits right.*)

LUCK: Well, take that poor peasant, Vanek. He and his father and brother make a bare living on their little farm. By making Vanek lucky, I can improve his life. Can intelligence bring Vanek a better life?

INTELLIGENCE: I think so. I will get Vanek to use his intelligence. You will see that it will do more for a man than just luck.

LUCK: I would like to see that. Luck is not a bad thing to have, but if you prove you can do more for Vanek than I can, every time we meet I will bow to you. Is it a bet?

INTELLIGENCE: Very well, it's a bet. And if *you* can do more, I will bow to you. (*They shake hands.*)

LUCK: Agreed, Mr. Intelligence. Take your turn first. We shall see what intelligence can do for a lad as poor as Vanek. (LUCK *exits left;* INTELLIGENCE *exits right.* VANEK'S FATHER *enters left.* VANEK *enters right, with brisk, alert steps. He goes to* FATHER.)

VANEK: Why must I spend my whole life plowing, Father? I think there are better ways of earning a living.

VANEK'S FATHER (*Astonished*): What are you saying, Vanek? Have you lost your wits?

VANEK: No, Father, I have found them. Our little farm is not big enough for all of us to make a good living. I must go to seek my fortune.

VANEK'S FATHER: But where will you go, Vanek?

VANEK: I will go to the King's palace and apprentice myself to the Head Gardener.

VANEK'S FATHER: And will that be better than staying here and working our little farm? At the King's palace there will always be someone to say, "Do this! Do that!" Here, you can be your own master.

VANEK: I know. I will have to work hard and learn to be a head gardener. Then *I* will be the one who says, "Do this! Do that!" If the King is pleased with my work, he will reward me.

VANEK'S FATHER: I really do not know what has happened to you, Vanek. But I will not stand in your way. If you leave, our little farm will go to your younger brother instead of to you. I will give you my blessing. Goodbye, and God go with you.

VANEK: Goodbye, Father. I will come back and see you when I have made my fortune. (*They shake hands.* VANEK *exits right;* VANEK'S FATHER *exits left. Curtain opens.*)

*   *   *

SETTING: *The King's garden. There is a stone wall up center with roses growing over it.*

AT RISE: VANEK *and* BORIS *are gardening around some plants in front of the wall.*

VANEK: Be sure to loosen the soil around the plants, Boris.

BORIS: Why, Vanek? The Head Gardener never had us do this before you came.

VANEK: It will make the plants grow better, Boris.

BORIS: All right, if you say so. But before you came we just pulled the weeds. (HEAD GARDENER *enters right. He watches* VANEK *and* BORIS *work for a moment.*)

HEAD GARDENER: I must say that the gardens are even more beautiful than they were. I have been Head Gardener for a long time, Vanek, and you have worked in the King's gardens for less than a year, but I feel that you know more about the plants than I do.

VANEK: It is very kind of you to say so, sir, but I don't think I do.

HEAD GARDENER: The King sent for me today. He is very pleased with the new rose garden you planted. He and the Queen and the Princess spent an hour in it yesterday, admiring the roses.

VANEK: I am glad to hear it.

BORIS: And how is the beautiful Princess? Has anyone been able to do anything for her yet?

VANEK: What is the matter with her?

BORIS: Don't you know? The Princess doesn't speak.

VANEK: How terrible! Can she hear?

HEAD GARDENER: Oh, yes! When she was a little girl, the Princess talked and laughed like everyone else. But, on her twelfth birthday, for no reason at all, she suddenly stopped talking. They say that no word has passed her lips from that day to this.

VANEK: But surely, a great king like her father can have the best doctors and the wisest men to help her.

HEAD GARDENER: Oh, yes! For a time people came every day to help the Princess talk. No one succeeded. But they still haven't given up hope.

BORIS: The King has sent messengers all over the world, promising his daughter's hand in marriage, and half his kingdom, to the man who can get the Princess to speak.

VANEK: Now that is a mighty offer. You say the Princess used to speak?

HEAD GARDENER: Indeed she did, until her twelfth birthday.

VANEK (*Slowly*): I think I can make the Princess speak.

BORIS (*Horrified*): You! Would you dare go before the King, the Queen, and all the court?

VANEK: Why not?

BORIS: And would not your tongue cleave to the roof of your mouth?

VANEK: Why should it? They are just people like ourselves—some better, some worse, but mortal people all the same.

HEAD GARDENER: You can say that to us, but what will you say when you stand before the King and all the grand ladies and gentlemen of the court in your gardener's clothes and your gardener's shoes?

VANEK: First, I shall clean my gardener's clothes and my gardener's shoes. Then I shall stand before the King. I shall bow (*He demonstrates with a gracious bow*), and say, "Sire, I am Vanek, the gardener, come to get the Princess to speak."

HEAD GARDENER: And the King will say, "Back to your gardening, Vanek. You are too poor and lowly to speak to a Princess."

VANEK: Poor and lowly I am, but that need not keep me from getting the Princess to speak. (COURT OFFICIAL *enters right, followed by* TWO GUARDS *carrying chairs, a cushion and material to drape over the chairs.*)

COURT OFFICIAL (*Directing the* GUARDS): Put His Majesty's chair here (*Pointing to center*), and Her Majesty's beside it. Put the Princess' chair here, beside the Queen's. The cushion for the Princess' little dog may go there. Now, drape the chairs and be quick about it. There is no time to lose. (GUARDS *drape the chairs.*)

HEAD GARDENER: What is happening, sir?

COURT OFFICIAL: The King has been much pleased with the garden. He has decided to hold court here today. You gardeners, pick up your tools and leave. Their Majesties will be here any moment. (*The* COURT OFFICIAL *fusses with the drapes. The* GUARDS *stand at each side of the stage. The gardeners gather their tools as the* COURT OFFICIAL *exits right.*)

VANEK: Now is my chance. I will get the Princess to speak today.

BORIS: I fear you will get into some kind of trouble, Vanek.

HEAD GARDENER: Hurry, here come Their Majesties now. (*Gardeners exit left, carrying their tools. The* KING *and* QUEEN *enter right. The* KING *escorts the* QUEEN *to her chair and when she is seated, takes his own chair. The* PRINCESS *enters right, carrying her little dog. She places the dog on the cushion, and takes her seat. The* GUARDS *stand, one by the* KING, *one by the* QUEEN. *The* HERALD *enters right, and stands left center.* TWO LADIES-IN-WAITING *enter right and stand behind the* PRINCESS.)

KING (*To* QUEEN): This was a very good idea you had, my dear. I would never have thought of holding court in the garden.

QUEEN: The gardens are so beautiful now, we should enjoy them as much as possible. (*The* COURT OFFICIAL *enters, and bows before the* KING *and* QUEEN.)

COURT OFFICIAL: Your Majesty, the doctor from Spain is here to see the Princess.

KING: Let him come forward. (*The* COURT OFFICIAL *signals the* HERALD *and steps aside and stands right.*)

HERALD: Doctor Hernandes Esteban, from Spain. (DOCTOR *enters right.*)

DOCTOR (*Bowing before the* KING *and* QUEEN *and then addressing the* PRINCESS): How are you today, my Princess? (PRINCESS *shrugs her shoulders, but says nothing.*)

Has she been taking the pills I left for her, Your Majesties?

QUEEN: She has, good doctor. I saw to it myself.

DOCTOR: And she has not been speaking?

KING: Not a word to anyone.

DOCTOR: Then I fear there is nothing more to be done. I have tried pills and powders, diet and exercise. It must be a magic spell, that only a witch can remove.

KING: We thank you for trying. (*The* DOCTOR *bows and exits right.*)

COURT OFFICIAL (*Stepping forward*): The Prince of Bavaria is here, sire. He wishes to speak to the Princess.

KING: Let him come forward. (*The* COURT OFFICIAL *signals the* HERALD *and steps aside and stands right.*)

HERALD: His Royal Highness, Prince Rudolph of Bavaria. (PRINCE RUDOLPH *enters, carrying a bird cage in which is a bird. The* PRINCE *bows to the* KING *and* QUEEN, *then goes down on one knee before the* PRINCESS. *He holds the bird cage before the* PRINCESS.)

PRINCE: My Princess, I have a gift for you. This little bird will sing you a most beautiful song, but it will do so only if you ask it to. You must say, "Sing, little bird, sing." It will not sing for me, only for a princess. Will you tell it to sing, my lady? (*The* PRINCESS *takes the bird cage and holds it in different positions to admire the bird. Her lips move, as if she were speaking, but she makes no sound. Then she graciously gives the bird cage back to the* PRINCE, *shaking her head sadly, and placing her forefinger on her lips.*)

QUEEN (*Kindly*): Thank you for trying, Prince Rudolph. I wish that you had been successful. (*The* PRINCE *gives the bird cage to* 1ST LADY-IN-WAITING, *bows to everyone, and exits right.* VANEK *enters left and signals to the* COURT OFFICIAL. *The* COURT OFFICIAL *whispers with* VANEK *and shakes his head.* VANEK *seems to be insisting and the* COURT OFFICIAL *points to the exit.* VANEK *still insists and the* COURT OFFICIAL *claps his hands and motions to* 1ST GUARD.)

KING: What is going on over there?

COURT OFFICIAL: It is only Vanek, one of the gardeners, sire. He wants to speak to the Princess. I have told him that a peasant's son may not speak to a princess.

KING: Ah! Vanek! I have heard that name. The Head Gardener speaks very highly of you, Vanek.

VANEK (*Stepping forward*): Thank you, sire. As I told the Court Official, I came because I would like to get the Princess to talk.

KING: Many have tried and failed. But you shall have your turn if you wish. (VANEK *bows to the* KING *and* QUEEN, *then, instead of addressing the* PRINCESS, *he kneels to talk to her little dog.*)

VANEK: I hear that you are a very clever animal, little white dog, and I would like to ask you a question. I have two friends, a sculptor, and a tailor. One time the three of us went deep into the forest. When night came, we were lost. We gathered a big pile of wood and built a fire as protection against wolves. We agreed to take turns staying awake to keep the fire burning.

COURT OFFICIAL: Vanek, you are wasting the King's time with your long story. If you wish to get the Princess to talk, speak to the Princess, not to her dog.

KING: This is an interesting story. Let him continue.

VANEK: Thank you, sire. (*The* KING *and* QUEEN *and* PRINCESS *listen interestedly.*) The sculptor took the first watch. To keep himself awake, he took a log and carved it into a doll. When his time was up, he woke the tailor. "I carved this doll to keep myself awake," he said. "If you feel like it, you can make her some clothes."

COURT OFFICIAL (*Interrupting*): Are you still interested in this long story, sire?

KING: More than ever. Stop interrupting!

COURT OFFICIAL: Very well, sire.

VANEK: The tailor opened his pack, and spent the time making clothes for the doll. Then he woke me. "See this doll," he said. "The sculptor carved her, and I dressed her. Why don't you teach her to talk." And believe it or not, I did. By morning, the doll could not only talk, but move about freely.

QUEEN: A remarkable story!

VANEK: Thank you, Your Majesty. Now, my question is this. Who should keep the doll? The sculptor says she is his because he carved her. The tailor says she is his because he dressed her. And I have my claim. What do you say, little dog?

PRINCESS: Why, it is plain that the doll belongs to you because you made her talk!

1ST LADY-IN-WAITING: She spoke!

2ND LADY-IN-WAITING: The Princess spoke!

ALL (*Ad lib*): She spoke! The Princess finally spoke. (*Etc.*) (*Everyone looks happy; the* KING *and* QUEEN *hug each other.*)

HERALD (*Running off right*): The Princess has spoken! The Princess has spoken!

PRINCESS: I was never able to say anything to people who were trying to get *me* to speak. But when this gardener spoke to my dog, I suddenly realized I *would* be able to speak at last. (*The* PRINCESS *and the* LADIES-IN-WAITING *go off to a corner of the garden with the dog, and talk quietly among themselves, ignoring the others.*)

KING: Our deepest thanks, clever Vanek, for getting the Princess to speak. What reward may I give you?

VANEK: Only the reward Your Majesty has promised to the one who could make the Princess talk—her hand in marriage, and half the kingdom.

QUEEN: You are only a peasant's son, Vanek. You cannot

marry a royal princess. Choose some other reward, and the King will give it gladly.

VANEK: But I want no other reward.

KING: Surely, Vanek, you must know that I could not allow my daughter to marry the son of a lowly peasant. A princess must marry a prince.

VANEK: But the King said that any man who could make the Princess speak could marry her.

KING: I did not suppose that anyone but a prince could do it. Name some other reward.

VANEK: A king must keep his word, sire. You *must* let me marry the Princess.

COURT OFFICIAL: A peasant does not tell a king what he *must* do.

VALEK: I insist that I be married to the Princess. A king *must* keep his word.

COURT OFFICIAL: Guards! Bind this saucy peasant! He should be executed, sire! (GUARDS *step forward.*)

KING: Guards, take him to Execution Hill, and cut off his head immediately. (*The* GUARDS *pounce on* VANEK *and start to drag him out.* PRINCESS *does not see them. As* VANEK *is dragged off, the curtain falls.*)

*   *   *

SCENE 2

TIME: *An hour later.*

SETTING: *Execution Hill. There is an execution block midstage.*

AT RISE: INTELLIGENCE *enters right and* LUCK *enters left. They meet at center.*

LUCK: Well, my friend, Mr. Intelligence, you did well by Vanek for a time. But, what can you do for him now?

INTELLIGENCE (*Sighing*): I'm afraid there is nothing I can do.

LUCK: Then I will take my turn. (LUCK *exits left.* INTELLIGENCE *exits right.* BORIS *and the* HEAD GARDENER *enter left.*)

BORIS (*Sadly*): Poor Vanek! I was afraid he would get into trouble.

HEAD GARDENER: It's a great pity. Where am I going to get such a good gardener?

BORIS: By tomorrow the King will be sorry about this.

HEAD GARDENER: That will not help Vanek. (*Two* WOMEN *and* MAN *enter. They go toward the block, and stand just behind it.*)

MAN: Is this where the execution will take place? (BORIS *and the* HEAD GARDENER *nod.*)

1ST WOMAN: Who is going to be executed?

HEAD GARDENER: Vanek, one of the King's gardeners.

2ND WOMAN: The scoundrel! What did he do?

BORIS: He made the speechless Princess talk, that's what he did.

1ST WOMAN: And for that he must lose his head?

HEAD GARDENER: He insisted that the King keep his word and allow him to marry the Princess.

MAN (*Shaking his head*): Only a brave man or a fool would argue with the King.

1ST WOMAN: I have never seen an execution. What will happen?

HEAD GARDENER: Hush! Here they come with Vanek now. You will see. (*The* COURT OFFICIAL *enters right and takes a position to the right of the block.* GUARDS *lead in* VANEK. *He is blindfolded, and his hands are bound behind his back. They take him to the left of the block.*)

1ST GUARD: Make way for the Headsman! (*The* HEADSMAN *enters left, carrying a large cardboard ax. He wears a black hood over his head and face. He leans ax against block.*)

HEADSMAN: Stand back!

2ND GUARD: Stand back!

COURT OFFICIAL: Do you have anything to say, Vanek? It won't do you any good, but you can say it, anyway.

VANEK: All I have to say is a king should keep his word. (*He kneels beside block.*)

COURT OFFICIAL: Headsman! Do your duty! (*The* HEADS-MAN *steps forward. All look on horrified. As he picks up ax, the handle breaks.*)

ALL (*Ad lib*): It broke! The Headsman's ax broke! (*Etc.*)

COURT OFFICIAL: What is the meaning of this?

HEADSMAN (*Stunned*): It never happened before, sir!

COURT OFFICIAL: Don't just stand there! Get another ax!

HEADSMAN: I don't have another ax, sir. Why should I have two axes to cut off one head?

COURT OFFICIAL: This is very irregular! Who has an ax? You (*Pointing to* 1ST GUARD), guard, get another ax for the Headsman!

1ST GUARD: I shall have to go all the way back to the castle, sir.

COURT OFFICIAL (*Loudly*): Then do so. And hurry! (GUARD *exits right.*)

BORIS (*Loudly*): Maybe Vanek isn't meant to have his head cut off.

COURT OFFICIAL: Of course he is meant to have his head cut off! The King himself ordered it.

1ST WOMAN (*Pointing off right*): Look at the road. Some-one is riding toward us for dear life! (*All look off right.*)

2ND WOMAN: He is waving a white flag!

HEAD GARDENER: Look! The royal coach is behind him!

COURT OFFICIAL: It's the Herald. He must have a message from the King.

MAN: He has jumped from his horse. Here he comes. (*The* HERALD *enters right.*)

HERALD (*Panting*): Stop the execution!

COURT OFFICIAL: What? What are you saying?

HERALD: The King has changed his mind.

COURT OFFICIAL: But, how did that happen?

HERALD: The Princess convinced the King. She said that Vanek was right. A king *should* keep his word.

COURT OFFICIAL (*Angrily*): A king should not let his daughter marry a peasant.

HERALD: That is what the King said. But the Princess said, "A king can do anything. A king can make a peasant into a prince."

COURT OFFICIAL: And what did the King say?

HERALD: The King said, "I never thought of that." So he sent me ahead to stop the execution, and the royal coach is behind me to take Prince Vanek home. (*Looking around*) Where is Prince Vanek? I hope he still has his head.

COURT OFFICIAL (*Rushing to* VANEK *and untying him*): I pray Your Highness will pardon me. I was only obeying the King's orders. This way to the royal coach, Your Highness. (VANEK *looks dazed as the* COURT OFFICIAL *ushers him off right.*)

BORIS: Hooray for the Princess!

1ST WOMAN: Long live Prince Vanek!

ALL (*Exiting right; happily*): Hooray! Hooray! Hooray! INTELLIGENCE *enters right.* LUCK *enters from left. As they meet, they bow to each other.*)

INTELLIGENCE: I must admit that you saved Vanek's life. That broken ax handle was a neat trick, Mr. Luck.

LUCK: And *I* must admit that without you, Mr. Intelligence, Vanek would still be plowing his father's farm—never to be made a prince.

INTELLIGENCE: We had better work together, Mr. Luck. Now that Vanek is a prince, and will someday be King, he will need both of us. Intelligence *and* Luck make a good team. (*Each bows to the other as the curtain falls.*)

THE END

Robin Hood Outwits the Sheriff

A story of an English folk hero

by Constance Whitman Baher

Characters

ROBIN HOOD

LITTLE JOHN
WILL SCARLET
ALLAN-A-DALE
FRIAR TUCK ⎫ *Robin's Merry Men*
KET
HUGH
WILL STUTLEY

MAID MARIAN
ELLEN
SHERIFF OF NOTTINGHAM
THREE MONKS
SIR RICHARD OF THE LEA
LADY ALICE, *his wife*
NELL
MARGOT
PEG

TIME: *Twelfth-century England.*
SETTING: *Sherwood Forest.*
BEFORE RISE: *The* SHERIFF OF NOTTINGHAM *enters, right,*

followed by THREE MONKS. 1ST *and* 2ND MONKS *carry a large chest, and* 3RD MONK *carries a bag over his shoulder.*

SHERIFF: Come, holy fathers, we have no time to waste. Prince John expects us in Nottingham by sunset.

1ST MONK: Have no fear, my lord Sheriff. Everything will go just as you have planned it.

2ND MONK: This time, we cannot fail.

3RD MONK: By sunset, Robin Hood will be ours.

SHERIFF (*Rubbing his hands*): Ah, what a treasure we shall bring to Prince John tonight! (NELL, MARGOT, *and* PEG *enter, left, carrying baskets of wild berries. They stop as they see* SHERIFF.) Out of our way, peasants. (*Women draw back in fear, trying to hide baskets under their shawls.* SHERIFF *goes over to* NELL.) But what have you here, woman? (*He pulls shawl from* NELL's *shoulders and takes basket from her.*) Ah, berries. I see.

NELL: They are but blackberries, my lord Sheriff. They grow wild here in the forest.

SHERIFF (*Taking baskets from* MARGOT *and* PEG): Wild blackberries, eh?

MARGOT: They are all we and our children have to eat, my lord Sheriff. Our sheep have been taken to pay the taxes, and our wheat is already in your granaries in Nottingham.

SHERIFF: Do not think you will soften my heart with tales of your poverty.

PEG: Please, let us keep the berries.

SHERIFF (*Slyly*): Perhaps you shall. (*Stepping toward women*) Tell me where Robin Hood and his men hide out, and you shall have your wretched berries back. (*Women look at one another.*)

NELL: We do not know, my lord.

SHERIFF: Of course you know Robin Hood. He has be-friended all the poor wretches in England. Now tell me where he hides, or you and your children can starve, for all I care.

PEG: We cannot tell you, my lord.

SHERIFF (*To* MONKS): Set down the chest. (*They do so.*) Open it. (SHERIFF *stands beside chest. To women*) I shall give you one last chance.

NELL (*Kneeling before* 1ST MONK): Please, reverend father, help us.

1ST MONK: Picking berries in the King's forest is a grave offense.

3RD MONK (*To* 2ND MONK): If you don't watch these peasants, they will steal the very trees from Sherwood Forest.

PEG (*To* MARGOT): These are strange monks, Margot, that do lack the spirit of charity.

SHERIFF (*To women*): Then you will not tell us?

NELL (*Rising*): No, my lord Sheriff.

SHERIFF: Then you shall go without your dinner tonight. (*He puts baskets into chest and closes it.*) Now, begone! And do not let me find you trespassing in Sherwood Forest again or you shall pay with your lives. (*Gesturing*) Now, out of our way!

MARGOT (*To* NELL *and* PEG, *as they start to exit right*): Oh, if only Robin Hood were here now.

SHERIFF (*Overhearing her words*): Aye, dames, talk of Robin Hood while you can. We'll find him—and we have a little surprise for him, too. Before the night is out, he'll be a prisoner in Prince John's dungeon! (*To* MONKS) Come! (*He and* MONKS *exit left; women exit right.*)

* * *

SETTING: *Robin Hood's den in Sherwood Forest.*

AT RISE: ROBIN HOOD *and his Merry Men, and* MAID MARIAN *and* ELLEN *are busy at their tasks—*MAID MARIAN *and* ELLEN *are tending to kettles and a spit set above a "fire"; some of the men are trimming off branches to make staffs; some are testing their bow-strings; others are mending arrows or practicing with quarterstaves.* ROBIN *sits on top of table at center, mending an arrow.* NELL, MARGOT, *and* PEG *rush in, right.*

NELL: Oh, Robin, Robin! (ROBIN *jumps down from table.*)

ROBIN (*Bowing*): Welcome, Nell. And Peg—and Margot —welcome to our grove. What brings you ladies to the greenwood?

PEG: Robin, we've come to warn you. The Sheriff of Nottingham is in Sherwood Forest.

WILL SCARLET: With his men-at-arms?

MARGOT: There were but three monks with him. We had been gathering wild blackberries, when they came upon us.

NELL: The Sheriff asked us where you dwelt, Robin, but we did not tell.

PEG: So he took the berries from us.

ROBIN: The knave! Since the Sheriff has taken your food, you must dine with us today.

NELL, PEG, *and* MARGOT (*Ad lib*): Oh, thank you, Robin. Thank you. (*Etc.*)

ROBIN: Later, when it is safe for you to return through the forest, my men shall take you home. (MAID MARIAN *goes to women.*)

MAID MARIAN: Come, ladies. Perhaps you'll help me in preparing our meal.

PEG: Gladly, Marian. (MARIAN *leads women to fire. The Merry Men gather about* ROBIN.)

ROBIN: So the Sheriff is looking for Robin Hood, is he? (*Turning to men*) Well, my Merry Men, what then?

LITTLE JOHN: Then Robin Hood's men shall look for the Sheriff!

ROBIN: Well said, Little John! We'll search old Sherwood and *find* this trespasser on the King's land.

FRIAR TUCK: I shall search the west path, Robin. (*Holding out his robe*) After all, I have a way with holy men. (*Laughing, as he goes to right*) Come, Will Stutley. You, too, Ket. I've a mind to teach the Sheriff a prayer or two. (*He,* STUTLEY, *and* KET *exit.*)

WILL SCARLET: Little John and I shall go toward Lincoln Pond.

ROBIN: Fair enough, Will. And I'll see to Wentham Grove.

LITTLE JOHN: Come, Allan. Sing us a song as we go.

ALLAN-A-DALE: A fair request. Hugh, will you guard the women?

HUGH: Aye, I will, Allan. Your pretty Ellen shall not come to harm. (ALLAN, LITTLE JOHN, *and* WILL SCARLET *exit.*)

ELLEN: Marian and I have twigs to gather, Hugh. Will you join us?

HUGH: Of course, my lady.

ELLEN: And you, good women?

NELL, MARGOT, *and* PEG (*Ad lib*): Of course, Ellen. (HUGH *and the women exit left.*)

ROBIN (*To himself*): Now, where did I put that arrow I was mending? (*He looks to left, standing with his back to right entrance, as* SIR RICHARD OF THE LEA *and* LADY ALICE *enter, dressed in ragged clothes. He quickly stoops, picks up quarterstaff, wheels about.*) Who goes there? (SIR RICHARD *jumps back.*) Ah, I see I startle you. But you startled me, as well. The next time you would sneak through a forest, do not break every twig in your path. Your clumsiness gives you away. But enough. What brings you to this wood? A poor answer, and this quarter-staff will rap your knuckles.

SIR RICHARD: I know not if my answer will be a good one, but I come to Sherwood Forest in search of one Robin Hood. It is said that he dwells in these woods.

ROBIN: You search for Robin Hood, eh? And what business have you with him?

LADY ALICE (*Falling to her knees*): Oh, kind woodsman, tell us where we may find him. The wicked Sheriff of Nottingham has taken our gold from us, and our lands, and soon he will take our home. They say no one but Robin Hood can help us.

ROBIN (*Twirling staff*): Then, my dear lady, you have done well. Your steps may be clumsy, but they have not led you astray. (*Bowing*) Robin Hood, at your service.

LADY ALICE (*Rising*): Oh, Robin, I am so glad we have found you.

SIR RICHARD: And I, too. I am Sir Richard of the Lea, and this is my wife, the Lady Alice. I fear our ragged clothes belie those noble titles, but in truth, little more remains to us than those names.

ROBIN (*Kindly*): Tell me the cause of your woes, and perhaps we shall be able to help you. I have my own quarrels with this Sheriff of Nottingham, and it is my pleasure to aid those who have felt the sting of his Norman greed. Tell me your tale. (*He sits.*)

WILL SCARLET (*Rushing in*): Robin! Robin! (*He sees* SIR RICHARD *and* LADY ALICE *and stops short, then whispers something to* ROBIN.)

ROBIN: Well done, Will Scarlet. Well done! The hound has found his quarry.

LITTLE JOHN (*Running on*): Aye, Robin, Will Stutley, Ket, and Friar Tuck are escorting our guests this very minute. Tell the others, Robin.

ROBIN (*Taking his hunting horn from his belt; to* SIR

RICHARD *and* LADY ALICE): You bring us good luck, Sir Richard. I shall summon the rest of my Merry Men, and then, I promise, you'll see how Robin Hood's justice is meted out in Sherwood Forest. (*Blows on horn*)

ALLAN ·(*Entering, out of breath; to* LITTLE JOHN): I've searched the whole south path, from Barnesdale Cave to Thurston's Den, and there's not a sign of him, Little John. (*The women, carrying kindling, enter left with* HUGH.)

MARIAN: We heard you call, Robin. Nothing is wrong, is it?

ROBIN: No, my love. Nothing at all. The Sheriff is about to pay us a visit, that's all.

ALLAN: They've found him!

LADY ALICE: The Sheriff is coming!

HUGH: Now we'll teach that proud tyrant a lesson or two. (FRIAR TUCK *enters, leading* SHERIFF, *who is blindfolded.*)

FRIAR TUCK: Look what I've brought you, Robin.

ROBIN (*Going to* SHERIFF *and untying blindfold*): Welcome to the Grove of the Trysting Oak, my lord Sheriff of Nottingham. (KET *and* WILL STUTLEY *enter, leading the* THREE MONKS, *also blindfolded.*)

SHERIFF (*Rubbing his eyes*): You rascal! You'll pay for this! (KET *and* WILL STUTLEY *undo* MONKS' *blindfolds.*)

1ST MONK: You rogues!

2ND MONK: Waylaying holy men in the forest!

3RD MONK: You should be taught a stern lesson for this!

ROBIN (*Walking toward* MONKS): And look what we have here. (MONKS *hold their robes tightly about them.*) Since when do you travel with such holy men, my lord Sheriff?

FRIAR TUCK: The Sheriff has turned religious, Robin. (*He laughs.*)

HUGH: But he goes a mite far into the forest to say his

prayers, eh men? (*All laugh.* MONKS *look to* SHERIFF, *who steps forward.*)

SHERIFF: Enough of your idle jests! I am escorting these holy men to their abbey and have given my word that they will reach their monastery in time for vespers. Now, let us be on our way. (SHERIFF *starts right, as if to exit, but* HUGH *and* LITTLE JOHN *quickly take his arms and hold him.*)

ROBIN: If all this be true, my good Sheriff, you shall pass on your way unharmed. We shall but detain you for a short while, as we have some small business with you. (*Walks to* LADY ALICE *and* SIR RICHARD) My Merry Men, these two poor travelers happened upon me in this grove, and they claim the Sheriff has done them grievous wrongs. (*Gesturing*) Sir Richard of the Lea, and his wife, the Lady Alice.

MARIAN (*Stepping forward and curtsying*): You are welcome to our home.

MEN (*Ad lib*): Aye, welcome to the greenwood. We are at your service. (*Etc.*)

SHERIFF: So you've come to this outlaw to plead your case. Ha! (STUTLEY *goes to hold* SHERIFF) Sir Richard comes a-begging to these ragamuffins—ha! (*Laughing*) You are a merry lot indeed.

ROBIN: Shall we show the Sheriff the justice of Saxon outlaws?

MEN (*Ad lib*): Aye, Robin. Let him see a true court of law. Aye, Sheriff, we'll show you! (*Men bring* SHERIFF *to bench at left and guard him there. They place a bench at right for* LADY ALICE *and* SIR RICHARD. ROBIN *sits on table, at center.*)

ROBIN: Now, good visitors, pray tell your story and my Merry Men and I shall listen. (*To* SHERIFF) I warn you, my lord Sheriff, my Merry Men shall be the jury, and

if you have indeed done some wrong to these poor gen-
tlefolk, you shall pay the penalty before you leave.

MEN (*Ad lib*): Aye! That you will, Sheriff. Listen to him,
Sheriff! (*Etc.*)

ROBIN (*Bowing*): My Lady Alice—

LADY ALICE (*Rising*): Kind woodsmen, once Sir Richard
and I owned many lands—fair fields of wheat and barley
farmed by good hands. In our woodlands roamed all
manner of wild animals, and when we had taken all we
needed for ourselves, we used to let the poor folk hunt
within them. Our estate was indeed one of the fairest in
the kingdom, and all who lived upon it dwelt in happiness—until King Richard departed for the wars in the
Holy Land, and his brother John became our ruler.

SIR RICHARD: Prince John summoned me to the Court and
bid me accept service with him as his tax collector.
(*Looking about*) In no great time, I learned that Prince
John wanted no ordinary taxes. He sought to plunder
this fair land of all its riches and to rob its people of all
they possessed.

SHERIFF: The man speaks treason!

ROBIN (*As* HUGH *and* LITTLE JOHN *restrain the* SHERIFF):
Silence, my lord Sheriff. The story is not yet told.

SIR RICHARD: Prince John promised that I should grow
rich, that a portion of all I collected would remain as my
private treasure, but I could not in all conscience accept
his offer. (*He pauses.*) I refused him, and the Sheriff of
Nottingham became tax collector in my place. To punish me for my "disobedience," the Sheriff exacted from
us three times the tax he asked of the other nobles.

LADY ALICE: He took our wheat fields, and our fields of
barley. He took our forest lands and the streams that
gave us water. He took our sheep and our horses, our
gold and anything we owned that might be of value.

(*Sadly*) The jewels and fine linens that my father gave to me as dowry have long since gone to fill the Sheriff's coffers. Only two days ago, I gave the Sheriff's men the last of my fine brocades.

SIR RICHARD: And we still have a debt of four hundred pounds. But we have nothing left to give to the Sheriff but our home and the small parcel of land on which it stands. After that, this greenwood must be our home, as it is yours, good men.

ROBIN: This is indeed a sorry tale, Sir Richard. My lord Sheriff, think you not this is a sorry tale?

SHERIFF: I think nothing, you rogue.

ROBIN: Well, then, what think you, my Merry Men?

MARIAN (*Stepping forward, to* SHERIFF): Do not ask any more of Sir Richard, my lord Sheriff.

WILL SCARLET: Let these good people keep their home. Prince John shall find enough tax money elsewhere.

MEN (*Ad lib*): Aye. They have paid enough. No more taxes. (*Etc.*)

ROBIN (*Stepping down from table*): Well, sir Sheriff, the verdict is that you must be more merciful with Sir Richard and Lady Alice.

SHERIFF: Merciful—bah! They owe me four hundred pounds, and four hundred pounds they shall pay.

ROBIN: I shall give you another chance, Sheriff. Perhaps you will reconsider.

LADY ALICE (*Kneeling before* SHERIFF): Please, kind Sheriff, leave us our home. (*She begins to cry silently.*)

ELLEN (*Kneeling before* SHERIFF): This lady's tears should be repaid by kindness, not by cruelty, my lord.

SHERIFF: Away with you, girl! Tears mean nothing to me. Four hundred pounds will not be raised by tears.

ROBIN: Enough! You have had your last chance, Sheriff, and now you shall see how Robin Hood's justice is meted out. Scarlet, bring in the chest. (SCARLET *exits with* KET.)

SHERIFF: The chest? That chest belongs to the holy monks, here.

1ST MONK (*Gruffly*): Aye. 'Tis property of the Church.

SHERIFF (*As* WILL SCARLET *and* KET *return with chest*): There is nought in the chest but candles and incense belonging to the monks. What right have you to touch it? (*Men set chest on table at center.*)

ROBIN: We shall soon see what right we have to touch this chest, good Sheriff. (*Suddenly*) But you speak true, Sheriff. I must not touch the chest without leave of these holy fathers. (*Going to* 1ST MONK) Holy father, I fear my men and I show disrespect toward your worthy self and your brothers. (1ST MONK *pulls hood tightly about his head.*) Pray, give me your hands and your forgiveness. (ROBIN *holds out his hands, and* 1ST MONK *reluctantly takes them.* ROBIN *looks at* MONK'S *hands and suddenly swings* MONK *about, holding out* 1ST MONK'S *left hand.*) Aha! As I thought! This is no monk's hand. Look—this is a hand that holds a bow. See where the feathered shaft has left its mark on his middle finger. (*Swiftly dropping* 1ST MONK'S *hand*) Tell us more, my lord Sheriff, about these monks who bear the marks of your Norman longbows. (*To* KET *and* STUTLEY) Come, men, let us see the Sheriff's soldiers in all their Norman finery. (KET *and* STUTLEY *pull* MONK'S *robes from them, revealing soldiers' uniforms underneath.* MONKS *quickly reach for their swords, but men hold them fast.*)

FRIAR TUCK: The next time you keep company with holy men, Sheriff, be sure that you are not cheated.

SHERIFF (*Angrily, as* LITTLE JOHN *holds him*): You'll pay for this!

ROBIN: My good Sheriff, I fear you are mistaken. You may

levy high taxes and exact great payments, but you forget that the price of deception is also high. You told us the chest was filled with candles and incense, my lord Sheriff. Again let us see if you spoke the truth. (*Opens chest; tipping it over so that its contents spill over the table— fine cloths, jeweled cups, golden plates, etc.*) Do you see candles and incense here? Indeed not! These are the treasures that only a tax collector would carry.

SHERIFF: Rogue! Varlet! You'll pay for your evil deeds, Robin Hood. I'll see that you pay with your life!

ROBIN (*To his men*): Ah, the Sheriff fears he will have no treasure to show Prince John. (*To* SHERIFF) We shall give you something to show to Prince John, my lord Sheriff, but all in good time. We must first settle an account or two. (*Counting on fingers*) Sir Richard's debt amounts to four hundred pounds, does it not?

SHERIFF (*Moodily*): Aye.

ROBIN: Now let us see. . . . As for what you and your men-at-arms owe to us— (SHERIFF *starts to protest, but men hold him firmly.*) You took us from our tasks today and instead of mending our arrows and practicing our marksmanship, we had to spend our time searching the forest for you and your men. For the time we spent searching Sherwood Forest, I shall charge you fifty pounds. (*Sifts through "treasure" and pulls out jeweled sword*) This sword is worth some fifty pounds, I warrant. (*He puts sword on small table at right.*)

LITTLE JOHN (*Helpfully*): I had to ford Bedwin's Stream as I searched the forest, Robin.

ROBIN (*Pointing to* LITTLE JOHN's *feet*): For Little John's wet feet, I charge you another fifty pounds. (*Takes gilded chalice from "treasure" and sets it on small table*)

WILL STUTLEY: And Ket and Friar Tuck and I led the Sheriff and his men safely through the forest to this grove.

ROBIN: And so you did. (*To* SHERIFF) Why, Sheriff, certainly you owe us much for protecting you from the dangerous outlaws who hide in Sherwood Forest.

FRIAR TUCK: Aye! We gave him safe conduct, did we not, men?

ROBIN (*Looking through treasure*): Let me see . . . this cloth (*Holding up wool cloth*) for keeping you safe from Gibbs, the villainous wool merchant.

2ND MONK (*Gruffly*): Gibbs, the villainous wool merchant —hah! There is no such man. You'll not trick us with fancy names.

LITTLE JOHN: Gibbs, the wool merchant? Never heard of him.

ROBIN (*Aside, to men*): Nor have I. (*Walking toward* 2ND MONK, *as he holds cloth*) Tell me, have you not heard of this villain? They say he is a vile rogue, who pulls the wool over his customers' eyes. (*Throws cloth over* 2ND MONK's *head. All laugh as* 2ND MONK *struggles to throw it off.*) And, now, where was I? Ah, yes, the other villains of the forest.

3RD MONK (*Grumbling*): A pack of worthless outlaws!

ROBIN (*Overhearing him*): Ah! You have reminded me, my goodly "monk." My men have kept you safe from Hatch, the hawk-nosed huntsman. They say he can smell a chest full of velvets seven leagues away. (*Pulling out long piece of velvet*) Ah, indeed! Had he smelled this, it would have gone hard with you. (*Tosses velvet onto table*)

1ST MONK: You rogues! The Sheriff of Nottingham and his men are not this easily beaten. You'll see.

FRIAR TUCK (*Taking long piece of brocade and walking toward* 1ST MONK): Ah, my reverend father—or should I call you my reverend archer? You are angered because you are not yet a true man of the cloth. (*Wrapping brocade around* 1ST MONK) Here, my good man, try this.

(FRIAR TUCK *winds cloth tightly around* 1ST MONK. MONK *hobbles about, trying to unwind the cloth as all laugh.*)

LADY ALICE (*Thoughtfully, as she watches* MONK): That brocade . . . I would swear 'tis some I myself gave to the Sheriff and his men. (ROBIN *picks up brocade after* MONK *has unwound it.*)

ROBIN (*Taking brocade to* LADY ALICE; *kneeling*): If this be yours, good lady, let me now restore it to you.

LADY ALICE (*Taking cloth*): Oh, Robin, you are too kind.

ROBIN (*Taking other cloths, sword, and gilded chalice*): The Prince will not miss these riches. And (*Setting them at feet of* LADY ALICE *and* SIR RICHARD) I think you shall put them to better use than would Prince John and the Sheriff.

SIR RICHARD: Robin, you have indeed come to our rescue.

ROBIN (*Looking to* SHERIFF *and then to cloths and other treasures*): These, I would think, are worth four hundred pounds, Sir Richard.

SHERIFF (*Fuming with anger*): Villains! You'll pay for your insolence!

ROBIN (*Reaching down into chest*): But what is this? (*Taking baskets from chest*) A strange kind of goods for a tax collector's chest.

NELL: Our blackberries!

MARGOT: Those are the baskets the Sheriff took from us!

ROBIN: Three baskets of (*Eating blackberry*) delicious wild blackberries. Oh, Sheriff, these berries must have cost you much. (*Walking to* SHERIFF) Why, had they been mine to sell, I should have asked for much gold in return for such sweet-tasting fruit. Tell me, what payment did the good women ask?

SHERIFF: Payment? Your jests are funny indeed. The Sheriff of Nottingham doesn't pay for what he wants. He takes it!

MONKS: Aye!

ROBIN: Then you have made a grave error, my lord Sheriff, for in Sherwood Forest, we keep strict accounts, and *everything* must be paid for. Will Scarlet, bring in the sack. (*He whispers something to* SCARLET, *who exits.*)

3RD MONK: You scoundrels! To think I carried that sack from Avondale to Hereford, and now it ends in the hands of these outlaws.

WILL SCARLET (*Returning with sack*): Here you are, Robin.

ROBIN: Thanks, good Scarlet. (*Taking small bag from the sack; holding basket and walking to* NELL) Now it seems, Nell, that you have one full basket of wild berries here. Is that not so?

NELL: Aye, Robin. It is indeed.

ROBIN: Hold out your hands, Nell. (*She does so.* ROBIN *holds up basket in one hand and bag in other, as if his arms were part of a scale.*) Ah, it is a fair balance. Here is your payment, Nell. (*He pours gold coins from bag into* NELL's *hands. Gold spills onto the ground, and others help her gather it in.*)

NELL: Oh, thank you, Robin.

ROBIN (*Going to* SHERIFF): And, for you, my lord Sheriff —your blackberries. (*Holding out handful of berries*) Here, Sheriff, try one.

SHERIFF (*Gesturing*): Take them away. I don't want them.

ROBIN: But they are yours. You have paid for them, my lord Sheriff. I would not want my men to think that the Sheriff would buy something he does not want. Here, show my men you like the blackberries of Sherwood Forest. Eat one, my lord.

KET (*As Merry Men draw closer; menacingly*): Aye, Sheriff. Show us that you like our woodland berries.

SHERIFF (*Reluctantly eating berry*): There.

MEN (*Cheering*): Aye!

ROBIN: You like the berries, my lord Sheriff! (*Taking out two more bags of gold*) Here, Margot and Peg, the Sheriff will buy your baskets as well. (*Hands bags to women, places baskets beside* SHERIFF)

MARGOT *and* PEG (*Ad lib*): Robin, you are so good. Thank you, Robin! (*Etc.*)

ROBIN: We have but one more account to settle—yours, my lord Sheriff. (*To* WILL SCARLET) Where is the last bag, Will? (WILL SCARLET *picks up bag and hands it to* ROBIN.) Well done, Will. (*To* SHERIFF) My lord Sheriff, we would not want you returning to Prince John with an empty hand. We promised we would give you something, and so we shall. (*Tossing bag in* SHERIFF's *direction, but over his head to where* LITTLE JOHN *is standing*) Here, my lord Sheriff, take this to your precious Prince. (SHERIFF *reaches for bag, but cannot catch it, and* LITTLE JOHN *catches it instead.*)

LITTLE JOHN: Here, my lord Sheriff. (*Tosses bag over* SHERIFF's *head to* WILL SCARLET)

WILL SCARLET: Try again, good Sheriff. (*Tosses bag to* LADY ALICE)

LADY ALICE (*Catching bag*): This bag of poor folks' tax money is heavy. (*Walking to* SHERIFF) But it should be enough to satisfy the Sheriff for some short while, I hope. (*Sets bag at* SHERIFF's *feet*)

WILL SCARLET (*As* SHERIFF *kneels to pick up bag*): Hurrah! The debt is paid! Well done, my lady.

FRIAR TUCK: At last the Sheriff kneels to justice!

SHERIFF (*Picks up bag and opens it, taking out a stone and holding it up*): A stone! You've filled the bag with stones! (*Merry Men all laugh.*)

ROBIN (*To* SHERIFF): You have brought us much merriment this day, my lord Sheriff, but we have detained you long enough. (KET *and* WILL STUTLEY *bring blindfolds.*)

Ket and Will Stutley shall escort you through the forest, and if you make haste, you shall be in Nottingham by sunset.

SHERIFF: And then Prince John shall hear of you and your disgraceful outlaw tricks. You'll pay for your deeds, Robin Hood. I shall return, and then you will know what happens to those who anger the Sheriff of Nottingham. I shall return with my men—

ROBIN (*Nodding his head*): Oh, indeed, Sheriff. But you'll have to find me first! (*He laughs.* KET *and* STUTLEY *quickly blindfold the* SHERIFF *and his men.*) Return quickly, men.

KET: Aye, Robin. We shall.

STUTLEY (*To* SHERIFF *and his men*): Come. (KET *and* STUTLEY *lead* SHERIFF *and his men off right.*)

ROBIN (*Looking about*): And now, men, a feast! Our visitors must have a taste of our woodland venison.

MEN: Aye!

LITTLE JOHN: The King's venison shall make us a kingly feast! (*All begin to prepare feast—bringing platters and goblets to upstage table, tending to the spit and kettles, etc.*)

MARIAN: Come, Ellen, help me fill the goblets. Come, Nell. (*Women fill goblets, as others bring more food and benches to the table. When table is ready, all sit around it.*)

LITTLE JOHN (*Rising and raising his goblet*): Good visitors and Merry Men, a toast! To Robin Hood!

SIR RICHARD (*Rising*): To Robin Hood! (LADY ALICE *rises next then* NELL, MARGOT, *and* PEG, *and then the others.*)

ALL: To Robin Hood! (*All drink toast, and sit down to begin feast. As others carve meat, fill plates and bowls, and begin to eat,* ALLAN *rises and begins to walk around the table singing.*)

ALLAN (*Singing to tune of "Coventry Carol"*):

Robin Hood and his merry men,
Clad all in Lincoln green,
In Sherwood Forest make their home—(*Bowing to*
   MARIAN)
Maid Marian is their queen.
While Richard, England's noble king,
Fights in the Holy Land,
The tyrant John sits on the throne,
Rules with an iron hand.
(ALLAN *leads singing, and others join in.*)
Robin Hood fights in freedom's cause,
Tyranny spurs him on—
Protecting honest English folk
Wronged by the cruel Prince John.
Sheriff of Nottingham, beware—
Look well where you do tread.
When England's rightful king returns,
Watch—or he'll have your head.
(ALLAN *steps forward as curtains begin to close, singing*
slowly.)
Robin Hood, clad in Lincoln green,
Dwelt with his merry men—
He robbed the rich to help the poor—
His like shall not come again.
(*Repeating last line, very slowly*)
His like shall not come again. (*Curtain*)

THE END

A Most Special Dragon

An old English tale

by David Ferguson

Characters

GLORIANA ⎫ *the King's children*
ERIC ⎭
MIKTA, *an enchanted dragon*
ZARTOUM, *a wizard*
SIR REDMOND, *a knight*
KING
GUARD

SCENE 1

TIME: *The Middle Ages in England.*
SETTING: *The courtyard of the King's castle. A long bench stands at center, covered with a cloth that reaches the ground. Two chairs are left and right of bench.*
AT RISE: GLORIANA *enters right, on tiptoe, and crosses to bench.*

GLORIANA (*Calling softly off right*): Come on! (ERIC *enters from right, also on tiptoe, and joins her.*)
ERIC (*Softly*): Is he still here? (*He looks around stage.*)
GLORIANA: Unless Sir Redmond found him. (*Calling*)

79

Mikta! Mikta! (MIKTA, *the dragon, slowly raises his head from behind the bench.*)

ERIC (*Happily*): There he is! (MIKTA *joins the children at center. They hug him.*)

GLORIANA: Did you miss us? (MIKTA *nods.*) Did Sir Redmond find you? (MIKTA *shakes his head emphatically.*)

ERIC: We're going to get Zartoum to help you. He's the best sorcerer in the world! (*There is a noise off left.*) What's that?

GLORIANA (*Looking off left*): It's Sir Redmond! He's coming! (MIKTA *and children hide behind bench.* SIR REDMOND *and* ZARTOUM *enter from left.* ZARTOUM *carries a thick book.*)

REDMOND: I tell you, wizard, I heard a noise out here. It's those children again, I'll wager.

ZARTOUM: But, Sir Redmond, their father *is* the King.

REDMOND: He's been gone for a year now, hasn't he? And you know what the law says.

ZARTOUM: Yes, sire. (*Reciting*)
"If the King shall be gone a year and a day,
Then the knight called Redmond shall hold sway."

REDMOND: Right! And tomorrow is the last day. If the King doesn't appear, *I* shall be king!

ZARTOUM: But, sire, he will surely come.

REDMOND: I would not be so certain. What if he's been eaten by a dragon?

ZARTOUM: I hardly think that is possible, sire. You have killed most of the dragons in the kingdom.

REDMOND: Aye, that I have, but some are still loose. Not until I cut off the head of *every* dragon will I be satisfied.

ZARTOUM: As you say, sire.

REDMOND (*Looking around stage*): Well, whoever made that noise isn't here now. I'm going to check the guards on the castle walls. (*He starts to walk off right.*)

ZARTOUM: Very good, sire. I shall stay here. I have some spells to perform.

REDMOND (*Scoffingly*): Ha! You haven't cast a spell properly in forty years. (*He exits right. The children run from behind the bench to* ZARTOUM.)

GLORIANA (*Anxiously*): Zartoum! If Father doesn't come back tomorrow, will Sir Redmond really be king?

ZARTOUM (*Comfortingly*): Yes, I'm afraid so, but don't worry. I'm sure your father will turn up. (MIKTA's *head pops up behind bench;* ZARTOUM *sees him.*) What's this? A dragon? (*He pulls his magic wand from his sleeve.*) All right, you beast! (*Waving wand at* MIKTA, *he chants some magic words.*) Reggabad, livvogad, froom! (*At last magic word,* MIKTA *quickly sets up a huge paper flower which has been hidden behind the bench, concealing his movements from audience. The children laugh, and* ZARTOUM *scratches his head.*) A flower? I was certain that was a spell for dragons. . . .

GLORIANA (*Still laughing*): That's all right, Zartoum. Mikta's a special dragon.

ZARTOUM: Is that so? Well, it wouldn't be a good idea to make him disappear, would it? (*He takes handkerchief from his pocket and wipes his brow.*) But he certainly startled me. (*A rubber ball is sewn into a fold of handkerchief.* ZARTOUM *throws handkerchief to floor, catches it, and puts it back in his pocket, showing no sign of surprise. The children stare at him, but say nothing.*) Well, now, what can I do for you?

ERIC: We need your help, Zartoum.

ZARTOUM (*Astonished*): My help? Whatever for?

GLORIANA: We have to make Mikta safe from Sir Redmond. (MIKTA *comes to stand beside her.*)

ZARTOUM: Oh. Yes, I see what you mean. (*He sits on bench and thumbs through his book.*) Let me see . . . flying

carpets, rabbits from hats, fish feathers, dragons . . .
here we are! Protecting dragons! (*Reading*)
A dragon, to be safe and sound,
Must take a potion, finely ground,
Of root and birch tree, mushroom stem,
Powdered lily and nolorem.

GLORIANA: What's nolorem?

ZARTOUM (*Closing book*): A rare, rare spice, with all sorts
of magical powers. It can change things into other
things, and change them back; it can protect all creatures from harm; and it can undo any charm in the
world.

ERIC: Do you have any nolorem, Zartoum?

ZARTOUM (*Sadly*): No, my lad. In all the kingdom there is
only one man who has nolorem—Sir Redmond!

GLORIANA: Oh, no!

ZARTOUM: Yes. He keeps it in the little bag around his
neck. (*Hopefully*) But perhaps we could get it from him.

ERIC: How? He'll never give it to us.

ZARTOUM: No, but perhaps we can borrow it. I have an
idea. Listen. . . . (*Children and* MIKTA *draw close to
him as the curtain falls.*)

*   *   *

SCENE 2

TIME: *The next day.*

SETTING: *The same as Scene 1.*

AT RISE: *A scarf, a feather, a cup, and other magic props
are on chair beside the bench.* ZARTOUM *and* REDMOND
enter left, talking. REDMOND *wears small bag on a ribbon
around his neck.*

ZARTOUM: I hope you'll stay and view my magic act, sire.
I have to practice it before I perform at court.

REDMOND (*Glumly*): Very well. Let's get on with it.

ZARTOUM: Thank you, sire. (*Indicating a chair*) Won't you sit down? (REDMOND *sits, arms folded, looking angry.* ZARTOUM *may perform a simple magic trick at this time.*) Well, sire, my first trick will be to summon ghosts, and make them disappear. (*He takes scarf from chair*) Would you tie this around your eyes, sire? It's necessary for the trick.

REDMOND (*Taking scarf disgustedly*): Oh, very well. This had better be good. (*Ties scarf around his eyes*) Is this all right?

ZARTOUM: Fine, sire. Now I'll summon the spirits. (*Chants mysteriously*)

Blemobeem, rackipas, steembog, garp.

Shooleram, quishquat, zinzam, marp!

Sky ghosts, sea ghosts, spirits of the deep,

I summon you now to awake from your sleep.

(GLORIANA *and* ERIC, *followed by* MIKTA, *tiptoe on from left and watch, as* ZARTOUM *brushes feather across* REDMOND's *face.*)

REDMOND (*Jumping up in terror*): What was that?

ZARTOUM: Be still, sire! The spirits are here! Do not anger them. (ZARTOUM *brushes feather across* REDMOND's *face again, and lifts small bag off his chest. He nods to* ERIC, *who unties ribbon.*)

REDMOND (*In terror*): What's that?

ZARTOUM: Be *still*, sire! (*He gives bag to* ERIC, *who rushes off with* GLORIANA. MIKTA *remains, staring at scarf.*) The ghosts are gone now, sire. You're safe.

REDMOND (*Nervously*): Bah, what foolishness! (*He unties scarf and throws it behind him. It lands on* MIKTA's *head.*) What else have you to show me?

ZARTOUM: Well, sire, I . . . that is, I . . . (MIKTA *removes scarf and throws it angrily over* REDMOND's *head.*)

REDMOND (*Jumping up*): What's this? (*Removing scarf*

and seeing MIKTA) Aha! A dragon! (*Calling*) Guard!
(REDMOND *runs after* MIKTA, *who rushes to right.* GUARD
enters, right, carrying a spear.) Stop it, you fool! (GUARD
begins to chase MIKTA. ZARTOUM *pulls out his wand
and points it at* GUARD.)

ZARTOUM: Screelly—scrally—scrop! (GUARD *freezes.*)

REDMOND: What are you doing?

ZARTOUM: Sorry, sire. I think I used the wrong spell again.
I'll try this one. (*Chants*) Screelly—scrally—whop!

REDMOND: I'll deal with you later, but now . . . (*Un-
sheathing his sword*) I'm after this beast! (*He leaps after*
MIKTA, *who flees in panic. They race around stage, as*
ZARTOUM *watches, waving his arms helplessly. If stage
has stairs to audience,* REDMOND *may chase* MIKTA *up
aisle and back onstage. Finally,* MIKTA *grabs scarf and
tosses it over* REDMOND's *head. As* REDMOND *struggles,*
MIKTA *runs off left.*) Stupid beast! (*Removes scarf; to*
ZARTOUM) Which way did he go?

ZARTOUM (*Pointing off right*): That way, sire. Hurry! You
may catch him. (REDMOND *rushes off right.* ZARTOUM
crosses to left and calls offstage.) Hurry up, there. (ERIC
*enters left, carrying small cauldron which he puts down
at center.* GLORIANA *follows him, carrying the bag of
nolorem.* MIKTA *hurries on last and joins the others.*)

ERIC: Here's the potion, Zartoum, mixed the way you told
me.

GLORIANA: Here's the nolorem.

ZARTOUM: Give it to me, quickly. (GLORIANA *gives sack to*
ZARTOUM, *who empties it into cauldron and begins stirring with his wand.*)

Stars of the east, shades of the west,
Song of the nightwind, hummingbird crest,
Spirit of good and heart of the earth,
Give to this brew the sorcerer's worth.
Rellarax, krekkafax, mailmin, broo;

Fellibob, viggagob, pullabof, voo.

(*He peers into cauldron.*) It's ready.

ERIC: Now what?

ZARTOUM: A cup. There, on the chair. (*He points to cup. GLORIANA gets it and brings it to him. He dips it into cauldron.*) Now, to sprinkle our scaly friend. . . . (*He dips his fingers into cup and pretends to sprinkle some of potion onto MIKTA, who squirms.*) Oh, my! Oh—oh. Too much, too much.

GLORIANA: What's the matter, Zartoum?

ZARTOUM: I used too much of the potion. There's no telling what will happen now. We'll have to wait and find out. (REDMOND *enters right with drawn sword*)

REDMOND (*Furiously*): You've bungled your last bungle! (*He rushes at ZARTOUM, who points his wand at REDMOND.*)

ZARTOUM: Hold! (REDMOND *freezes.*)

REDMOND: What's this, more trickery?

ZARTOUM: I cannot be harmed while I am under the protection of the King. Only he can touch me.

REDMOND: But *I* am the king!

ZARTOUM (*Lowering his wand*): No, not until the sun sets.

REDMOND (*Sheathing sword*): Very well, wizard. See if the King can protect you from—(*He reaches for bag of nolorem, discovers it is gone, and speaks frantically.*) Where is it?

ZARTOUM (*Innocently*): What, sire?

REDMOND: My nolorem! It was in the sack around my neck. (*Seeing sack on floor*) There it is! (*He grabs sack.*) It's empty! (*To* ZARTOUM) What did you do with it? (*He sees cauldron.*) No . . . no, you couldn't have!

ZARTOUM: Ah, but I did!

REDMOND: And that dragon—did you give any to him?

ZARTOUM (*Innocently*): What of it? Perhaps I did.

REDMOND (*Suspiciously*): Nothing, nothing at all. But the

dragon must be killed! (*He draws his sword.* MIKTA
hides behind ZARTOUM.)

GLORIANA: Do something, Zartoum!

ZARTOUM: I can't. The sword is charmed.

ERIC (*To* REDMOND): Why kill Mikta? He can't hurt you.

ZARTOUM: That's right, sire. He can't hurt you, unless . . .
unless . . . So that's it! (ZARTOUM *points his wand at*
MIKTA.)

River of fire, winter of heat,
Turtle feathers, and lemon sweet,
Creature of land, or creature of sea,
Assume the shape that thou shouldst be!

(*Lights go out. Thunder or a loud crash is heard offstage. In the darkness,* MIKTA *goes off and* KING *enters
to take his place. Lights go on. At the sight of* KING,
ZARTOUM *falls to his knees,* REDMOND *cringes, and* ERIC
and GLORIANA *run to him.*)

ERIC *and* GLORIANA (*Happily*): Father!

ZARTOUM: Your Majesty!

REDMOND (*In terror*): No! (*He falls to his knees.*) Have
mercy, your Majesty!

KING: Silence! (*To* ZARTOUM) It was Redmond who had
me changed into a dragon by an evil sorcerer, a year ago.

ZARTOUM: So that's why he wanted to kill all the dragons!

KING: Yes, but luckily, you saved me.

ZARTOUM: What shall we do with him now?

KING: Let me see . . . perhaps we can arrange it so that
he will be harmless, and the children can still have a
dragon to play with.

ZARTOUM (*Chuckling*): You mean. . . .

KING: Yes. Can't you transfer the spell?

ZARTOUM: A little nolorem should fix him. (*He dips cup
into cauldron and sprinkles* REDMOND *with liquid.*)

Thou who dared to change the King,
Become the same: a dragon-thing!

REDMOND: No! No, not that! (*He jumps up and rushes off left.*)

KING: Stop!

ZARTOUM: Don't worry, sire. The potion will soon take effect.

REDMOND (*Off left*): Oh, no!

ZARTOUM (*Pointing left*): Here he comes now. A new friend for the children . . . a most special dragon! (MIKTA *enters left, and the children run to hug him, laughing.*)

KING (*Laughing*): So Redmond is the dragon now!

ZARTOUM: Yes, Your Majesty. The potion will make anyone a friendly dragon—even Sir Redmond! (KING *and* ZARTOUM *laugh, as curtain falls.*)

THE END

The Wise People of Gotham

An English folk tale

by Eleanor D. Leuser

Characters

HERALD ⎤
JOHN
RICHARD
HARRY
TIMOTHY
ROBERT
GAVIN ⎬ *townspeople*
MARTIN
FAIR ELLEN
MARY
BETSY
ELIZA
ALICE
JOAN ⎦
LORD HIGH CHANCELLOR
STRANGER

SCENE 1

TIME: *A long time ago in England.*
SETTING: *A square in the town of Gotham.*
AT RISE: HERALD *is standing on a stone or a small platform*

as JOHN, RICHARD, HARRY, TIMOTHY, ROBERT, GAVIN, MARTIN, *and* FAIR ELLEN *enter and gather about him, talking among themselves.*

HERALD: Come ye! Come ye! All good people of Gotham, I have a message from your king. (*Townspeople grow quiet as* HERALD *continues.*) The new king of England has just learned of your fair village of Gotham. He has also learned that never in the last one hundred years has Gotham been visited by royalty. He feels that this has been a grievous wrong which should be righted. Therefore, he is sending his Lord High Chancellor to Gotham to make arrangements for a royal visit, and bids you welcome him. That is all. (HERALD *turns and exits.*)

JOHN: This is not good.

RICHARD: If the King comes, he will not be satisfied just to *see* our town. He will want to raise our taxes.

HARRY: He will probably plan to make public roads out of our farm lands.

TIMOTHY: He will take our best men to Court with him to act as his advisers. Our town will suffer.

ROBERT: It would be better if no outsider came for another hundred years, especially one from the Court.

GAVIN: And most especially the King.

MARTIN: But what can we do about it?

JOHN: There must be something.

FAIR ELLEN (*Jumping up on the stone*): Listen, good people—all of you. I have an idea!

ALL (*Crowding around her; ad lib*): What? How? Tell us! (*Etc.*)

FAIR ELLEN: When the King's Lord High Chancellor arrives, let all our townspeople pretend to be foolish and act half-witted. The Lord High Chancellor will be amazed and return to the King. His Majesty, hearing such a tale, will never wish to visit such a town.

JOHN (*Doubtfully*): But the King might punish *us*, the people of Gotham.

FAIR ELLEN: He would never punish us, for he would think we knew no better.

RICHARD (*Hesitating*): I do not know. I am afraid it might not work.

FAIR ELLEN (*Coaxingly*): But if the King does not come, he will forget about us. Then there will be no tax. Everything will be as it has been for another hundred years.

HARRY: It might be worth trying.

TIMOTHY: How would we go about it?

FAIR ELLEN: Let me talk to the women of the town. We will make the plans, if you will go along with us. Everything will be in readiness when the Lord High Chancellor appears.

ROBERT: Anything will be better than having the King come—

GAVIN: And tax us and upset all our lives.

MARTIN: I say Fair Ellen should do as she sees best.

RICHARD: Yes, yes, go ahead. Plan for us all to be exceedingly crazy.

FAIR ELLEN: I promise, you'll never be sorry. I shall gather together the women of Gotham, and we shall make our plans. (FAIR ELLEN *exits as the curtain falls.*)

*   *   *

SCENE 2

TIME: *Two weeks later.*
SETTING: *The same as Scene 1.*
AT RISE: *The* LORD HIGH CHANCELLOR *enters.*

LORD HIGH CHANCELLOR (*Looking all around*): I wonder where everyone is. (*Calling*) Ho, good people of Gotham! Come hither. I come from your king. Ho, there, I say!

(TOWNSPEOPLE *peer out briefly from behind tree, bench,
and platform, then draw back as* JOHN *enters. He is
pushing a wheelbarrow upside down.* LORD HIGH CHAN-
CELLOR *looks surprised*) Fellow, what on earth are you
doing with your wheelbarrow upside down?

JOHN (*Looking stupid*): Why, good sir, 'tis to make sure
that no one will put anything in it. (*He laughs foolishly
and wheels wheelbarrow offstage.*)

LORD HIGH CHANCELLOR: Methinks I never saw one so
foolish in my life. (*Looking offstage*) Aha, here come
some village women. (BETSY, MARY, ELIZA, *and* ALICE
*enter, carrying boxes, pans, and butterfly nets. They
chase each other about the stage.*)

BETSY (*Almost knocking down* LORD HIGH CHANCELLOR,
*as she pretends to catch something in net, just above his
head*): Oh, I beg pardon, sir. I thought I had it.

MARY (*Approaching* LORD HIGH CHANCELLOR): It's there!
It's there! (*She almost knocks his hat off.*)

LORD HIGH CHANCELLOR (*Crossly*): My good ladies, what
are you doing?

ELIZA: We are trying to catch the sunshine, sir.

LORD HIGH CHANCELLOR (*Astounded*): Catch the sunshine!
Are you crazy?

ALICE (*Winking at others*): Of course not, good sir. (*Gesturing toward backdrop or toward wings*) You see, our
houses have become so overshadowed by these large trees
that they are quite dark inside.

BETSY: We are trying to catch the sunlight to put inside
our houses. Then they will be light as day.

LORD HIGH CHANCELLOR: 'Tis a witless idea. Catch sunlight indeed!

MARY (*Looking sad*): Oh, what a pity. We thought it would
work.

RICHARD (*Entering*): I've been listening to you stupid
women, and I have a better idea.

WOMEN (*Excitedly, ad lib*): What? How? Tell us! (*Etc.*)

RICHARD: I'll get the other men of Gotham to help me take the roofs off the houses. Then the sunlight will pour in.

WOMEN (*Ad lib*): Wonderful! Wonderful! A fine idea! (*Etc.*)

LORD HIGH CHANCELLOR: You numskull! The rain and the wind will come in, too. Leave the roofs alone and cut down some of the trees.

ALL (*Ad lib*): Why didn't we think of that? Naturally. Of course! (JOAN *enters, carrying a large feather.*)

JOAN (*Crying*): Oh, dear! Oh, dear!

LORD HIGH CHANCELLOR: Now, what is the matter with you, my girl? Why all this weeping?

JOAN: Oh, good sir, this feather has lost its bird, and it is feeling so sad about it.

LORD HIGH CHANCELLOR: It would be more to the point if the *bird* were feeling sad about losing its feather. Is there no one with any sense in this town?

JOAN (*Hesitating*): Why, there is one person—

LORD HIGH CHANCELLOR: Go and fetch that person immediately, whoever it is.

JOAN: It's Mistress Ellen, sir. She's the brightest of us all.

LORD HIGH CHANCELLOR: Bring her here immediately. I cannot stand one more of these half-wits. (JOAN *exits briefly and returns with* FAIR ELLEN, *who comes dancing in and curtsies to the* LORD HIGH CHANCELLOR. *He addresses* ELLEN *severely.*) The townspeople say you have good sense. Well, you'd better try to give some of it to your neighbors. They don't seem to have any at all.

FAIR ELLEN: Oh, yes, sir!

LORD HIGH CHANCELLOR: Now, listen. Tell these people of Gotham that before the King comes to visit them, he must receive the first installment of their taxes. It seems they have never paid any taxes at all. When your people have proved their good faith in this matter, then the King will be pleased to visit Gotham. Now I must be gone. (*He leaves, muttering to himself and shaking his head.*)

FAIR ELLEN (*Standing on the stone as the townspeople gather round her*): Good people, you were all most beautifully mad. Yet we must all be even more foolish than before if any other nobleman from the Court comes to visit us. Now I have an idea about the taxes—(*All gather still closer about* FAIR ELLEN, *and as she begins to whisper her plan, the curtain falls.*)

*   *   *

SCENE 3

TIME: *Two months later.*

SETTING: *The same.*

AT RISE: JOHN *is mending a net.* BETSY, ALICE, MARY, *and* ELIZA *each have a mirror into which they are gazing.* MARTIN *has a huge sieve into which he is trying to pour water.* JOAN *is running about wildly.* GAVIN *and* HARRY *are holding a white rabbit.* FAIR ELLEN *enters and all stop their activities.*

FAIR ELLEN (*Out of breath*): 'Tis good you are practicing your madness, for I have come to tell you that a stranger is coming down the road. I feel sure by his dress that he is from the King. Now, you each know what you are to say and do?

ALL (*Ad lib*): Yes, yes, we know. We are ready. (FAIR ELLEN *runs from one to the other, whispering in their ears, as they resume their activities.* STRANGER *enters and watches them quietly for a moment before he speaks.*)

STRANGER: Good day, my good people. You all look very

busy. (*He goes up to* JOHN, *who works intently on his net.*) What are you doing, my man?

JOHN (*Making an O of his thumb and forefinger and holding it up in the air*): I'm taking holes out of the air and sewing them together to make a net. (*He smiles foolishly.*)

STRANGER: Marry, good man, you are cleverer than I. (*He goes up to the women, who immediately close their eyes and hold up their mirrors as if to look in them.*) Good women, are you looking in your mirrors to see how fair you are?

BETSY (*Giggling*): Oh, no, good sir.

ALICE: We are just trying to find out how we look when we're asleep.

ELIZA: That's why our eyes are closed.

MARY: Isn't it a good idea, sir?

STRANGER: Hm-m. A clever idea—or is it a foolish one? I begin to wonder. (JOAN, *who has started to run around again, bumps into him.*)

JOAN: I'm sorry, good master. I was just trying to catch something very important.

STRANGER (*Curiously*): And what is that?

JOAN: My shadow!

STRANGER: Why on earth would you want to catch your shadow?

JOAN: Then it could help me in my work. At present it does nothing but follow me around.

STRANGER: I'll wager if you catch it, it will be the first shadow in captivity. (*He goes up to* MARTIN, *who is trying vainly to pour water into his sieve.*) What is your trouble, good fellow?

MARTIN: I do not know what is the matter, sir. This sieve will not hold a drop of water.

STRANGER: I cannot believe what I see or hear. No people can be as witless as these. (*Raising his voice*) Good people of Gotham, you have not yet sent your yearly taxes to the King. I have come to see what is the matter. (GAVIN *and* HARRY *come forward.* HARRY *carries white rabbit.*)

GAVIN: Oh, but we did, my lord.

HARRY: We tied the money around the neck of our pet hare and sent the hare on its way to the King.

GAVIN (*Pointing to the rabbit*): And here it is. It came back without the money, so it must have reached there.

STRANGER (*Groaning*): But don't you know that London, where the King is, is a good fifty miles from here? How much money did you send with this hare?

HARRY: We put a thousand gold pieces in a purse and tied it around the hare's neck.

STRANGER: A pox on such stupid fellows to waste so much money in such a stupid way. I cannot understand this situation at all. Methinks there is something queer going on. Begone, all of you, while I think this through. (*As all start to leave, he speaks to* FAIR ELLEN) Wait, girl! You stay. You look as if you had some wits as well as beauty. I would talk with you. (*All but* FAIR ELLEN *exit.*) What is your name, good woman?

FAIR ELLEN (*Curtsying*): I am called Fair Ellen.

STRANGER: Perhaps, Fair Ellen, you can tell me what is happening in this town. Perhaps the King can help—

FAIR ELLEN: Why doesn't the King leave our people alone? He must know that we are poor and witless.

STRANGER: I have a feeling that those townsfolk are too witless to be true. I noticed you flitting from one to the other and whispering in their ears. I feel that some trickery is being played upon the King.

FAIR ELLEN: Oh, sir! Why would the people of Gotham do such a thing?

STRANGER: That's what I want to know. Tell me, Fair Ellen, and I will try to understand.

FAIR ELLEN: But will the King understand also?

STRANGER: I, personally, will see that the King does understand.

FAIR ELLEN: Then I shall tell you. We feared that if the King came to visit us, he would demand more taxes from us, take away our farm lands for roads, and send our best men to his Court.

STRANGER: You have an unfortunate opinion of your king. What then?

FAIR ELLEN: We thought that if we pretended to be mad, his messengers would go back and report that the whole village was crazy. Then the King would never bother to come here, and we would be forgotten.

STRANGER: I have the feeling that you were the one who invented this scheme to keep your village of Gotham safe. Is that not so?

FAIR ELLEN (*Smiling*): I had some small hand in it.

STRANGER: I thought so. The King has need of such as you at Court to help him solve his problems.

FAIR ELLEN: If the King were only like you, I would gladly go to the Court. You are so wise and understanding.

STRANGER (*Taking off his cape and revealing royal emblem on his coat*): I *am* the King!

FAIR ELLEN (*Startled, then curtsying low*): Oh, Your Majesty, what have I done?

KING: Do not be alarmed, Fair Ellen. You have done nothing but good.

FAIR ELLEN: I am not certain whether I have been more wise or more foolish. I thought I was fooling both *thee* and the King.

KING: Your game has ended better than you think. In Gotham, you have made both wise and foolish things seem the same. It was a merry foolery, and it would have been a wise device if your King had turned out to be as stupid as you thought. I will leave your town of

Gotham to its own manner of living. But, I hope, Fair Ellen, that I may take you with me. Never have I seen so fair and wise a maid.

FAIR ELLEN: Whether I am wise or foolish, Sire, I do not know. But now that the trickery is ended, I will gladly go with thee.

KING (*Taking* FAIR ELLEN *by the hand and calling*): Good people of Gotham! Good people of Gotham, I have good news for you! (*They enter, crowding around.* KING *mounts platform.*) I am your king.

TOWNSPEOPLE (*Ad lib*): The King! He is the King! (*Etc.*)

KING: I proclaim the village of Gotham to be free from taxes forever, and the town shall be under my personal protection. You have shown yourselves to be more clever than mad, and I have great need of such people as you. (*Turning to* FAIR ELLEN) And Fair Ellen shall come to my Court and be my bride! (*He takes her hand, and she steps onto platform alongside the* KING.)

TOWNSPEOPLE (*Ad lib*): Hurrah! Fair Ellen shall be Queen! Hurrah for the King! (*Etc.*) (*Curtain*)

THE END

The Stolen Tarts

A tale of merry old England

by Lida Lisle Molloy

Characters

SPY ⎫ *royal pages*
SPRY ⎰

QUEEN OF HEARTS

KNAVE OF HEARTS

KING OF HEARTS

ROYAL GUARDS

SETTING: *The royal kitchen.*

AT RISE: SPY *and* SPRY *enter.* SPRY *runs around room, turning somersaults, leaping and dancing.* SPY *pokes his nose into everything—the oven, the pantry, the cupboards.*

SPRY (*Turning a somersault*): It's the King's birthday!

SPY (*Peering into pantry*): That means the Queen's tarts! Hooray! The pages who mix the pastry will have tarts to eat with their supper.

SPRY: Will they be currant tarts or plum tarts, I wonder? I like plum tarts best.

SPY: They will be gooseberry tarts, as always, Spry. Don't you know that for hundreds of years every King of Hearts has had gooseberry tarts on his birthday—royal gooseberry tarts made by the Queen's own hands?

SPRY: But suppose a queen cannot make good tarts? Or suppose she burns them?

SPY (*Bringing a huge bowl from the pantry*): All queens make excellent tarts, Silly Spry. Most of them do, anyway. There was one a hundred years ago who let them burn to a crisp while she tidied her hair looking into a polished copper kettle.

SPRY (*Taking a very large and a small spoon from work table and trying to juggle them*): What happened to her?

SPY: She disappeared. There was a new queen the next year who *could* bake tarts, they say.

SPRY (*Making faces at himself in a shiny kettle*): I hope our Queen makes good tarts. She is so beautiful and kind.

SPY (*Bringing a huge baking pan from pantry*): Kind, indeed! She is as young and merry as any lady-in-waiting. It will surprise me if she can make pastry half so fine as the Queen Mother. (QUEEN OF HEARTS *enters, looking frightened.* SPY *and* SPRY *jump to attention.*)

QUEEN: Well, Spry. Well, Spy.

SPY *and* SPRY (*Bowing in unison*): Your Majesty.

QUEEN: We are to have the honor of making cherry tarts for the King's birthday.

SPY *and* SPRY (*Bowing*): Gooseberry tarts, Your Majesty.

QUEEN: G-gooseberry tarts? (*Hastily*) But, of course, gooseberry tarts.

SPY: Does Your Majesty desire a bit of butter?

SPRY: A pastry fork?

QUEEN (*Crossing to worktable*): Fetch me a jar of the best honey, if you please.

SPY (*Amazed*): Honey, Your Majesty? The Queen Mother never used honey.

QUEEN (*Regally*): Honey, *if* you please, Spy.

SPY *and* SPRY (*Bowing*): Yes, Your Majesty. (*They go into pantry.*)

QUEEN: Oh, dear! How does one make tarts, anyway? (SPY *and* SPRY *re-enter, carrying between them huge jar labeled,* ROYAL HONEY.) Thank you, Spy. Thank you, Spry. Now fetch me . . . ah, three measures of fine barley flour . . . a—a dozen large sticks of cinnamon . . . a cheese—yes, goat's milk cheese! And a crock of the best gooseberry jam. (*Pages look at each other and shake their heads.*)

SPY *and* SPRY: Yes, Your Majesty. (*They go into the pantry.*)

QUEEN: The Counselors of the Kingdom will be here to taste the tarts. And the Poet is to make rhymes about them. (*Sighing*) Oh, dear! (SPY *and* SPRY *re-enter, carrying long sticks of cinnamon, large box labeled* BARLEY FLOUR, *jar labeled* ROYAL GOOSEBERRY JAM, *and package labeled* GOAT'S MILK CHEESE. *They put items on worktable.*) Oh, my! What a lot of ingredients. Thank you, Spy. Thank you, Spry. You may go now.

SPY (*Bowing*): It is the custom for the royal pages to stir and blend, Your Majesty.

QUEEN (*Firmly*): Then I shall start a new royal custom. From this day the tarts for the King's birthday shall be made in secret by the Queen.

SPY *and* SPRY (*Bowing*): Yes, Your Majesty.

QUEEN: And, Spy, if a page so much as puts an eye to the keyhole, he shall be made to sit with the ladies-in-waiting at dinner.

SPY: Yes, Your Majesty. (*The pages bow and exit hastily through door.*)

QUEEN (*Uncertainly*): Oh, dear! Oh, me! These tarts will be very bad. And then what will happen to me? Perhaps I shall disappear like that other queen—poor thing!— who stopped to tidy her hair and let the tarts burn. (*Puts *ingredients, except cheese and honey, into bowl and begins to stir. She puts a finger into the mixture and licks it, then makes a face.*) If I put in plenty of honey that should help. (*She pours honey into bowl and stirs. Finally she holds up cheese.*) Whatever shall I do with this cheese? I can't stir it in; the batter is quite bumpy already. If I throw it out the window the gardener will find it. Perhaps I can carry it up to my chamber under my apron and feed it to the royal white mice. Now . . . (*She pours the mixture into the baking pan and spreads the jam on top.*) Now . . . that doesn't look so bad. They may turn out extremely well after all. (*She puts baking pan into oven.*) I am sure my hair is hanging in wisps and there must be a spot of flour on my nose, but I will not look to see. No one shall ever read in the royal archives that *I* let the birthday tarts burn. (*She pulls a stool near the oven and sits down, hiding the cheese behind her.*)

SPY *and* SPRY (*Entering, bowing*): Your Queenship!

QUEEN: Well, Spy! Well, Spry!

SPY: His Majesty, the King, begs to know if the royal tarts are baked.

QUEEN: Tell His Majesty the royal tarts are baking in the royal oven. (*The pages bow and leave.*) Oh, dear! Oh, me! (QUEEN *begins to weep into her apron.*)

KNAVE OF HEARTS (*Looking in at window, rear*): Aha!

QUEEN (*In surprise*): Oh!

KNAVE (*Jumping into the room*): The royal birthday tarts, is it not so?

QUEEN: Yes, good Knave.

KNAVE: You have never made tarts before, Your Majesty? And the tarts are not good?

QUEEN (*Nodding*): I'm afraid they are dreadful. Will you look at them for me, Knave?

KNAVE (*Looking into the oven*): Ah-h!

QUEEN: They are very bad, dear Knave?

KNAVE (*Nodding*): Very!

QUEEN: What shall I do? Think, wise Knave, think. If something is not done I may disappear like that other queen who burned the tarts. Are you thinking, Knave?

KNAVE (*Sitting on table, swinging his legs*): I am thinking . . . I have it. (*Bravely*) I shall steal the tarts.

QUEEN (*Frightened*): What if you are discovered?

KNAVE: I shall be beaten with a thousand and one stripes —or beheaded.

QUEEN: Not beheaded, good Knave. I could not have you beheaded. It is much too bloody.

KNAVE: Or banished, Your Majesty.

QUEEN: No, no! You shall never be banished. You tell such nice stories, such funny stories, Knave.

KNAVE: But what if I wish to be banished?

QUEEN: Funny Knave, how could you?

KNAVE: Listen well, Your Majesty. I am heir to the Kingdom of Dreams, sent to the Kingdom of Hearts in my youth to be educated. But a fortnight ago my father sent a messenger praying me to come in all haste, as he lies ill and would have me reign in his stead. His Majesty, the King of Hearts, will not give me leave to go. He vows I know so little law I could not govern a flock of geese. (*Sighs*) He, too, likes my stories.

QUEEN (*Touched*): Dear Knave, you must steal the tarts! (*She takes pan of tarts from oven. There is a knock on door.*)

KING OF HEARTS (*From offstage*): The Lords of the Kingdom await the tarts, my Queen.

QUEEN: When the tarts have cooled, dear King. (KNAVE *takes pan and jumps out window. She pretends to be alarmed.*) Oh! Oh! They are gone!

KING (*Entering*): What is it, my Queen? What has alarmed you?

QUEEN: The tarts! The royal gooseberry tarts have been stolen.

KING: What scoundrel has done this? (*Calling*) Ho, Spy! Spry!

SPY *and* SPRY (*Entering*): Your Majesty?

KING: The royal tarts have been stolen. Command His Excellency, the Chancellor, to summon the guards.

SPY *and* SPRY: Yes, Your Majesty. (SPRY *leaves,* SPY *runs to window.*)

KING (*Storming*): He shall be hanged, this rogue! He shall be lashed . . .

SPY: I see the thief, Your Majesty! It is the Knave of Hearts. He is running along the currant row with the royal baking pan in his hands.

KING: Ho! Knave! Fetch back the tarts and you shall not even receive a beating.

SPY: Your Majesty, he has tripped and spilled them, every one.

KING: Spilled them! My precious gooseberry tarts!

SPY: Your Majesty, the royal guards have caught him.

KING (*Pacing the floor*): What punishment is fitting for such a Knave? A hundred lashes would be a feather-weight of justice. He shall be beheaded.

QUEEN (*Hastily*): And ruin the polish on the headman's ax? No, indeed, Your Majesty. He should be banished from this fair Land of Hearts, banished to pine for it and to grieve over his wicked deed.

KING: He shall know the full weight of our displeasure. Banish him I shall. (GUARDS *enter leading* KNAVE.) Have you anything to say, Knave, in defense of your wicked self?

KNAVE (*Kneeling*): Nothing, gracious and merciful King. I saw the royal tarts and I was tempted.

KING: There is naught to do but banish you, Knave. You must leave our palace and presence forever. (*Lower*)

Knave, the tarts were superior, were they not? The royal
Counselors vowed one so young and fair as the queen
could not bake tarts for the birthday feast. I wagered my
crown against them.

KNAVE (*Solemnly*): My Lord, in all the world were never
such tarts as those.

KING: Whisper this to my Counselors before you go,
Knave. I command you.

KNAVE: It shall be done, Your Majesty. (*Music is heard
from offstage.*)

KING: Come, gentle Queen, to the birthday feasting.

QUEEN: Your Majesty, I fear there is flour upon my nose.
Let me brush it away.

KING (*Delighted*): Flour on your nose? So there is. Leave
it! The Chancellor must see it. They have often heard
the Queen Mother say that none but a true cook wears
a smudge of flour. (KING *starts toward door.*)

QUEEN (*To* KNAVE): Farewell, kind Knave. (*Whispering*)
The goat's milk cheese behind the stool. Could you steal
that?

KNAVE (*Bowing*): Farewell, my Queen. (*Whispering*) The
cheese is as good as stolen! And when I have come to
the Kingdom of Dreams I shall dispatch my fleetest
messenger with the royal recipe . . .

QUEEN: For tarts, dear Knave?

KNAVE: For tarts. (QUEEN *turns and exits on the* KING's
arm.)

KNAVE (*Reciting to audience*):
The Queen of Hearts
She made some tarts;
(Oh! woeful tarts were they!)
The Knave of Hearts
He stole the tarts
To save the Queen that day.
The King of Hearts

Called for the tarts
And vowed the Knave should die;
But fair young Queen
Did intervene.
"O, banish him!" did cry.
Thus, good friends,
Our story ends
With good will and with laughter.
And may you all *(Bowing)*
Both grown and small
Live happily hereafter.
(He doffs his cap in sweeping bow and then goes to win-
dow. With one leg over the sill, he remembers the cheese.
He picks up the cheese, hides it under his coat and slips
out window, whistling. Curtain)

THE END

King Arthur and His Knights

Scenes from the legends of King Arthur

by Olive J. Morley

Characters

KING ARTHUR
QUEEN GUINEVERE
MERLIN
SIR ECTOR
SIR KAY
SIR ULFIAS
SIR BRASTIAS
SIR BAUDWIN
ARCHBISHOP
BOY
SIR LANCELOT
SIR GAWAINE
SIR BORS
SIR BEDIVERE
LADIES

SIR LIONEL
SIR AGRAVAINE
SIR PERCIVAL
SIR GARETH
SIR GAHERIS
SIR LUCAN
SQUIRES
PAGES
SIR GALAHAD
OLD MAN
SIR MORDRED
LANCELOT'S KNIGHTS
THREE QUEENS
TWO HERALDS
LADY OF THE LAKE

SCENE 1

TIME: *Early sixth century.*
SETTING: *Outside a cathedral, in England. At center is a sword set in an anvil and stone.*

AT RISE: SIR ULFIAS, SIR BRASTIAS, SIR BAUDWIN, SIR
  ECTOR, SIR KAY *and the young* ARTHUR *come onstage
  from the cathedral. The older* KNIGHTS *talk together at
  center.* KAY *and* ARTHUR *move down right, chatting
  softly.*

ULFIAS: If the rightful heir to King Uther is not found,
  it will be a bad thing for the realm.
BRASTIAS: A fearful thing! Wrangling and bloodshed!
  (*They continue talking.*)
KAY (*To* ARTHUR): You go on and untether our horses,
  Arthur. Then we shall get a good start. (ARTHUR *exits.*
  KAY *suddenly sees the sword.*) My lords, look! (*Goes up
  to sword*) This was not here when we came. (*All turn.*)
KNIGHTS (*Ad lib*): A sword! A naked sword stuck in an
  anvil! What can it mean? Who put it there? (*Etc.*)
KAY (*Reading inscription on sword*): "Whoso pulleth this
  sword from the stone and anvil is rightful King of all
  England." (ARCHBISHOP *enters from cathedral.*)
BAUDWIN (*To* ARCHBISHOP): My Lord Archbishop, the
  sign we have prayed for has been sent to us! (*Leads
  ARCHBISHOP to stone, where he reads inscription si-
  lently.*)
ARCHBISHOP: Why, my lords, this may offer the true test!
  You must all attempt to pull out the sword. (*Knights in
  turn attempt to pull out sword and fail.*) He is not here
  who shall draw the sword, but no doubt God will make
  him known. Now leave the sword and go to the tourna-
  ment, my lords. (*Talking excitedly, knights exit, except
  KAY. ARCHBISHOP exits into cathedral.*)
KAY (*Going right and beckoning offstage*): Arthur! Hurry!
ARTHUR (*Entering*): Our horses are ready, Kay.
KAY (*Playfully arrogant*): *Sir* Kay, now! Don't forget, I
  was knighted at All Hallows.

ARTHUR (*Grinning, speaking with mock servility*): Sir Kay!
(*Pointing to sword*) Whose sword is that?

KAY: Oh, it's the most wonderful thing. I'll tell you as we
go along. (*Suddenly clapping his hand to his side*) Why
I've forgotten *my* sword! Run back and get it for me,
there's a good fellow.

ARTHUR: All right. I'll take a shortcut home.

KAY: Thank you, Arthur. I'll go ahead slowly. (KAY *exits
and* ARTHUR *runs off in opposite direction.* MERLIN *enters and stands looking at the sword. Suddenly* ARTHUR
re-enters, out of breath, with a small BOY.)

ARTHUR: You say they've *all* gone to the tournament from
Sir Ector's house?

BOY: Yes, the whole household. You'll find no one there.
But, I must hurry—I want to see the jousts. (*He runs
off.* ARTHUR *stands looking at the sword.*)

ARTHUR: My brother Kay shall not be without a sword.
Why not this one? (*He runs to sword and pulls it out
easily.*) A fine sword this!

MERLIN (*Coming forward*): Is it not too heavy for so light
an arm?

ARTHUR (*Laughing*): *Heavy*, old man? No! Not for me.
I shall soon be a knight! (*Runs off, brandishing sword*)

MERLIN (*Softly*): And more than a knight! (*Curtains close
for a moment to denote the passage of time. When they
are opened,* SIR ECTOR *and* KAY *stand center,* SIR ECTOR
looking at the sword, which he holds. ARTHUR *stands
with* ULFIAS, BRASTIAS, *and* BAUDWIN, *watching.* ARCH-
BISHOP *stands near cathedral, holding book.*)

ECTOR (*To* KAY): Once more, Kay, how came you by this
sword?

KAY: I told you, Father, from that anvil. (*Pointing*) See,
the anvil is empty now.

BAUDWIN: He is right, Sir Ector. It *is* the sword from the
anvil.

ECTOR (*Looking keenly at* KAY): But when you tried to draw it before, you could not do so.

KAY: It—it came out quite easily this time. (ARTHUR *shifts his feet uneasily.*)

ECTOR: My son, you are a knight now. A knight's word is his bond. Will you swear upon the Holy Book that you have drawn the sword from the anvil? (KAY *hesitates, then as* ARCHBISHOP *comes forward holding book, places his hands on it.*)

KAY: I swear—that this sword—was drawn from the anvil.

ECTOR: By you?

KAY (*Dropping his hands suddenly*): No—I cannot do it. (*Pauses*) My brother, Arthur, drew the sword.

ALL: Arthur!

ECTOR: Arthur! Come here! (ARTHUR *steps forward.*) Now speak truth, boy. A kingdom stands on your words. Did you, in fact, draw out this sword, unaided, from the anvil?

ARTHUR: Why, yes, Father. I seized the hilt, and just drew it out. (SIR ECTOR *looks at him piercingly. Then he walks silently to the anvil, and replaces the sword. He tries it.*)

ECTOR: Now it is fixed and immovable. Come here, Kay. Try to draw it. (KAY *tries to pull out sword and fails. He steps back.*) Now, Arthur. (ARTHUR *steps up and with one movement draws the sword, waving it aloft. There is a gasp.*) Rightful—King—of all England! (*He falls on his knees before* ARTHUR, *as does* KAY.)

ARTHUR: But, why are you kneeling to *me*? My own father, my brother?

ECTOR (*Rising, putting his hand on* ARTHUR'S *shoulder*): Arthur, I was never your father, though you were brought up as my own son. All you older men will remember that years ago King Uther and his Queen had a child. It was believed that the child died. It now appears the child stands before you here. It was a wild, stormy night when the boy was born, and on that night there came to our castle gates none other than Merlin, the great magician, bearing in his arms a newborn child. He told me and my lady that we were to bring the little one up as our own son, with our own child, Kay . . . that this boy was not to know his true parentage till the time was ripe. Even *we* did not know until now whose child we were nourishing.

ARTHUR: Why was I not brought up as a prince, in my own parents' palace?

ECTOR: Merlin has great wisdom, Arthur. Perhaps he knew that you should be reared in the strict discipline of an ordinary castle, first a page, then a squire, taking the hard knocks that must come to a boy in that training. For you are to be King of all England, Arthur—

MERLIN (*Entering suddenly*): And the greatest knight in the world! (*All turn to look at him.*)

BRASTIAS: It is Merlin!

ARTHUR (*In awed tones, to* ARCHBISHOP): May I lay this sword on the high altar, my Lord Archbishop? It seems it is a holy thing.

ARCHBISHOP: Go, lay it there, my son.

KAY: But then you will have no sword, Arthur!

MERLIN: Arthur shall be given a sword. With that he shall vanquish his enemies. Accept this youth as your king, my lords. He is the true son of Uther Pendragon. (*Lays his hand on* ARTHUR's *shoulder*) All my wisdom and knowledge shall be at your command, my king.

ALL: Hail, Arthur, King of all England! (*They kneel before him as curtains close.*)

*   *   *

Scene 2

Before Rise: Arthur *and* Merlin *walk on, talking together.*

Merlin: And now, Arthur, that you are settled on the throne of this land, and have overcome so many enemies, there is something else, surely?

Arthur: What else?

Merlin (*Looking at him shrewdly*): A king must have a queen.

Arthur (*Laughing*): So my barons have told me—but I said I would not choose without your approval.

Merlin: Is there any lady your gaze has favored?

Arthur (*Eagerly*): Oh, there is but one now! There have been others; I did not love them. The one I want to marry is the daughter of King Leodogrance—Guinevere.

Merlin: Guinevere . . . I wish that your eyes had alighted on anyone else.

Arthur: But she is the most beautiful lady in the realm! And—I love her, Merlin.

Merlin (*Sighing*): It is because she is the most beautiful lady that I fear for you, Arthur. Others will love where beauty is.

Arthur: I want my queen to be loved and worshiped by all my knights.

Merlin: Yet if you marry this peerless girl, have a care of your knights. Admit none to your court that is not trusty and true.

Arthur: I shall have the best in the whole realm. You seem to have gone into one of your trances, Merlin. (*Half jokingly, as* Merlin *stares fixedly ahead*) Tell me, what do you see?

Merlin: I see—much fighting. But a king must expect that. And I see. . . .

ARTHUR: Happiness?

MERLIN: Ah yes, I see that . . . and I see sorrow, too. But I see greater things than all these. I see something that will go on to the end of time. . . . (*Turning sharply*) Do you know what King Leodogrance will give as Guinevere's dowry? The Table Round.

ARTHUR: That great circular table? Tell me, Merlin, what is its significance, why is it round?

MERLIN: Its shape is round, for the earth is round. The sun is round. A circle is endless. It has no break. The Table Round is meant to seat the most valiant knights in all Christendom. And it will be yours! You are to establish an order of chivalry that will inspire men long after you and your matchless knights are dead. They will hear your tales in boyhood, and later they will go out to succor the helpless, to rescue the innocently imprisoned, to right the wrong! The Table Round will never die! (*Pauses*) But you must have your sword. Look over there at the lake. (*Points off right. An arm in a white sleeve appears from the wings, holding aloft a sword.*)

ARTHUR: An arm rising from the lake, clothed in white samite, with a sword. (LADY OF THE LAKE *enters.*) And a girl is stepping from the water.

MERLIN: That is the Lady of the Lake. Go forward to her, and she will give you the sword.

LADY OF THE LAKE: Come, Arthur, receive your sword. (*He takes sword, and the arm slowly recedes. He comes center, as* LADY OF THE LAKE *slips off.*)

ARTHUR: What a fine sword! (*Draws it from its scabbard and examines it*) Why, it has a name—Excalibur!

MERLIN: That is your sword. Never let it drop from your hand in any fight you are engaged in, and no harm can come to you.

ARTHUR (*Holding it up*): Excalibur! (*Blackout.*)

*   *   *

TIME: *Some months later.*

SETTING: *The Round Table at Camelot. Around it are placed the seats of the knights.* ARTHUR's *seat faces the audience. One seat, beside his, is covered.*

AT RISE: MERLIN *stands with* SIR ULFIAS, SIR KAY, SIR ECTOR, SIR BORS, SIR BEDIVERE, SIR LANCELOT *and* SIR GAWAINE, *as all admire the table.*

ECTOR: Is there any order in sitting, I wonder?

BEDIVERE: Perhaps the oldest knights near the King.

MERLIN: There is no preference for age, sir knights, at this table. It is round. (*He points to the chairs.*) Come, find your places. Each knight has his. (*They go round, finding their places.*)

BORS: But what is this covered seat?

MERLIN: That is the Siege Perilous. No man may sit on that but the purest knight in the world.

GAWAINE: Lancelot—surely.

LANCELOT (*Shaking his head*): I am not the purest knight. Perhaps he is not yet come.

MERLIN (*Looking at him shrewdly*): You are right. He is *not* yet come. But perhaps through you he may be led here. (*The sound of triumphal music is heard.* TWO HERALDS *enter, and give a long fanfare on their trumpets.* KING ARTHUR *enters with* QUEEN GUINEVERE. *Her* LADIES *follow her.*)

ALL: Hail, Arthur, King of all England! (*They kneel.*)

ARTHUR: Welcome, my knights, to Camelot. I present to you my Queen, Guinevere.

ALL: Hail, Guinevere, Queen to King Arthur! (*They kneel to her.*)

GUINEVERE (*To* ARTHUR): My lord, I am honored to be your queen. (*Looking around*) What a wonderful kingdom is Camelot, and what noble knights you have gathered about you. (*Lovingly*) I know that I shall be happy here.

ARTHUR: My queen, I hope you shall always reign happily in Camelot. (*To* KNIGHTS) It is my aim to make this band of knights a great fellowship, bound together by ties of brotherhood and chivalry. This table is to be the symbol of our deathless union. We are to be the greatest knights in all Christendom. My men are to be ready to do battle in a just cause, to right the wrong, to help all women in distress, to be true to the holy vows of knighthood. All men must know us, throughout the ages, as the pattern of chivalry. Will you swear to this?

KNIGHTS: We swear.

ARTHUR (*In ringing tones*): Then let us be known as the Knights of the Table Round! (*Curtain*)

*   *   *

SCENE 3

TIME: *A few months later.*

SETTING: *The throne room at Camelot; the same as Scene 2.*

AT RISE: GUINEVERE *is sitting on a low bench, at left, working at an embroidery frame. She sighs, takes the crown from her head, and sits looking at it.* LANCELOT *enters.*

LANCELOT: Do I intrude, madam?

GUINEVERE (*Smiling*): No. You are welcome.

LANCELOT: I came—to see if I could find you. You dropped this from your gown as you passed through the hall. (*Hands her a small ornament*)

GUINEVERE (*Softly*): Thank you, Lancelot. (*He turns to go, reluctantly.*) Stay with me awhile. (*He sits beside her.*) The crown is heavy at times and then I wonder if I shall be able to wear it as it should be worn.

LANCELOT: But, my lady, all the court worships you.

GUINEVERE: *All* the court? I am not sure. There are some I mistrust. Morgan le Fay, for one.

LANCELOT: She is the King's sister! She could not wish you anything but well.

GUINEVERE: She dabbles too much in necromancy. Merlin does, too, but his is a *good* magic. He loves Arthur truly, but with Morgan le Fay, I feel there is evil somewhere. (*She shivers*) And I do not trust Sir Agravaine.

LANCELOT: He is nephew to the King!

GUINEVERE: Yes, that is why I fear him. I think he envies other knights who are braver than he is, and that is wrong in a knight of the Round Table. I believe his envy is dangerous—and perhaps to *you.*

LANCELOT: I am sure you are mistaken. His courage has been proved in battle.

GUINEVERE: Perhaps. (*Pauses*) Would you do battle for my sake, Lancelot?

LANCELOT: I would.

GUINEVERE: Would you fight for me, and save me from danger—and death?

LANCELOT: I would brave death itself to save you from any evil that could befall you.

GUINEVERE: I believe you would. (*She rises and gives him the ornament he had found.*) Keep this for my sake. (*He kneels and kisses her hand. She stands looking at him for a moment, then exits.* LANCELOT *stands and slips the ornament on a chain he wears.*)

LANCELOT: My talisman—from the loveliest lady on earth. (*Curtain*)

*   *   *

SCENE 4

SETTING: *The same as Scene 3.*

AT RISE: SIR LANCELOT, SIR BORS, *and* SIR LIONEL *are at center, surrounded by* SIR GAWAINE, SIR KAY, SIR AGRA-VAINE, SIR PERCIVAL, SIR ECTOR *and* SIR GARETH.

GAWAINE: Lancelot, the King will be glad to see you.

AGRAVAINE: And the Queen, too.

KAY: They thought some mischief might have befallen you when you did not return.

BORS (*Teasingly*): Or that the lady who called for your help might have beguiled you to stay away from today's feast.

LANCELOT: My friends, do not trouble me with your banter. The girl came with a request, and I have fulfilled it. You will know when I tell the King. (*The knights talk together. A light suddenly shines on the Siege Perilous.* LANCELOT *moves toward it. No one else notices.*) My lords! (*They turn. The light vanishes.*) Did you see the light on the Siege Perilous?

PERCIVAL: Why, no. Was there one?

LANCELOT: Yes—a shining light. And I thought I saw letters engraved. . . . (*Sounds of talking are heard from offstage, and then* KING ARTHUR, QUEEN GUINEVERE, LADIES *enter, along with* SIR BEDIVERE, SIR GAHERIS, SIR LUCAN, SIR BRASTIAS, *and* SIR BAUDWIN.)

ARTHUR: Why, Lancelot! (*Takes both* LANCELOT's *hands*)

GUINEVERE: We feared so much that some misfortune had overtaken you.

LANCELOT: Madam, I thank you for your concern. But, here I am, safe, as you can see.

ARTHUR: What was the adventure? Were King Pelles and his daughter in danger?

LANCELOT: Sire, it was not an adventure, but a strange

request. The girl who called for me took me to an abbey, where twelve nuns brought forward a youth, whom they had brought up. They begged me to knight him.

ARTHUR: Did you knight him?

LANCELOT: Yes. He kept vigil all night kneeling before the altar. Then, in the morning I knighted him.

ARTHUR: What was his name, and where was his home?

LANCELOT: His name is Galahad. (*Slowly*) I know not where he was born.

ARTHUR: It is a pity you did not bring him to Camelot, but perhaps we shall yet see this young knight. Now, come, my friends, take your seats. (ARTHUR *and* KNIGHTS *sit at round table or stand behind it, and* GUINEVERE *and* LADIES *sit at smaller tables up right and left. Meanwhile,* SQUIRES *and* PAGES *enter and pass around baskets of bread. Suddenly, a loud clanging sound is heard from offstage.* PAGE *runs in.*)

PAGE (*To* ARTHUR): Sire, all the windows and doors have shut by themselves! (*From offstage a knocking is heard, and an* OLD MAN *enters, leading a* YOUTH *in a scarlet tunic.* LANCELOT *rises with a look of startled recognition.* OLD MAN *leads the* YOUTH *to* ARTHUR, *and he kneels to him.*)

OLD MAN: Sire, I bring here a young knight of noble lineage. Through him the marvels of this court shall be fully accomplished.

ARTHUR: Sir, you are welcome, and the young knight. (*To the* YOUTH) What is your name? (*He does not answer.* OLD MAN *leads him to the Siege Perilous. He uncovers it, revealing gold letters which* LANCELOT *reads.*)

LANCELOT (*Reading*): "This is the Siege of Galahad, the High Prince."

ALL: Galahad!

OLD MAN: Here is your place. (GALAHAD *sits in the siege. He looks around, wondering, and bows and smiles to*

LANCELOT *in recognition. Suddenly a spotlight appears on the wall. All strain to look at it, then cringe away, cover their eyes and sit bowed.* GALAHAD *alone gazes at it. Suddenly light dims and all raise their eyes.*)

ARTHUR: The Holy Grail!

LANCELOT (*To* GALAHAD): Did you see it?

GALAHAD: It was covered with white linen. I could not see it clearly. Slowly it was borne aloft and out through the window.

ARTHUR: I believe that it is through you, Galahad, that the quest of the Holy Grail will be achieved.

LANCELOT: I vow to seek the Holy Grail!

GAWAINE: I here make a vow that I shall labor for a year and a day, and shall not return until I have seen it.

KNIGHTS: And I! And I!

GALAHAD: I, too, vow to seek till I behold with these eyes the Holy Grail!

ARTHUR: Oh, Gawaine, Lancelot! You have almost killed me with your vow, for you have bereft me of my truest knights! Some of you may die in the quest!

LANCELOT: That would be a great honor. (*Some* KNIGHTS *gather around* ARTHUR, *talking quietly. Other* KNIGHTS *break up into groups, bidding farewells to their* LADIES. GUINEVERE *and* LANCELOT *come down right.*)

GUINEVERE: Oh, Lancelot, Lancelot, you have betrayed me, to leave my lord thus!

LANCELOT: Madam, I shall come again—as soon as I may. (*He takes her hand and kisses it. She turns away, weeping.*)

GUINEVERE: Alas, that I ever saw you! (*Takes a chain with a cross from her neck and places it around his neck*) May you have good conduct and safety—as may all the whole fellowship. (LANCELOT, *his hand on the cross, goes up to* ARTHUR. *Silently, they clasp hands.*)

LANCELOT (*As* KNIGHTS *assemble to join him*): Now let us

pray God's blessing on our adventure—then to our
quest! (*As* GALAHAD *leads,* LANCELOT *and* KNIGHTS *of
the quest follow.*)

GALAHAD: The Holy Grail!

KNIGHTS: The Holy Grail! (*They exit.* ARTHUR *and*
GUINEVERE *watch them go off.* ARTHUR *raises his hand
in parting salute, then* GUINEVERE *waves. Curtain.*)

*   *   *

SCENE 5

TIME: *Thirteen months later.*

SETTING: *The throne room, as in Scene 4.*

AT RISE: *The full court is assembled. The* KNIGHTS *who
have returned from the quest are welcomed.* LANCELOT
and BORS *are center, and* ARTHUR *and* GUINEVERE *are
with them.*

ARTHUR: At last your quest is over, and once again I have
my Round Table. But two seats, alas, cannot be filled.
You are sure, Sir Bors, that Sir Percival really died in
that far city?

BORS: Yes, sire. He is buried near Sir Galahad.

GUINEVERE: And the young knight, Galahad, really saw
the Holy Grail?

BORS: He alone, of us all, had the full vision which is only
granted to the pure in heart.

LANCELOT: Alas, yes!

BORS: The earth could no longer hold him. (*There is a
moment of awed silence.*)

ARTHUR: Now let us give welcome to those who have returned. (*To a* PAGE) Boy, tell the cooks to serve dinner
in half an hour. Meanwhile, our weary knights can wash
off the dust from their journey. (*All start to exit in*

groups. ARTHUR *lingers, talking first with* BORS, *while* LANCELOT *and* GUINEVERE *speak together, downstage.*)

GUINEVERE (*Sadly*): Lancelot, you are changed!

LANCELOT: Madam, I have been on a high quest, and seen strange visions, of which I cannot speak. . . . To come back—is like coming back to earth from some other region. But, always, my lady, I am at your command. (BORS *has now gone out, and* ARTHUR *comes toward* LANCELOT. GUINEVERE *withdraws, and* ARTHUR *and* LANCELOT *are now alone.*)

ARTHUR: Ah, Lancelot, it has been a strange place without you at this Table! After your high adventures, can you still join in those more earthly ones to which we are pledged at Camelot?

LANCELOT (*Eagerly*): Oh, yes! I wish always to be a knight of the Round Table! (GAWAINE *enters.*)

GAWAINE: Sire, there is a knight arrived who wants an audience with you. He did not give his name, but he said that he was a near kinsman to you.

ARTHUR: A near kinsman? (*He paces about, then speaks quickly*) Tell him I will see him alone.

GAWAINE: Sire!

LANCELOT: Is that safe? Suppose he is an enemy?

ARTHUR: I have no fear for personal safety. Admit him. (LANCELOT *and* GAWAINE *exit.* ARTHUR *resumes pacing.* MORDRED *enters.*) Your name, sir knight?

MORDRED: My name is Mordred.

ARTHUR: Mordred! (MORDRED *bows.*) What brings you here?

MORDRED: I wish to enter the fellowship of the Table Round—sire. (*He kneels.* ARTHUR *raises him, and looks earnestly into his face.*)

ARTHUR: Is that your true wish, Mordred? Or are you after—higher game?

MORDRED: I wish to be one of this band of knights. I do not know what you mean by "higher game."

ARTHUR: Do you not? (*He turns away, and stands in thought with his back to* MORDRED, *who watches him. Then* ARTHUR *wheels round, and speaks with strong emotion.*) Mordred, I will do all that I can to advance you in this court, but I cannot make you my heir.

MORDRED: I am next of kin.

ARTHUR: Not in the legitimate line. And the Queen may have sons.

MORDRED: But if she does not, then surely I—

ARTHUR: My boy, you do not understand the laws of this realm. The people would never accept as king any but the legitimate heir. So if your idea of coming here was only the succession, you had best go back.

MORDRED: No! I *want* to remain! I *want* to become a knight of the Table Round.

ARTHUR: Can you take the vow? It entails self-sacrifice, and danger.

MORDRED: I can take the vow.

ARTHUR: Then I will admit you. (*He takes* MORDRED'S *hand.*) But—be loyal, Mordred. Remember, it is the *Round* Table. No one has precedence.

MORDRED: I will remember. (ARTHUR *stands looking at him earnestly. Curtain.*)

*   *   *

SCENE 6

BEFORE RISE: *A party of May Day revelers, including* LANCELOT, GUINEVERE, *other* KNIGHTS *and* LADIES, *come dancing on, laughing and singing.* LANCELOT *carries a crown of spring flowers which he places on* GUINEVERE'S *head. All clap happily and dance off, as* MORDRED *and* AGRAVAINE *enter.*

MORDRED (*With a sardonic smile*): Did you see that little byplay, Agravaine?

AGRAVAINE: I did. Lancelot advances in favor daily, both with the King and the Queen.

MORDRED: So I notice.

AGRAVAINE: There *could* be a way of breaking up that happy trio.

MORDRED (*Too eagerly*): How?

AGRAVAINE (*With a sharp glance*): You want it, too?

MORDRED: Perhaps.

AGRAVAINE: Then listen. The King could be persuaded to go hunting, and stay from home one night. Might it not be possible for us to lure Lancelot to *her* on that particular night? She might even send for him herself to amuse her with his songs—if it were suggested to her, from the right quarter. Perhaps a lady-in-waiting. Then *we* could break in upon them, and accuse the Queen of falseness to her lord. And that, in a queen, is *treason,* Mordred!

MORDRED: But, the punishment for treason is death at the stake! I do not want the Queen's *death,* Agravaine.

AGRAVAINE: Oh, it would never come to that! Somehow, he would contrive to deliver her from that fate! But it would drive a stake between the King and Lancelot— and destroy that presumptuous knight's power forever!

MORDRED: We both want the same things, Agravaine—for different reasons! (*Softly*) But it is a plan worth trying. We will be truly brothers in this. (*They grasp hands.*)

AGRAVAINE: Come, let us not be seen talking together. (*They move offstage. Revelers enter joyously and dance singing across the stage. Curtain.*)

* * *

TIME: *A few weeks later.*

SETTING: *Before Lancelot's castle of Joyous Gard. There is a lake on the backdrop.*

AT RISE: ARTHUR *and a band of* KNIGHTS, *including* MORDRED, AGRAVAINE *and* GAWAINE, *are at right.*

ARTHUR (*Calling*): Lancelot, bring forth the Queen!

LANCELOT (*Appearing on parapet*): My Lord Arthur, I cannot bring her to certain death. I only rescued her, and brought her to this my castle of Joyous Gard, because your barons had tied her to the stake for treason, and of that she is innocent.

ARTHUR: Lancelot, word was brought to me that you had betrayed me.

LANCELOT: Those who brought you that word were my enemies.

ARTHUR: You have killed many of my knights, amongst them Sir Gareth and Sir Gaheris, your own friends.

GAWAINE (*Fiercely*): You have slain my brothers!

LANCELOT: It grieves me that I killed your brothers, Gawaine. But I was surrounded by many knights as I fought my way to the stake. I did not know whom I struck down. My one thought was the Queen's safety. (*To* ARTHUR) Sire, I have many times fought for the Queen, and I have fought for you, and you have rewarded me with your trust. Evil men have laid this trap for me—it is not of my making.

GAWAINE: False miscreant knight! I will avenge my brothers' deaths!

LANCELOT: No man calls me miscreant knight! I will take up your challenge, Gawaine! (ARTHUR *draws* GAWAINE *back and talks urgently with him.* LANCELOT'S KNIGHTS *enter, and he comes down from parapet to join them.*)

ARTHUR (*Stepping forward*): Sir Lancelot, I am deeply moved by your defense. But you have broken the most solemn rules of the Table Round. You have fought your own brothers-in-arms, and defied your king. There is war between us.

LANCELOT: My lord, if that is your wish, so be it. But I beg of you and Sir Gawaine not to come into the field, lest harm befall you from me. For when I fight, *I fight to win!* (*Both sides withdraw, and stage lights go out. Sounds of battle and swords clashing are heard. When stage lights come on,* ARTHUR *and* LANCELOT *are fighting with swords, center. They parry, and then with a swift stroke* LANCELOT *sweeps the King's sword from his hand and lunges forward.* ARTHUR *falls.* LANCELOT *places his foot on* ARTHUR'S *chest.*) Yield, knight!

ARTHUR: You have me in your power, Lancelot. Strike.

LANCELOT (*In horror*): The King! (*He kneels and helps* ARTHUR *to rise.*) Oh, my lord, I could never kill the man who knighted me! (*Picks up Excalibur and hands it to* ARTHUR)

ARTHUR (*Deeply moved*): That was a knightly act! (LAN-CELOT'S KNIGHTS *enter, leading* GUINEVERE.)

LANCELOT: My Lord King, I bring back to you Guinevere, your Queen. She has been true and loyal to you. (AR-THUR *takes her hands.*) And now, my lord, I leave your realm, and go to my lands overseas.

ARTHUR: But, Lancelot, you cannot leave us now!

LANCELOT (*Shaking his head*): Alas, no. I would not stay to be any cause of contention between you, my King and Queen, nor among your knights. I cannot break up the Table Round. It is better for me to leave it. (*He goes to wall at rear, then turns*) Oh, beloved Camelot! I leave my heart with you! (*Curtain*)

*   *   *

Scene 7

TIME: *Two months later.*

SETTING: *The same as Scene 6.*

AT RISE: ARTHUR *sits on the low wall at the back, looking utterly dejected.* SIR LUCAN *and* SIR BEDIVERE *are with him.*

ARTHUR: So it has come to this! Mordred seizing my kingdom when I was away! I should have let Gawaine and Lancelot fight it out between them, but when Gawaine went dashing after him like an angry boy I had to follow, or all my fellowship of knights would have been broken up. And now they are broken up in any case— for Mordred's followers are all dead on the field, and all mine, but you two.

BEDIVERE: But, sire, Lancelot still lives.

ARTHUR: Ah, yes . . . but not here. (*He stands and gazes out over lake at rear.*) It was near here that I was given my sword Excalibur. (*Turning*) You had best inquire at the castle if we can have lodging for the night. Lancelot would not grudge it to me, I know.

BEDIVERE: We will, my lord. (*He and* SIR LUCAN *exit.* ARTHUR *looks again over the water.*)

ARTHUR: Serene, that water—like glass. And all my realm ravaged! (MORDRED *enters.* ARTHUR *wheels around.*) Mordred! Traitor! Come, meet me in fair fight! (*They draw. The fight is furious. Finally,* ARTHUR *wounds* MORDRED, *and he falls to the ground.* ARTHUR *bends over him.*) Repent! You are killed, Mordred! (*With his last dying strength,* MORDRED *knocks Excalibur from* ARTHUR'S *hand and thrusts his own sword into him. Then* MORDRED *falls back with a groan and dies.* ARTHUR *falls nearby.* SIR LUCAN *and* SIR BEDIVERE *enter, and rush to* ARTHUR'S *side.*)

BEDIVERE: My lord Arthur!

LUCAN: And Mordred! They are dead! (ARTHUR *groans*.)

BEDIVERE: The King lives! We may yet heal him! Run,
Lucan, to the castle, and fetch possets and healing potions. (LUCAN *runs off*.)

ARTHUR (*Weakly*): No—it is too late—too late. Bedivere!

BEDIVERE: My lord?

ARTHUR: Take my sword Excalibur and throw it into the
lake. Go—quickly.

BEDIVERE (*Picking up Excalibur*): I cannot throw this
beautiful sword away! (*He goes to wall, stands examining sword for a minute, then hides it quickly near
wall and returns to* ARTHUR.)

ARTHUR: What saw you?

BEDIVERE: I saw the waters lapping and the waves ebbing
. . . nothing more.

ARTHUR: You lie! Go, throw it. (BEDIVERE *takes the sword
and "throws" it over the wall, where a hand clothed in
white reaches up to take the sword, then vanishes with
it*.) What saw you?

BEDIVERE: A hand, clothed in white samite, arose and received the sword.

ARTHUR: Ah, its work is done. And mine, too. Take me
to the water's edge. (LUCAN *appears, bearing bandages,
and* BEDIVERE *beckons to him. Both support* ARTHUR
and bring him to the wall, up left. THREE QUEENS *appear, dressed in black. They stretch out their arms to*
ARTHUR *and take him from the knights*.) Farewell, my
true knights. I go—to the Isle of Avalon—to be healed
of my wounds. Perhaps . . . I will—come—again. (*Exits, as if carried by* THREE QUEENS. GUINEVERE *enters,
dressed as a nun, and* LANCELOT *follows.* LUCAN *and*
BEDIVERE *beckon them to wall*.)

GUINEVERE (*Looking out at water and calling*): Arthur!

BEDIVERE: Lady, it is too late. He is dead. (*She raises her hand in farewell, as does* LANCELOT. *Then she kneels by the wall in grief, her back to the audience.*)

LANCELOT: My lady, come from this place of sorrow. (*Then, as if noticing her habit for the first time*) Are you taking the vows of a nun?

GUINEVERE (*Slowly rising*): Because of my frailty the noblest band of knights in all of history was broken up. What is there left for me to do but pray? (*He moves to take her hand, but she beckons him away*) No, Lancelot. You must go to your lands abroad.

LANCELOT: Perhaps I, too, will seek a hermitage. For us it is a long farewell. (*They stand looking at each other, raise their hands in salute, and go out separately.*)

LUCAN: And so the Table Round is broken up.

BEDIVERE: No! Who knows—Arthur may come again, and yet lead the Britons! But, if not—the table was a circle. A circle never ends. (*In ringing tones*) As long as there are men to defend the weak, and to right the wrong, the Table Round will never die! (*Curtain*)

THE END

Pierre Patelin

A French folk tale

by Helene Koon

Characters

PIERRE PATELIN, *a clever lawyer*
WILHELMINA, *his wife*
MR. JONAS, *a draper*
TIBALD, *a shepherd*
JUDGE

SETTING: *A street in a small French town. At left is Pate-lin's house; the front of house is open, revealing small table and stool and a bed. At right is the draper's shop and house, also open at front.*

AT RISE: PIERRE *is lying in bed, facing the wall, and* WILHELMINA *is sitting on the stool, mending.*

WILHELMINA: Pierre! Pierre!

PIERRE: Mm-m-m-m-m?

WILHELMINA: Pierre, you haven't said one word this morning. You just lie in bed all day long, and there's not a thing in the house to eat! And here I sit putting patches on patches. (*Holding up ragged gown*) Look at that! A beggar wouldn't wear it. And that's my best dress!

PIERRE: What do you want me to do?

WILHELMINA: You might at least say you're sorry.

PIERRE: I'm sorry.

WILHELMINA: Is that all?

PIERRE: Can I help it if no one in town needs a good lawyer?

WILHELMINA: You used to have lots of clients. What happened to them?

PIERRE: Wilhelmina, people don't like it when you're smarter than they are.

WILHELMINA: How smart do you have to be to starve to death?

PIERRE: If only I had a case—just one case!

WILHELMINA: Oh! I can't stand it! I can't stand it! (*She throws down her mending and bursts into tears.*)

PIERRE (*Jumping out of bed*): That does it!

WILHELMINA: What?

PIERRE: Do you think I like being hungry? Or seeing you cry your eyes out for a new dress? No! I can't stand it either! (*Starts to put on his shoes*) I'm going shopping!

WILHELMINA: Shopping! Whatever for?

PIERRE: For clothes, of course—or at least some cloth to make some.

WILHELMINA: Where's your money?

PIERRE: I don't need any.

WILHELMINA: You're out of your mind!

PIERRE (*Measuring her*): Let's see—two and a half yards for you, three for me. What color do you like? Green? Red? Purple?

WILHELMINA (*Sarcastically*): Don't you think you'd better hurry, before all the cloth is sold?

PIERRE (*Grandly*): Wilhelmina, I forgive you. You don't believe me, but I forgive you.

WILHELMINA (*Sarcastically*): Thanks very much.

PIERRE: If I don't bring home the most beautiful cloth in the world, you may kick me.

WILHELMINA: Why don't I just kick you now and save you the trouble of going? (*She prepares to kick him.*)

PIERRE (*Dodging her and going to door*): Ah, ah, ah! Wait and see! Wait and see! (*He walks out of house into street.* WILHELMINA *shrugs, picks up her mending and exits left into kitchen.* JONAS *enters his shop.* PIERRE *crosses to the shop and enters.*) Well, well, Mr. Jonas! And how are we today?

JONAS (*Grumpily*): Hello, Patelin. What do you want?

PIERRE: Oh, nothing. Not a thing! I just stopped by to see how you were getting along.

JONAS (*Shrugging*): Not so good, not so bad.

PIERRE: Oh, you mean just so-so! (*Laughs loudly*) Say, that's pretty good!

JONAS: What?

PIERRE: You know—business—cloth—"sew-sew." (*He laughs.*)

JONAS: Hmph!

PIERRE (*Suddenly stopping laughing*): Say that again.

JONAS: Say what again?

PIERRE: That, that *hmph.*

JONAS: No.

PIERRE: Please—for me.

JONAS: Look here, Patelin, I have better things to do than stand around saying *hmph* just to please you.

PIERRE: You did it! You said it again! Oh, thank you, thank you!

JONAS: What are you thanking me for?

PIERRE: For saying *hmph* again! When you say *hmph,* you sound exactly like your father.

JONAS: My father?

PIERRE: Yes, oh, yes! Please, please say it again!

JONAS: Like this? (*Squares his shoulders and poses*) Hmph!

PIERRE: That's it! That's it! (*Pretends to dry a tear*) Oh, how I miss that good old man!

JONAS: Ah, Mr. Patelin, it does my heart good to know someone remembers him.

PIERRE: Oh, I do, I do! And I'm not the only one. There are lots of people in this town who couldn't forget him even if they tried.

JONAS: Ah, thank you, thank you!

PIERRE: And if anybody did forget, they have only to look at you. You're the spitting image of him.

JONAS: You think so?

PIERRE (*Nodding*): The spitting image! His walk (JONAS *walks.*), his smile. . . . (JONAS *smiles.* PIERRE *tries to take a piece of cloth while* JONAS *is posing, but* JONAS *catches him and grabs it.*)

JONAS: Did you come here to buy something, Patelin, or just to talk?

PIERRE: Maybe a little of both, Mr. Jonas. I was sitting at home with my wife, and we got to talking about your father, and I just had to stop by and see his old shop.

JONAS: Well, now you've seen it.

PIERRE (*Shaking his head*): Alike as two peas! Every time you open your mouth, your father comes out! (JONAS *claps his hand over his mouth.*) He was so good, so kind, so trusting. . . . (PIERRE *feels cloth on counter.*) What a wonderful piece of wool! Do you make it from your own sheep? Your father always kept a special flock.

JONAS: So do I, Patelin. I still have the same flock, but my fool of a shepherd has lost some of them.

PIERRE: You don't say! (*Feels cloth again*) Hm-m-m-m-m. . . .

JONAS: You couldn't find better wool anywhere in the world.

PIERRE: I'm not really in the market for wool, but I'm tempted, I'm tempted!

JONAS: Business bad, Patelin? Short of cash?

PIERRE: No, certainly not! As a matter of fact, I just happen to have a couple of hundred francs lying around. (*He starts to walk off with cloth, but* JONAS *is holding the other end, and bolt unrolls.* PIERRE *smiles.*) This cloth is good and strong.

JONAS (*Pulling* PIERRE *toward him*): Oh, it's strong all right. (*Confidentially, in* PIERRE'S *ear*) And cheap! I wouldn't tell everybody that, but for you, Mr. Patelin, very cheap!

PIERRE: I believe you, I believe you! But I shouldn't—not right now.

JONAS: Come, come, come, Mr. Patelin! You need the cloth and you have the money. What's stopping you? This will make an elegant suit. Clothes make the man, you know. And maybe one of these days we'll hear a little gossip around town—a new judge has been appointed—and his name is Mr. Patelin.

PIERRE: Ho! Ho! Ho! You must have your little joke— just like your father! (*Draping the cloth around him*) I must say, it would make a beautiful dress for my wife.

JONAS: Oh, yes, yes!

PIERRE: And, as you say, I could use a new suit.

JONAS: Certainly! Certainly! Well—well?

PIERRE: Well—I'll take it!

JONAS: That's the way to do business! How much do you want? What color do you like? Green? Yellow? Red? Blue?

PIERRE (*Still holding the same piece of cloth*): This is it, the blue! How much is it?

JONAS (*Slyly taking the two-franc price tag off the cloth and substituting a twenty-franc tag*): Well, now, I wouldn't do this for anyone else, but just for you, Mr. Patelin, because you knew my father, shall we say— twenty francs a yard?

PIERRE: Twenty francs a yard! Do you think I'm a fool?

JONAS: I swear that's exactly what it cost me.

PIERRE: Then you're a fool.

JONAS: It's good cloth, Mr. Patelin.

PIERRE: Well, every man has a right to his little profit. I'll take it.

JONAS: You will?

PIERRE: Measure it out. Two and a half yards for my wife, three for me. Five and a half yards.

JONAS (*Measuring and cutting*): One—two—four—

PIERRE (*Catching* JONAS' *error*): Four?

JONAS (*Laughing nervously*): Ha, ha! I always forget. *Three!* Three—four—five. I'll make it six. You won't mind the extra ten francs?

PIERRE: Not when I'm getting my money's worth. Now, what do I owe you?

JONAS: Six yards—twenty francs a yard—that makes exactly two hundred—

PIERRE: *Two* hundred?

JONAS (*Laughing*): Ah, *one* hundred twenty francs.

PIERRE: That's better.

JONAS: And a good bargain, too.

PIERRE: Oh, absolutely, absolutely! (*Takes cloth and starts out*) I'll drop by tomorrow and pay you for it.

JONAS: What! (*Grabs cloth*) Oh, no you don't!

PIERRE (*Not letting go*): Well, you don't think I carry that much money around with me, do you? For people to steal? Your father trusted me many times, Mr. Jonas. You ought to be more like him. (JONAS *drops the cloth in amazement, then recovers, catches the cloth, and begins a tug of war which lasts through the next speeches.*)

JONAS: It's bad business to sell on credit.

PIERRE: Do I ask for credit? For a month? A week? A day? Come to my house at noon and you'll get the money.

JONAS: I like payment—in good, solid francs.

PIERRE: Well, it's just waiting for you. I tell you what, Mr.

Jonas—when I left my house to come here, my wife was just putting a nice fat goose on the fire. Why don't you have lunch with us? Your father always liked a nice tender bite of goose.

JONAS: Well—maybe. It's true I haven't been to your house for a long time. I'll come at noon, Mr. Patelin, and I'll bring the cloth with me.

PIERRE: Oh, I wouldn't dream of bothering you! I'll carry it! (*As* JONAS *protests*) No, no, no! I can't let *you* carry it for *me!*

JONAS: But I'd rather—

PIERRE: Never! (JONAS *does not let go.* PIERRE *throws his end over* JONAS' *head and walks away a few steps*) Just forget the whole thing, then.

JONAS (*Fighting his way out of the cloth*): Mr. Patelin! Mr. Patelin! I didn't mean that! Here—here—(*He folds the cloth neatly and puts it on* PIERRE's *arm.* PIERRE *lets it drop.*) Now, don't be angry. Please take it. Please, I insist. (JONAS *gives him cloth again, and* PIERRE *lets the cloth remain on his arm.*) I'll come over for lunch, Mr. Patelin—just don't forget the money!

PIERRE: I won't forget! We'll celebrate with a bottle of good wine and a nice fat goose! Don't be late!

JONAS: I won't! I won't! (*As* PIERRE *crosses the street, humming,* JONAS *bursts into laughter*) The fool! A great bargain! And on top of that a good lunch! Oh, for a customer like that every day! (*He exits right into house, laughing.* PIERRE *enters his own house, puts cloth on the bed and sits in front of it.*)

PIERRE: Wilhelmina! Wilhelmina, my dear! Oh, Wilhelmina!

WILHELMINA (*Entering from left, carrying mending*): What's the matter?

PIERRE (*Picking up dress she was mending*): What's this

old rag? (*Throws it in the corner*) We can use it for the cat's bed. Didn't I promise you a new dress?

WILHELMINA: You did. Several times.

PIERRE: Well, it's here! Good woolen cloth fit for a queen! (*He shows it to her.*)

WILHELMINA: Oh! Where did you steal it?

PIERRE: I didn't steal it.

WILHELMINA: But you didn't have a penny when you left. How much was it?

PIERRE: One hundred twenty francs.

WILHELMINA: What!

PIERRE: Plus one bottle of red wine and a roast goose.

WILHELMINA: Pierre! We don't have a hundred twenty francs *or* a bottle of red wine—or even a bit of roast goose, you goose! Who on earth would be stupid enough to give us any goods before we had paid for them?

PIERRE (*Interrupting*): Not stupid, my dear Wilhelmina, not stupid at all. A very, very shrewd man, it was.

WILHELMINA: Who was it?

PIERRE: None other than the chancellor of fools, the king of baboons, the emperor of idiots—that worthy gentleman across the street, our neighbor, the draper.

WILHELMINA: Jonas?

PIERRE: Himself.

WILHELMINA: I don't believe it.

PIERRE: There's the cloth. Six yards of his best wool.

WILHELMINA (*Examining it*): How come? That old skin-flint wouldn't trust his own mother.

PIERRE: Ah, Wilhelmina, you don't appreciate my legal mind! I made him think he was the greatest man in the world. I laid it on thick!

WILHELMINA (*Laughing*): Pierre, you're a genius! And when does he expect to be paid?

PIERRE: At noon. (WILHELMINA *stops laughing abruptly.*)

WILHELMINA: Good heavens! What are we going to do? A hundred twenty francs!

PIERRE: He'll get it—and his wine—*and* his goose! (*Gets into bed*) Now listen. As soon as he gets here, you tell him I've been sick in bed for the last two months.

WILHELMINA: That's all I should do?

PIERRE: Well, it would help if you could cry a little. (*She nods.*) And if he asks for his money, tell him he's crazy —I haven't been out of bed. You can leave the rest to me. (JONAS *enters his shop, then starts to cross to* PIERRE'S *house.*)

WILHELMINA (*Looking out*): He's coming! He's coming! Oh, dear, I'm frightened!

PIERRE: Don't worry about a thing! (*He hides the cloth under the bedclothes, and* WILHELMINA *picks up her old dress and sits on the stool, pretending to mend.* JONAS *knocks.*)

WILHELMINA: Come in.

JONAS (*Entering*): How do you do, Mrs. Patelin. (WILHELMINA *meets him at door.*)

WILHELMINA: Sh! Don't talk so loud.

JONAS (*Lowering his voice*): How is your husband?

WILHELMINA: Oh, Mr. Jonas, how can you be so cruel as to ask?

JONAS: Cruel? Me?

WILHELMINA: When you know he's been in bed for the last eleven weeks! My husband, Pierre Patelin! Once a great lawyer, now a poor wreck on his deathbed!

JONAS: What?

WILHELMINA: But, of course. Everyone knows how ill he has been.

JONAS: Ill! Then who just took six yards of cloth out of my shop?

WILHELMINA: How should I know? It wasn't Pierre.

JONAS: There's something funny here. Your husband came to my shop this morning.

WILHELMINA: Impossible.

JONAS: He bought a hundred twenty francs' worth of wool, and I'm here to collect. Where is he?

WILHELMINA: Don't shout. He gets little enough sleep as it is. You come in here squealing like a stuck pig, and he's been in bed for twelve weeks without three nights' sleep. (*She cries.*)

JONAS: But he can't be! He was in my shop not fifteen minutes ago! (PIERRE *groans.*)

WILHELMINA (*Pointing to* PIERRE): See—see! He's been there thirteen weeks without a bite to eat!

JONAS: He was in my shop just a few minutes ago and he bought six yards of wool. Blue wool!

WILHELMINA: Please, Mr. Jonas! Can't you see how sick he is? Speak quietly! Noise upsets him!

JONAS (*Taking a deep breath*): Mrs. Patelin—your husband, Pierre, the lawyer—came into my shop and bought six yards of blue cloth! And—and he told me to come here for the money!

WILHELMINA (*Laughing loudly*): Very funny! Today? When he's been in bed for fourteen weeks, half dead all that time? (*She pushes him.*) Get out of this house. Get out!

JONAS: If he doesn't want the cloth or hasn't the money, I'll be glad to take it back. But I know he has it. I talked to him myself. Six yards of blue wool! Blue, blue, blue wool!

WILHELMINA: I don't care if it was gold, gold, gold silk! He hasn't been out of the house in fifteen weeks.

JONAS: Now you listen to me! If you think I'm going to be taken in by—

PIERRE (*Groaning*): Ah-h-h! Wilhelmina! Wilhelmina,

come raise my pillow. (*She rushes to his side.*) And please—keep quiet. I hear a donkey braying. Oh-h-h! Everything is black and yellow! Help! Help! Drive these nightmares away!

JONAS: Patelin!

WILHELMINA: My poor Pierre!

JONAS (*Approaching bed*): My dear Mr. Patelin, I've come for the money you promised me.

PIERRE (*Sitting up suddenly, staring at* JONAS): Ha! The dog is out! Shut the door before the cat comes in! (*Falls back, raising his feet stiffly in the air*) Ah, rub my feet! Tickle my toes. Drive this pain away! (WILHELMINA *motions for* JONAS *to tickle* PIERRE's *foot. When he takes one foot,* PIERRE *suddenly brings both feet together, pinching* JONAS' *hand.* JONAS *cries out and pulls his hand away.*) Look, there! (*Points upward*)

JONAS: Where? Where?

PIERRE: It's a bird! No, it's a bee with Jonas the draper hanging on his back! Catch him quickly! (PIERRE *jumps up and starts dashing around room. He catches* JONAS *and begins to tickle him.* JONAS *pulls free.*) There he goes! And there's the cat! Right after him! (*Darts at* JONAS, *who jumps back, alarmed.*) Get him! Get him! Oh-h-h! (PIERRE *falls back on bed as if exhausted*)

WILHELMINA (*To* JONAS): Now see what you've done!

JONAS (*Staring at* PIERRE): But this morning—did he get sick after he came home?

WILHELMINA: Are you starting that again?

JONAS: I should have insisted on immediate payment. I know Patelin! (*To* WILHELMINA) Tell me, do you have a goose roasting on the fire?

WILHELMINA: A goose on the—? We don't even have a fire! Oh, please! Just go away and leave us alone! (*Cries very hard, watching slyly to see the effect*)

JONAS: Oh, dear, oh, dear, please don't cry like that! I must think! (*Pantomimes scene in his shop*) I'm sure I had six yards of cloth, and he chose the—the blue— didn't he? Or did he? Of course! I gave it to him myself. Yet—(*Looks at* PIERRE) He's sick, all right. (*To* WILHELMINA) Sixteen weeks, you say? (*She nods.*) But—he was in my shop. "Come to my house," he says, "and have some roast goose," he says, "and a bottle of red wine!" he says.

WILHELMINA: Maybe your memory's gone bad. You ought to make sure before you accuse people. I'll bet the cloth is still in your shop.

JONAS: Wait here. (*He dashes into street, crosses to shop and looks through bolts of cloth. As* JONAS *exits,* PIERRE *sits up.*)

PIERRE: Is he gone?

WILHELMINA: Careful! He might come back!

PIERRE: We did it! We put it over! Good Wilhelmina! Sweet Wilhelmina! (*They laugh.* PIERRE *gets out of bed, and they begin to dance about.* JONAS *runs out of shop and re-enters* PIERRE'S *house.*)

JONAS (*Entering*): Aha! I thought so! A nice bit of trickery! Where's my money?

WILHELMINA (*Still laughing*): Other people cry for joy, but I'm laughing because I'm miserable. Look at him! (*She laughs harder.*) Poor Pierre! And it's all your fault! You drove him crazy!

PIERRE (*Grabbing the broom*): Ha! A guitar! (*Makes strumming sounds and pretends to play it*)

JONAS: Stop this nonsense! Please! My money or my cloth!

WILHELMINA: Haven't you done enough? (*Looks at him closely*) Oh! Now I see! You're the crazy one! (*She pretends to be afraid, runs behind* PIERRE) Oh, help, Pierre! He's a crazy man!

JONAS (*Going to* WILHELMINA): Now you stop that! (PIERRE *swings the broom and gives* JONAS *a swat.*) Hey! What's going on here? That's a funny way to be sick!

PIERRE: Aha! Are you a man or a mouse?

JONAS: What?

PIERRE: It's a mouse! The mouse in the moon, and he's made of blue cheese! I'm just the cat to catch him! (PIERRE *chases* JONAS, *and* WILHELMINA *joins in. She trips* JONAS *so that* PIERRE *can hit him with broom.* PIERRE *occasionally hits* WILHELMINA *by mistake.*)

WILHELMINA: Oh, I'm afraid! I'm afraid! Help me, Mr. Jonas, help!

JONAS: Dear lady, I can't even help myself! (*Suddenly* PIERRE *stops, drops the broom and falls down on floor as if dead.*)

WILHELMINA: He's dead! He's dead! And you killed him, Mr. Jonas! It's all your fault! (*At the window*) Help! Help! Somebody! Mr. Jonas has killed my husband!

JONAS: Mrs. Patelin! That's not true! (*Shouting out the window*) That's not true! I didn't do it!

WILHELMINA (*Running into street*): Yes, he did!

JONAS (*Following her into street*): No, I didn't! (*Looks around*) I—uh—I think I'd better go! Somebody might just believe you! (*He runs across street to his shop.* WILHELMINA *re-enters her house. She and* PIERRE *burst into laughter and exit left into kitchen. As* JONAS *re-enters his shop,* TIBALD *enters street from rear, and* JONAS *sees him.*) The very man who stole my sheep! (*To* TIBALD) You, shepherd! Stop, thief!

TIBALD (*Stopping*): Are you talking to me, Mr. Jonas?

JONAS: I certainly am, robber!

TIBALD: Me? A robber?

JONAS: Yes!

TIBALD: Oh.

JONAS: And I'm going to see you hanged for it, too.

TIBALD: Now, Mr. Jonas, why would you do a thing like that?

JONAS: If you think you can get away with stealing my sheep—

TIBALD: You have it all wrong, Mr. Jonas.

JONAS: Where are the sheep, then?

TIBALD (*Sadly*): Dead, sir.

JONAS: Aha!

TIBALD: But I didn't kill them. They just fell sick. Hoofsickness, it was. One, then another. First thing I knew, six sheep up and died.

JONAS: With a little help. (*Draws his finger across his throat*)

TIBALD: I never—never! Please, Mr. Jonas!

JONAS: Get out of here, you thief! You're going to pay for this! (*Looks toward* PIERRE's *house*) Someone has to pay!

TIBALD: Why me?

JONAS: You just wait! You'll see! (*He goes into shop and exits right into house.*)

TIBALD: Oh! Oh! Oh! What do I do now? What I need is a good lawyer! Only whom can I get? I don't know anybody except—wait a minute! Patelin! They say he can talk the arm off a brass monkey! And there's his house! (*He knocks, and* PIERRE *comes to door immediately.*) Are you Mr. Patelin?

PIERRE: I am.

TIBALD: Well, I'm a shepherd. I take care of sheep. (*Pause*) And—well—some of those sheep died.

PIERRE: With a little help, no doubt.

TIBALD: Well, just a little. (PIERRE *nods wisely.*) But now they want to hang me! Oh, help me, Mr. Patelin, help me!

PIERRE: Hang you, eh? (TIBALD *nods.*) Well, I might—I just might—be able to save you!

TIBALD: Oh, thank you, Mr. Patelin, thank you!

PIERRE: But I warn you, going to court is expensive.

TIBALD: I'm only a poor shepherd, but I have a little saved up.

PIERRE: What do you think you could pay?

TIBALD: Do you think five—that is—four hundred francs would be enough?

PIERRE: Hm-m-m-m. Well, we might just scrape through. I realize you're a poor man. Of course, I don't take less than a thousand, usually, but did you say five hundred?

TIBALD: I did! I did!

PIERRE: Better make it six.

TIBALD: Six? Six, if you say so.

PIERRE: I think we can win. That is, if you do as I say.

TIBALD: Anything.

PIERRE: That's the spirit! Now listen. When we get to court, you mustn't say a single word but "baa." You understand? (TIBALD *shakes his head.*) Bleat—like a sheep.

TIBALD: Oh.

PIERRE: No matter what anyone says, you just say "baa." Pretend you *are* a sheep.

TIBALD (*Dropping to his knees and butting* PIERRE): Baa! Baa!

PIERRE: That's it! Wonderful! Even if they call you a crook, a liar, a thief.

TIBALD: Baa.

PIERRE: Perfect! Even if *I* talk to you.

TIBALD: Baa.

PIERRE: Your case is as good as won! Now don't forget— baa!

TIBALD: Baa-a-a-a!

PIERRE: And *don't* forget the money! You understand?

TIBALD: Oh, yes, Mr. Patelin. Six hundred francs.

PIERRE: Good. (JUDGE *enters, carrying bench, which he*

sets up in street. PIERRE *looks out window.*) The judge
is here. We must have him hear your case.

JUDGE: Hear, hear! The judge is here! (JONAS *enters at
right into shop.*) Now if anyone has business here, let's
get it over with. Court wants to adjourn. (PIERRE *and*
TIBALD *enter street.*)

PIERRE (*Going to* JUDGE): Hear! Hear! Bless you, judge!

JUDGE: Bless you, dear sir! (JONAS *comes into street and
approaches bench.* PIERRE *tries to hide his face, and*
TIBALD *hides behind the bench.*)

JONAS: Your honor! Your honor!

JUDGE: Yes?

JONAS: My lawyer isn't here yet, but he's on his way.

JUDGE: You're the plaintiff, aren't you? (JONAS *nods.*)
Well, what's your complaint? And where's the defendant?

JONAS: Right there, your honor. (*Points to* TIBALD) That
lummox of a shepherd hiding away as if he couldn't say
baa. He looks very gentle, your honor, but he's as wild
as a wolf.

JUDGE: Since both parties are here, I'll start the questioning. Did he work for you?

JONAS: He did, your honor. I treated him like a son, and
he repaid me by killing my best sheep.

JUDGE: Did you pay him well?

PIERRE (*Pulling up his collar to hide his face*): Your honor,
he never paid him a penny.

JONAS: That's not true—(*Recognizes* PIERRE) You!

JUDGE: Why are you covering your face, Patelin?

PIERRE: Your honor, I have a terrible toothache.

JUDGE: Oh, that's too bad. I had one myself just the other
day. Tell you what to do. Put three hairs from the tail
of a white horse into a tub of ice-cold water and soak
your feet in it. It'll draw the ache into your toenails and

all you have to do then is clip them off. The pain will
go at once. Try it and see.

PIERRE: Oh, thank you, your honor. I'll try it right away!

JONAS (*Staring at* PIERRE): It *was* you, wasn't it? Six yards
of wool. Where's my money?

JUDGE: What are you talking about?

PIERRE: He seems confused, your honor.

JONAS: *I'm* confused? You thief! You—

PIERRE: Your honor, I think I understand. It's amazing
how muddled people can get without legal training. I
think he means he could have made six yards of woolen
cloth from the sheep this poor man is supposed to have
stolen.

JUDGE: It seems that way. Come, come, Mr. Jonas. Finish
your story.

JONAS: Your honor, he took six yards of sheep this morning. (To PIERRE) You thief!

JUDGE: Six yards of what?

PIERRE: Your honor, let's call the defendant. He'll make
more sense.

JUDGE: Good idea, Patelin! Where's the shepherd?

TIBALD: Baa.

JUDGE: What's this, a man or a sheep?

TIBALD: Baa.

PIERRE: Your honor, I think he's a little—(*Taps his forehead*)

JONAS: Listen here! (*Points to* TIBALD) He can talk, and
he's not—(*Taps his forehead, then turning on* PIERRE
angrily) What are you doing here, you robber. Where is
my cloth?

JUDGE: Cloth? What are you talking about, man? Get back
to your sheep!

JONAS: Yes, yes, your honor! That shepherd there—he took
six woolly yards—

JUDGE: Six woolly what?

JONAS: Pardon me, your honor. I meant, six woolly sheep! That's it, sheep! And this—this shepherd told me I'd get my money for the wool as soon as—I mean, this shepherd was to watch my flocks, and when I went to his house, he pretended to be sick. Ah-h-h-h! Patelin! (*To* JUDGE) He killed my sheep and said they died of hoof-sickness!

JUDGE: Who? Patelin?

JONAS: I saw him take that cloth. I *saw* him! And he swore he didn't kill them—and his wife swore he was sick and said he never killed the cloth—and then he—he—oh, I don't know what I'm saying!

JUDGE: Silence! I've heard all I can stand. Now tell me the truth about the blue sheep and the woolly money or out you go! This is your last chance!

PIERRE: Your honor, this poor man seems feverish. Maybe we ought to call a doctor. At times it sounds as if he's worried about some money he owes this poor shepherd.

JONAS (*To* PIERRE): Thief! Robber! Where's my wool? I know you have it! And you're not sick either!

PIERRE: Who's not sick?

JUDGE: Who has what?

JONAS: I'll talk about that later. Now I want to take care of *this* thief! (*Points to* TIBALD)

PIERRE: This poor shepherd doesn't know court procedure, your honor. I'll be glad to defend him.

JUDGE: You won't get anything out of it, Patelin.

PIERRE (*Piously*): Ah, but I'll be doing a good deed. That's enough for me.

JUDGE: You're an honest man, Patelin.

PIERRE: Thank you, your honor. (*Taking* TIBALD *by the arm*) Come along, my good man. This is all for your own good. Now, just answer my questions truthfully.

TIBALD: Baa.

PIERRE: Come, now. I'm your lawyer, not a lamb.

TIBALD: Baa.

PIERRE: Tell me, did this man ever pay you for taking care of his sheep?

TIBALD: Baa.

PIERRE (*Pretending to lose his temper*): Idiot! I'm your lawyer, trying to help you! Answer me!

TIBALD: Baa.

JONAS: Your honor, that shepherd can talk if he wants to. He talked to me this morning.

PIERRE: Apparently everything happened to you this morning, Mr. Jonas. (*To* JUDGE) Your honor, it seems to me this man should go back to his sheep. He understands them better than he does people. It doesn't look to me as if he had enough brains to kill a fly, let alone a sheep.

JONAS: Liar! Liar! Liar!

JUDGE: I honestly think they're both crazy.

PIERRE: Your honor is a great judge.

JONAS: I'm crazy? (*To* PIERRE) You scoundrel! Where's my wool? (*Pointing to* PIERRE *and* TIBALD) Your honor, there are the thieves!

JUDGE: Silence!

JONAS: But your honor—

JUDGE: Silence, I say! Trouble, trouble, trouble everywhere I go. Case dismissed!

JONAS: Is there no justice?

JUDGE: Are you making fun of justice?

JONAS: Oh, no, no, no, your honor, but—

JUDGE: You hire half-wits and don't pay them. You come here shouting about cloth which has nothing to do with the case—and you expect justice?

JONAS (*Almost in tears*): My cloth! My money! My sheep!

JUDGE: Silence—for the last time! (*To* TIBALD) Shepherd, or whatever your name is—

TIBALD: Baa.

JUDGE: Baa, then. Go home, Baa, and never let me see you again!

PIERRE: You're free, Tibald! Thank his honor!

TIBALD: Baa.

JUDGE (*Shaking his head and wiping his brow*): I hope I never have to go through anything like this again. Court is adjourned. (*He picks up bench and starts to exit at rear.*) Goodbye, Mr. Patelin. Don't forget—three hairs from the tail of a white horse.

PIERRE: Thank you, your honor. I won't forget. (JUDGE *exits.*)

JONAS: Thieves! Scoundrels! Liars! You—you—

PIERRE: You'll get a sore throat shouting like that, Jonas.

JONAS: Justice may be blind, but I'm not! Didn't I see you dancing and singing this morning?

PIERRE: Are you sure you didn't dream all that?

JONAS: But—but—you may have fooled the judge but you can't fool me. I'll fix you next time. (*Stamps into shop and exits right into house.*)

PIERRE (*Laughing*): Well, Tibald, my boy, wasn't that a great bit of work?

TIBALD: Baa.

PIERRE: Yes, yes! Brilliant!

TIBALD: Baa.

PIERRE: Everyone's gone now. You can talk. I say, you can talk now. There's no one here. (*Holds out his hand*) Where's the money?

TIBALD: Baa.

PIERRE: I can't stand around all day. What is this?

TIBALD: Baa.

PIERRE: Listen, I'm a busy man!

TIBALD: Baa.

PIERRE: Yes, yes, you did very well, but now it's all over. Six hundred francs, please.

TIBALD: Baa.

PIERRE: Five?

TIBALD: Baa.

PIERRE: Four? Three? Two?

TIBALD (*Handing him his shepherd's crook*): Baa.

PIERRE: You mean that's all I get?

TIBALD: Baa.

PIERRE: I'll take you back to court, you thief! Robber!
 (*He tries to strike* TIBALD.)

TIBALD (*Dodging* PIERRE's *blows*): Baa! The judge said he
 never wanted to see me again! (*Runs off at rear, laughing*) Baa! Baa!

PIERRE (*Looking after him*): I suppose you'd say it serves
 me right. (*Shrugs*) Anyway, it was a great idea. (*He
 exits as curtain falls.*)

THE END

The Price of Eggs

A French folk story

by Mary Ann Nicholson

Characters

WIDOW ⎱ *French peasants*
NEIGHBOR ⎰
STRANGER, *a young peasant*
VILLAGE MAGISTRATE, *an older man*

TIME: *A summer morning.*
SETTING: *A French village street.*
AT RISE: WIDOW *is sweeping the doorstep in front of her house and stops to greet her* NEIGHBOR *who is passing on her way to market.*

WIDOW: Good day to you, Neighbor. I see you are off to market.

NEIGHBOR: And good day to you, Widow. I have not seen you for a long while, not since your late husband's funeral.

WIDOW (*Sadly*): May heaven keep him.

NEIGHBOR: How do you get along these days, Widow?

WIDOW (*Sighing*): I manage, though I do have to work hard. I have my goats and my chickens. With the money I get from selling the eggs, I buy more chickens. I'm not starving.

NEIGHBOR: Indeed, you are a lucky woman to be able to say that. My husband has gone away to the iron ore mines. He sends home his week's pay for me to buy food and shoes for our children, but it is never as much as we need.

WIDOW: Alas, times are hard for everyone. Every day one sees a stream of men going past the door on their way to work in the iron ore mines. Look, here comes one now. (*Ragged* STRANGER *enters from right, walking wearily. As he approaches the two women, he stumbles and slumps onto doorstep.*)

STRANGER: I beg your pardon, my good women, but I must sit down. I am too weary to walk another step without rest.

NEIGHBOR: You must have come a great distance. I suppose you are on your way to find work in the iron ore mines like all the others.

STRANGER: Yes, I am on my way to the mines. I have walked from a province beyond this one and still have many miles to travel.

WIDOW: You may rest awhile on my doorstep if you wish; it's clean and it's free.

STRANGER: Thank you, madam. If I had some food, I might have more strength to continue my journey. Could you spare a crust of bread, kind woman? I have had nothing to eat all day.

WIDOW (*Coldly*): I have little enough to eat myself. I am a poor widow alone in the world. I cannot help every stranger who passes by.

NEIGHBOR (*Whispering to her*): You could sell him some of your eggs, Widow. Take pity on him, he is so tired and hungry. Surely, you can't refuse him a little kindness. Remember, we, too, know what it is to be hungry. Help him.

WIDOW (*Reluctantly, to* STRANGER): I could sell you a

dozen eggs. They were fresh from under the hens this morning. You could eat them on your way.

STRANGER: How wonderful they would taste, but I have no money to pay you for them. I cannot give you anything but a promise to pay at some later date.

WIDOW: I would be a fool to do business that way.

NEIGHBOR: Good Widow, how can you be so mercenary? He is starving and you do nothing. Give him some eggs.

WIDOW: Give him eggs? Certainly not. How you talk! No wonder you are always poor.

NEIGHBOR: Then accept his promise to pay. He has an honest face. I'm sure you can trust him.

WIDOW (*Giving in*): All right, but he will have to take yesterday's eggs which I cooked this morning. I shall get a good price for my best *fresh* eggs in the market.

STRANGER: Cooked eggs will be very welcome, and I won't have to worry about breaking them. Thank you, kind and generous Widow. You have my word of honor that I will pay for the eggs when I come back this way again, no matter how long it takes me to make my fortune at the iron mines. (WIDOW *goes into house and returns with a dozen hard-boiled eggs in a kerchief which she hands to* STRANGER.)

NEIGHBOR: Heaven preserve you, Stranger. (STRANGER *exits, down left.*) Don't you feel a little lighter in your heart for having helped a stranger, Widow?

WIDOW: No, I only feel lighter in my larder. I will never see him again, thanks to you. It's the last time I'll listen to you.

NEIGHBOR: Heaven will bless you many times for your kindness today, wait and see. (WIDOW *turns and shuts door in anger. Curtain.*)

*   *   *

SCENE 2

TIME: *Ten years later.*

SETTING: *Same as Scene 1.*

AT RISE: STRANGER *enters, dressed in fine clothes. He is accompanied by the* NEIGHBOR.

NEIGHBOR: When I saw you in the marketplace, I didn't recognize you at first. Ten years can make a lot of difference in people. When you were here before, you were in rags.

STRANGER: I have been blessed with prosperity from my work in the iron ore mines. Now I am part owner of those mines. I can repay my debt to the widow who gave me a dozen eggs when I needed food. Does she still live here?

NEIGHBOR: Yes, she does, but I rarely see her. She has become a miser and is so bitter with the world that she can't say a kind word about anybody. Your paying the debt will please her very much.

STRANGER (*Knocking on door*): I hope it will be a happy surprise.

WIDOW (*Now older and very cranky*): Who's there? Who's knocking? (*She opens door a crack and peeks out.*)

STRANGER: It is I, good Widow. I have come to pay you for the dozen eggs you gave me ten years ago. (*She comes out eagerly.*) You see, I have never forgotten your great kindness to me. I want to keep my promise to pay. Here are two bags of gold for you. (*Holds out bags*)

WIDOW: Only two bags of gold? It will take all you possess to pay me after ten years.

STRANGER: How can that be?

NEIGHBOR: I see trouble brewing for you, Stranger. I warned you she had become greedy. I'll run and fetch the Village Magistrate. He is wise in handling such matters. (*Hurriedly, she exits right.*)

STRANGER: Just a moment, old Widow. Your neighbor is fetching a magistrate. Perhaps he can solve this difficulty. I don't understand why a dozen eggs should be worth more than two bags of gold, even with interest on the debt for ten years.

WIDOW: The Magistrate will understand and protect a poor old widow's rights. (NEIGHBOR *enters, breathless, with an aged* MAGISTRATE.)

NEIGHBOR: Here is the Magistrate. Now you can tell him your story, Widow.

WIDOW: Well, Your Honor, if I had not given this man a dozen eggs, I would have hatched a dozen chickens from them. And, from those dozen chickens I would have had more eggs and more chickens. In these ten years I would have had thousands of chickens, and I, too, would be rich.

MAGISTRATE: What you say sounds logical enough. (*Turning to* STRANGER) Has she left any point out, Stranger?

STRANGER: Not that I can see, Your Honor.

MAGISTRATE: Ahem, ahem, then I shall proceed with the verdict. . . .

NEIGHBOR: Wait a minute, Your Honor. I have just remembered something. (*She whispers excitedly to* MAGISTRATE. *He registers surprise and smiles slyly.*)

MAGISTRATE: Before I offer you my decision, I want to ask the Widow if she will do me one favor.

WIDOW (*Curious*): What is that, Your Honor?

MAGISTRATE: Will you cook me some ears of corn? I'm thinking of planting a garden.

WIDOW: You must be joking, Your Honor. Everyone knows you can't grow corn that has been cooked.

MAGISTRATE: Aha, there you see. Then you have forgotten

that the eggs you gave this stranger were hard-boiled.
How did you think you were going to hatch chickens
from cooked eggs?

WIDOW (*Eager to retreat*): You are right, Your Honor, I
have been very foolish. I will be satisfied with the two
bags of gold the Stranger offered.

MAGISTRATE: Not so fast, old Widow. You should be
taught a lesson for your meanness. (*To* STRANGER) Sir,
pay her no more than the price of a dozen hard-boiled
eggs.

STRANGER: If it's all right with you, Your Honor, I would
rather give her the two bags of gold to show my gratitude
to her for the kindness she showed me ten years ago.

MAGISTRATE: You are very generous and forgiving, Stranger. I hope that after today, the Widow will know better
than to count her chickens before they are hatched.
(*Curtain falls, as* STRANGER *hands bags of gold to*
WIDOW.)

THE END

The Musicians of Bremen Town

A story of old Germany

Adapted from *Grimms' Fairy Tales*

by Walter Roberts

Characters

NARRATOR	FARMER
DONKEY	FARMER'S WIFE
CAT	ROBBER CHIEF
DOG	TWO ROBBERS
ROOSTER	

TIME: *Once upon a time, in Bremen.*

SETTING: *The stage is bare, except for a black wooden box at right.*

AT RISE: CAT *is sitting on wooden box. At left of box* DOG *stands; at right,* ROOSTER; *and at rear left,* DONKEY. NARRATOR *enters, carrying book from which he reads. He stands down right.*

NARRATOR (*Reading*): Once, long ago, there lived on a farm a donkey (DONKEY *brays*), a cat (CAT *meows*), a dog (DOG *barks*), and a rooster (ROOSTER *crows*). They lived in a warm barn where they had always been very happy (*All nod*), until one day they overheard the farmer talking to his wife. (*All lean toward left and cup their*

hands to their ears, listening. FARMER *and* FARMER'S
WIFE *enter left, conversing.*)

FARMER: I am going to get rid of all the animals. They are
too old to do their jobs on the farm any more, so I am
going to sell the donkey for glue . . .

DONKEY: For glue!

FARMER: And drown the cat in the creek . . .

CAT: In the creek?

FARMER: And shoot the dog . . .

DOG: With a gun?

FARMER'S WIFE: And on Sunday we will roast the rooster
for dinner.

ROOSTER: Awk! Dinner! (FARMER *and* WIFE *exit left.*)

NARRATOR: Now they were a very sad donkey, and cat, and
dog, and rooster. (*All moan and cry.*) They didn't know
what they could do. (*All shake their heads.*) They had to
leave the farm. (*All nod.*) But where could they go, and
what could they do to earn a living? (*All shrug.*) Then
the donkey had an idea.

DONKEY: I have an idea!

CAT, DOG, *and* ROOSTER (*Excitedly*): What? What?

DONKEY: Why don't we become famous singers? (*All look
at him in surprise.*)

NARRATOR: The others were surprised. They looked at
each other and thought about the idea. They were only
animals. Did animals become famous singers? (*They
shrug.*) It *might* be possible. It certainly wouldn't hurt
to try! So it was agreed that they would run away to
Bremen Town and become famous singers! (*They nod
happily.*) Why, they'd be rich overnight. (*They nod.*)
And the farmer would never know what happened to
them. (*They shake their heads, pleased about this.*) Just
for practice, they decided to try out a song together before they left. (*They group, leaning toward center like
an amateur quartet. Each makes his own animal sound*

several times. NARRATOR *winces a little, but he speaks diplomatically.*) And it wasn't as bad as it might have been. In fact, it was quite good—for a start.

ROOSTER: That was quite good!

NARRATOR: None of them had any idea how far it was to Bremen Town, for they had never been out of the barnyard before, so they decided to take a lunch. (*Animals collect items from behind box.*) The donkey took some hay, the rooster took some corn, the dog took a bone, and the cat took a mouse she had been saving for Sunday. Then they set out for Bremen Town to become famous musicians. (*Animals exit right in order named, carrying their food.*) The donkey (DONKEY *brays musically*), the cat (CAT *meows musically*), the dog (DOG *barks musically*), and the rooster (ROOSTER *crows musically*).

Just before dark, that same day, on a lonely stretch of road about halfway between the farm and Bremen Town, the four animals decided to sit down and rest. They were very tired. (ROBBER CHIEF *and* TWO ROBBERS *enter left, carrying table laden with food, money, and valuables, and set it down at left. They stand around table and begin to count their money silently, as animals drag in wearily from the right, without food, and sit near box.*)

DONKEY: I am very tired.

CAT: How much farther is it to Bremen Town?

DOG: Perhaps we are lost!

ROOSTER: I am *so* hungry.

DOG: I could even eat a mouse!

NARRATOR: They had eaten their lunches long ago, and now they were hungry. (*Animals nod sadly.*) Well, they had come this far, and at least nobody had sold them for glue, or shot them, or drowned them in a creek, or cooked them for Sunday dinner. (*All nod happily.*) For now, they'd just have to try to sleep and not think about being hungry. Tomorrow, when they came to Bremen Town, everything would be fine. (*All lie down;* ROOSTER *perches on box*.) No sooner had they settled down, than the rooster began to shout.

ROOSTER (*Pointing left excitedly*): I see a house! I see a house!

CAT (*Sitting up straight*): A mouse? Where's a mouse?

ROOSTER: Not a mouse—a *house!*

NARRATOR: They all looked. (*Animals stare at* ROBBERS.) Sure enough, it was a house with a big fire burning, lots of food on a table, and even money scattered all around. (*Animals gasp*.) The animals looked at one another. They had an idea! Why didn't they sing a nice song for these obviously rich people and earn themselves a good supper? (*All nod and group to sing.* NARRATOR *leans forward and uses secretive tone*.) Now, what the animals didn't know was that this house was inhabited by desperate and cruel robbers who would stop at nothing. (ROBBERS *growl at audience*.)

ROBBER CHIEF: I would stop at nothing!

TWO ROBBERS: Neither would we!

NARRATOR: And all the great amount of food and money they had in the house was stolen!

ROBBERS: Right!

NARRATOR: But our musicians didn't know this, so they sang. (*Animals sing as before, discordantly.* ROBBERS *freeze in terror. When song ends, all hold their positions as the* NARRATOR *speaks*.) The robbers were frightened by the terrible noise. They thought it must be the king's army coming to capture them. If so, the only escape from the hangman was to hide in the woods. (*With a terrifying shout,* ROBBERS *rush across stage, push wildly through animals, and exit right*.) The musicians looked at one another in amazement. They certainly had not expected *this* to happen. They had sung their very best.

DOG: Why did they run away?

CAT (*Hurt*): We sang our very best.

NARRATOR: They were all a little hurt. (*Animals drop their heads and nod sadly.*) But soon they figured it out! (*They look up and smile at each other.*) It was obvious that these people had liked their song so much that they had rushed off to get their friends. That was it! Of course!

ANIMALS (*Together*): Of course! (*Animals congratulate each other.*)

NARRATOR: The animals wondered what they could do while they waited for the audience to come.

CAT. Maybe we could eat.

DOG: Of course!

DONKEY: We'll have a nice dinner before the audience comes.

NARRATOR: So they went into the house and ate all they could—and then they ate some more! (*Animals go to table and pantomime eating.*) It grew late and they were tired and warm and full. But still no audience came. Perhaps the three men had to go a long way to find their friends, and might not even be back until morning. The animals thought they'd better lie down and be rested for their performance. Certainly, they were a tired donkey (DONKEY *stretches, yawns, brays.*), cat (CAT *stretches and meows.*), dog (DOG *yawns and barks.*), and rooster (ROOSTER *stretches, yawns, and crows.*). So they all lay down and fell asleep. (*Animals sit on floor around table and go to sleep.* ROBBERS *sneak in right, and cross to box.* NARRATOR'S *voice becomes very dramatic.*) Meanwhile, outside the house, the robbers crept back up close to see who it was who had found their hideout.

ROBBER CHIEF: I wonder who has found our hideout.

1ST ROBBER: I don't know.

2ND ROBBER: Neither do I.

NARRATOR: Well, they had to find out who it was and then get rid of them. (ROBBERS *nod.*) The Robber Chief pointed to the bravest of the robbers. (ROBBER CHIEF *points at* 1ST ROBBER.) He was the one who would go in! (1ST ROBBER *squeals with fear, covers his eyes, and trembles. Others push him toward table.* 1ST ROBBER *starts to move cautiously toward table.*) So the brave robber moved with cunning and stealth toward the dark house, making his way silently into the black interior. Outside, his two companions waited and listened.

ROBBER CHIEF (*Whispering loudly*): Wait!

2ND ROBBER (*Also whispering*): Listen!

NARRATOR: For a long moment, all was silent in the house, and then what they heard was enough to strike terror into the hearts of even the most terrible robbers. (*They gasp and stare toward table in amazement.*) For, inside the dark house, their companion had stepped on the tail of the old cat. (1ST ROBBER *steps on* CAT's *tail.* CAT *jumps up and screeches;* 1ST ROBBER *screams.*) And this so upset the donkey that he woke up kicking everything —mainly the robber. (DONKEY *brays and pantomimes kicking* 1ST ROBBER. DOG *and* ROOSTER *jump up;* DOG *barks loudly and grabs* ROBBER's *leg and* ROOSTER *flaps arms wildly and crows.* ROBBER *moans and tries to pull leg away. Noise stops.*) Outside, the robbers were too afraid to run. (1ST ROBBER *staggers toward box and sits down.* ROBBER CHIEF *and* 2ND ROBBER *gather around him.*)

1ST ROBBER: I have been badly beaten by *twenty* horrible villains! No—there were *fifty* of them!

2ND ROBBER: We can see that!

ROBBER CHIEF: Let's get out of here! (*He runs off right, followed by others.*)

NARRATOR: The poor animals, who didn't know *what* had actually happened, decided to have another supper (*Animals shrug, then gather around table*), while they waited for the audience to come to hear them sing. So they waited and ate, and waited and ate, but the audience never did come.

DOG (*Sadly*): I guess the audience isn't going to come.

CAT: It doesn't matter much, though, for we have plenty of food.

ROOSTER: And plenty of money to buy more! (*Animals nod happily.*)

DONKEY: We even have a warm house to live in, which is much nicer than the old barn ever was.

NARRATOR: So the animals stayed there for the rest of their lives, and everything worked out fine. Except that Bremen Town missed out on a fine quartet, made up of a very happy donkey, and cat, and dog, and rooster. (*Animals form a group and sing discordantly.* NARRATOR *closes book, shakes his head, and exits right, as curtain falls.*)

THE END

Merry Tyll and the Three Rogues

A German folk tale

by Adele Thane

AUTHOR'S NOTES

Tyll Eulenspiegel is a well-known character in German and Dutch stories and many are the tales told of his pranks. Contrary to general belief, Tyll is not a fictitious character, but actually lived in medieval times. He was born in Kneitlingen, Germany, at the end of the 13th century and died in Mollen about 1350. His tombstone still stands in the cemetery, carved with the figures of an owl (*Eulen,* in German), and mirror (*Spiegel,* in German), the symbols of Tyll Eulenspiegel's wisdom and truth.

A Franciscan monk, Thomas Murner, was the first to record Tyll's pranks in 1493. In these early tales, Tyll is a boorish peasant who works his way across Europe, outwitting innkeepers and merchants. In later versions, however, his character undergoes a transformation and he is represented as a sort of jester, a clever fellow whose wit delights the people while his irreverent mischief-making is the despair of respectable society. He wanders about the countryside to fairs and markets, praising what is good and beautiful and making sport of vanity and conceit.

Merry Tyll and the Three Rogues is freely adapted from three of the original tales.

Characters

VEGETABLE WOMAN	YOUNG WOMAN
LACE MAKER	FOUR CHILDREN
TOY MAKER	TYLL EULENSPIEGEL
PIE MAN	OLD LADY
TRINKET VENDOR	TWO STUDENTS
VILLAGERS	THREE ROGUES
SIR POPINJAY	PETER SIMPLE
BEGGAR GIRL	COW
YOUNG MAN	SHERIFF
WAITRESS	

SETTING: *The marketplace of a town in Germany in the early 14th century. Five booths are up right and left, and a large frame with a closed curtain is on an elevated platform up center. Table and chairs of a street café stand at right center.*

AT RISE: VEGETABLE WOMAN, LACE MAKER, TOY MAKER, PIE MAN, *and* TRINKET VENDOR *are calling out their wares.* WAITRESS *is wiping café table.* VILLAGERS *and* CHILDREN *enter right and left and walk about, talking and buying. In crowd are* SIR POPINJAY, BEGGAR GIRL, YOUNG MAN, YOUNG WOMAN, *and* OLD LADY.

VEGETABLE WOMAN: Come, buy my fresh turnips! Sweet white turnips! Carrots crisp and golden! Who will buy?

LACE MAKER: Fine laces here! Laces woven of silk and linen! Laces fit for a queen! (SIR POPINJAY, *arrayed in frills and ribbons, stops at booth.*) Laces for your cuffs, sir? (POPINJAY *daintily selects several yards.*)

TOY MAKER: Toys! Toys! Tin toys, wooden toys! Toys for girls and boys! Spinning tops and jumping jacks! Toys! (FOUR CHILDREN *surround the* TOY MAKER.)

PIE MAN: Pies, hot pies! Right out of the oven! Sweet to eat! Apple, currant and quince! Buy a pie! (BEGGAR GIRL *reaches for pie and he restrains her.*) Here now, where's your money?

BEGGAR GIRL: I haven't any money.

PIE MAN: Well, you can have this one.

BEGGAR GIRL: Oh, thank you, Mr. Pie Man! (*She eats it.*)

TRINKET VENDOR: Trinkets for sale! Beads and brooches! Bangles and bracelets! (*To* YOUNG MAN *and* YOUNG WOMAN, *who are holding hands.*) Buy a pretty locket for your lady-love? Buy a wedding ring? (*They giggle self-consciously, and he buys the locket.* CHILDREN *turn away from the toys and wander over to frame with closed curtains. A stuffed owl is on top of frame.* BEGGAR GIRL *joins them.*)

1ST CHILD: What do you think this booth is?

2ND CHILD: I don't know, but (*Pointing*) there's an owl on top.

3RD CHILD: That's not a real owl. It's stuffed.

4TH CHILD: Maybe it's a cage full of birds.

1ST CHILD: Maybe it's a cage full of animals!

2ND CHILD (*Timidly*): *Wild* animals?

3RD CHILD: Say, that would be great! Lions and tigers!

4TH CHILD: Oh, I'll bet it's only something you shoot at for prizes.

1ST CHILD: Let's take a peek. (*They are about to open curtains when* TYLL EULENSPIEGEL *pops his head out.*)

TYLL (*In a high-pitched voice*): Hello, boys and girls! (*They jump back, startled.*)

2ND CHILD: Oh! It's a puppet!

3RD CHILD: It's too big for a puppet.

4TH CHILD: *Are* you a puppet?

TYLL: If *you* are a puppet, then *I* am a puppet!

4TH CHILD: I'm not a puppet. I'm a person.

TYLL: So am I. See? (*He steps out from between curtains.*

He is dressed as a jester and wears a cap with bells. He grins impishly.)

1ST CHILD: What's your name?

TYLL: Merry Tyll Eulenspiegel.

2ND CHILD: Eulenspiegel? That's a queer name.

3RD CHILD: What does it mean?

TYLL: "Eulen" (*Pointing to stuffed owl*)—that means "owl". And "spiegel" (*Pointing to frame*)—that means "glass"—a looking-glass. So, Eulen-spiegel—Owl-glass.

4TH CHILD: It sounds silly—Owl-glass.

TYLL: It's not silly at all. Quite the contrary. An owl is wise. And a mirror reflects the truth.

1ST CHILD (*Indicating empty frame*): But there *isn't* any mirror. There's nothing there.

TYLL (*With a bow*): *I* am the mirror.

CHILDREN: *You!*

TYLL: Yes! I show people as they really are. I am their true reflection. Watch! (*He calls to crowd.*) Step right up, good people! Right this way! See yourself as others see you! See yourself for what you are! It won't cost you a penny. Take a free look. (*Crowd gathers around, puzzled.*) Who will be first? (POPINJAY *mounts platform.*) Ah, Sir Popinjay! Stand here, if you please. (TYLL *leads him in front of curtains, then exits behind them.* POPINJAY *starts to posture and pose. Suddenly curtains part and* TYLL, *inside the empty frame, pretends to be* POPINJAY's *reflection by imitating his exaggerated gestures and facial expressions. Crowd roars with laughter.*)

POPINJAY (*Contemptuously*): You are an impudent scamp! You do not show me my true self. It's all a hoax.

TYLL: Very well, I will show you your true self now. Here you are. (*Hands* POPINJAY *a cream puff*)

POPINJAY: What's this? A cream puff!

TYLL: That is you—a pastry shell filled with froth and thin air.

POPINJAY: Bah! (*He exits, as* TWO STUDENTS *enter and join crowd.*)

TYLL: All right! Who's next? The young couple in the front row there. Come up and take a look into your hearts. (YOUNG MAN *and* YOUNG WOMAN *shyly hang back but crowd pushes them onto platform.*) Ah, there is no love like true love. (*He holds up cardboard cutout of two red hearts joined by arrow.*) Marry her quickly, young man. Many another is looking sweetly at her. (*He gives them hearts and crowd applauds.*) Now then— that little old lady. (*Points to* OLD LADY *who is helped up onto platform.*) Granny, your face may be wrinkled and your hair white with the snows of winter but the freshness of spring is in your heart. Allow me. (*He bows and presents her with bouquet of flowers, which he takes from behind curtain.*)

OLD LADY: Blessings on you, my boy. May you never lose the joy of life. (*She leaves.* STUDENTS *elbow their way through crowd and up onto platform.*)

1ST STUDENT (*Arrogantly*): Ho there, prankster! We are two students from the university. You seem to be such a clever fellow, we'd like to ask you some questions.

TYLL: Ask away. I'm ready.

2ND STUDENT: You're pretty cocksure for a fool.

TYLL: Folly is next to wisdom, but the wise ones don't know that.

2ND STUDENT: Well, let's see if your brains are as long as your ears. (*He shakes the drooping ears of* TYLL's *jester cap, jingling the bells.*) Here is the first question. How many gallons of water are there in the sea?

TYLL (*Quickly*): Four hundred and eighty million, seven hundred and thirty thousand, two hundred and sixty-four gallons—and two-thirds for good measure.

2ND STUDENT: Can you prove it?

TYLL: Easily. If you will stop all the rivers and streams

from flowing into the sea, and stop the rain from falling,
I will measure out the gallons and you can count them.
Four hundred and eighty million, seven hundred and
thirty thousand, two hundred and sixty-four—

2ND STUDENT: Enough! Enough!

TYLL (*Finishing*):—and two-thirds for good measure!
(*Crowd applauds.*)

1ST STUDENT (*Sarcastically*): You think you're pretty smart,
don't you! Well, answer me this. How many days have
passed since the birth of Adam?

TYLL: That's soon reckoned. Seven, sir.

1ST STUDENT: Only seven? Since Adam? How do you figure
that?

TYLL: Well, there are seven days in a week, aren't there?
Sunday, Monday, Tuesday, Wednesday, Thursday, Fri-
day and Saturday. And when these days have passed,
they begin all over again. It will go on like that until
Judgment Day.

1ST STUDENT (*Turning away, annoyed*): Hm-m-m, quite
so, quite so.

2ND STUDENT: Now, owl of wisdom, where is the center of
the earth? Answer that if you can! (TYLL *is silent.*
STUDENTS *nudge each other.*)

1ST STUDENT: There, we've stumped him at last! (TYLL
shuts his eyes. Crowd murmurs anxiously. TYLL'S *eyes
open and he recites in a clear voice.*)

TYLL:
Far is near, and near is far,
And the center of earth is where we are.
(*He points to the spot where they are standing.*)

2ND STUDENT: What rubbish! Do you expect me to believe
that?

TYLL: Then take a yardstick. Here, I'll get you one. (TYLL
hands yardstick to 2ND STUDENT.) Take this yardstick
and measure from here all around the earth and back

again. If you find that I am off a fraction of an inch, you can have me put in jail for a liar.

2ND STUDENT (*Angrily throwing down yardstick*): Are you trying to make a monkey out of me?

TYLL: It's the other way around, sir. *You* are trying to make a monkey out of *me*. (STUDENTS *stamp off.* TYLL *calls after them.*) If you want to know anything else, come back tomorrow and I'll tell you! (*Trumpet sounds offstage.*)

VILLAGERS (*Looking off right; ad lib*): It's the jugglers and acrobats! They're here! Let's go! (*Etc.*)

CHILDREN (*Ad lib*): Look! There's a puppet show! And clowns! Come on! (VILLAGERS *and* CHILDREN *go off right with* TYLL.)

VEGETABLE WOMAN (*To other vendors*): Go along and see the sights. I'll mind your wares. There won't be any customers for a while. (*Vendors exit.* VEGETABLE WOMAN *places stool where she can watch festivities off right while she knits. Two* ROGUES *enter left and sneak up to booths, as* VEGETABLE WOMAN *turns and catches them.*) Hands off! There's nothing here for the taking. Move on, or I'll call the sheriff. (ROGUES *go to café table and sit.*)

1ST ROGUE: This is a scurvy way to make a living. I haven't had a good meal for a week.

2ND ROGUE: I wish Willy would come. He said he'd meet us here. Where do you suppose he is?

1ST ROGUE: Picking rich men's pockets to fill his own and forgetting all about us. (3RD ROGUE *runs in left.*)

2ND ROGUE: Willy! Where have you been?

3RD ROGUE: Never mind that. Listen! (*He sits between them.*) Would you two like to play a trick and share in what we win?

1ST ROGUE: What will it get us?

3RD ROGUE: Well, for one thing, we'll each have a cut of

prime beef hanging in the pantry without paying a brass
button for it.

2ND ROGUE: What are you talking about?

3RD ROGUE: There's a simpleton on his way here to sell his
cow. We must make him believe that the cow is a goat.

1ST ROGUE: How will we do that?

3RD ROGUE: You two go off there (*Pointing left*) and wait
until you see me arguing with him. Then one after the
other, you walk over to us and pretend that you don't
know me. When I ask you if the animal is a cow, you
must swear it is a goat. Leave the rest to me. Now, off
with you! Here he comes. (1ST *and* 2ND ROGUES *exit
quickly, left.* TYLL *enters right unnoticed by* 3RD ROGUE,
*and conceals himself behind curtains in his booth, peek-
ing out at intervals.* PETER SIMPLE *and his* COW *trudge
slowly down center aisle, go up on stage.* PETER *stares
stupidly about.*)

PETER: Where *is* everybody? (COW *shrugs and moos.*)

3RD ROGUE (*Standing and crossing to* PETER): Good morning, my lad. That's a fine animal you have there.

PETER: Do you want to buy it?

3RD ROGUE: Oh, no. I'd have no use for a goat. (COW *gives
a start of surprise.*)

PETER: *Goat!* Pshaw! It's the finest cow that ever came to
market, or my name isn't Peter Simple.

3RD ROGUE: Well, Peter Simple, may I suggest that the
next time you come to market to sell a *cow,* you *bring*
a cow.

PETER: But I *have* brought a cow! (COW *moos, nodding
head.*) Look again.

3RD ROGUE: I don't have to look again. I can tell with both
my eyes shut that (*He closes his eyes and feels* COW's
head)—this is a *goat.*

PETER: Haw, haw! Where have you been all your life that
you don't know a cow from a goat?

3RD ROGUE: I know the difference between them, and I say this is a goat!

PETER: And I say it is a *cow!*

3RD ROGUE: A goat!

PETER: A cow!

3RD ROGUE: Come, come, let's not quarrel over the matter. (1ST ROGUE *enters.*) We will consult this bright-looking person. My good man, will you tell me, is that a cow or is it a goat?

1ST ROGUE: How you talk! Why, it's as plain as the nose on your face that it's a goat.

PETER: You're wrong. It's a cow. At least I think it's a cow. (*Appealing to* 1ST ROGUE) Isn't it a cow?

1ST ROGUE (*Shaking his head*): No.

PETER (*Timidly*): No?

1ST ROGUE (*Definitely*): *No!*

PETER: Oh, dear! How did I ever make a mistake like that? (Cow *moos.*) Yes, Gretel? (Cow *moos again.*) What's that? You *are* a cow? (*Beaming with delight*) Gretel says she is a cow!

3RD ROGUE: What nonsense! Now, listen here. I am willing to wager fifty gold pieces that this poor animal is a goat.

PETER (*Gasping*): Fifty gold pieces!

3RD ROGUE: That's right. Let the next man who comes this way judge between us. If he says this is a cow, I will pay you fifty gold pieces. If he says it is a goat, you will give the animal to me. Do you agree? (PETER *hesitates;* Cow *moos "yes".*)

PETER: Gretel says yes. She's positive she's a cow.

3RD ROGUE (*As* 2ND ROGUE *enters*): Here comes a solid citizen. Ask him yourself.

PETER (*To* 2ND ROGUE): Good sir, there is a great argument between us and we want you to judge who is right. Would you kindly tell us what this animal is?

2ND ROGUE: What is it? Why, can't you see for yourself what it is?

PETER: Oh, yes, sir. I say it is a cow, but these gentlemen say it's a goat.

2ND ROGUE: Well, I've never heard anything like this! Are you blind? Can't you see it is a goat? And a scrawny, sickly goat at that.

PETER: But—but it is a cow! Her mother was a cow! Her grandmother was a cow! I raised her for a cow. She says she's a cow. (Cow *moos*.)

2ND ROGUE: Don't you believe her. It's all in her imagination. (ROGUES *laugh*.)

3RD ROGUE: Come along, old nanny goat. (ROGUES *exit left with* Cow, *whistling merrily.* PETER *stands staring after them.* TYLL *steps out from behind curtains and comes down to* PETER.)

TYLL: Hello, Peter. Did you get a good price for your cow?

PETER (*Blankly*): What cow?

TYLL: Why, the cow you just sold to that fellow.

PETER: That was no cow. It was a goat.

TYLL: No, Peter, *you* are the goat. Those rascals have played a trick on you.

PETER: You mean it was a cow after all? I knew it ought to be. What shall I do? I can't go home empty-handed. Mother will be so angry. That cow was all we had in the world. I'll go and tell the sheriff.

TYLL: No. I have a plan to get even with them—more than even.

PETER: Will I get my cow back?

TYLL: Indeed you will, Peter. If three rogues can whistle a cow away, Tyll Eulenspiegel can whistle it back again. (*He takes a whistle from his pocket and blows a toot on it.*) With this ordinary whistle, I'll play a trick worth three of theirs. (*Vendors and* WAITRESS *return.* TYLL *calls them together and points off left.*) Do you see those three fellows over there with a cow? Well, I'm going to make their acquaintance and pretend to buy the cow. Then I'll invite them to eat with me at the café. (TYLL *speaks to* WAITRESS.) Serve us whatever we order. And when I blow on this whistle and ask for the bill, simply say, "It's already paid." Not a word more. Do you understand?

WAITRESS: Yes, but it *won't* be already paid. I'll get into trouble and lose my job.

TYLL: Stop worrying. The bill will be paid, I promise you. Now, stand in the doorway and be ready to wait on me.

LACE MAKER: What about us?

TYLL: Well, when I buy something from any of you and start to pay for it, I'll blow my whistle and you say the same thing: "It's already paid." If you do exactly as I tell you, we will all be laughing until next Christmas. Peter, get out of sight behind those curtains. (PETER *hides behind* TYLL's *booth, and vendors go to their booths.* TYLL *crosses to left*) Remember—when I blow on my whistle, you say: "It's already paid for." (*He exits.* CHILDREN *run on from right playing tag, then run off as* TYLL *enters left with* ROGUES *and* Cow. *He ties* Cow *to his booth.*)

TYLL: There you are, Gretel. (*He turns to* ROGUES) Well, my friends, now that we've settled on a price for this cow—

3RD ROGUE (*Interrupting*): One hundred gold pieces it is, and that's a fair price for such a fine animal.

TYLL: Suppose we seal the bargain by eating a good meal together. (*He points to café table.*) Sit down and be my guests. Order anything you like.

1ST ROGUE: I'll have something of everything.

2ND ROGUE: That suits me.

3RD ROGUE: Me, too.

TYLL (*To* WAITRESS): Four orders of something of everything. (WAITRESS *exits and returns with plates of food. If desired,* VILLAGERS *and* CHILDREN *may enter and perform folk dance as* TYLL *and* ROGUES *eat. When they finish eating,* TYLL *takes whistle from his pocket and beckons to* WAITRESS.) A very tasty meal, my girl. Figure up the cost, and I will pay you. (*He blows once on whistle.*)

WAITRESS: It's already paid for. (TYLL *blows two short blasts and puts whistle away.* WAITRESS *leaves.* ROGUES *exchange amazed looks.*)

1ST ROGUE: Already paid for?

2ND ROGUE: That's what she said.

3RD ROGUE: It's mighty queer.

TYLL (*Rising*): Come, let's see what the vendors have to offer. (*He leads way to booths.*) I want to buy each one of you a gift before we part company. Look around and pick out something.

TRINKET VENDOR: Rings and stickpins! Cuff links of pearl! A gold watch chain for the gentleman!

3RD ROGUE: I'll take the watch chain. And a couple of rings, too.

1ST ROGUE: I'll take the cuff links and a stickpin.

TYLL (*To* TRINKET VENDOR): How much do I owe you? (*He blows once on his whistle.*)

TRINKET VENDOR: It's already paid for. (TYLL *blows whistle twice and joins* 2ND ROGUE *at* LACE MAKER'S *booth.* 1ST *and* 3RD ROGUES *come down center.*)

1ST ROGUE: How does he do it?

3RD ROGUE: It's that whistle.

1ST ROGUE: Do you think it's magic?

3RD ROGUE: It could be. If we had a magic whistle like that, we'd be rich.

1ST ROGUE: Shall we steal it?

3RD ROGUE: Not a chance. He's too sharp. We'll have to buy it.

1ST ROGUE: Buy it? With what?

3RD ROGUE: With this. (*He takes money bag from pocket and jingles coins. As he does so,* TYLL *blows whistle once, then twice.* 2ND ROGUE *comes to them with bundle of lace.*)

2ND ROGUE (*Pointing toward* TYLL *who is talking to* LACE MAKER): It happened again. He just blew on his whistle, and presto! "It's already paid for."

3RD ROGUE (*Taking* TYLL *aside*): That's quite a remarkable whistle you have there. I'll give you twenty-five gold pieces for it.

TYLL (*Indignantly*): What! Sell my marvelous whistle for only twenty-five gold pieces! You must be joking.

3RD ROGUE: I'll double that—fifty gold pieces.

TYLL: Preposterous! Haven't you noticed how valuable it is? It's worth much more money because it pays for everything I buy, no matter how expensive it is.

3RD ROGUE: Seventy-five. (TYLL *shakes his head.*) One hundred. And that's all I have.

TYLL (*Hesitantly*): Well—all right, but only if you include the cow.

1ST ROGUE (*Impatiently*): Oh, let him have the cow! What's one cow when we can toot together a whole herd with that whistle?

3RD ROGUE: That's true. (*He exchanges money bag for whistle.*)

TYLL: Here it is—and may it serve you as you deserve to be served. (*He nods at vendors, who smile and nod understandingly. With mock bow,* TYLL *leaves* ROGUES, *who immediately turn their attention to the whistle.* TYLL *quickly slips behind curtains into his booth. Unnoticed,* TYLL *and* PETER *peer out through curtains of booth to watch following scene.*)

3RD ROGUE: I can't wait to try it! (*He turns to* TRINKET VENDOR.) Look sharp, fellow! I'm going to buy everything you have. (*He blows long blast on whistle.*)

TRINKET VENDOR: It will cost you two hundred gold pieces.

3RD ROGUE: Two hundred gold pieces! What are you talking about? It's already paid for. (*He blows another blast.*)

TRINKET VENDOR: It's no such thing! If you want my trinkets, you'll have to pay for them.

3RD ROGUE (*Shaking his fist*): Don't you try to double-cross me! I say it's already paid for! (*He blows fiercely a third time.*)

1ST ROGUE: Oh, give me the whistle! You're not blowing it right. It's five toots, not three. (*Goes to* PIE MAN *and selects some pies*) Three apple pies and seven currant and fifteen quince—that's my favorite. (*He blows five short squeaks on whistle.*)

PIE MAN: Where's your money?

1ST ROGUE: Who needs money? It's already paid for. (*He repeats five squeaks.*)

PIE MAN: You can blow on that thing till you burst, but it won't do you any good. No money, no pies.

2ND ROGUE (*Snatching whistle*): Dunce! You're doing it all wrong! It's two long and two short—like this. (*He demonstrates.*)

1ST ROGUE (*Snatching whistle back*): Who are you calling a dunce? It's five short.

3RD ROGUE: No! Three long! (*ROGUES continue to argue, grabbing whistle and blowing it. At peak of uproar* SHERIFF *arrives.*)

SHERIFF: What's going on here? Are these rascals making trouble?

VENDORS (*Ad lib*): They're stealing my toys! My pies! My lace! Scoundrels! Thieves! (*Etc.*)

VEGETABLE WOMAN: They take things and don't pay!

2ND ROGUE: No, no, sheriff! We have a whistle that pays for everything.

SHERIFF: A *what*?

2ND ROGUE: A magic whistle. (*He shows it to* SHERIFF.)

SHERIFF (*Laughing*): That thing? Why, you can buy one of those anywhere for a penny. Now, return that bundle of lace you've taken and be quick about it. You, there! (*To* 3RD ROGUE) Empty your pocket! Hand over those rings! You rogues won't have any use for rings or lace or pies where you're going. Come along now. It's off to jail you go. (*He leads* ROGUES *off left*.)

CHILDREN (*Singing*):

Off to prison they must go, they must go, they must go!
On a whistle they will blow, toot, toot, tooting!

(TYLL *emerges from booth and steps onto platform*.)

TYLL (*Speaking from his platform*): Well, my good people, did you enjoy the show? (*Crowd shouts its approval.* TYLL *bows*.) Thank you. And now it is time to pay the actors. (*He shakes* 3RD ROGUE's *money bag and opens it.* WAITRESS *comes onto platform*.) Ten gold pieces for our leading lady and ten for the props we ate. (*He counts money into her hands*.) Ten gold pieces for each of our featured players. They didn't miss a single cue. (*Vendors line up on platform and* TYLL *pays them*.) And twenty gold pieces for Peter and his cow. Without them, there wouldn't have been any show. (*He gives coins to* PETER, *who jingles them in* Cow's *ear*. Cow *moos happily*.) That leaves ten gold pieces for Tyll Eulenspiegel and his merry pranks! (*All cheer and applaud, as curtain closes*.)

THE END

King Midas

Adapted from the Greek myth

by Mercedes Gardner and Jean Shannon Smith

Characters

KING MIDAS
PRINCESS CORA, *a young girl, his daughter*
ANTONIUS, *the King's barber*
BACCHUS, *a clever Greek god*
VOICE FROM OLYMPUS
VOICES OF THE REEDS

SETTING: *An anteroom in the palace of King Midas. There are two doorways, the one at right leading to palace, the one at left to the rose garden, which is visible from audience. A few rocks and some tall reeds are at one side of the garden.*

AT RISE: *The stage is empty. Then* KING MIDAS *is heard shouting from off right.*

MIDAS (*Offstage*): No—no—no! (*He backs in through doorway at right, as if being pestered by members of his court.*) No—no—no! (*Slams door and locks it.*) No more interruptions. I have business to attend to. Important business. (*He turns from door, and, rubbing his hands greedily, hurries to large chest and opens it. He dips his*

*hands into chest and lets coins run through his fingers.
Then he raises his head and looks up.*) Ah! Gold, beautiful gold! I ask you, Jupiter—I ask you, gods of this land
—is there anything so splendid as gold? (*He takes a
small bag of gold from inside his robe and holds it up
to admire. Then he goes to table, weighing bag in his
hand.*) Ah, more—more shining yellow beauties for my
treasure chest. How many are there? Twenty? Thirty?
We shall see. (*He starts to open bag, but is interrupted
by* PRINCESS CORA, *who enters from the garden and
stands outside the door at left. She carries a red rose.*)

CORA: Father! Father!

MIDAS (*Quickly putting bag into chest and closing lid*):
Yes? Yes, daughter?

CORA: Open the door, Father, please? (MIDAS *crosses to
open door.* CORA *steps through. He puts his arm about
her shoulder in a brief gesture of fondness.*)

MIDAS: And what does my Princess want?

CORA (*Holding out the rose*): See, Father, I have brought
you a lovely rose.

MIDAS (*Taking rose, impatient but not unkind*): Very
nice. Thank you, CORA. Now run along. I am very busy—

CORA (*Disappointed*): Oh, Father—you've forgotten! You
promised to walk with me to the Cave of the Oracle.

MIDAS: Walk? To the cave? (*Puts rose into vase on table.*)
Of course, my dear—and I shall. But, some other time.
I am very busy now. I have important business to attend
to—most urgent.

CORA (*Sighing*): Oh, it is so hard to be the daughter of a
king! I have so little to do! No one to go walking with
me. (MIDAS *pats her shoulder as he escorts her to the
door left.*)

MIDAS: There, there, Cora, we shall go to the Cave of the
Oracle another time. Run along now, dear—there's a
good girl.

CORA (*Kissing his cheek*): That's a promise? You won't
forget?

MIDAS: No, dear, I promise, I won't forget. (CORA *goes
through doorway and exits.* MIDAS *locks door, crosses to
chest and is about to open it when* ANTONIUS, *the barber,
enters right and knocks on door.*) By Jupiter—now who
is that? (*Crosses to door*) Who is it?

ANTONIUS ("*Singing*"): It is I—Antonius. (NOTE: AN-
TONIUS *may "sing" his lines throughout.*)

MIDAS (*Irked*): That barber! (*Raising voice*) Go away,
Antonius. I am busy.

ANTONIUS ("*Singing*"; *very persuasively*): Now, now, King
Midas. Busy or not, it is time for your haircut. Let me
come in.

MIDAS (*Opening door*): Oh, very well, but I am busy.
Can't you come back another time? (ANTONIUS, *who
carries a basket with his barber implements, towel and
cape, comes into room. He studies* MIDAS, *then flips a
lock of* KING's *hair.*)

ANTONIUS: Of course, of course I can come back, if you do
not care how you look!

MIDAS (*Crossly*): What do you mean? How *do* I look?

ANTONIUS (*Turning away, shuddering*): Like a—a moth-
eaten lion!

MIDAS: That bad?

ANTONIUS: May the gods strike me down if I am not telling the truth! (*Coaxingly*) Please, now, King Midas, let
me tidy you up. It will not take long. (*Takes* MIDAS'
hand and leads him to a chair)

MIDAS: A moth-eaten lion, eh? Well! Very well, Antonius,
you may cut my hair. But make it fast. I have important
business. (MIDAS *sits.* ANTONIUS *whips out a cape and
puts it over* MIDAS. *Then he takes out comb and scissors
and studies* MIDAS' *long hair.*) Well, well, barber, get on
with it.

ANTONIUS: I will—I will, Your Highness. (*Steps back; looks at* MIDAS) It was just that—

MIDAS: Just what?

ANTONIUS (*Leaning down and speaking very confidentially*): I—I have heard talk in the village—

MIDAS: Talk? What kind of talk? (*Whips off cape and stands up*) Something about me? What are my people saying?

ANTONIUS (*Gently pushing him down and putting cape back in place*): Not about you, King Midas. I should not have mentioned it.

MIDAS (*Growing angry*): You're enough to make a man lose his temper. Tell me what they are saying!

ANTONIUS: Well— (*Hesitates*) I thought perhaps you knew, but it must be just a rumor.

MIDAS (*Angrily*): Now, you have aroused my curiosity, Antonius. Tell me what you have heard—or by Jupiter, I'll have your tongue cut out!

ANTONIUS: All right, Sire, although it is just talk, they do say the god Bacchus has been seen here about.

MIDAS (*Whipping off cape again and standing up*): Bacchus! A god, the favorite of all gods! Here?

ANTONIUS (*Gently pushing him into chair again*): Please, Sire, do sit down. (*Poises scissors and comb again*)

MIDAS (*Musing aloud*): Bacchus, one of the cleverest and wisest of gods. Oh, how I should like to talk to him.

ANTONIUS (*Surprised*): You? Why? You are already clever and wise.

MIDAS (*Very pleased*): Thank you, Antonius.

ANTONIUS (*Expansively*): It is nothing but the truth, Sire. They say you are most clever in making money. They say you are most wise in ways of saving it. They say that you have cellars full of gold. (MIDAS *whips off cape and jumps to his feet. He grabs* ANTONIUS *by the collar, and shakes him.*)

MIDAS: That is a lie! Do you hear me? I do not have *cellars* full of gold! No—no—no—*no*!

ANTONIUS (*Choking, pleading*): Please—please—you are choking me!

MIDAS (*Reluctantly letting go of him*): Mind you now, do not repeat such a wild falsehood.

ANTONIUS (*Recovering*): No, no, Your Majesty. I won't.

MIDAS (*Sitting*): Of course—I do have *some* gold, that is true. But *cellars* full of gold? No! (ANTONIUS *puts cape over* MIDAS *and starts to work on hair.*)

ANTONIUS: Yes? (*Encouragingly*) Yes?

MIDAS (*Musing aloud*): *Cellars* full of *gold*! (*Rubs hands together*) Ah—that would indeed be glorious! Splendid. Someday I shall have more gold, and more—maybe enough to fill a cellar— (CORA *comes to garden door. With her is* BACCHUS, *disguised as a poor man wearing a ragged cloak.* CORA *knocks at the door.*)

CORA (*Calling*): Father, Father, please open the door.

MIDAS (*Starting to get up*): It is Cora.

ANTONIUS: Please, Sire, allow me. (*Crosses and opens door.* CORA *and* BACCHUS *come into room.*)

CORA: Oh, Father, I am so sorry to interrupt you, but I found this poor man wandering along the sea.

MIDAS (*Fondly*): Ah, dear daughter, such a tender heart. (*Then briskly*) But why have you brought him to me?

CORA: He is lost. I thought that you could help him find his way.

MIDAS: I will have one of my servants assist him.

CORA (*Coaxingly*): But first—may he have something to eat? He is hungry.

MIDAS: Take him to the kitchen and have the servants feed him.

CORA: And he is tired—so tired. Please, could he not rest here?

MIDAS: Here? Dear girl, I am busy.

CORA (*Pleading*): Please, Father, just for a moment. He is *so* weary. Let him rest here. For me?

MIDAS (*Sighing*): Very well, daughter, if that is what you want. (*To* BACCHUS) Sit down, man. (BACCHUS *nods to* MIDAS. *He crosses to a chair, then suddenly removes his ragged cloak and stands revealed in white robes as a god.*)

ANTONIUS (*Dropping his comb and scissors*): A god—he is a god. (*Falls on his knees*)

CORA (*In awe*): You are a god!

BACCHUS (*Quietly amused*): I am Bacchus.

MIDAS (*Whipping off cape and leaping to his feet*): Bacchus! (*Bows, then ingratiatingly*) Oh, wise and clever Bacchus, to whom I am most devoted. You honor us with your presence. I make you welcome. (*To* CORA) Run, child, have food and drink brought.

CORA (*Laughing excitedly and happily*): Yes, yes, Father, I will bring it myself. (*She exits.* MIDAS, *seeing that* ANTONIUS *is still on his knees on the floor, gives him a kick, hiding this action from* BACCHUS.)

MIDAS: Antonius!

ANTONIUS (*Getting to his feet at once*): Yes, King Midas?

MIDAS: Be off with you, barber!

ANTONIUS (*Scarcely able to take his eyes from* BACCHUS): But your hair—

MIDAS: Later, barber, later. (*Shoos* ANTONIUS *toward the door*)

ANTONIUS: But, but I—(*Trying to dodge around* MIDAS *to see* BACCHUS.)

MIDAS: Off with you now.

ANTONIUS (*Looking for an excuse to linger*): My scissors, my comb! (*He starts to go back for them, but* MIDAS *takes him by the arm and pushes him out.*)

MIDAS: Out! (*Shuts the door firmly on* ANTONIUS, *but does not lock it.* ANTONIUS *goes off.* MIDAS *turns to* BACCHUS,

ingratiatingly.) Are you quite comfortable, mighty Bacchus?

BACCHUS (*Quietly amused at* MIDAS): Oh, quite.

MIDAS: You are not in a draft?

BACCHUS: I am fine, thank you. It is most pleasant here.
(CORA *enters, carrying tray with cheese, grapes, plates
and knives. She sets the food on table, then crosses to
side table and brings goblets and wine bottle.*)

MIDAS: Come, Bacchus, do us the honor of supping with
us. (BACCHUS *and* MIDAS *sit down at table.* CORA *fills
goblets, as they eat and drink and continue to talk.*) I do
hope you will forgive my daughter, Bacchus. Telling
me that you had lost your way. Ha-ha! (*Laughs*)

CORA: But, Father—

MIDAS (*Patting* CORA'S *hand*): Such a wise and clever god
could not lose his way! Cora, you are a foolish girl!

BACCHUS: But it is quite true.

MIDAS (*Stunned*): True?

BACCHUS: I had indeed wandered astray.

MIDAS (*Embarrassed*): But—but you who have been a
tutor to the young gods of Olympus—how is it possible
for you to get lost?

BACCHUS: When I am deep in thought I sometimes forget
where I am. You might say, "When Bacchus is lost in
thought, he has also lost the path."

MIDAS: That is very clever.

CORA (*Concerned*): You should be more careful—you
might have fallen into the sea.

MIDAS: Yes, yes—is it truly wise to wander about?

BACCHUS (*Laughing softly*): I find, King Midas, that there
is always some mortal *eager* to help *me*.

MIDAS: Help you? To be sure, mighty Bacchus, we mortals
—I—I would do anything in the world to please you.
(*Offers* BACCHUS *food*) More cheese? More grapes? (*Picks
up wine bottle*) More wine? (BACCHUS *shakes his head*

to each offer, but MIDAS *does not notice.* MIDAS *notes that wine bottle is empty*) Cora, fetch more wine.

CORA: Yes, Father. (*She exits.*)

BACCHUS: You need not have bothered, King Midas. I must be going.

MIDAS: Please, Bacchus, I beg of you, do not hurry off.

BACCHUS: I must.

MIDAS: Wait, I shall have two of my most trusted servants escort you.

BACCHUS (*Rising from the table*): For your great kindness to me, I shall grant your fondest wish.

MIDAS (*Quivering in anticipation*): Oh, thank you, great Bacchus.

BACCHUS: What shall it be?

MIDAS: I—I—wish that—

BACCHUS (*Strolling around the room*): What could you possibly wish for, King Midas? You have a large kingdom, and you are famous for your roses. You have a magnificent home, and a sweet and loving daughter—

MIDAS (*Nodding*): I know. (*Thinking aloud*) But what is my fondest wish! Bags of gold? Chests of gold? Cellars of gold? Mountains of—

BACCHUS (*Pausing at treasure chest, rubbing hand over it*): Hm-m-m-m. Well, King Midas?

MIDAS (*Rubbing hands together greedily*): I—I wish that everything I touch would turn to gold.

BACCHUS (*Touching* MIDAS *on shoulder*): So be it, King Midas. Everything you touch shall turn to gold. (*Turns and goes toward garden door*)

MIDAS: Everything I touch! (*Spellbound and so eager for the charm to start he is hardly aware that* BACCHUS *is leaving. He looks at his hands.*) And when—when will this—this power be mine?

BACCHUS: You shall see, King Midas. You shall see. (BAC-CHUS *exits.*)

MIDAS: Thank you, thank you, mighty Bacchus. (*Discovers* BACCHUS *is gone, shrugs*) Well, that is the way of the gods, I suppose. (*Rubs hands greedily*) Oh, I wonder when my power will come upon me. (*Notices comb on floor*) What's this? The barber's comb? (*Stoops over, picks it up. He is about to put it into basket, stops, stares at it curiously.* NOTE: *There are gold-painted duplicates of comb and other props which are shown to audience when* MIDAS *has "golden touch."*) Hm-m-m, I did not know Antonius had a golden comb. (*Looks around and sees scissors*) And—his scissors. (*Picks up "golden" scissors*) Why, I do believe they are gold, too! (*He drops comb and scissors into basket and hurries to table. He picks up a knife, closes eyes tightly as he turns it over slowly.*) Can it be—is it possible that the power is on me—already? (*Opens eyes slowly. Astonished*) Gold! The knife has turned to gold. Is it true? Is it really true! (*Eagerly grabs a plate*) Gold! Gold! It *is* true! Oh, by all the gods! (*Picks up "golden" rose. In doing so, he turns gold side to audience*) And the rose, too! It has turned to gold. I shall have cellars and cellars full of gold. I shall be the wealthiest man in the whole world! (*Paces about excitedly. He pauses at table and holds up "golden" goblet.*) A toast! A toast to *me!* To King Midas! (*Puts goblet to lips, nothing comes out. He looks into goblet*) What is this? No wine? It doesn't look empty. (*Stares into goblet, then slowly tips it over. Nothing pours out*) Gold—the wine has turned into gold. (*He frantically tries a grape. There may be some gilded grapes under the others. He holds up "gold" grapes.*) Solid gold! The grape—everything has turned to solid gold. Oh, no—no—no—no! Oh, I shall starve to death! (*Slumps into chair, stunned into shock.* CORA *enters. She carries wine jug. Seeing her father alone and dejected, she puts jug on table and runs to his side.*)

CORA: Father, what is it?

MIDAS: Oh, Cora— (*Buries his face in his hands.* CORA *sits on floor at his feet, looking up at him.*)

CORA: Tell me, Father, what has happened.

MIDAS (*Puts his arm around her shoulder. As he touches her, she turns to a "solid gold statue."* NOTE: *An amber spotlight will make* CORA's *white dress look like gold, and she seems "frozen" like a statue. He reacts with horror as the truth dawns on him*): My daughter—my Princess! Oh, Cora—you *too* have turned to gold. (*Leaps to his feet*) What have I done—what have I done? (*Raises arms heavenward*) Merciful gods! Hear me! I beg you, please, free me from this terrible curse. Please —Bacchus—Jupiter—help me!

VOICE FROM OLYMPUS (*Offstage, as though thundering down from a great distance*): So—you wish to be free of your golden touch?

MIDAS: Yes, oh, yes! Please—release me!

VOICE: Are you willing to take your punishment for your greedy wish?

MIDAS: Punishment? Yes, I will accept my punishment— anything, mighty gods—*anything.*

VOICE: Anything?

MIDAS: Anything to have my daughter back!

VOICE: Go you, then, King Midas, to the River Pactolus. Plunge your head and body into the magic water and wash away your cursed touch. Bring water from the river to release your daughter.

MIDAS (*Starting at once for door to garden*): I will, oh, I will. Thank you, thank you. (MIDAS *exits through garden. As* MIDAS *exits,* ANTONIUS *appears at other door. He knocks, then tries door. It opens, and he sticks his head in. He sees* CORA, *enters hesitantly.*)

ANTONIUS: Princess, where is your father? (*He approaches her, peers at her, leans down*) Princess Cora! (*Touches*

*her lightly, then examines her more closely, touches her,
and pulls back stunned.*) Gold! She is solid gold! Oh, by
all the gods, the King's daughter has turned to gold.
(*Backs away from her. He sees the gold knife, rose, etc.,
on table; picks up rose.*) And the rose—solid gold. What
has happened in this house? (*Runs to basket and takes
out his comb and scissors*) My comb—gold! My scissors
—gold! (*Pleased, he picks up basket to leave. As he
passes* CORA, *he stops.*) By the gods, there is a curse upon
this house. (*Hurries on to the door, but stops as* MIDAS
*enters through garden. He carries a vessel of water. He
has the collar of his cape turned up to cover the donkey
ears which have appeared on his head as his punishment.
He approaches* CORA, *dips his fingers into water and
sprinkles her with it.*)

MIDAS: Oh, magic water from the River Pactolus, free my
daughter. Free the Princess from her golden prison.
(CORA *begins to move her hands, head, then stands up.*)

CORA (*Bewildered*): My, I must have fallen asleep. (MIDAS
leans against table, obviously relieved.)

MIDAS: Yes, daughter— (CORA *rubs her hand across her
forehead as if still dazed.*)

CORA: It—it seems as though I interrupted you, Father.
What was it you were doing?

MIDAS: I—that is—I—

CORA: Now I remember. Bacchus was here. And then—

MIDAS: Do not trouble yourself, child. Bacchus had to
leave and—

CORA: And—you were having your hair cut. Now, I remember—

MIDAS (*Grasping this explanation eagerly*): Yes, yes, Cora,
that is right—

CORA (*Turning to* ANTONIUS, *who is about to try to sneak
out*): Oh, Antonius, do finish Father's hair. And then,
Father, may we take our walk to the Cave of the Oracle?

MIDAS: Anything to please you my daughter. In fact, we can go right now. I do not need my hair cut today.

CORA: Oh, Father, of course you do. You look like a shaggy lion. You cannot be seen in public *that way*.

MIDAS: Very well. Run along now until I am ready, and then we will go for our walk.

CORA: Do a good job, Antonius. (*She exits.*)

ANTONIUS: Yes, Princess. (MIDAS *turns and busies himself sprinkling water on the grapes, cheese and wine.*) Come now, King Midas. It is time for your haircut. (MIDAS, *with his back to* ANTONIUS, *shakes his head*) Now, now, Sire, you heard what your daughter said. (MIDAS *sighs, turns slowly, with resignation.*)

MIDAS: I know. Like a shaggy lion. (*He sits in chair.* ANTONIUS *laughs as he places cape over* MIDAS. *He takes out his scissors, comb, brush, etc., and turns down collar on* MIDAS' *cape.*)

ANTONIUS (*Continuing to talk*): True—a shaggy moth-eaten lion. (*He suddenly sees donkey ears, stops, stunned.*) King Midas! By all the gods, you have the *ears of a donkey!* (MIDAS *slumps in his chair.*)

MIDAS (*Dejectedly*): I know, I know, Antonius, I know. This is the punishment the gods have placed upon me.

ANTONIUS: The ears of a donkey! Oh—oh—oh— (*Starts to laugh.*) The King— (MIDAS *whips off cape, jumps to his feet, and grabs* ANTONIUS *by his shirt.*)

MIDAS: You—you, barber—you will not tell a single living soul! (*Shakes* ANTONIUS) Do you hear! You will not tell anyone about my donkey ears. If you do, I will have your tongue cut out.

ANTONIUS: I will not tell a single person. I swear it!

MIDAS (*Letting go of* ANTONIUS): See that you don't! Promise!

ANTONIUS: I promise, by all the gods on Mount Olympus. I promise.

MIDAS (*Sitting*): Well. Do something, barber. Fix my hair so the ears will not show.

ANTONIUS (*Frantic for a moment*): Dress your hair so the donk— (*Claps hand over his mouth*) —will not show? Yes, Sire. (*Rummages in basket and comes up with turban. Places it on* KING's *head with a flourish.*) There! How is that? (MIDAS *reaches to head, feels that ears are concealed just as* CORA *enters.*)

CORA: Oh, you look splendid, Father. May we go now? (MIDAS *stands, takes her hand.*)

MIDAS: Yes, my dear. (*As they start toward door, he looks back at* ANTONIUS, *who is shaking with suppressed laughter.*) Remember, barber—you promised! (MIDAS *and* CORA *exit.* ANTONIUS *gathers up his comb, etc., stuffs them into basket, giggling nervously*)

ANTONIUS: I must not tell—I must not tell that the King has the ears of a donkey. The ears of a donkey. Donkey ears! (*His laughter grows: he slaps his thigh and laughs long and hard before he can control himself.*) And I must not tell. Oh, oh, I cannot keep such a secret! It will slip out—I know my wagging tongue. What shall I do? What shall I do? (*Runs about the stage, laughing and exclaiming*) Donkey ears! (*Then soberly*) I cannot tell anyone or he will cut out my tongue. Oh, I have to tell it—I must— (*Runs to garden, stares down at the rocks and reeds*) I know, I shall dig a hole and tell my secret to the earth. It will be safe there. (*Removes a couple of rocks, leans over and sings his secret into hole*) The King has donkey ears! (*Quickly places rocks back over hole, then stands up and sighs with relief*) Now the King's secret is safe forever. (*Takes up basket and exits.*)

VOICES OF THE REEDS (*From offstage, softly, then growing louder until they can be clearly understood.*): The King has donkey ears. The King has donkey ears. The King has donkey ears. (*This continues as* BACCHUS *enters garden and pauses, listening. Then he crosses to reeds and bends his head toward them, listening.*)

BACCHUS: What is this? The reeds are singing? (*He listens again.*) So—the King has donkey ears. The secret is out! A man, greedy and foolish as King Midas, cannot long keep it a secret. (*Begins to laugh softly, then louder as he exits.*)

VOICES OF THE REEDS (*As curtains start to close*): The King has donkey ears . . . (*Curtain*)

THE END

One Wish Too Many

A tale of old Holland

by Jean Feather

Characters

PETER HOOTSON
GRETCHEN, *his wife*
OLD MAN

MRS. VAN HOEK
WILHELMINA, *her daughter*

SCENE 1

TIME: *Long ago.*

SETTING: *Cutaway of sitting rooms of two adjoining houses —Hootson house, left, and Van Hoek house, right. Street runs in front of houses. Exits from each sitting room lead to other rooms of houses.*

AT RISE: *No one is in* VAN HOEK *home.* PETER *is seated at table in the* HOOTSON *home.* GRETCHEN *enters the room.*

GRETCHEN: Dinner's ready, husband.

PETER (*Standing up*): Good! It smells wonderful.

GRETCHEN: It's your favorite stew.

PETER: With lots of onions? (GRETCHEN *nods.*) And carrots? (*She nods again.*) And big, juicy chunks of meat? (*As she nods*) Good. I'll have three helpings. (OLD MAN

191

enters downstage and walks along street in front of houses.)

GRETCHEN: You have three helpings of whatever I cook. (OLD MAN *knocks on door of* HOOTSONS' *house.*) Now, who can that be?

PETER (*As* GRETCHEN *goes to door*): Not someone come to dinner, I hope. (GRETCHEN *pantomimes opening door to* OLD MAN.)

OLD MAN: Good wife, I've traveled a long way today, and I'm hungry. I wonder if you could spare a little food?

GRETCHEN: Ah, no doubt you smelled our stew. A pity, but we have only enough for ourselves.

OLD MAN: Perhaps a little bit of bread? I could eat it out here. . . .

PETER (*Crossing to* GRETCHEN's *side; roughly*): We don't share our food with beggars. Begone!

GRETCHEN: If you want to eat, go work for your food. Leave us alone. (*She closes door, and they exit left, as* OLD MAN *makes his way along street, muttering.*)

OLD MAN: Surely someone has a little food to share. (*He knocks at* VAN HOEKS' *door.* MRS. VAN HOEK *enters right and answers door.*)

MRS. VAN HOEK: Good evening.

OLD MAN: Good evening. I come this way but once a year, and so I'm a stranger to your village, good wife. I've traveled a long way today.

MRS. VAN HOEK: Oh, do come in. You look so tired and cold.

OLD MAN: Thank you. (*He enters.*)

MRS. VAN HOEK (*Indicating chair*): Please sit here. (*He sits, wearily sighing.*) Are you hungry? Have you eaten?

OLD MAN: Not since yesterday, good wife.

MRS. VAN HOEK: Why, you have come at a good time! We have just made a kettle of soup. (*Calling*) Wilhelmina! (*To* OLD MAN) That's my young daughter. (WILHELMINA *enters and curtsies to* OLD MAN.) Wilhelmina, set another place at the table. We'll share our soup with this traveler.

WILHELMINA: But, Mother . . . there's scarcely enough for two.

MRS. VAN HOEK: I know, dear, but you can add a little more water. (WILHELMINA *exits right.*)

OLD MAN: Have times been hard in the village this winter?

MRS. VAN HOEK: The crops were not good. But we manage. I weave very good cloth, and my daughter takes a piece to market to sell every week. That buys thread for next week's weaving, and enough food for both of us.

OLD MAN: Perhaps I'd better move on. You can scarcely afford to share with a stranger.

MRS. VAN HOEK: Nonsense. There's always enough to share, if we want to.

OLD MAN: You're very kind. I'm sorry I can't pay you for my supper in guilders, but I can grant you a wish.

MRS. VAN HOEK (*Cheerfully*): Now what could I wish for? I have a fine daughter, and together we earn enough. We don't need anything else.

OLD MAN: I can see I'd better wish for you.

MRS. VAN HOEK (*Chuckling*): Yes, you do that.

OLD MAN: I wish that the first thing you do tomorrow will last all day.

WILHELMINA (*Entering*): Supper's ready, Mother.

MRS. VAN HOEK: Did you hear that, Wilhelmina? I'm to have a wish. Whatever I do first tomorrow will last all day.

WILHELMINA: It had better be something good, then.

OLD MAN: I think it will be.

MRS. VAN HOEK: I hope so. Anyway, let's have supper now. (*They exit right. Curtain.*)

*　　*　　*

SCENE 2

TIME: *The next morning.*

SETTING: *The same as Scene 1.*

AT RISE: HOOTSON *house is empty.* WILHELMINA *and* MRS. VAN HOEK *enter their sitting room, right.*

MRS. VAN HOEK: My goodness, we did oversleep. You'd better go straight to market as soon as I measure the cloth. I'll get it off the loom. (*She exits right.*)

WILHELMINA: Yes. Someone is sure to ask the measure of the cloth.

MRS. VAN HOEK (*Re-entering*): Here we are. (*Stretches out right arm and measures lengths of cloth*) Exactly three meters. You should get a good price, Wilhelmina.

WILHELMINA: I hope so, Mother. I'll get my shawl. (*She exits.* MRS. VAN HOEK *folds cloth; in a moment* WIL-HELMINA *re-enters, carrying another piece of cloth.*) Mother, I found this on the loom. Where did it come from?

MRS. VAN HOEK (*Putting down first piece of cloth and taking second*): Why, I don't know. I've never seen it before.

WILHELMINA: It's nearly the same length as the cloth you wove.

MRS. VAN HOEK: Let me see. (*Measures it*) That's right, three meters. (*She and* WILHELMINA *look at each other.*) Come, show me just where you found it.

WILHELMINA (*As they exit*): It was right there on the loom. . . . (*They re-enter at once, carrying a third piece of cloth.*)

MRS. VAN HOEK: I don't believe it. I just don't believe it. Where could the cloth be coming from?

WILHELMINA: Mother, it must be your wish.

MRS. VAN HOEK: But, Wilhelmina, that poor old man who was here yesterday? How could he grant a wish?

WILHELMINA: Measure this piece of cloth, Mother.

MRS. VAN HOEK (*Slowly*): I suppose I should. (*They measure the third piece*) Exactly three meters. (WILHELMINA *exits quickly.*) I don't understand this. There's the piece of cloth I finished weaving last night, but. . . . (*Looking at second and third pieces*)

WILHELMINA (*Re-entering with a fourth piece of cloth*): Look, Mother. You see what's happening. As soon as you measure one piece of cloth, another appears on the loom. Come, measure this one. (*They do.*) Exactly the same. Here, give me all four. I'll take them to the market. And you go on measuring, Mother. Measure cloth all day. (WILHELMINA *dashes into the street, as* MRS. VAN HOEK *exits right.* GRETCHEN *enters left and looks into street. She calls to* WILHELMINA *as she passes.*)

GRETCHEN: Good day, Wilhelmina. Did your Mother weave all that cloth?

WILHELMINA: No. I mean yes. Oh, I'm in such a hurry, Mrs. Hootson. Excuse me. (*She runs offstage.* GRETCHEN *looks after her, puzzled, as in the next house* MRS. VAN HOEK *carries in a piece of cloth, measures it, exits and re-enters with another piece of cloth which she begins to measure as curtains close.*)

* * *

SCENE 3

TIME: *One year later.*

SETTING: *Same as Scene 1.*

AT RISE: VAN HOEK *house is empty.* PETER *stands in sitting room, left, looking into street.* GRETCHEN *enters left.*

GRETCHEN: No sign of the old man yet?

PETER: No. Gretchen, this is a foolish waste of time. I've been standing here since three o'clock.

GRETCHEN: And what have I been doing? Slaving in the kitchen, cooking the grandest meal that old man will ever have.

PETER: But, Gretchen—

GRETCHEN: You keep watching. I don't want him to go to Van Hoeks' again. They got plenty out of him last year. Why, in one day Wilhelmina sold enough beautiful cloth to keep them for years.

PETER: But, Gretchen, how do you know he's coming back today?

GRETCHEN: He told the Van Hoeks that he comes to our town once a year. And this is the day. This time, I'll have my wish.

PETER: Gretchen, it's past our suppertime. I'm starving.

GRETCHEN: You watch. (*She starts to exit.*)

PETER (*Looking out window as* OLD MAN *enters*): Gretchen, someone's coming.

GRETCHEN: Where? (*Running to window*): It's the same old man, I'm sure. I knew he'd come. (*She goes into street to meet* OLD MAN) Good evening, sir. How nice to see you again.

OLD MAN: Good evening.

GRETCHEN: Would you like to come into our house and rest a while, and share our simple supper?

OLD MAN: Thank you. (*They go inside.*) You're very kind.

GRETCHEN: This is my husband, Peter Hootson. (*Men bow to each other.*) Won't you come into the kitchen? We'll eat right away. (*They exit left. Lights dim to denote the passing of several hours.*)

OLD MAN (*Entering with* GRETCHEN *and* PETER *as lights go up*): Thank you for a most delicious dinner. Now I

must be on my way. But, before I go, I must show my
gratitude by letting you have a wish.

GRETCHEN (*Quickly*): I wish that whatever I do first tomorrow I'll keep on doing all day.

OLD MAN: Granted. And may you have the fortune you
deserve. Good night to both of you. (*He enters street and
walks offstage, right.*)

GRETCHEN: Peter, Peter, we'll be rich! The richest people
in the world.

PETER: How? What will you wish for?

GRETCHEN: Can't you guess what I'm going to do tomorrow? I'm going to count gold pieces.

PETER: What?

GRETCHEN: Gold pieces! How much gold do you think
we'll have if I go on counting it all day?

PETER: Gretchen, my dear, you are a clever woman! What
a job! Counting gold pieces all day! It will be a joy to
watch. But what are you going to put them in, my dear?

GRETCHEN: Oh, my goodness, I never thought of that.

PETER: We have one chest, but that won't hold nearly
enough. And where will we store it?

GRETCHEN: Oh, dear!

PETER: You know, we ought to have a lot of small bags
ready. Then, as fast as you count the gold, I can fill the
bags and carry them up to the attic.

GRETCHEN: Yes, they'd be safe up there. I know what I'll
do. I'll stay up all night making bags. I'll get my scissors
and some old cloth. You fold up this tablecloth. I'll work
here. (*She dashes off quickly as* PETER *folds up table-
cloth. She returns with scissors and a small piece of
cloth.*) I'll cut out a couple of little bags and sew them
up. See what you think of the size. (*Clock strikes twelve
as she is cutting.* PETER *watches.*) There now, I'll sew
this one up. (*She goes on cutting the material into small
scraps.*) Peter . . . Peter!

PETER: My dear, you're cutting that too small. You're chopping it into tiny pieces.

GRETCHEN (*Frightened*): Peter, I can't stop cutting.

PETER: Nonsense. Of course you can stop.

GRETCHEN: I can't. It's my wish, don't you see?

PETER: But it's not morning yet.

GRETCHEN (*Still cutting*): I know. But it is tomorrow already—it's after midnight, isn't it? This must be the tomorrow I wished for.

PETER: But you intended to be counting gold.

GRETCHEN: Yes. But I'm not. I'm cutting cloth. (*She continues to cut, without a pause. She starts on the table-cloth.*)

PETER: Gretchen, stop. You're cutting up our good table-cloth.

GRETCHEN: I can't stop. (*She cuts tablecloth into strips.*)

PETER: Yes, you can. Here, give it to me. (*He grabs table-cloth from her. She starts cutting his tie.*) Stop! You're cutting up my clothes. Stop! (*He runs into the street carrying the tablecloth as she begins to cut the curtains.*) Gretchen, you'll ruin us! (*He runs down street and pounds on* VAN HOEKS' *door, then runs back to look at* GRETCHEN.) Gretchen, stop cutting things. Go to bed! Gretchen! (MRS. VAN HOEK *enters right and answers door.* WILHELMINA *follows her.*)

MRS. VAN HOEK: Who is it? Why, Mr. Hootson, what's the matter?

PETER: Oh, Mrs. Van Hoek, it's my wife. She's cutting up the curtains! (*In Hootson house,* GRETCHEN *begins cutting rug.*)

MRS. VAN HOEK: Cutting up the curtains!

PETER: She's cutting up everything. Even my tie! (*Waves tie*) She won't stop!

MRS. VAN HOEK: But, why?

PETER: It's the wish. That terrible old man granted her wish.

WILHELMINA: But surely she didn't wish to be cutting up cloth.

PETER: No. She planned to be counting gold pieces all day. Oh, it's my fault, too! When I pictured her counting gold, did I say, "We'll ask everyone in our village to come and get a basketful of gold pieces?" Did I? No. I said, "Make a lot of bags so I can put the gold in them and store it in the attic." Then the clock struck twelve. Tomorrow came and she was still cutting cloth for bags of coins!

MRS. VAN HOEK: Oh, dear!

PETER: Will she stop, Mrs. Van Hoek?

MRS. VAN HOEK: Not till midnight, I'm afraid.

PETER: But she'll get tired, won't she?

MRS. VAN HOEK: I didn't. I measured cloth all day. We had hundreds of pieces.

WILHELMINA: We've sold some every week and we still have lots in the storeroom.

PETER: But all we have are strips of tablecloths and curtains. If only Gretchen and I hadn't been so greedy! (*As curtains close,* GRETCHEN *continues to cut up rug.*)

THE END

A Gift for Hans Brinker

A tale of Holland

Adapted by *Adele Thane*

from Mary Mapes Dodge's *Hans Brinker,
or The Silver Skates*

Characters

HANS BRINKER
GRETEL, *his sister*
HILDA VAN GLECK
PETER VAN HOLP
LUDWIG VAN HOLP
ANNIE BOUMAN
RYCHIE KORBES
CARL SCHUMMEL
VOOSTENWALBERT SCHIMMELPENNINCK
KATRINKA FLACK
JACOB POOT
BEN DOBBS
DAME BRINKER
MADAME VAN GLECK, *Hilda's mother*
RACE OFFICIAL

SCENE 1

TIME: *A winter morning, long ago.*
SETTING: *The bank of a canal near Amsterdam. The bank*

*is separated from the canal by a stone wall, which runs
across back of stage.*

AT RISE: HANS *and* GRETEL *are seated near entrance to
canal at left, tying on wooden skates.* HANS *finishes and
stands up.*

HANS: Hurry up, Gretel! It's so cold when we're not skating.

GRETEL: I'm hurrying as fast as I can.

HANS: Here, I'll do it. (*He kneels beside her and tugs at
skate laces.*)

GRETEL (*Crying out in pain*): Ouch! Don't pull so hard,
Hans! The leather lace is cutting into my foot.

HANS: I'll tie it higher up.

GRETEL: You can't. The laces are not long enough.

HANS: Then you'll just have to grin and bear it—or not
skate at all.

GRETEL: Oh, Hans! Not skate?

HANS (*Getting an idea*): I'll fix it! (*He takes off his cap and
removes inner lining which he folds into a pad across*
GRETEL'S *instep.*) Now—can you stand some pulling?

GRETEL: Pull away! (*She presses her lips together tightly,
and* HANS *yanks lace over pad and ties it.*) There! I'll
race you to the bridge! Catch me if you can! (*They run
on their skates to canal entrance and off. A moment later
they appear behind wall, "skating" across from left to
right and off.* NOTE: *The motion of skating can be easily
imitated, since only the upper half of the body is seen
over top of wall. Voices are heard off right and* HILDA
VAN GLECK, PETER *and* LUDWIG VAN HOLP, ANNIE BOU-
MAN, RYCHIE KORBES, CARL SCHUMMEL, *and* VOOSTEN-
WALBERT SCHIMMELPENNINCK *enter, carrying skates and
chattering excitedly.*)

ALL (*Ad lib*): Such news! What a prize! Silver skates!

Think of it! Isn't it splendid? I hope I win! So do I! (*Etc.*)

ANNIE (*Waving in direction of canal*): There's Katrinka! Yoo-hoo, Katrinka! Come here! (KATRINKA FLACK *enters, carrying skates. The others crowd about her.*)

CARL: Have you heard?

LUDWIG: You must enter!

ANNIE: We are!

RYCHIE: You're one of our best skaters!

KATRINKA (*Laughing*): Don't all talk at once! I can't understand. Hilda, you tell me.

HILDA: There's going to be a grand skating match on my mother's birthday, and she will give prizes to the best skaters.

RYCHIE: A pair of silver skates!

ANNIE: With bells on them!

HILDA: The girls' pair is to have bells, and there is another pair for the boys with an arrow engraved on the sides. (HANS and GRETEL *skate into view behind wall.*)

CARL (*Looking over wall*): There's a pretty pair of ragamuffins! (RYCHIE *goes to wall and looks over.*)

RYCHIE (*With a sneer*): They're wearing wooden skates. Maybe they were a present from the king.

KATRINKA: Who ever heard of wooden skates! (PETER *looks over wall.*)

PETER (*Watching* GRETEL *skate*): That girl skates well! It will be a joke on us if she is in the race and wins.

RYCHIE: If she's in the race, I won't enter.

KATRINKA: Neither will I.

CARL: Don't worry, girls. Those young beggars don't stand a chance of winning with wooden skates.

PETER: No one should object to good skaters in a race just because they are poor.

LUDWIG (*Looking off right*): Why, here comes Jacob Poot! And there's someone with him—a stranger.

Voost: That's Jacob's English cousin. He has such a funny name—Ben Dobbs. He's here on a visit.

Jacob (*Entering from right with* Ben): Hello, everybody! This is my cousin, Benjamin Dobbs, from England.

Ludwig: Do they skate in England?

Ben: Yes—I mean, ja!

Jacob: He doesn't speak Dutch very well, but he wants to learn. And he wants to see some of our big cities, like Amsterdam.

Ben: Ja, ja!

Jacob: He skates better than he talks. (Ben *nods*.) We're on our way to Amsterdam now. Will any of you come with us?

All: I will! I will!

Jacob: We'll be there in half an hour. Come along! (*They go out left*.)

Peter (*To* Hilda, *who holds back*): Aren't you coming, Hilda?

Hilda: Go ahead, Peter. I'll catch up with you.

Peter: What's the matter?

Hilda (*Pointing off left*): I want to speak to the little girl and her brother. (Gretel *enters from left with* Hans. *They sit to remove their skates*.)

Peter: Ah, ha! I know what you're up to, and I'm going to help you. (*The others skate into view behind wall and then off.* Hilda *and* Peter *turn to watch them*.)

Gretel (*Laughing as she unties her skates*): Oh, Hans, you looked so funny when you fell down!

Hans: Well, you skated right into me.

Gretel: I couldn't stop. I tried to.

Hans (*Removing his skates*): These wretched wooden things! As soon as they become damp, they stick and trip us.

Hilda (*Approaching* Gretel): What is your name, little girl?

GRETEL: Gretel—and this is my brother Hans.

HILDA: I'm glad to see you, Hans. I am Hilda van Gleck, and this is my friend, Peter van Holp. (*Boys shake hands.*) You look cold, Gretel. You should dress more warmly.

GRETEL (*Embarrassed*): I have nothing else to wear.

HANS (*Gruffly*): My sister has not complained of the cold.

GRETEL: It is nothing. I am warm enough—too warm when I am skating.

PETER: You skate very well—and so does Hans. I hope you will both enter the race.

HANS: What race?

PETER: In honor of Madame van Gleck's birthday. The prize is silver skates.

GRETEL: Silver skates! Oh, Hans!

HILDA: Anyone can enter.

HANS (*Shaking his head*): No. Even if we did enter, we could skate only a few yards. (*Holding up his skates*) Our skates are made of wood, you see. We can't afford real ones.

GRETEL: But I love them. Hans carved them, and he carves beautifully. He made this chain, too. (*She shows* HILDA *the chain around her neck.*)

HILDA (*Looking at it*): Which of you is the better skater?

GRETEL: Hans!

HANS: Gretel!

HILDA (*Smiling*): I can't buy each of you a pair of skates, but here are eight silver pieces. Decide between you which has the better chance of winning the race, and buy the skates accordingly.

HANS: We can't take your money—thank you just the same.

HILDA: Why not?

HANS: Because we haven't earned it.

HILDA (*Putting money into his hand*): Then carve me a chain like Gretel's.

HANS: Oh, I will, gladly. But not for money. (*He tries to return money to* HILDA.)

HILDA: No, no, keep it. That is a poor price for such a pretty chain.

HANS: You shall have it tomorrow.

PETER: I wonder, Hans, if you would carve one for my little sister? It would make such a nice present. Here are eight silver pieces.

HANS: I'd be glad to.

GRETEL: Oh, Hans, it will buy another pair of skates!

HANS: Thank you, Master Peter.

HILDA: We'll expect to see you both in the grand race. Come, Peter! (*She exits followed by* PETER.)

GRETEL: Hans, do you remember when the stork settled on our roof last summer? Mother said it would bring us luck. And it has! To think that we shall have *real* skates at last!

HANS: You shall have them, Gretel. I will go without. (PETER *and* HILDA *skate into view behind wall.*)

GRETEL: Hans, go without skates? Why? You have the money to buy them.

HANS: I will spend it for other things. You need a warm jacket.

GRETEL: No, I don't. I'm not cold. Please buy the skates.

HANS (*Resolutely*): No, Gretel, I can wait. Some day I'll have enough money to buy a fine pair.

GRETEL: I know what you can do! You can get a pair a little too big for me and a little too small for you, and we can take turns using them.

HANS: Nonsense, Gretel! You could never skate with a big pair. No, you must have a pair to fit exactly, and you must practice every chance you have until the race. You shall win those silver skates!

GRETEL (*Hugging him*): Hans, you're the best brother in the world!

DAME BRINKER (*Calling from off right*): Hans! Gretel!

HANS: Here we are, Mother! (DAME BRINKER *enters, carrying a parcel.* GRETEL *runs to her.*)

GRETEL: Oh, Mother, the most wonderful thing has happened! Hans has enough money to buy new skates for both of us. Sixteen silver pieces!

DAME BRINKER: Where in the world did you get all that money, Hans?

GRETEL (*Before* HANS *can answer*): Miss Hilda and Master Peter gave it to him. They said we were to skate in the grand race.

DAME BRINKER: *Gave* you the money?

HANS: No, Mother. I am to carve a chain for Miss Hilda and another one for Master Peter's sister.

GRETEL: But Hans says he won't buy any skates for himself.

DAME BRINKER (*Puzzled*): Don't you want new skates, Hans?

HANS: Oh, yes, I do, Mother—very much. But you need so many things.

DAME BRINKER: Nonsense! The money was given to you to buy skates and that's what you will use it for.

HANS: But your spinning wheel needs a new treadle.

DAME BRINKER: You can make it.

HANS: And you need wool, and meal, and . . .

DAME BRINKER: There, there, that will do! Your silver can't buy everything. Now, go to Amsterdam and get the skates. (*He sits and starts to tie on his wooden skates.*) Here, Gretel, take this penny, and while Hans is trading for the skates, you can buy a waffle in the marketplace.

GRETEL: Let me stay with you, Mother. Hans will buy me the cake.

DAME BRINKER: As you will, child. Hans, take these stockings to the hosier and sell them. (*She hands him the parcel*). He will give you four pennies and then you can buy four waffles.

GRETEL: Oh, my! Don't break the waffles, Hans. Button them under your jacket carefully.

HANS: Don't worry, I'll be careful.

GRETEL: Hurry back! We'll race on the canal tonight, if Mother lets us.

DAME BRINKER: Of course.

HANS: I'll be back before you know it! Goodbye! (*He exits left and skates into view behind wall, then off.* GRETEL *and* DAME BRINKER *wave, as curtain falls.*)

*   *   *

SCENE 2

TIME: *The day of the race.*

SETTING: *The same as Scene 1. A small table has been set up center in front of the wall.*

AT RISE: VOOST *runs on from right, carrying his skates and waving a small Dutch flag.*

VOOST (*Calling back over his shoulder*): Hurry up, everybody! It's almost time for the race! (JACOB, BEN, RYCHIE, HILDA, PETER, KATRINKA, LUDWIG, CARL *and* ANNIE *enter carrying skates and flags. They stick their flags into holders attached to wall at regular intervals.*)

KATRINKA: Hilda!

HILDA: Yes?

KATRINKA: Are the Brinkers going to race today?

HILDA: Indeed they are!

CARL: What! On wooden skates?

HILDA (*Exchanging a smile with* PETER): They have real skates now. They have been practicing on them every day.

CARL: Where did *they* get real skates?

RYCHIE: Hilda and Peter gave them the money.

CARL: Hilda! Peter! Are you crazy? What if they should win?

PETER: We didn't *give* them the money. Hans *earned* it. He made a chain for Hilda and one for me to give my little sister, and we paid him for them. Besides, they deserve to win. They are the best skaters on the canal.

ANNIE (*Looking off right*): Here they come, with their mother.

JACOB: And Madame van Gleck is right behind them.

LUDWIG: Who is that man with your mother, Hilda?

HILDA: He is the official who will start the race. (DAME BRINKER *enters, followed by* HANS *and* GRETEL, *proudly carrying their skates.* HILDA *and* PETER *greet them, then turn to welcome* MADAME VAN GLECK. *The* OFFICIAL *places two cases with silver skates on table. He then crosses and stands beside entrance to canal.*)

MADAME VAN GLECK: Good afternoon, my young friends. I know you are all eager for the race to begin, so I won't make any long speeches. Here are the rules. The girls and boys are to race until one girl and one boy win. You will start from that point (*Pointing off left*), and skate to the third flagstaff beyond the bridge (*Pointing up right*), circle it, and then come back to the starting point. The girls will race first. (*Girls exit left, and boys line up along wall to watch race.* MADAME VAN GLECK *gives a signal and* OFFICIAL *blows a whistle.*)

BOYS: They're off! (*Girls skate past behind wall and out of sight right. Boys shout encouragement to their favorite. The cheering continues in background.*)

HANS: Who's ahead?

PETER: Three are in the lead.

DAME BRINKER: Gretel?

HANS: Yes, you can see her red skirt.

JACOB: Now it's the girl in white!

PETER: Hilda!

LUDWIG: The one in blue is gaining.

PETER: That's Annie!

CARL: Come on, Katrinka!

HANS: Come on, Gretel! Gretel!

PETER: She's gaining, she's gaining!

CARL: She's passing Annie!

VOOST: And Hilda! (GRETEL *skates into sight behind wall ahead of others.*)

ALL: Hurray! Gretel!

HANS: Gretel has won!

OFFICIAL: The winner of the girls' silver skates—Gretel Brinker! (*General applause.*) Now, the boys will race. (*Girls enter from left, passing boys on their way to the race.* GRETEL *runs to her mother and hugs her.* MADAME VAN GLECK *raises her hand to give signal for boys to start when* PETER *re-enters, wearing his skates, and sits on a bench.*)

GRETEL: What's the matter with Peter? Something has happened. (PETER *bends over, working at one of his skates.* HANS *hurries in, also wearing his skates.*)

HANS: What is it, Peter?

PETER: My skate strap is broken.

HANS: Here, take mine.

PETER: Don't be silly! Get back in the race.

HANS: No. (*He pulls strap from his skate.*)

PETER: I won't take it.

HANS: You must. (*He puts strap in* PETER'S *skate.* PETER *protests, but* HANS *pushes him off left just as* OFFICIAL *blows his whistle.* HANS, *his skates in hand, joins girls at wall. The boys skate into view behind wall.*)

HANS: Go on, Peter!

ANNIE: Come on, Voost!

KATRINKA: Faster, Carl!

RYCHIE: Ben! Ben Dobbs!

HANS: It's Peter! He's going to win!

KATRINKA: No, it's Carl!

GRETEL: They're right together!

DAME BRINKER: Who?

GRETEL: Peter and Carl. (*They speed by, side by side, leading others.*)

ANNIE: It's over.

DAME BRINKER: Who won?

HANS: It has to be Peter.

HILDA: They were right together. It must be a tie. (MADAME VAN GLECK *holds up her hands for silence as boys enter and wait for the announcement of the winner.*)

OFFICIAL: The winner of the boys' silver skates is Peter van Holp!

GRETEL, ANNIE, HILDA *and* HANS (*Together*): Hurray, Peter! (MADAME VAN GLECK *takes silver skates from table.*)

MADAME VAN GLECK: Gretel Brinker! (GRETEL *steps to table.*) Peter van Holp! (PETER *steps to table.*) It is a pleasure to award these silver skates—to the fleetest!

PETER (*Turning to* HANS): I couldn't have won these without your help, Hans Brinker. Thank you for lending me this strap. (*He returns it to* HANS.) It was the kindest thing anyone ever did for me. I will never forget it.

HANS: It was nothing.

PETER (*Holds out the silver skates*): I want you to have them, Hans.

HANS: You won them, Peter.

PETER: Because of you.

HANS: No—because of a penny skate strap.

DAME BRINKER (*Putting her arm around* HANS): I am proud of you, my boy. You have won a great deal more than a pair of silver skates.

PETER: Three cheers for Hans Brinker, the noblest fellow in Holland! (*He takes a flag from wall and others do same.*) Hip, hip—
ALL: Hurray! (*They cheer three times, waving their flags, then shout—*) Hans Brinker! (*Curtain*)

THE END

The Tiger, the Brahman, and the Jackal

A folk tale of India

by Gladys V. Smith

Characters

Two Children	Water Buffalo
Narrator	Tiger
Tree	Brahman
Road	Jackal

BEFORE RISE: NARRATOR *enters in front of curtain and sits down left.* Two CHILDREN *enter and stand at right.* TREE *enters left and crosses stage with wavy motion.*

1st CHILD (*Pointing at* TREE): Look at that! Can that be a tree?

2ND CHILD: It doesn't look like a tree.

NARRATOR: Of course it's a tree, a pipal tree. If you had lived in India, as I have, you would know a pipal tree when you see one. (TREE *exits right.*)

2ND CHILD: Then it will be in the play. (ROAD *enters and walks across stage.*)

1ST CHILD: What's that? Is it a road?

2ND CHILD: It doesn't look like a road.

NARRATOR: Of course it's a road, a country road. If you had been in India, as I have, you would know a country road when you see one.

1ST CHILD: And it will be in the play. (*As* ROAD *exits left,* WATER BUFFALO *enters right and crosses stage.*)

2ND CHILD: What a funny cow!

1ST CHILD: Look at its horns!

NARRATOR: Silly children! That is no cow. It is a buffalo, a water buffalo. (WATER BUFFALO *exits.*) If you had been in India, as I have . . .

2ND CHILD: You would know a water buffalo when you see one! And it will be in the play.

1ST CHILD (*As* BRAHMAN *enters and crosses stage from left to right*): But this time I know. This is the Brahman, the poor old Brahman. He is not very wise, and he is always in need. (BRAHMAN *exits.*)

2ND CHILD (*As* JACKAL *enters right, crosses stage*): And there goes the jackal, the clever young jackal. You will soon find out how clever *he* is! (JACKAL *exits left.* CHILDREN *join* NARRATOR *down left to watch play as the curtain rises.*)

*   *   *

SETTING: *The stage is bare, except for cage left center, with* TIGER *in it.*

AT RISE: TREE *and* WATER BUFFALO *stand near* ROAD, *at right.* TIGER *roars loudly.*

NARRATOR: A Bengal tiger, the fiercest of beasts! And he is caught in a cage. There is trouble brewing. (BRAHMAN *enters and walks near cage and stands.*)

TIGER: Oh, Brahman! Sweet Brahman!

BRAHMAN: Yes, tiger!

TIGER: Good Brahman! Wise Brahman!

BRAHMAN: Do not flatter me, tiger.

TIGER: Dear, good, sweet, wise Brahman. Please let me out of this cage.

BRAHMAN: I don't trust you, tiger. Your teeth are too long and sharp.

TIGER: Kind Brahman! Please let me out! It is so lonely here.

BRAHMAN: There is an evil gleam in your eye.

TIGER: How can you say such things, dear Brahman? Let me out, and I will do your work forever.

BRAHMAN: I wish I could believe you. But, no. Your claws are too long.

TIGER: Just think. You would never need to work again! Only open the door. I will be your slave.

BRAHMAN: Do you really mean that? If I really had someone to cook my rice and wash my linen, how happy I would be! Remember your promise.

TIGER: Sweet Brahman! (BRAHMAN *opens cage door.* TIGER *pounces at him.*) Foolish one! Stupid one! You should have more sense. What a good dinner you will make. But you are a bit thin.

BRAHMAN: Oh, please, Sir Tiger, remember your promise.

TIGER: Pooh! What is a promise to a tiger? (*As he paces around* BRAHMAN) I hope you are more tender than you look.

BRAHMAN: Do not eat me, I beg of you. Give me another chance. I saved your life. Now spare mine.

TIGER: Very well. I will prove to you how foolish you are. Ask the first three things you meet if I have been unfair. If even one thing agrees with you that I have been unfair, I will let you go. But don't say I didn't warn you. Be off, stupid one. You will soon be back—for my dinner. (TIGER *sits upstage.*)

BRAHMAN (*Walking toward* TREE): Surely the whole world must know how cruel the tiger has been to me. I am sure this pipal tree will help me. O tree, beautiful tree. Hear my story.

TREE: I am listening.

BRAHMAN: An angry tiger was in a cage. He promised to serve me if I would let him out, but when I freed him, he sprang on me and said he would eat me. I ask you, did he treat me fairly?

TREE: All day long men come to me for shelter from wind and rain. I give them shade from the sun's hot rays. Do men give me even a cup of water in return? Not they. The tiger has treated you as fairly as men treat me.

BRAHMAN: Alas!

TREE: Do not expect me to feel sorry for you. Good day!

BRAHMAN: What misfortune! But I have two more chances. Surely this water buffalo will help me. (*Goes over to* WATER BUFFALO) Water buffalo, please listen to my story.

WATER BUFFALO: I am listening.

BRAHMAN: When an angry tiger promised to be my slave, I let him out of his cage. Then he said he would eat me. Tell me. Was that fair?

WATER BUFFALO: Foolish man! When I was young and strong I was well fed. Now that I am old, people expect me to work for nothing. No. I do not pity you. Good day.

BRAHMAN: Ah, me. What shall I do? Is there no end to my trouble? There's the road. I shall ask the road. It is my last chance. (*Walks over to* ROAD) Mr. Road, hear my story. A Bengal tiger was in a cage. He promised to be my slave forever, if I let him out. So I freed him, but he pounced on me and started to eat me. Was that fair?

ROAD: Fair? It is the way men treat me. See how they trample over me. They do not even keep me clean.

BRAHMAN: Ah, me!

ROAD: No one offers to help me. Why should the tiger help you? Good afternoon.

BRAHMAN: There is no hope for me. I may as well go back to the tiger. (*As he turns to leave,* JACKAL *enters.*)

JACKAL: Friend Brahman, why are you so sad?

BRAHMAN: Ah, jackal, you will never see me again. I am about to be eaten by a tiger.

JACKAL: A tiger?

BRAHMAN: A Bengal tiger. You see, the tiger was in a cage. I came walking by.

JACKAL: Dear me! What a story! Please explain it to me again.

BRAHMAN: Certainly. The tiger was in the cage and I let him out.

JACKAL: I shall never get this straight until I have seen the tiger. Please take me to him. (*They go to* TIGER.)

TIGER: What took you so long? You know how hungry I am!

BRAHMAN: Yes, yes. But before we begin, I must tell my story to this jackal. I can't seem to make him understand.

TIGER: Not understand? He must be stupid. Hurry up! I am hungry.

BRAHMAN (*To* JACKAL): You see, my friend, it was like this. The tiger was in the cage, and I came walking by.

JACKAL: Oh! My poor head! My poor head! You were in the cage. The tiger came walking by.

TIGER: Fool! *I* was in the cage.

JACKAL: Surely. I mean, I was in the cage. Dear me! That doesn't sound right. How dizzy I am!

TIGER: Silly fellow.

JACKAL: I must take this slowly. My poor head is spinning. Let me see. The tiger was in the Brahman, and the cage came walking by. No, no. That is not right. You may as well eat the Brahman. I shall never understand.

TIGER: See here! Don't you dare say that. You shall understand. Listen to me! I am the tiger. Do you understand that?

JACKAL: Yes, Sir Tiger.

TIGER: And this is the Brahman. Do you understand that?

JACKAL: Yes, Sir Tiger.

TIGER (*Pointing to cage*): And this is the cage. Do you understand that?

JACKAL: Yes—er—no—that is, not quite. . . .

TIGER: What? You dare to tell me that you still do not understand?

JACKAL: There is just one thing, just one little thing.

TIGER: I am at the end of my patience. Hurry up! What is the one thing that you do not understand?

JACKAL: Please, sir. How did you get in?

TIGER: How did I get in? Foolish one, there is only one way. Everyone knows that.

JACKAL: And how is that?

TIGER (*Jumping into the cage*): *This way,* of course. Now do you understand?

JACKAL (*Locking the cage door*): I certainly do. And if you don't mind, we will let you stay right where you are. (*Turning to* BRAHMAN) As for you, friend Brahman, be glad that you can cook your own rice for the rest of your life. (BRAHMAN *embraces* JACKAL, *as curtain falls.*)

THE END

Finn McCool

A tale about an Irish folk hero

by May Lynch

Characters

FINN McCOOL   GRANNIE
UNA, *his wife*   MRS. O'MALLEY
OWEN ⎤   MRS. SHANE
JOHN ⎥   CUHULLIN
JAMIE ⎬ *his children*
MEG ⎥
CELIA ⎦

SETTING: *The interior of Finn McCool's cabin, on top of Knockmany Mountain, in Ireland.*

AT RISE: UNA *stands at a washtub, wringing out a piece of clothing. She places it on top of a basket of laundry at her feet.* OWEN, JAMIE, *and* JOHN *are sitting nearby.*

UNA: There! That's the last of my washing, and I must say it was a big one.

OWEN: I'll say it was. I carried six buckets of water up Knockmany Mountain this morning.

JOHN: And so did Jamie and I. We do it all the time.

OWEN: You didn't carry six buckets, John.

JAMIE (*Laughing*): No, Owen, but you spilled half of yours.

218

OWEN: I did not, Jamie McCool!

JAMIE: You did, too.

OWEN (*Loudly*): I did not!

UNA: Children! Stop that brawling and squalling. My, I'll be glad when your father, Finn McCool, finds us a spring up here near the house.

JOHN: He says that there's water right out there under those two rocks.

JAMIE: Yes, and he's going to move them someday.

OWEN (*Interrupting*): Someday! Someday! He keeps saying *someday*, but *someday* never comes.

UNA: Owen McCool, don't speak that way of your father. After all, the dear man is very busy and tired—and—and busy. (MEG *and* CELIA *enter*.)

CELIA: Mother! Mother! Guess what!

MEG: Grannie Owen and Mrs. O'Malley and Mrs. Shane are coming up Knockmany Mountain right now.

UNA: Your grannie hasn't been here in a long time. Put on the teakettle, Meg. Celia, dear, lay the cloth. And Owen, hang these things out on the line, like a good boy.

OWEN: I have to do *everything*.

JAMIE: I'll help you. Come on. (*He picks up basket of laundry. The two boys exit.*)

JOHN: I'll fix the fire. (UNA *and the girls tidy up the room, as* JOHN *kneels at fireplace*.)

CELIA (*At window*): Here they are. I see them coming up the path.

JOHN (*Opening the door*): Welcome, Grannie. Good day, Mrs. Shane. Good health to you, Mrs. O'Malley. (GRANNIE, MRS. O'MALLEY, *and* MRS. SHANE *enter. All exchange greetings. The girls kiss* GRANNIE.)

GRANNIE: Well, I must say, Knockmany Mountain gets steeper every year. I'm puffing from that long walk.

MRS. O'MALLEY: I am, too. And that wind gets stronger and stronger.

MRS. SHANE: Una, however do you manage in winter when that cold wind howls and blows and screams? Aren't you afraid to be up here?

UNA (*Laughing*): No, indeed. Finn McCool wouldn't live anywhere else in the world. (*Ladies glance at each other with knowing looks.*)

GRANNIE: Where is Finn today?

JOHN: He's somewhere about. He's busy, I guess.

UNA: He's such a busy man, you know.

MRS. SHANE: It's too bad he's too busy to find a spring up here. Those poor lads of yours shouldn't have to carry water all the way up the mountain.

JOHN: We really like to do that, Mrs. Shane. Besides, our father says that someday he is going to let my brothers and me help him split open those rocks out there. There's water under them. (*Ladies shake their heads.*)

MEG: Grannie, Mother, Mrs. O'Malley, Mrs. Shane, do sit down and have a cup of tea. (*Ladies sit, as girls serve them tea and pass a plate of cakes.*)

GRANNIE: It's good to see you, Una. Since Finn built this house on top of the world, we seldom get together.

MRS. SHANE: Is it true, Una, that Finn came up here to get away from Cuhullin?

UNA: Goodness, no.

JOHN: Who is Cuhullin?

MRS. O'MALLEY (*Quickly*): Nobody important, John.

MRS. SHANE: *Nobody important?* He's a giant. That's who he is.

JOHN: Finn McCool, our father, is a giant, too.

MRS. SHANE: Oh, but Cuhullin is very strong. There's not a man so strong within a hundred miles of our town of Dungannon.

GRANNIE: Except maybe my son-in-law, Finn McCool.

MRS. SHANE: The talk around Dungannon right now is

that Cuhullin once stamped his foot and all of Ireland shook and trembled.

JOHN: Why would he do that?

MRS. SHANE: To show that he had beaten ever single giant in Ireland except Finn McCool, whom he can't find.

MRS. O'MALLEY (*Nervously*): I don't like to frighten you, Una, but there is talk in town that Cuhullin is on his way here to find Finn.

GRANNIE: But there's nothing to be afraid of, Una. You can all come down to my cottage and hide until Cuhullin goes away.

MRS. SHANE: Yes, you'd better.

MRS. O'MALLEY: Get the children and Finn right away, Una. My Mr. O'Malley heard only this morning that Cuhullin was thundering toward Dungannon.

MRS. SHANE: They say he'll stamp Finn into pancakes when he finds him.

JOHN: But why?

GRANNIE: It's an old story, John. Finn used to brag about how much stronger he was than Cuhullin. Of course, Cuhullin heard about it and he began to look for Finn McCool.

MRS. O'MALLEY: And he's never found him. Come, Una. Come with us.

UNA: Why, we have nothing to be afraid of. Finn will take care of us.

LADIES (*Ad lib; excitedly*): Please come right away. We're frightened. (*Etc.*)

UNA: No, we'll be perfectly safe. (*Thinks for a moment*) But I just remembered I must do some baking.

JOHN: You just did your week's baking, Mother. (UNA *starts to mix flour and salt in a bowl, as* GRANNIE *and other ladies rise.*)

UNA: Did I indeed, John? (*To ladies*) Must you go so soon,

ladies? (*They nod and start toward door.*) Finn will be sorry he wasn't here to see you. Come again soon.

GRANNIE: We will, Una. (*Aside*) Poor Finn will be no more. Poor Finn McCool. (*They exit.*)

CELIA: Mother, is it true what they said about Cuhullin? (UNA *shrugs and continues mixing.*)

UNA (*To herself*): I need some iron skillets. (*Picks up two skillets*) Here they are.

MEG: I'm scared, Mother.

UNA (*To herself*): One bite of bread with a skillet in it will take care of Cuhullin. (*She starts to cover the skillets with dough.* FINN *enters.*)

FINN: I'm a dead man. I've been to Dungannon, and the giant Cuhullin is on his way to town looking for me. He told somebody he'd squeeze me into a sausage.

GIRLS: Is he big?

FINN: Big he is. Too big for me to handle. And *I'm* too big to hide from him.

UNA: You leave everything to me, Finn. I'll handle Cuhullin. Meg, give your father that old long nightdress of mine and find the baby's bonnet in the drawer. (*To* FINN) And *you* put on the nightdress and the bonnet and hide in that bed over there. (*She puts bread into oven.* MEG *exits.*)

FINN: Right here? Hide here in the open? (UNA *nods her head. He exits and returns wearing a long white nightgown and a bonnet. He climbs into bed, as* MEG *re-enters.*)

UNA: Girls, get Jamie and Owen and gather lots of kindling. Then build a great big fire right on the very tip of Knockmany Mountain.

CELIA: But a fire on the mountain means that we are welcoming a stranger. The only stranger is—is Cuhullin.

MEG: I'm too scared to move.

UNA: Go! Get your brothers to help you. (*To* JOHN) You,

son, stand where the wind will carry your whistle. As soon as you see Cuhullin coming up the mountain, you must let out your long, loud whistle.

FINN: Ooooh! Ooooh! I'm scared out of my wits. Cuhullin will make a grease spot of me. He'll chew my darling children up alive and carry off my good wife.

UNA: Nonsense! You just listen to my plan. I've already made bread Cuhullin will never forget, and now if I take a cobblestone and make it look like a cheese— (*She sits on edge of bed and whispers in* FINN's *ear. Both of them burst into loud laughter. She whispers again, pointing to the oven. Loud whistle is heard.*) Cuhullin is coming! (*She pulls the covers around* FINN.) Now keep the bonnet on and remember *who* you are! (*She hands him stone and a round cheese from table.*) Now, don't roll on this cheese. (*A loud banging at door is heard.*)

CUHULLIN (*Shouting from offstage*): Is this where you live, Finn McCool? Open up, if you're a man. (UNA *opens the door, looks surprised.*)

UNA: Well, I wondered if I heard someone at the door. It's so windy I don't always hear people knocking. Come in, stranger. Welcome.

CUHULLIN (*Entering*): Does Finn McCool live here?

UNA (*Sweetly*): He does, indeed.

CUHULLIN: Is he home?

UNA: Dear me, no! He left here an hour ago. Somebody said a giant named Cuhullin was down in Dungannon looking for him. Finn went right down to make pudding out of him.

CUHULLIN: Mm-m-m.

UNA: Did you ever hear of Cuhullin, poor thing?

CUHULLIN: That's me.

UNA: Oh, you poor man. Finn is in a terrible temper. Don't let him find you.

CUHULLIN: I've been wanting to meet him for years. I notice he doesn't let *me* find *him*.

UNA: Well, wait for him then. But don't say I didn't warn you.

CUHULLIN: I'll wait.

UNA: Don't be nervous. Here, to keep yourself from being scared, and while you're waiting, would you do me a favor? (*He nods.*) Would you turn the house around? Finn always turns it around in the fall when the wind blows at the door. It makes it warmer in winter.

CUHULLIN: Turn the house? Nothing easier. (*He exits. A loud noise is heard from offstage.* UNA *goes to door.* FINN *groans.*)

UNA (*Calling*): That's better. Thank you very much. Now, would you do something else? Finn has been meaning to pull those rocks apart and find us a spring, but he hurried off, and I do need water. (*She steps back toward* FINN *as a loud crash is heard.*) Good heavens! He pulled apart those rocks with his bare hands and made a spring! (FINN *groans.* CUHULLIN *enters.*)

CUHULLIN: What now?

UNA: That's a good little job finished. Now you come and have a bite to eat. Even though you think Finn is your enemy, he would want me to be kind to anyone in our home. Here's a cup of tea and I have some hot bread right in the oven. (*She takes out loaves of bread.* CUHULLIN *bites into the bread.*)

CUHULLIN: Blood and thunder! I just broke my two front teeth. What did you give me to eat, woman?

UNA: Only what Finn always eats. He and our little child in the bed have these biscuits all the time. (*She indicates bed.*) Try another one.

CUHULLIN: Jumping shamrocks. My teeth are ruined. Take this stuff away. What a toothache! (*Holds jaw*)

FINN (*In a deep voice*): Give me something to eat. I'm hungry! (UNA *takes a loaf of bread to* FINN, *and he pretends to eat it.*) Yum!

CUHULLIN (*Amazed*): I'd like to see that child. He must be some boy!

UNA: Get up, dearie, and show the man that you're Finn's little son.

FINN (*Jumping out of bed*): Are you strong like my father?

CUHULLIN: Toads and snakes! What a gigantic child!

FINN: Are you strong? Can you squeeze water from a stone? My father can, and so can I. (*He hands white stone to* CUHULLIN, *who squeezes it.*) Ah, you *can't* do it. (FINN *takes stone, throws it on bed, then picks up cheese, unseen by* CUHULLIN, *and squeezes it until water drips from it.*) My father, Finn McCool, taught me to do that. He can stamp a man to pancakes.

UNA: Into bed, son. You'll never grow strong and big like your father if you don't get your rest.

CUHULLIN (*Nervously*): I think I'd better go. I never saw the like of that child. What must his father be like!

FINN: Will Father hurt that little man, Mother?

UNA: No, dearie. (*To* CUHULLIN) You are the lucky one that Finn isn't home. That temper of his! (CUHULLIN *exits, running.* FINN *and* UNA *laugh. The children come running in.*)

MEG: Mother, what did you do to Cuhullin?

JOHN: He was holding his jaw and crying about a toothache.

OWEN: I heard him muttering about pancakes and a baby giant.

JAMIE: I watched from the bushes. He pulled those rocks apart one—two—three. And now we have a spring.

UNA: And he turned the house around. It's warmer already.

MEG: How did you do it, Mother?

FINN: Ah, your mother is a clever woman. She makes rocks out of cheese.

UNA: Your father fooled him. Cuhullin tried to squeeze water from a rock, but Finn squeezed water from *cheese*. Cuhullin never knew the difference.

FINN: And she put iron skillets into her bread and served them for biscuits.

UNA: But your father fooled him. He just nibbled around the crust.

OWEN: Why are you wearing that silly outfit, Father?

UNA: You should have seen how your father fooled him, pretending he was a baby giant. (*All laugh.*)

FINN: Now if somebody will help me out of this night-gown, I'll lie down and have a rest. A busy man like me gets very tired. (*Curtain*)

THE END

The Bridge to Killybog Fair

An Irish tale

by Frances B. Watts

Characters

TERENCE LEPRECHAUN
SEAN PIXIE
MICKEY, *a country lad*
KATHLEEN, *his sister*
THOMAS ⎱ *drummer boys*
COLIN ⎰

FARMER HANNIGAN
MRS. HANNIGAN
TIM ⎱ *their children*
JUDY ⎰
FOUR O'LEARY LASSIES
TWO PIGS

TIME: *A short time before noon, on St. Patrick's Day.*

SETTING: *The woods near the hamlet of Killybog, in Ireland.*

AT RISE: TERENCE LEPRECHAUN *stands down right, blocking the entrance to bridge.* SEAN PIXIE *enters, skipping and chanting.*

SEAN: The fair, the fair, the Killybog Fair. Cross over the bridge, and I'll soon be there. . . . The top o' the mornin' to you, Terence Leprechaun!

TERENCE: Ah, it's you, Sean Pixie. I was thinking it might be a human being.

SEAN: And what are you doing loitering here by this bridge? It's St. Patrick's Day. Sure, and you'll be going to the Killybog Fair. 'Tis a great day for the Irish.

TERENCE: Aye, it's a great day, all right. For today, at last, I'm going to have me revenge.

SEAN: Revenge? Revenge on whom, may I ask?

TERENCE: On people. They keep stealing my nice shamrocks that I grow. Such wanton greed enrages me!

SEAN: They do not realize the shamrocks are yours, no doubt.

TERENCE: They know all right. And they've been robbing me blind for years. They leave me hardly enough shamrocks to give to my friends for good luck on St. Patrick's Day. (KATHLEEN *and* MICKEY, *carrying baskets, enter. They skip and sing to the tune of "The Farmer in the Dell."*)

KATHLEEN *and* MICKEY:
  We're going to the fair,
  We're going to the fair,
  Heigh-ho, the derry-o,
  We're off to the Killybog Fair.

KATHLEEN: Ah, look here by the bridge, Mickey! A wee leprechaun and pixie!

MICKEY: Begorrah! To see fairies is a sign of good luck, I think.

TERENCE: Have another think, me lad. 'Twill be a sad day for the two of you, and no mistake.

KATHLEEN: What do you mean by that, sir?

TERENCE: I mean I'll not be letting you cross this bridge, that's what I mean.

MICKEY: But it's the *only* way we country folks can get to the Killybog Fair!

TERENCE: It is indeed.

KATHLEEN: But we must get to the fair, and we must be there by noon if we are to get a booth. We have barley cakes to sell, and our mother sorely needs the money they will bring.

TERENCE: Then it's a sad day for your mother, too. For you'll not get to the Killybog Fair. (KATHLEEN *and* MICKEY *step up center.*)

KATHLEEN: What shall we do, Mickey? He truly means not to let us cross.

MICKEY: Leprechauns, I hear, will cast evil spells if they are angered. 'Tis best not to argue with him.

KATHLEEN: I agree. Leprechauns are touchy and peculiar. Let's sit on those stumps and hide in the shadowy bushes. Perhaps the leprechaun will soon go away. (*They hide in the foliage far up left.*)

SEAN: Now they are going home and will miss all the fun, poor dears! 'Tis a hard heart you have, Terence. They be only innocent children.

TERENCE: Bah! Children are the same as other people— wicked and self-centered. (THOMAS *and* COLIN *enter, beating drums and singing appropriate song.*)

THOMAS (*Stopping*): Look, Colin. A wee leprechaun is blocking the bridge!

COLIN: See the pixie, too, Thomas. Fairies are rare, uncommon sights. Come, wee chappie, step out of the way so me friend and I can go to the Killybog Fair.

TERENCE: Small I may be, but power I have to keep you right here. And that I intend to do, me lad.

THOMAS: I say now, 'tis important we get to the fair before high noon.

COLIN: Aye. It's drummer boys we are. They are having a St. Patrick's Day parade at the Killybog Fair. Sure, and it's to start at noon, but it cannot start without us.

TERENCE: You'll not be changing me mind. The bridge stays blocked to the likes of you. (THOMAS *and* COLIN *stand up center*)

THOMAS: We cannot hold up the parade. Already, I'm sure, folks are lining up to see it.

COLIN: Aye. We cannot disappoint them. We'd best fight

and force our way across the bridge. We are two strapping lads, and he is just a bit of a sprite. (*They go back and fight and tussle with* TERENCE, *who takes wand from his pocket and flourishes it.*)

TERENCE: So it's force you're resorting to, is it? Such pugnacity! Well, me magic wand here is stronger than any lad!

THOMAS: Begorrah! He's going to cast a spell!

COLIN: Let's make a run for it!

TERENCE: Too late, me wicked lads. (*Waves wand and chants*)

Walk ten paces back, then turn about-face.

Speak not again, and stay in your place.

(THOMAS *and* COLIN *follow directions, as if in a trance. They end up at back of stage, facing audience.*)

SEAN: Faith, and you've cast the Transfixion Spell! They cannot move again until you give them leave.

TERENCE: Aye. And I may never break the spell a-tall.

SEAN (*Shaking fist*): 'Tis a cruel leprechaun you are, Terence. Were pixie magic as powerful as leprechaun magic, I'd break the spell myself.

TERENCE: Mind your own business, Sean. 'Tis revenge for my stolen shamrocks I want, and revenge I'll have.

SEAN: Very well. But, if you don't mind, I'll stay on to see how things turn out. (*Sits down, sulkily.*)

MICKEY: 'Tis lucky *we* did not anger the leprechaun. Look what has happened to Thomas and Colin.

KATHLEEN: Poor lads! Is there no way we can help them?

MICKEY: I wish we might. But no human being, I've been told, can break the spell of a leprechaun. We must keep silent for now. (FARMER HANNIGAN, MRS. HANNIGAN, TIM, JUDY, *and* TWO PIGS *enter.* FARMER *and wife are leading* PIGS. PIGS *grunt and struggle occasionally during following encounter.*)

FARMER (*To* PIGS): Come on, Maggie. Come on, Maureen.

We'll never get to the fair if you keep balking like this.

PIGS: Oink! Oink!

MRS. HANNIGAN: Saints preserve us! There's a pixie and a leprechaun! I've not seen a sprite in many a day.

JUDY: Aren't they cunning!

FARMER: Cunning, aye. But this little leprechaun is blocking the bridge.

TIM (*Pointing to* THOMAS *and* COLIN): Look at Thomas and Colin over there, Papa. Why are they standing so still?

FARMER: I don't know, and we've no time to ask. . . . (*To* TERENCE) Come, little one, move out of the way. It's in a hurry we are to get to the Killybog Fair.

TERENCE: It's here I'll keep standing. You'll not cross this bridge today.

MRS. HANNIGAN: But we must get across. We're taking our pigs to sell at the fair. We must get there by noon to sell at a good price.

JUDY: With the money, Papa will buy me a trinket.

TIM: And I'll have a ride on the Swing Boats.

TERENCE: Hah, greedy children! It's breaking me heart you are.

FARMER: Come now, be reasonable. Let us cross over the bridge.

TERENCE: Not for all the shamrocks in Ireland.

MRS. HANNIGAN (*Slyly*): How about gold then? Leprechauns like gold, do they not? We've a whole pot of gold I'll bring you tomorrow, if you'll be letting us cross the bridge today.

TERENCE: So it's bribery you're using! If you have all that gold, why must you be selling your poor pigs? Bribery! Lies! False promises! (*Stamps with rage*) Are you taking heed, Sean? Am I right about human beings?

SEAN: You are only seeing in them what you want to see. They have good traits as well, Terence.

TERENCE: They have none! If I could find but one good quality in just one human being, I'd give up my plans for revenge.

FARMER (*Pointing skyward*): Look! Look at that giant eagle!

TERENCE *and* SEAN (*Starting to run with fear*): Where? Where?

FARMER: Up there. You'd better run. Sure and I've heard that eagles kidnap fairy creatures. (FARMER *signals family to sneak across bridge. They start across.* TERENCE *spies them and waves his wand*)

TERENCE: Trickery! Did you ever see such trickery, Sean? (*He performs the spell-casting ritual. All become spellbound.*)

SEAN: Glory be, Terence! You've bewitched the whole family, even their pigs. Have you no pity?

TERENCE: Even less than I had before. Greed, pugnacity, bribery, trickery. That's all I've been seeing today. What is worse, the farmer was so wrapped up in his own interests that he was not even concerned about his spellbound neighbors. Such selfishness!

SEAN: Aye. But there's still a lot of good in folks, me friend.

TERENCE: Pah!

KATHLEEN: Oh, dear, the poor Hannigans! Perhaps we should go to the village for help.

MICKEY: But we cannot get to the village without crossing the bridge.

KATHLEEN: Aye, I forgot. But we must do something. It's nearly noon. (FOUR O'LEARY LASSIES *enter, skipping.*) Begorrah! Here come the O'Leary lassies! We ought to warn them!

MICKEY: Sh-h! We will, if we get the chance. But we dare not anger the leprechaun by letting him see us do it.

1ST LASS: Look! A dear little leprechaun and a pixie!

2ND LASS: I have heard that there are fairies in this wood. But never have I set eyes on one till now.

3RD LASS: Nor I!

4TH LASS: Perhaps it is the magic of St. Patrick's Day that has given us the power to see them.

1ST LASS: Will you please step aside, little fellow? We must go to the Killybog Fair.

TERENCE: Step aside I will not. And you'll not be crossing this bridge today, me fine lassies.

2ND LASS: But we simply have to be there, Mr. Leprechaun.

3RD LASS: Aye. We have promised to dance at the St. Patrick's Day celebration. Right after the Mayor speaks, we are to do an Irish dance.

4TH LASS: And our sweethearts are waiting for us, besides.

TERENCE: You'll neither dance nor see your sweethearts, for you'll not be crossing the bridge today. (LASSIES *step up center*)

1ST LASS: What are we going to do?

2ND LASS: Sure and the Mayor will be all riled up if we do not come.

3RD LASS: Aye, and our sweethearts, too.

4TH LASS: (*Pointing to the spellbound folks*): I wonder why our neighbors over there do not come to our aid. Surely Farmer Hannigan or Thomas and Colin ought to offer to help us.

1ST LASS: Alas, men no longer offer to help lassies in distress. Faith, the age of chivalry is dead for sure.

MICKEY (*Beckoning stealthily to* LASSIES): Psst! Come here! (LASSIES *tiptoe to hiding place*) Be careful! The leprechaun has cast a spell on our neighbors over there because they angered him.

KATHLEEN: We have barley cakes to sell at the fair. But we are waiting here, hoping the leprechaun will go away.

1ST LASS: But we cannot wait, Kathleen.

2ND LASS: We are due to dance very soon.

3RD LASS: We simply must find a way to cross the bridge!

KATHLEEN: Whatever you do, do not anger the leprechaun. He'll bewitch you to be sure.

4TH LASS: I know! Let us feed him a bit of blarney, sisters!

1ST LASS: Aye! Let's dance for him as well. Dancing and blarney should sweeten him up! (*They go back to bridge.*)

2ND LASS (*To* TERENCE): We've just been talking about you, sir. And none of us has ever beheld a leprechaun so handsome.

3RD LASS (*Touching his beard*): Such a beautiful silky beard! Sure, the fairy king himself could not have one as fine.

4TH LASS: And such eyes you have! Indeed, they're as bright as the morning sun.

1ST LASS: Such a bonnie leprechaun deserves a pretty dance. Don't you agree, sisters?

LASSIES: Aye, that he does. (LASSIES *dance and sing "Did You Ever See a Lassie."*)

2ND LASS: Did you like our dance, sweet leprechaun?

TERENCE: Sweet leprechaun, indeed! I'll have no part of your flattery and conceited show-off ways. Do you think I don't recognize Irish blarney when I see it?

3RD LASS: Please don't be angry. We hoped it would soften your heart. We just have to get to the Killybog Fair!

TERENCE (*To* SEAN): Did you observe them, Sean? What have I been telling you? Human beings have no good traits a-tall, a-tall. Pugnacity, bribery, greed, trickery, flattery, conceit. These are the qualities people possess.

SEAN: Ah, if only I could stop your cruelty. You are being far too hard on them, Terence.

TERENCE: Not hard enough! These lassies will pay for their treacherous flattery. (*Waves wand, and the spell-casting ritual is repeated.*)

SEAN (*Hiding eyes*): Aye, it's cruel, cruel, cruel you are!

KATHLEEN: Oh, oh, the poor lassies!

MICKEY: I can hardly believe my eyes! Already the leprechaun has bewitched ten people and two pigs. We must bring help somehow.

KATHLEEN: Who is there to help? Most everyone is at the fair and we cannot get to Killybog without crossing the bridge.

MICKEY: Mother is at home. Perhaps she will have an idea. Let us go.

KATHLEEN: All right. But first let us eat a barley cake. I am truly starving.

MICKEY: I am hungry, too. It must be lunchtime. (*They take cakes from basket and eat.*)

KATHLEEN: 'Twould be nice if we could share our cakes with our poor neighbors.

MICKEY: Aye, but they are so enchanted that they probably cannot feel hunger.

KATHLEEN: What about the leprechaun and the pixie? They must be hungry.

MICKEY: The leprechaun? Would you be giving our barley cakes to him? To him, who holds our good neighbors spellbound?

KATHLEEN: Leprechauns must get hungry as well as people. Besides, if folks have been stealing his shamrocks, he has reason to be angry.

MICKEY: Yes. But there is no reason for him to be so unforgiving.

KATHLEEN: Perhaps it is hard for leprechauns to be forgiving. So let us show him that people, in spite of their faults, know what it is to forgive.

MICKEY: It's right you are, Kathleen. Let us offer him some cakes. (*They tiptoe timidly to bridge.*)

TERENCE: Ah, back again, I see.

KATHLEEN: No, we never left.

MICKEY: We have been watching and hiding in the shadows yonder.

SEAN: Then you have been seeing these terrible happenings here. 'Tis best you run along home right now, me dears.

KATHLEEN: That we will soon do. But first we wish to offer you both some barley cakes. You are very hungry, no doubt.

TERENCE: Can I believe me ears? It is generous you're being! Are you not angry with me for the spell I've cast on your neighbors?

MICKEY: We are very angry, yes. But, if you are hungry, we will not begrudge you some barley cakes.

SEAN (*Delighted*): Take notice, Terence. The children are not only generous, but they have it in their hearts to forgive. Your heart holds only revenge.

TERENCE (*Hanging head*): 'Tis ashamed I am. Aye, in forgiveness I am sadly lacking. I have been berating people and alas, I am no better than they.

MICKEY: Then why not forgive us all, Mr. Leprechaun? It is easy to forgive.

KATHLEEN: 'Tis simply a matter of letting love cast out hate.

SEAN: Break the spells, Terence! Release the poor souls!

TERENCE: That I will. I said I would if I found one human being with one good quality. Indeed, I have found two with several good qualities.

KATHLEEN: Oh, Mr. Leprechaun, please hurry!

TERENCE (*Waving wand at spellbound ones, who follow directions*):

Stretch your arms and turn about.

My wicked spell is now cast out.

THOMAS (*Still dazed*): What happened?

COLIN: What has been going on?

TERENCE: I was angry with you and cast you all under a wicked spell. But now, because these good children taught me how to forgive, you are free again.

JUDY: Why were you angry with us in the first place?

TERENCE: Because people have been taking my lovely shamrocks from my cave beyond the brook. But I see now that my anger was much worse than your offense.

FARMER (*Shamefaced*): Many a time, I must admit, I have taken one of your shamrocks. It's sorry I am now.

COLIN: We all have taken shamrocks at one time or another, I'm sure.

MRS. HANNIGAN: Had we known they belonged to you, sir, we never would have done such a thing.

SEAN: See, Terence. I told you they were innocent. They truly did not know those shamrocks were the private property of a leprechaun. Everyone in Ireland likes shamrocks for a little bit of luck.

TERENCE: It's a highly suspicious nature I have. That I must try to correct, too.

1ST LASS: Are we free to go to the fair now? May we cross the bridge?

TERENCE: You all are as free as Ireland herself.

ALL: Hooray! Then it's on to the Killybog Fair!

KATHLEEN (*To* TERENCE): Won't you and your friend join us?

TERENCE: It's thoughtful you are as well, me dear. We will come. But do not be surprised if we become invisible while there.

SEAN: Aye. Irish fairies grow shy in those great Fair crowds. But come, let Kathleen and Mickey lead the way! Their loving forgiveness has saved the day!

ALL: Aye! Kathleen and Mickey shall lead the way! (*All sing to the tune of "The Farmer in the Dell," as they cross over the bridge*)

We're going to the Fair,
We're going to the Fair,
Heigh-ho, the derry-o
We're off to the Killybog Fair.
(*Curtain*)

THE END

The Leprechaun Shoemakers

An Irish folk tale

by Frances B. Watts

Characters

PATRICK ⎱ *leprechaun shoemakers*
DANNY ⎰

MRS. PIXIE

KEVIN ⎱ *her children*
KATHLEEN ⎰

MR. BROWNIE

MRS. BROWNIE

EILEEN ELF

BEGGAR FAIRY

FAIRY LADIES-IN-WAITING

TIME: *Early morning on St. Patrick's Day, long ago.*

SETTING: *A leprechaun shoe shop in an Irish woodland. Two cobbler's benches with tools stand right, a work-basket between them. Gaily-painted chairs and table are left.*

AT RISE: PATRICK *sits at cobbler's bench, stitching and tapping a slipper. He sings to the tune of "When Irish Eyes Eyes Are Smiling."*

PATRICK (*Singing*):
　　Oh, I make shoes for fairies,
　　And I'm proud of every pair,
　　For my shoes for Irish fairies

239

Are the best that one can wear.
I use the finest leather,
And I have a steady hand.
Yes, the shoes I make for fairies
Are the best shoes in the land.
(DANNY *rushes in.*)

DANNY: Brother, I just heard the grandest piece of news!

PATRICK: Did you now, Danny? And what was that, pray tell?

DANNY: I was chatting with the troll who lives by the knoll. He said that the Fairy Queen is looking for a leprechaun to be her own special shoemaker. Her old shoemaker has retired from the business.

PATRICK: Sure, and I hope she finds a good one. Her delicate royal feet should be shod in nothing but the most elegant shoes.

DANNY: Would it be too much to hope that the Fairy Queen might choose us?

PATRICK: It's highly unlikely that she will. Our Irish woodlands are full of experienced leprechaun shoemakers. You and I are new at the business. Young upstarts, so to speak.

DANNY (*Sitting on his bench and sighing*): Aye, that is true. The only order we've had is for those house slippers we're making for old Mrs. Woodsprite. And there's not a single gold piece in our pot. We'll starve at this rate.

PATRICK: Cheer up, Danny me lad. Today is St. Patrick's Day, which is a lucky day for leprechauns. Perhaps we'll have a bit of luck soon.

DANNY: I hope so, Patrick. Ah, if only the Fairy Queen would choose one of us for her own special shoemaker, we'd become rich and famous overnight!

PATRICK (*Handing* DANNY *a slipper*): Here, you'd better get to work. Shoes aren't made with daydreams, you know.

DANNY (*Shading eyes and peering toward left*): Wait! Here come some pixies. Perhaps they're customers! (MRS. PIXIE, KEVIN *and* KATHLEEN *enter left.*)

PATRICK (*Bowing*): Good morning, pixies. May we be of service?

MRS. PIXIE: Do you leprechauns make shoes for pixies?

DANNY (*Prancing about as he recites*):
> Do we make shoes for pixies?
> Listen to her talk!
> Why, we make shoes for every sprite
> That ever learned to walk!

(*Counts off names on fingers*)
> We make shoes for elves and naiads,
> Brownies, trolls, and gnomes and dryads,
> Woodsprites, treesprites, nymphs, and nixies—
> So we *certainly* make shoes for *pixies*!

PATRICK: Enough of your nonsense, Danny. (*To pixies*) Do pardon my brother. He fancies himself a poet, and often gets carried away.

MRS. PIXIE: Since you have assured us that you are shoemakers, perhaps I will give you an order. My children, Kevin and Kathleen, need new play shoes.

KEVIN: Our shoes must be pointed, leprechauns.

KATHLEEN: And we want the toes to curl up like shepherds' crooks.

PATRICK: No, no. We do not make shoes with curled toes.

MRS. PIXIE: And why not, may I ask? All the pixie children are wearing pointed, curled-up toes this year.

PATRICK: Sure, and it may be the fashion. But my brother and I refuse to make them. Curled toes pinch young growing feet. What's more, they are ugly and unnatural. We make only graceful and beautiful shoes.

MRS. PIXIE: You're very particular for upstart shoemakers, I must say!

DANNY (*Aside*): He's going to ruin us for sure! (*To*

PATRICK) If the pixies like curled-up toes, Patrick, what will it matter if we make them that way?

PATRICK: It will matter a great deal, Danny. For unless we make shoes that are graceful and beautiful, we cannot consider ourselves good shoemakers.

KEVIN (*Stamping his foot*): We want shoes with pointed toes!

KATHLEEN: That curl up like shepherds' crooks!

PATRICK: No, children. But I can make you some pretty shoes that will give your toes plenty of room to grow.

MRS. PIXIE: Never mind. If you refuse to make the shoes we want, we'll take our business to the leprechaun who dwells in Mushroom Hollow! (MRS. PIXIE, KEVIN, *and* KATHLEEN *exit*.)

DANNY: How do you expect to get business when you insult the customers?

PATRICK: I don't insult them. I simply insist on making them shoes that are the very best.

DANNY: But what about us? If we don't get some orders soon, we'll starve to death. We've had nothing but parsnips for weeks.

PATRICK: Don't worry. Someday we'll find fairies who appreciate good shoes. (*Pauses*) I'll go brew us some parsnip tea. That might cheer us up. (*Exits right*)

DANNY (*Pacing stage, grumbling*):
    Parsnip tea! Parsnip tea!
    That's lean fare for the likes of me.
(*Rubs his stomach*)
    Ah, how my poor tummy aches
    For whipped cream tarts and sugar cakes,
    And all the sweets a leprechaun
    Is very apt to dote upon.
    Parsnip tea! Parsnip tea!
    That's lean fare for the likes of me!

(*Peers left*) Ah, here come some brownies. Perhaps I can fill an order before Patrick returns! (Mr. *and* Mrs. Brownie *enter left.*)

Mrs. Brownie: You're a leprechaun shoemaker, I take it?

Danny: Aye. Me brother, Patrick, and I have recently set up shop. But our shoes are excellent, nonetheless.

Mr. Brownie: My wife is interested in walking shoes. Could you show us some of your leather?

Danny (*Taking a strip of leather from workbasket*): This is the leather we use for walking shoes. As you see, it is of the highest quality. And the shoes will cost you only two pieces of gold.

Mrs. Brownie (*Feeling it*): What lovely leather!

Mr. Brownie: Two pieces of gold! Have you none cheaper than that?

Danny: Alas, my brother insists on using only the finest leather. (*Digs in basket, and holds up another strip of leather.*) However, here is a piece of inferior leather that he was intending to throw away. We'd charge only a piece of silver for shoes made of this.

Mr. Brownie: That's more like it. (*To* Mrs. Brownie) Sit down, my dear, and allow him to measure your foot. (Mrs. Brownie *sits on bench.* Danny *measures her foot.* Patrick *enters, carrying two cups and saucers.*)

Patrick: The tea's ready, Danny. (*Stops in surprise and sets cups on bench*) What's going on here? (*Picks up leather*) What are you doing with this shoddy leather which I asked you to throw away?

Danny: Mrs. Brownie, here, wishes us to make her a pair of walking shoes out of it.

Patrick (*Tossing leather under bench*): Never! We do not make shoes with inferior leather.

Mr. Brownie: But my wife and I are not particular about the quality of the leather you use.

PATRICK: Ah, but *I'm* particular. There's the catch. A good shoemaker makes good shoes. And good shoes are made of good leather. It's as simple as that.

DANNY: Sure, and you'll change your mind, Patrick. Just this once.

PATRICK: No. The shoes will be made of fine leather, or they will not be made at all.

MRS. BROWNIE: We will have to go elsewhere then.

MR. BROWNIE: That we will, my dear. You're not the only leprechaun shoemakers in the woodland. (MR. *and* MRS. BROWNIE *exit.*)

DANNY (*Tearing his hair*): You've done it again, Patrick! Talk about being shoemakers for the Fairy Queen! We'll be lucky if we sell a pair of shoes in our lifetime!

PATRICK: Only a flimsy sort of shoemaker would make a flimsy pair of shoes. We must have courage to stand by our beliefs.

DANNY: *Your* beliefs, you mean. Right now I'd be willing to make shoes out of peat, if that would earn me money for a sugar cake.

PATRICK: You don't mean that, Danny. It's your empty stomach that makes you rave so. (*Hands him a cup*) Here, have some parsnip tea.

DANNY (*Sipping tea*):
Parsnip tea! Parsnip tea!
That's lean fare for the likes of me!

PATRICK (*Peering toward left*): Ah, here comes a pretty elf maiden. Perhaps we will have better luck this time. (EILEEN ELF *enters.*)

EILEEN: Good morning. I'm Eileen Elf.

PATRICK (*Bowing*): Good morning, Miss Elf. May we help you?

EILEEN: Yes. I am a dancer, and I need a new pair of dancing shoes.

DANNY: A dancer! Fancy that! Would you be so kind as to dance for us, Miss Elf?

EILEEN: Certainly. (*She dances a sprightly Irish jig. Leprechauns applaud.*)

PATRICK: A fine dancer like you will want fine shoes, no doubt.

EILEEN: Yes. The very best. The style must be graceful and simple, with plenty of room in the toes. And the leather must be of the highest quality.

PATRICK: Good! I have a sketch of just such a shoe. (*Pulls sketch from basket*) Is this what you had in mind?

EILEEN: Exactly! I'll order a pair just like that. Will you have them ready by six o'clock this evening?

PATRICK: I'm afraid not. It will take at least three days to make shoes as fine and delicate as these.

EILEEN: But I must have them by six! The St. Patrick's Day Fairy Frolic is being held on the green tonight. The Fairy Queen will be there. And my sisters and I have been asked to dance "The Fairy Ring"!

DANNY: Surely, if we hurry, we can have them done by six, Patrick.

PATRICK. Yes, we could. But they'd soon fall apart at the seams. Hurriedly made shoes are slipshod shoes. Only a slipshod shoemaker would make them. We refuse to do so.

EILEEN: Oh dear, I'll have to hurry and find another shoemaker then. I must have new shoes tonight! (*Exits*)

DANNY (*Moaning*): Patrick, if you turn away one more customer, I'll leave and start a business of my own. I respect your workmanship, but, oh, my, I'm so tired of parsnips! (*Sits on bench and groans*)

PATRICK: Aye, I know how you feel, lad. Still, if we wish to be known as excellent shoemakers, we must make only excellent shoes.

DANNY: But if our diet doesn't improve soon, we'll dry up and blow away in the wind. Then we'll never be known as anything!

PATRICK (*Peering left*): Hush, here comes another customer!

DANNY (*Holding out arms; reciting*):
　Oh, powers that be,
　Let this one choose
　A pair of well-made
　Graceful shoes!

(BEGGAR FAIRY, *walking with cane, enters left*.)

PATRICK (*Bowing*): Good morning, Madam Fairy. Are you interested in a pair of new shoes?

BEGGAR FAIRY (*Showing her bare feet*): *New* shoes? I don't even have *old* shoes. Alas, I'm just a poor old beggar fairy.

DANNY (*Worried*): Then you have no money for shoes?

BEGGAR FAIRY: Not a penny. My, I do wish I could afford some though. I'm always stubbing my bare toes. You don't have any old shoes lying about, by any chance?

PATRICK: Perhaps we can work out an arrangement. I'll make you some *new* shoes now, and you can pay me when you have the money.

BEGGAR FAIRY: How generous you are! So many leprechauns are interested only in hoarding gold.

DANNY: But, Patrick, we cannot afford to be generous to beggars! What are you thinking of?

PATRICK: I'm thinking that this poor fairy needs shoes. So she shall have them. (*Shows leather and a sketch to the* BEGGAR FAIRY) You will have none but the best, my dear. I will use the softest leather, and the shoes will be made in the most graceful lines. It will take me a week to finish them, but, I assure you, they will be perfect.

BEGGAR FAIRY: You will go to all this trouble for a beggar?

PATRICK: Of course, for my greatest joy in life is making excellent shoes.

DANNY: Alas, my greatest joy in life is *eating*.

PATRICK: If you will please be seated, Madam Fairy, I will measure your foot.

BEGGAR FAIRY: A little later, Mr. Leprechaun. Right now, there is something else I must do. (*She claps her hands three times, and the* FAIRY LADIES-IN-WAITING *enter*.)

DANNY: What beautiful fairy maidens!

PATRICK: Who are you?

1ST LADY: We are Fairy Ladies-in-Waiting.

2ND LADY: We wait upon the Queen.

3RD LADY: How we love our Queen!

BEGGAR: Come, ladies, show the leprechauns who I really am. (LADIES *stand in a circle around* BEGGAR FAIRY. *When they move away, her cape has been removed, and she is wearing white dress and crown.* NOTE: *She may have slippers in her cape pocket, which she puts on to complete her costume as* FAIRY QUEEN. *Her cane, to which a star may be attached, is now her magic wand.*)

PATRICK *and* DANNY (*Bowing low*): The Fairy Queen!

QUEEN: You may rise now.

PATRICK: Your Majesty, we cannot understand your presence here. Why are we so honored?

QUEEN: The explanation is simple. I am looking for a leprechaun to be my own special shoemaker. At last, I have made my choice. (*Touches* PATRICK *with wand*) Patrick Leprechaun, from this day forward you will be known as the Queen's Royal Shoemaker!

PATRICK: You have chosen *me*, Your Majesty? Sure, and I'm naught but a young upstart.

QUEEN: Nevertheless, you are the kind of shoemaker I have been looking for. I came here disguised as a beggar. Not only were you generous enough to work without payment, but you insisted on making perfect shoes. If you will make perfect shoes for a beggar, then I know you shall truly make shoes that are fit for a queen.

PATRICK (*Bowing*): You are so kind, Your Majesty. Aye, and I had a feeling that St. Patrick's Day would bring us a bit of luck.

QUEEN (*To* LADIES): Will one of you please hang up the royal sign? (1ST LADY *exits and returns with a sign, reading*, THE QUEEN'S ROYAL SHOEMAKER. *She hangs sign on back wall.*)

DANNY (*Reading sign with awe*): The Queen's Royal Shoemaker! Fancy that! (*To* PATRICK) Well, Patrick, I'll pack up my gear and go along now. You won't be needing the help of a slipshod shoemaker like me anymore.

PATRICK: Don't leave, Danny. Indeed, I'll need your help. No doubt I'll be having lots of customers from now on. Besides, if you really put your heart into your work, you can easily change your ways.

DANNY: Do you really think so?

PATRICK: I'm sure of it!

QUEEN: Danny, if you follow your brother's fine example, you are bound to become an excellent shoemaker in time. Come, you may both start to work right now. For I truly need new shoes, and so do my ladies-in-waiting. (PATRICK *and* DANNY *start measuring the feet of the* FAIRY QUEEN *and* LADIES. *As they work they sing a variation of the opening song.*)

PATRICK *and* DANNY (*Singing to tune of "When Irish Eyes Are Smiling"*):

> Oh, we make shoes for fairies,
> And we're proud of every pair,
> For our shoes for Irish fairies
> Are the best that one can wear.
> We use the finest leather,
> And we have a steady hand.

Yes, the shoes we make for fairies
Are the best shoes in the land.
(*Curtain*)

THE END

The King and the Bee

A tale of ancient Israel

by Virginia Payne Whitworth

Characters

LORD CHAMBERLAIN
KING SOLOMON
BEE
KEEPER OF THE ROYAL OINTMENT
PAGE
QUEEN OF SHEBA

TIME: *Many years ago.*

SETTING: *King Solomon's garden. Ornamental vases stand at right.*

AT RISE: *Soft, appropriate music is heard, then fades, as* LORD CHAMBERLAIN *enters.*

CHAMBERLAIN (*Pounding on floor with staff, and intoning*): Make way for His Majesty, the King!" Make way! Make way! King Solomon in all his glory enters the royal garden! (KING SOLOMON *enters.*)

SOLOMON: Peace, Lord Chamberlain! There is no one here. The garden is quite deserted.

CHAMBERLAIN: As you will, sire.

SOLOMON: You may go. I wish to be left alone, to think—maybe to sleep a little.

CHAMBERLAIN: To sleep—here—in the garden?

SOLOMON: Yes, to sleep, and perhaps to dream of the coming of the great queen from the land of Sheba.

CHAMBERLAIN (*Bowing himself out*): I go, sire, but I shall be not far off, should you require me.

SOLOMON: Very well, Lord Chamberlain. (*Yawning*) Ah, this heat! It makes me drowsy. (*Stretching out on bench*) The stillness is good. I can almost hear the flowers growing in the ground. Even the bees sound only faintly in the distance. This crown is too heavy for a hot day. (*He takes off crown and lays it on the ground.*) There! That's better. (*As he closes his eyes, music begins softly, suggesting the humming of bees.* BEE *enters, moving about in an aimless kind of dance. The music grows louder.*)

BEE: This must be the king's garden. I've never seen so many flowers. (*Bends over flowers, as if gathering honey.*) Mm-m-m! This is very good honey. (*She suddenly sees* SOLOMON.) A man! (*She quickly moves a few steps away. He does not move, so she tiptoes back.*) I wonder if he is asleep. (*She peers into his face and as she bends over him, her wings touch his face. He wakes and waves his hand to brush her away. Frightened, she strikes out with her stinger, and pricks his nose.*) Oh! What have I done? I fear I have pricked his nose! (*She runs away again.*)

SOLOMON (*Putting his hand to his nose and looking around*): What is this? What has hurt me? Oh, my nose! My nose! Who's here?

BEE: Oh, dear, oh, dear! I'm so frightened! (*Looks at stinger*) I've broken the point of my stinger! (*Hides behind a bush*)

SOLOMON: Who speaks? I hear a little voice crying that she is frightened.

BEE (*Amazed*): He understands me! No human being has ever understood me before. It must be the great and wise King Solomon!

SOLOMON: Step forth, creature. Name yourself.

BEE (*Coming forward timidly*): It is only I, sire. One of the humblest of the Lord's creatures—a honeybee.

SOLOMON: Do not be afraid. Only tell me why you struck me just now. (*Taking her arm*)

BEE: Do not kill me, sire. I did not mean any harm. I was curious to see whether you were asleep, and as I bent over to look, you woke very suddenly with a jump. When I am frightened or startled I always strike out with my little stinger—and so I did this time. Forgive me, Your Majesty.

SOLOMON: How do you know that I am king? See, I wear no crown.

BEE: No, but you understood my language. No one but the wisest of the wise may do that.

SOLOMON: I was dreaming of the lovely Queen of Sheba, and you disturbed me.

BEE: I am sorry, sire. Please, sire, let me go free!

SOLOMON: What if I do?

BEE: Maybe sometime I can show my gratitude. Maybe I can be of service to you, who knows?

SOLOMON (*Laughing*): Ho! That is very kind of you, little creature! Service to me, eh? Well, as you say, who knows? (*Feeling his nose*) Who knows— hm-m-m! The place is very sore, little creature, and is beginning to swell, I fear.

BEE: Your Majesty, do not lock me up in a cage! Pray, do not keep me within walls and under a roof. I could not bear to be away from the bright sunshine and the free, fresh outdoor world.

SOLOMON: Very well, you may go. (*Releasing her*) Remember your promise! (*Laughing*)

BEE: Yes, sire! I thank you! You may count on me, sire! (*She goes over wall.*)

SOLOMON (*Clapping his hands*): Ho! Lord Chamberlain!
(LORD CHAMBERLAIN *runs in.*)

CHAMBERLAIN: Your Majesty! Has anything harmed you?
Where is your crown? Oh, here it is upon the ground!
(*Starting*) Your nose! Sire!

SOLOMON (*Feeling it*): Is it that bad?

CHAMBERLAIN: Your Majesty! What has befallen you?

SOLOMON: A little creature in gauze and velvet, and carrying a small dagger, has just been interfering with the
royal rest. (*Laughing*)

CHAMBERLAIN: May I not call in the doctors, Your Majesty? Truly, your nose is becoming—shall I say—

SOLOMON: It is, indeed, Lord Chamberlain, but a bit of
ointment will fix it up. Send for some, will you?

CHAMBERLAIN (*Calling very loudly*): Keeper of the Royal
Ointment! Come into the king's garden!

SOLOMON: I hope I shall not frighten the Queen of Sheba.

CHAMBERLAIN (*Announcing*): The Keeper of the Royal
Ointment. (KEEPER, *carrying many boxes and jars on a
tray, enters and bows.*)

KEEPER (*Standing before* KING): I am the Keeper of the
Royal Ointment, Your Majesty.

SOLOMON: Well, you should have something there that
would help me.

KEEPER (*Taking out large magnifying glass*): May I examine Your Majesty's royal nose? (*He secretly takes piece of
putty from hand or pocket and sticks it on* KING's *nose*)

SOLOMON: Do, please.

KEEPER (*After studying the nose*): Ah, yes, just as I feared.
I shall have to remove a small object. (*Takes large tongs*)
This won't hurt much, Your Majesty. There! Out it
comes! (SOLOMON, CHAMBERLAIN, *and* KEEPER *all jump.*)

SOLOMON: Oops!

CHAMBERLAIN: Did you get it?

KEEPER: I did. Here is the royal poultice. (*Places the poultice on* KING'S *nose.*)

CHAMBERLAIN (*Taking out bright silk scarf*): Here is His Majesty's silk kerchief to hold it in place.

KEEPER: Tie it firmly in the back.

CHAMBERLAIN: There we are.

SOLOMON: How does it look? (*Takes up mirror*) Dear me, what a strange sight I am!

CHAMBERLAIN (*Placing crown on* SOLOMON'S *head*): Your Majesty's crown.

SOLOMON: I don't think that helps much, do you, Keeper?

KEEPER (*Bowing*): Your Majesty, you must leave the poultice on until two suns have set.

SOLOMON: I believe the village children know more about bee stings than you do. They simply put wet mud or clay on the spot, and in an hour or so the whole matter is forgotten. (*Sound of gong or trumpet*)

CHAMBERLAIN (*Looking off*): The Queen of Sheba approaches! (QUEEN *enters, preceded by* PAGE, *who carries two enormous bouquets of flowers.* CHAMBERLAIN *and* KEEPER *kneel.* SOLOMON *bows.* QUEEN *curtsies to him.*)

QUEEN: Hail, O King! Your Majesty, I, the Queen of Sheba, have journeyed for many days over seas and deserts to see the great and wise Solomon.

SOLOMON: I, Solomon, am deeply honored, lovely queen!

QUEEN (*Looking curiously at* SOLOMON'S *bandaged nose*): Pardon the question, Mighty King, but is Your Majesty the victim of some illness?

SOLOMON (*Touching the bandage*): You mean my nose? Nay, I am the victim of my friend, the Keeper of the Royal Ointment. He insists that I keep this stupid poultice on until two suns have set. I have received a very slight injury.

QUEEN: I see. As you have been told, I come here to test

the great wisdom of Solomon. I have heard it said that Solomon can always give the correct answer to whatever question is asked him.

SOLOMON: It has been my good fortune to be able to solve some of the problems puzzling my people.

QUEEN: Do you draw these answers all from the greatness of your own brain?

SOLOMON: I am always helped by divine guidance and the world around me, Sheba. It has taught and will teach me many things. What is your question, gracious queen?

QUEEN: Stand forth, page. You see here two bouquets of flowers, both colorful, both fragrant—but only one of them is real. The other is the work of one of my most skillful artisans. Can you tell me without touching them, which is the real one?

CHAMBERLAIN: How beautiful they both are!

KEEPER: No one could tell the difference!

QUEEN: Look well, O King. Use all the wisdom in your power. Call on all your senses save those of taste and touch.

SOLOMON (*Looking closely at bouquets*): They are both perfect in fragrance, too, you say?

QUEEN: Yes, but one is the work of God, and one the work of man.

SOLOMON: Here, Lord Chamberlain, I command you to untie this scarf. I care not if the Queen *does* gaze upon my nose. I must test the fragrance of these flowers. (CHAMBERLAIN *unties it.*)

KEEPER: Alas! I fear the worst!

SOLOMON: You are always fearing the worst, Keeper. Try expecting the best, for a change.

QUEEN: Solomon is as handsome as the world has reported him.

SOLOMON (*Bowing*): Sheba is as gracious as she is beautiful.

Come, Page, let me smell these flowers properly. Hm!
Quite marvelous! Both have the fragrance of a thousand
gardens, and the colors are nature's own!

CHAMBERLAIN: The King's wisdom will fail him.

KEEPER: I fear so. (*Buzzing grows loud.*)

SOLOMON: Hush! What is that I hear? (BEE *comes in.*) I
thought I heard you, little friend. What? Where are you
going? (BEE *circles around the two bouquets, finally
pausing at one and burying her face deep in the flowers
to draw out honey.*) I see! I see! The little creature keeps
her promise! Thank you, little friend! (BEE *dances away;
others do not notice her.*) This, O Queen, is the real
bouquet. There are the honey-laden flowers of nature,
as my little friend well knew. The others, beautiful as
they are, never grew in the earth, but came from the
hand of man.

CHAMBERLAIN: Great King Solomon!

KEEPER (*At the same time*): How did he guess?

SHEBA (*At the same time*): Wise he is, indeed!

SOLOMON (*Leading* QUEEN *to the window*): Look among
my garden flowers, O Sheba. There you will see the
little creature who wounded me earlier. Now she makes
amends by solving your riddle.

QUEEN: Ah, yes, I see! The little bee flying from flower to
flower. You are wise in your friendship with all the
earth's creatures, for even the tiniest can sometimes
serve you.

SOLOMON: Now may I lead you to the feast that is prepared
for Solomon's royal guest?

CHAMBERLAIN (*Pounding floor with staff and intoning*):
Make way, make way, for the Queen of Sheba, the royal
guest of His Majesty, King Solomon, the wise! Make
way! (CHAMBERLAIN *leads the way out followed by* SOL-
OMON *and* QUEEN. KEEPER *lifts up two large vases,*

in which PAGE *places the bouquets. They go out after others.* BEE *re-enters, music grows louder. She dances around flowers, hovers over real ones as curtain falls.*)

THE END

The Magic Grapes

An Italian folk tale

by *Eleanor D. Leuser*

Characters

PIETRO	CROSS WOMAN
SHEPHERD BOY	TWO CHILDREN
FARMER	BEGGAR
WOODCUTTER	POLICEMAN

SETTING: *Country road in Italy long ago. A grape arbor stands near the road.*

AT RISE: SHEPHERD BOY *is seen picking grapes here and there and tasting them. He hastily moves to one side as* PIETRO *rushes in, pursued by* FARMER. PIETRO *gets half way across stage, then turns to listen as* FARMER *stands in opening of arbor and shakes his fist at him.*

FARMER (*Shouting*): Off my land! Get out of my sight!

PIETRO: But I wasn't doing anything.

FARMER: Stay off my land! Keep out of my orchard! By the hair of a hundred foxes, I vow I will have the police after you if I catch you again. Be gone! (*He watches as* PIETRO *exits, then muttering to himself, goes back into grape arbor. As soon as he is out of sight,* PIETRO *puts his head around corner. When he is convinced* FARMER *is really gone, he walks slowly back to grape arbor and sits*

258

down on stone near it, his head resting on his hands.
SHEPHERD BOY *looks at* PIETRO *thoughtfully, then comes up to* PIETRO *with a half-skipping step and taps him on the shoulder.* PIETRO *starts and looks up.*)

PIETRO: Who are you?

SHEPHERD BOY: You may call me Rocco or Angelo or Nino or anything else you wish, but I'm a Shepherd Boy, magic or not as you please, from the Enchanted Country which lies, no man is just sure where. (*He throws his cap into the air and catches it.*) What is the matter with you? You seem to be in trouble.

PIETRO (*Sadly*): Oh, I'm always in trouble. I can't seem to keep out of it, even when I am as innocent as a bambino. You see, no one likes me.

SHEPHERD BOY: That is bad! What makes you think so? You do not look like such a disagreeable fellow.

PIETRO: It's always the same everywhere I go. I have even left my village to seek my fortune elsewhere, where nobody knows me. But my misfortune follows me.

SHEPHERD BOY (*Sympathetically*): Tell me about it. Perhaps I can help you.

PIETRO: First, I met a woodcutter. I was only trying to get out of his way, when I stumbled against his wood and knocked it over. What names the fellow called me!

SHEPHERD BOY: I suppose it took you a long time to help him pick up all the wood?

PIETRO: Well, no . . . I didn't stop. I was in too much of a hurry to get to this next village and start trying my fortune.

SHEPHERD BOY: Oh, I see!

PIETRO: Then I met a cross woman on the road. She was carrying a bird on her head and a cat under her arm. It looked so ridiculous that I . . .

SHEPHERD BOY: You laughed at her, of course, and the cross woman shook her finger at you.

PIETRO (*Surprised*): How did you know?

SHEPHERD BOY: Well, it seemed just what you would have done. Anything more?

PIETRO (*Slowly*): There were two children coming this way. They were playing ball, and I caught it and just to play a little joke on them, I threw it far off.

SHEPHERD BOY: And they didn't like it?

PIETRO: No. One began to cry, and the other ran after me with a stick.

SHEPHERD BOY: I begin to see why nobody likes you. Anything else?

PIETRO: Only an old beggar. He wanted a slice of my bread, and I needed it for myself. There was no reason for him to call me selfish. (*Shrugging*) It is names and bad looks everywhere I go. I am most unfortunate.

SHEPHERD BOY: What about this farmer? How did you get in trouble there?

PIETRO: I had hired out to this farmer thinking that now I would certainly make good. He sent me to a field to bring home some cows. Unfortunately, I was so interested in the beautiful scenery that I was looking around, and the cows got away from me. I forgot to close one of the gates, and a stupid bull slipped through. You can guess the rest.

SHEPHERD BOY: Yes, indeed. But I know this farmer well. He is a good-hearted fellow. Didn't he give you another chance to prove yourself?

PIETRO: He did put me in the orchard to watch the trees to see that no birds ate the fruit. I closed my eyes for only a moment—I was so tired—but he says he found me asleep. He shouts that I am no good to work for anybody, that I think only of myself.

SHEPHERD BOY: So he chased you out here. I see. I see a great deal more than you think.

PIETRO: If you do, perhaps you can help me. I want to do

well and be liked, but I don't know how to go about it.

SHEPHERD BOY: Most of your trouble seems to come from thinking about yourself all the time. We'll have to change all that. Will you do exactly what I say?

PIETRO: Try me! I really want to change my luck.

SHEPHERD BOY (*Taking large bunch of grapes from arbor*): It's very simple. See these grapes. They're magic. Take them.

PIETRO (*Taking them*): Shall I eat them?

SHEPHERD BOY: You would think of that first. Listen, you must not eat a single, solitary one yourself. But you must give some to everyone you meet.

PIETRO (*Surprised*): As you say. But it's a very queer idea. I cannot see how this will help me.

SHEPHERD BOY: Here comes your first customer now. (WOODCUTTER *enters, carrying a load of wood.*)

PIETRO (*Backing up*): Oh, no, I can't. That is the woodcutter who called me names.

SHEPHERD BOY (*Giving him a push*): Go ahead! You must do as I say. Remember the grapes are magic. (*The* SHEPHERD BOY *watches as* PIETRO *goes hesitatingly to meet the* WOODCUTTER.)

WOODCUTTER: Ah, here is this boy again! Out of my way before you cause my wood to tumble.

PIETRO (*Trembling*): Please, Signor Woodcutter, all I would do is offer you some of these grapes. Your throat must be dry on such a hot day.

WOODCUTTER (*Surprised*): Hm-m. The boy is not so bad after all. Yes, I'll take some. (*He breaks off a few and goes off eating them.*)

PIETRO: Well, that was not so hard after all. (CROSS WOMAN *enters with her bird and cat.* PIETRO *goes up to her.*)

PIETRO: Will you have some grapes, good lady? Perhaps your bird would like some, too? I am sorry that I have nothing for your cat.

CROSS WOMAN (*Smiling a little*): Well, well, that's a different tune you sing now, young master. I'll try your grapes. You're a good boy! (*She takes some and goes off slowly.*)

PIETRO (*Delightedly*): I feel happy! People are beginning to like me. (Two CHILDREN *come down the road, enter, quarreling.* PIETRO *runs up to them.*)

PIETRO: Here, forget your quarreling. See what I have for you. (*Holds up grapes*)

1ST CHILD: Well, I'll be eaten by little wolves! It's the boy who threw our ball away this morning.

2ND CHILD: He's offering us his grapes now, though. I'm going to take some. Thank you, boy. (*They both take some grapes and go off singing.*)

PIETRO: This is wonderful—marvelous. I feel like a new person! (BEGGAR *comes down the road leaning on a stick. He sits down on the stone by arbor.*) Good sir, will you have some grapes? I do not have many left but you are welcome to what I have. (*He hands* BEGGAR *rest of grapes.*)

BEGGAR: It is a good boy who shares the last of what he has. Thank you, little master. (*He rises slowly and walks off with difficulty,* PIETRO *looking after him as the* SHEPHERD BOY *comes forward.*)

PIETRO: Did you hear? The Beggar called me a good boy. (FARMER *suddenly appears, sees* PIETRO *and shakes his fist at him.*)

FARMER: What did I tell you? I don't wish to see you again. Begone!

PIETRO: But I am not on your land. And I am trying to change myself.

FARMER (*Still angry*): I warned you. Now I'm going to get a policeman. (*He runs off left.*)

PIETRO (*Sadly*): Nothing is changed. All my troubles will

begin over again. You will see. He's gone to get the policeman.

SHEPHERD BOY: I'll go to get your new friends. (*He exits. In a moment,* FARMER *re-enters with* POLICEMAN.)

FARMER: Arrest this boy. He is making a nuisance of himself.

POLICEMAN (*Taking hold of* PIETRO): What has he been doing?

FARMER: Nothing at this moment. But I can prove that he is lazy, selfish, and good for nothing—a public nuisance. SHEPHERD BOY *re-enters with* WOODCUTTER, CROSS WOMAN, CHILDREN, *and* BEGGAR.)

SHEPHERD BOY (*Walking over to* FARMER): Not so fast, good farmer. I think I can prove otherwise.

WOODCUTTER: Why, the lad is good. He shared his grapes with me.

CROSS WOMAN: He is considerate. He even thought of my bird and my cat.

CHILDREN: He made us forget our quarreling.

BEGGAR: He gave me the last of what he had.

POLICEMAN (*Releasing his hold*): This does not sound like a bad boy.

FARMER (*Bewildered*): He does not seem like the same boy I knew this morning. I must have made a mistake. Let him go.

POLICEMAN: Be sure you need me if you call me again. (*He goes off, followed by the others.* FARMER *goes back into orchard, then suddenly turns and calls.*)

FARMER: If you want a job again—I might have one for a lad who is all the things these people say of him. Perhaps this morning we both made mistakes, eh?

PIETRO: Thanks, good Farmer, thanks! I will show you what I can do. (*As* FARMER *goes off,* PIETRO *turns to* SHEPHERD BOY, *who has been standing at one side.*) This is all due to you, Shepherd Boy. The grapes *were* magic.

SHEPHERD BOY (*Twirling his hat*): That's the funny part of it, young Pietro. The grapes weren't magic at all. I only told you they were. These people could all have picked them for themselves. They grew on the roadside.

PIETRO: But what made them seem like magic?

SHEPHERD BOY: You made others feel happy by sharing something with them. It works like magic because folks can't help liking you and thinking you're a pretty good fellow. I'll tell you a secret. It doesn't have to be grapes. Anything will do.

PIETRO (*Slowly*): I see! I was stupid, thinking of myself all the time—even when I thought I was working. A thousand thanks, Shepherd Boy. You may be magic or not, but to me those grapes will always be enchanted. They taught me to think of others first and changed my fortune. (*Curtain*)

THE END

The Magic Box

An old Italian tale

by Mary Nygaard Peterson

Characters

TONIO, *a rich farmer*
PIETRO, *his servant*
ANTON ⎫
CARLO ⎬ managers
ANGELO ⎭
DONIZETTI ⎫
SIGNORA DONIZETTI ⎪
SIGNORA ROSSINI ⎬ *neighbors*
GROSSI ⎭
BARTOLOMEO, *banker*
ANGELICA
OLD WOMAN
GUIDO ⎫
VINCENTE ⎬ *Tonio's sons*

SCENE 1

TIME: *Long ago in Italy.*
SETTING: *The main room of a prosperous farm home.*
AT RISE: TONIO, *richly dressed, is pacing back and forth.*
  Impatiently, he pulls bell cord up left.

PIETRO (*Entering right*): You wish to hear the managers' report, sir?

TONIO (*Impatiently*): I suppose so. What a nuisance! Send them in and let us have it over with.

PIETRO (*Bowing and backing out*): Very well, sir. (TONIO *sits behind desk.* ANTON, CARLO, *and* ANGELO *enter and bow.*)

TONIO: Well? Let's hear it. Who will be first—Anton?

ANTON: The fields look fine, sir. There will be a good harvest soon.

TONIO: Good. See to it. (ANTON *bows.*) And you, Carlo?

CARLO (*Bowing*): The vines are loaded with grapes, sir. I have been thinking of having the pickers start with the harvest. There is a good olive crop, too. The branches are almost breaking under the weight of the fruit.

TONIO: Good, good. You will do what needs to be done. You will have charge of the winepress, also.

CARLO: As you say, master.

TONIO (*Nodding toward* ANGELO): And what do you have to report?

ANGELO: I am happy to say that the sheep are healthy. The shepherds work hard.

TONIO: That is what I like to hear. You have all done very well. You may go. (ANTON, CARLOS, *and* ANGELO *bow and exit.* TONIO *speaks to himself.*) At last! I am an hour late already. If I don't hurry, the beautiful Angelica will give her smiles to someone else. (*He rises and walks to exit left.*)

PIETRO (*Entering right*): Sir!

TONIO (*Testily*): Yes, Pietro?

PIETRO: You have visitors, sir.

TONIO: Oh, bother! Who are they?

PIETRO: Friends of your father, sir. Your neighbors, I believe.

TONIO: Fuddy-duddy meddlers, no doubt. I'll see them.

(PIETRO *goes to door right and opens it with a flourish.*
SIGNORA DONIZETTI, SIGNORA ROSSINI, DONIZETTI, *and*
GROSSI *enter.*) To what do I owe the pleasure of your
company, my friends? (*They look uncertainly at each
other.*)

SIGNORA DONIZETTI (*Hesitantly*): Tonio, we have known
you since you were a mere bambino.

TONIO (*Impatiently*): Yes, yes, Signora Donizetti, I know.
My father thought a good deal of all of you. If there is
anything I can do for you now—(*He sits behind desk.*)

DONIZETTI: Tonio, as old friends of your family, we feel
it is our duty to call your attention to certain matters.

TONIO: Oh? And what might these matters be?

GROSSI: First, it is the matter of your wheat.

TONIO: Yes, yes. What about my wheat?

SIGNORA DONIZETTI: It should have been cut last week. All
your neighbors have finished their harvests. Yours is not
yet started.

TONIO: What difference does it make? A week or two one
way or another—

GROSSI: The difference, Tonio, is that your wheat is now
shriveled. Big patches have fallen to the ground. You
will not get top price, and you will not get as many
bushels to the acre.

TONIO: I will have to talk to Anton about that. I am sure
it can't be as bad as you think.

GROSSI (*Shaking his head*): It is bad, Tonio. I know wheat.

TONIO (*Rising*): Is that all? I am late for an appointment
in town.

SIGNORA DONIZETTI: There is more, Tonio.

TONIO (*Sitting again*): Yes?

DONIZETTI: Your vineyard, Tonio. It has not been cared
for all summer. The weeds are about to choke out the
vines. The grapes have not been picked, though they
are past their prime.

TONIO: But there is still time. The days are warm.

SIGNORA ROSSINI: You don't understand, Tonio. They have to be picked at just the right moment or the wine will be thin and sour.

TONIO (*Upset*): This is hard to understand. Carlo assured me this very morning that the vineyards and olive orchards were never better.

SIGNORA ROSSINI: That was true earlier in the season, Tonio, but I am afraid Carlo has been idle. The olives are infected with oil flies. You will lose almost the entire crop.

TONIO (*Grimly*): I shall certainly speak to Carlo in the morning. It is probably a good thing my father had such big flocks of sheep. At least the meat and the wool will bring in enough money so that we can live comfortably this winter.

GROSSI: Don't be too sure of that, my friend. My shepherds say that you have very few lambs this year. They think your men have stolen them.

SIGNORA ROSSINI: I have heard the same. My husband's men say that your shepherds are feasting on lamb and mutton almost every day. Even the dogs grow fat on the parts that are thrown away.

TONIO (*Grimly*): I will soon put a stop to that—if it is true.

DONIZETTI: You will find it true.

SIGNORA ROSSINI: Yes, Tonio. We did not want to interfere, but we were afraid you would lose your land if you did not have enough money to pay the taxes.

TONIO (*Alarmed*): Lose the land! Heaven forbid! If my brother should come back from the war and find the land taken away from us, he would be furious.

GROSSI: I shouldn't be surprised.

TONIO: What can I do? You have said my wheat is ruined, the grapes and olives of no account, the lambs stolen.

How can I pay my taxes? I was depending on the harvest.

SIGNORA DONIZETTI (*Simply*): We will pray for you.

SIGNORA ROSSINI: My family will light candles.

TONIO: You are very kind, but it seems that something more ought to be done right away.

GROSSI: Nothing more can be done this year. The mischief is already done. Perhaps next year you could get some better managers.

DONIZETTI: We are sorry to have brought you so many worries. (*Neighbors move toward door*) You can rely on us. We will all light candles and remember you in our prayers.

TONIO (*Escorting them to door*): Thank you, my friends. You have been most helpful. (*They exit.* TONIO *paces back and forth.*)

PIETRO (*Entering right*): You wish to go to town now, sir?

TONIO: No, it is too late. Besides, I am not in the mood. (TONIO *continues to pace.*)

PIETRO: Something is troubling you?

TONIO: Yes. The neighbors brought me very bad reports about our estate. They say everything has been badly managed since my father died.

PIETRO: That is true, Master.

TONIO: Then why wasn't I told? Why didn't *you* tell me?

PIETRO: It is not a servant's place to tell the master such things, Signor.

TONIO: You are right, as usual, Pietro. But what can I do? (*He slumps into chair. There is a knock on door left.* PIETRO *opens it.*)

PIETRO: Signor Bartolomeo. (BARTOLOMEO *enters.*)

TONIO (*Rising*): Come in, Signor Bartolomeo. Will you sit down? (PIETRO *exits right.*)

BARTOLOMEO: Thank you. (*Sits*) In going over your accounts, Tonio, I find that you have made no deposits since your father passed away, but there have been many withdrawals. I hope you have not decided to do business with another bank.

TONIO: No, no. As it happens, I have not had any funds to deposit yet.

BARTOLOMEO: That is unusual, isn't it?

TONIO (*Uneasily*): Well, uh—I have needed the money to run the estate. My expenses have been heavier than I expected.

BARTOLOMEO: So I have observed. But that is your affair. What I am worried about for you is that you will not have enough money to pay the taxes. They are soon due, you know. Would it help if I were to sell part of the estate for you?

TONIO (*Nervously*): No, no. We can't do that. I will find a way to pay the taxes.

BARTOLOMEO (*Rising and going to door*): I hope so. If you change your mind, let me know. (*He exits.* TONIO *buries head in arms.*)

PIETRO (*Entering right*): I was just thinking, sir. There is someone who might be able to help you.

TONIO. Yes?

PIETRO: There is a wise woman who lives in a cave on the mountainside.

TONIO: The *Witch* Woman?

PIETRO (*Reprovingly*): Some call her a witch, perhaps—mostly children and superstitious people. I think she is just very old and very wise. I have known her all my life.

TONIO (*Pacing up and down*): I don't know. I don't see how she could help me.

PIETRO: She has helped many others. Asking costs little.

TONIO: You are right. I will consult her at once. (*There*

is a quick knock at the door left and ANGELICA *bursts
in.*)

ANGELICA: Tonio, my love, what happened to you? I have
waited for you all day. I have been so worried—and so
lonely!

TONIO (*Wearily*): I have been busy, Angelica.

ANGELICA (*Pouting*): All day? What has kept you so busy?

TONIO: Business, Angelica. Taxes and accounts.

ANGELICA: Oh, bother the business! Come along, Tonio.
You promised to take me sailing today. Remember?

TONIO: I'm sorry, Angelica. I can't. I have to go see someone who can help me with the estate.

ANGELICA (*Pouting*): But you will come to see me as soon
as you return? You will come tonight? Please? (*She tries
to put an arm around his shoulders.*)

TONIO (*Moving away*): I don't know, Angelica. I'll see.

ANGELICA (*Flouncing toward door*): If you ever want to see
me again, you'd better come! I mean it.

TONIO: I'll see, Angelica. (*Curtain*)

*   *   *

SCENE 2

BEFORE RISE: *The* OLD WOMAN'S *mountain cave.* TONIO
sits on one side of a tiny fire, the OLD WOMAN *on the
other.*

WOMAN: Why have you come, young man? Not many find
their way so far up the mountain.

TONIO: I am in trouble, and my father's faithful old servant, Pietro, told me that you might be able to help me.

WOMAN: Tell me what is troubling you.

TONIO: It is almost a year now since my father died. His

estate was the largest in the province. This very cave was on his land.

WOMAN: Then you must be speaking of my old friend, Signor Guido Tomba.

TONIO: Yes. He left the finest land in the country to my brother and me. My brother went off to war and I was left to manage the estate.

WOMAN: You have managed well, young man?

TONIO (*Sighing*): That is my trouble, Old Woman. I have managed very badly.

WOMAN: How could that be? Didn't Guido Tomba teach his sons all they needed to know about managing land?

TONIO: He did. The fault is all mine. I have been lazy and pleasure-loving. I left the management of the estate to others, and now I find that they have neglected or stolen everything. I don't even know how I can pay the taxes. If my brother should come back and find out how I have mismanaged the estate, he would have me thrown into prison, or even killed. (*He buries his head in his arms.* OLD WOMAN *pokes fire thoughtfully.* TONIO *raises his head.*) Can you help me, Wise One? Can anyone help me?

WOMAN: Perhaps. Wait here. (*She exits.* TONIO *sits with head in arms. A few moments later, she re-enters with a small box.*) I have here something which may be helpful to you. (TONIO *looks up eagerly.*) It is a magic box. Every morning, at daybreak, while the dew is still on the grass, you must carry this box over every part of your estate. Shake just one grain of the magic dust over every pasture, field, orchard, vineyard and flock. You will see an immediate improvement, I promise.

TONIO: Is that all?

WOMAN: That is all. But you must go every morning, without fail, while the dew is still on the grass. That is the most important part.

Tonio (*Rising*): I will do as you say. God bless you, Old Woman. I feel you have helped me. (*They exit.*)

* * *

Time: *Many years later.*
Setting: *The same as Scene 1.*
At Rise: Tonio *sits behind desk; before him stand* Guido *and* Vincente.

Tonio: My sons, I have called you to me to discuss your future plans. I have worked hard for many years and have built up a large inheritance for you. I think you are old enough now to manage your own affairs. Guido, as the elder, you will be manager. Vincente, you will be under the direction of your brother.

Guido: There is something I think I must tell you, Father.

Tonio: And what is that, my son?

Guido: I'm going off to war, Papa—today. I'm sorry I have to tell you in this way.

Tonio: Ah, history repeats itself. I had hoped I could keep you both here with me.

Guido: Leaving you is all that makes me sad. As for managing the estate—that is not to my liking. I shall be glad to let Vincente do it. He has always been interested in fields and flocks and vineyards. He takes after you, Papa.

Tonio (*Smiling*): You might be surprised how little interest I took in fields and flocks and vineyards when I was your age.

Vincente: Really, Father? As long as I can remember you have gone out each day to inspect every corner of the land.

Tonio: Believe me, I learned to do that from fear of losing my life. (*He chuckles.*) I haven't thought of these things for a long time.

VINCENTE: What do you mean, Father?

TONIO: Something that happened almost thirty years ago. My father called my brother and me to him in this very room to tell us he wanted to retire. My brother was not interested in the land. He wanted to be a military man —to travel in faraway places and have adventure.

VINCENTE: Like *my* brother!

TONIO: Yes.

GUIDO (*Impatiently*): What happened, Papa?

TONIO: When Father died, I had to manage the estate. I did not worry about it too much, at first. My father had many servants and managers. I thought they would continue to work, and I could live the life of a rich gentleman. Within a year, their neglect almost drove me into the hands of the tax collector.

VINCENTE: What did you do, Father?

TONIO: Well, first I listened to the advice of my neighbors —my father's friends.

GUIDO (*Impatiently pacing about*): I think you must have done more than that, Father.

TONIO (*Slyly*): Come to think of it, I *did* go to consult the Old Woman on the mountain— They called her the Witch Woman sometimes.

GUIDO (*Incredulously*): You *didn't*!

TONIO (*Nodding sagely*): Oh, but I did, son. I went right up the side of that mountain (*He gestures*) to what is now called "Witch's Cave."

GUIDO: How ridiculous! To think that my own father—

VINCENTE (*Interrupting*): What did the Witch say, Father?

TONIO: She gave me a magic box that she said would help me keep the estate.

GUIDO (*Disgustedly*): This is incredible. Even *children* know better than to consult witches and employ magic.

VINCENTE: How did the magic box save our estate, Father?

TONIO: When I had told the Old Woman the whole story,

she went into the cave and brought out the box. She said I must carry it to the farthest corners of the estate every morning, while the dew was still on the grass, and shake just one grain of magic sand on each field and pasture, flock, vineyard and orchard.

GUIDO: And did it work?

TONIO: Yes.

GUIDO: Incredible.

TONIO: You must remember, I was desperate and afraid, and willing to try anything.

GUIDO (*Surprised*): Afraid? Of what?

TONIO: Of my brother. He had the devil's own temper. I was afraid that if he came home and found I had mismanaged the estate . . .

GUIDO: And did he come back?

TONIO: No, son. He never came back.

VINCENTE: You know, I don't see how one tiny grain of sand—even magic sand—could cause a whole field, pasture, flock, or orchard to prosper.

GUIDO: I think there was more than *magic* involved.

TONIO: You are right, son. There were some happenings even *I* had not foreseen.

GUIDO (*Grinning*): Such as?

TONIO: Well, when I took the magic box into the barns and stables early that first morning, I found myself the only human being on the premises. The cows were waiting to be milked; the animals to be fed; and the stalls to be cleaned. There was not a stable boy or a milkmaid to be seen, and the place was filthy. I tell you, I got those sleepy servants out of their beds and on their feet before they knew what had hit them.

GUIDO (*Smiling*): I should like to have been there.

TONIO: As I went from acre to acre of the estate, I found the same state of affairs. There were no workers in the fields, orchards, pastures, or vineyards. The dogs, alone, were still faithful. They were guarding pitiful remnants of the flock. I suppose it was natural that, since the master slept, the servants felt they could do likewise.

VINCENTE: How about the second day?

TONIO: That morning—and every morning after that—those who wanted to work were up and about while the dew was still on the grass. Those who did not want to work left the estate and tried to find an easy life somewhere else.

VINCENTE: Do you still have that magic box, Father?

TONIO: Indeed, I do. (*He reaches into desk and brings out box. He sets it on the desk before him.*)

GUIDO (*Looking at the box closely*): You have never opened the box, have you?

TONIO: There was no need to.

GUIDO: I would like to open it.

TONIO (*To* VINCENTE): And you? Have you any objection?

VINCENTE (*Indifferently*): Let him open it. I intend to supervise the estate each day, and I don't think it needs any more magic dust.

TONIO: Good lad. (*To* GUIDO, *handing him the box.*) Open it, if you like.

GUIDO (*Opening the box and holding up a handful of sand*): Sand—just like the sand at the foot of the cliff.

VINCENTE (*Looking into the lid*): Here, I think, is the real magic. It is not in the sand. (*He reads from the lid.*) "The Master's Eye is needed over all."

TONIO: You are right. The magic has been in the words all these years—not in the sand. It is, as Guido says, just ordinary sand. (*Marching music is heard from the street.*)

GUIDO: I must go. Goodbye, Father.

TONIO (*Putting right hand on* GUIDO's *head*): Bless you, my son. Go with God.

GUIDO: Goodbye, Vincente. (*They shake hands.*) Magic sand or no magic sand, I know you will do a better job than I ever could do.

VINCENTE: Thank you, Guido. Nevertheless, hurry back. Half of the estate will be waiting for you—and it will not be run down. (*Curtain*)

THE END

The Ogre Who Built a Bridge

A Japanese folk tale

by Frances Mapp

Characters

STORYTELLER   CARPENTER
STAGEHAND   OGRE
TWO WOMEN   THREE OGRE CHILDREN
GRANDFATHER

TIME: *Long ago in Japan.*

SETTING: *A row of four chairs is up right center with a sign reading* SMALL VILLAGE. *Down right is a diagonal screen labeled* WOODS. *Up left center there is a screen labeled* RIVER, *with a roll of blue cloth at its base that can be unrolled toward the audience. A piece of curved cardboard labeled* BRIDGE *is behind screen. At left of river, there is a sign reading* TO LARGE VILLAGE, *with an arrow pointing offstage. A low stool stands down left.*

AT RISE: CARPENTER, GRANDFATHER, *and* TWO WOMEN *are seated on chairs.* THREE OGRE CHILDREN *are behind screen labeled* WOODS. OGRE *is behind screen labeled* RIVER. STORYTELLER *enters, carrying a rolled scroll, and stands down left.* STAGEHAND *follows, carrying a large gong. He strikes it once and then sits on stool.*

STORYTELLER (*Bowing to audience*): Ah, so! Welcome to Japan, the Land of the Rising Sun! In my country, as in yours, we have many stories told from one generation to another. Here is a tale, told by my grandmother's grandmother to her, and by my grandmother to me—the story of The Ogre Who Built a Bridge. (STORYTELLER *unrolls and holds up the scroll with* THE OGRE WHO BUILT A BRIDGE *printed vertically in Oriental script.*) Many suns ago, there was a small village. It stood beside a swift and rumbling river. (STAGEHAND *unrolls blue cloth.*) The village was a place of beauty and peace and its people led happy lives, except—as you say in America—for one small fly in the ointment. There was no bridge across the river. (TWO WOMEN *come forward to edge of river.*)

1ST WOMAN: Indeed, it is a fine day today. The clothes we wash in the river will shine.

2ND WOMAN: It is good to hear the song of the birds and feel the sun warm our backs. (*They kneel beside river and pantomime washing clothes.*)

1ST WOMAN: My fisherman husband brought many fish home last night. (*Makes face*) But his tunic smells of the sea and fish scales.

2ND WOMAN (*Laughingly*): You shall have to scrub harder than I, Mistress Sukaro. It is only my best kimono that will be dipped in the river today. (*Pretends to hold up kimono*)

1ST WOMAN: How beautiful the colors are! (*Enviously*) You must be selling much pickled octopus and grilled eel in the marketplace to buy cloth like that.

2ND WOMAN: The cloth is not new, and will be hard to replace. No one in our small village has such fine kimono cloth any more. (*They stand.*)

1ST WOMAN: Ah, so! The Festival of the Moon Blossoms is approaching and I would like a new kimono.

2ND WOMAN: And I also. I would like to shop in the large village across the river. (*Pointing across river*) I have heard that the shopkeepers have much fine cloth, patterned with butterflies of a thousand colors and with cherry blossoms as pink as persimmon.

1ST WOMAN (*Nodding her head*): Yes, and also many other things—nets so strong a tortoise could not escape, incense to burn in our shrines, and gold bells that tinkle in the wind. (*Sadly*) But we cannot cross the river!

2ND WOMAN: I know. The river is fierce and strong, and its rushing waters tear down the bridges our men build as though they were toothpicks in the wind. Even in Elderly Grandfather's time, men tried many times over to build a sturdy bridge, but no man has ever succeeded. (GRANDFATHER *comes forward.*) Greetings, Honorable Grandfather. (*She bows*) We were just speaking of you.

GRANDFATHER (*Bowing*): Ah, so! I am flattered.

2ND WOMAN: Tell us, Wise One, why this river cannot be crossed. We have heard tales of the many beautiful and useful goods that may be bought in the large village across the river.

1ST WOMAN: But it is impossible to see this with our own eyes.

2ND WOMAN: Is there no way to reach the large village across the river?

GRANDFATHER: Patience, my daughters, patience! You are mere women and do not understand the difficulties in building a bridge to stretch across this great river. Our best carpenters cannot conquer the force of these rushing waters. And our village council is quite aware of the need for trading with the large village across the waters.

1ST WOMAN: But they do nothing!

GRANDFATHER: Ah, but they do. The council has sent for

the best carpenter in all of Japan to come to our village and build us the bridge we need.

2ND WOMAN: That is wonderful news! A carpenter of such fame will conquer this troublesome river in no time at all! (TWO WOMEN *return to their chairs;* GRANDFATHER *remains.*)

STORYTELLER: And so it was that the very renowned carpenter came to the small village. (CARPENTER *comes forward.*) The first thing he did was to inspect the great river, where he met Elderly Grandfather. (STAGEHAND *strikes gong.*)

GRANDFATHER (*Bowing*): We are honored that you will devote your valuable time to our poor problem.

CARPENTER (*Bowing in return*): It pleases me to be of help, for I have no fear of your great river. My bridges stand over many rivers in Japan, and one shall stand here to glorify my name.

GRANDFATHER: It will not be an easy task.

CARPENTER (*Confidently*): Even though the river current is strong, it shall not bother me.

GRANDFATHER (*Chuckling*): Listen to the river. It is saying, "Never, never, never will you build a bridge over me!" And no man ever has.

CARPENTER: Oh, but *I* will.

GRANDFATHER: I will leave you to your musings, my son. Good fortune in your undertaking! (*Returns to chair.*)

CARPENTER (*Bowing to audience*): I would not want the old one to know that, despite my boasting, this river is truly a fearsome sight to me. Never have I built a bridge over such a river as this. How am I to anchor the beams that will support the bridge in this swirling, churning rush of water! To fulfill my task will be difficult, but I have made a promise to the villagers, and I cannot give up. I must build a bridge!

STORYTELLER: As the carpenter looked out at the tossing water, he suddenly saw something enormous rise slowly to the surface from a pool of foaming bubbles. (OGRE *slowly comes out from behind screen, wearing a fierce red mask.*) A horrible creature gradually emerged from the river, spilling water as it rose like a thousand waterfalls. (STAGEHAND *strikes gong.*)

CARPENTER (*Frightened*): Ai, yi! What frightful monster is this!

OGRE (*Roaring*): Carpenter, why do you stand there as pale as a water shrimp? Have you never seen such a magnificent creature before?

CARPENTER (*Stammering*): I—I don't think so.

OGRE: Speak up! Your voice squeaks like a mouse!

CARPENTER: W-who are you?

OGRE: I am the ogre of the swirling river, and all men fear me. (*Pauses*) Don't you?

CARPENTER: Yes, Ogre. I was not prepared for your terrifying appearance. The river is so deep that I could not see the bottom. (*Pointing off left*) And so wide that the opposite shore is only a misty strip floating in the haze. It is a river to be feared as much as you are feared.

OGRE: How true! The old men of the village know me, and they quiver and shake, as you do now, when they see me. (*Laughs loudly*) That is why I come up for air every hundred years. It's such fun to scare people. (*Roars*) How's that?

CARPENTER: Why, it was awful!

OGRE: Amazing, am I not? And scary, too.

CARPENTER: Quite so, Most Honorable Ogre. In truth, you are most beautifully hideous.

OGRE (*Delighted*): I am so glad you like me.

CARPENTER: But you must be a kind ogre or the villagers would have warned me against you.

OGRE (*Indignantly*): Of course! I haven't eaten anyone for many suns now. And I am very intelligent. You want to build a bridge over this river, isn't that so?

CARPENTER: Yes, that is so. But how did you know?

OGRE: Because I am smarter than any small human like you. And you are worried about building the bridge. I know that, too.

CARPENTER: Yes, that is true.

OGRE: You can stop worrying, for I will build the bridge for you. What is impossible for a small creature like you is nothing for a great ogre like me.

CARPENTER: Now you are bragging. I am the best bridge-builder in all of Japan, and I say it cannot be done.

OGRE: Ho! Ho! Ho! Foolish small mortal, I could have the bridge built before breakfast tomorrow morning.

CARPENTER: Could you really?

OGRE (*Indignantly*): An ogre never lies. Of course I could. I will have the bridge built by morning. You will see.

CARPENTER: Can I believe you? It would be a miracle.

OGRE (*Shouting*): I told you an ogre never lies! Your problem is solved.

CARPENTER: Then I am truly grateful. You must let me give you a gift in return for your help. Tell me, what could I give you?

OGRE: Ah, a gift! Hm-m-m. What useful gift could you give to a magnificent and mighty ogre like me?

CARPENTER (*Anxiously*): Oh, please think of something! My promise to the villagers must be kept.

OGRE: Well, let me see. (*Pauses*) Ah, I have it! You may give me one of your ears.

CARPENTER: One of my ears! But I only have two, and they are very precious to me. How would I enjoy the song of the nightingale?

OGRE (*Coldly*): Nevertheless, I am building you a bridge

that no human could possibly build. And besides, you have already promised me a gift.

CARPENTER: But what will I do with only one ear? What am I to do?

OGRE: Since you are so troubled, I will give you a chance to save your precious ear. I will build your bridge tonight, and if you can tell me what my name is by tomorrow morning, I will let you keep your ear. Is it a bargain?

CARPENTER: I'm afraid I must accept your terms. I cannot break my promise either to the villagers or to you.

OGRE (*Laughing*): Aha! Instead of two ears, I'll soon have three.

STORYTELLER: With that, the ogre disappeared as suddenly as he had come. (OGRE *moves behind screen.*) With a loud gurgle and a churning roar, he vanished into the murky water of the river, leaving only a few bubbles to show that he had been there at all. (CARPENTER *sits by the river and dozes restlessly.*) All that night, the carpenter tossed and turned in his sleep. Whenever he closed his eyes, he saw the ogre grinning and holding out his hand for the gift. (*While* CARPENTER *sleeps,* OGRE *comes out and places curved piece of cardboard labeled* BRIDGE *over the river.*) As the first faint light of morning streaked the sky, the carpenter awoke, anxious to see if the bridge was truly built. (CARPENTER *awakes.*) He looked up, and there stood the most magnificent bridge he had ever seen. Its great curving arch stood over the tumbling waters sturdy and strong, and yet it was as graceful as a willow tree. The ogre had built a bridge finer than the master carpenter of Japan could possibly have built.

OGRE: Well, Carpenter, how do you like my bridge?

CARPENTER (*Dismally*): It is the most splendid bridge I have ever seen.

OGRE: Far better than any human hands could have built?

CARPENTER (*Nodding*): Yes, it most certainly is.

OGRE: Then you must keep your promise and either tell me my name or give me your ear.

CARPENTER: Mighty Ogre, I worried so about the bridge last night that I gave no thought to guessing your name. I beg of you, please give me one more day.

OGRE (*Laughing*): And what good will that do you? It is plain to see that I will win. But I will be generous and allow you another day. (*Laughing*) You will never, never guess my name! (*Goes behind screen as* STAGEHAND *strikes gong.*)

CARPENTER (*To audience*): I must discover the ogre's name.

STORYTELLER: The poor carpenter was beside himself with worry. In desperation he turned from the river and walked slowly toward the wooded hills behind the small village. (CARPENTER *walks slowly toward woods and stops at one side of screen.*) He walked on and on, trying desperately to think of the ogre's name. Before long he was deep in the woods, many miles from the little village by the river. (THREE OGRE CHILDREN *come from behind screen and dance in a circle.*)

CARPENTER (*Aside; to audience*): Ah, me, what are these children doing in the deepest part of the woods?

CHILDREN (*Chanting*):
While the ogre's away,
His children will play!

CARPENTER: Fried dragonflies! These are not ordinary children—they are ogre children. I must creep away before they see me. (*Pauses*) But wait! Maybe they will give me a clue to the ogre's name.

CHILDREN:
Our father's the ogre who lives in the river,
Making the villagers quiver and shiver!

Mr. Ogre, Mr. Ogre, Mr. Ogre Roku!

CARPENTER: So that's his name! Ogre Roku! I am saved! (OGRE CHILDREN *move behind screen.* CARPENTER *returns to river.*)

STORYTELLER: As soon as the carpenter arrived at the river, the ogre appeared. (OGRE *comes from behind screen.*)

OGRE: Well, carpenter, are you ready to give me your ear?

CARPENTER: No—I want to try to guess your name first. Are you the Ogre of the Terrible River?

OGRE (*Scornfully*): No! You will never guess, carpenter.

CARPENTER: Are you the Ogre of the Rushing Waters?

OGRE: I am not! Do you give up? I told you I would win! Give me your ear, and give it to me now!

CARPENTER (*Shouting*): Wait! I know it! It is Ogre Roku! That is your name. Ogre Roku—the Red Ogre!

OGRE (*Angrily*): How did you know? (*He begins to move slowly behind screen.*)

CARPENTER: I'll never tell you, Ogre Roku!

STORYTELLER: And with that, the great red ogre vanished into the river with a tremendous swoosh. (OGRE *disappears behind screen.*) But the bridge still stood, forming a perfect arch over the rushing water. (GRANDFATHER *and* TWO WOMEN *come forward.*) All the people in the small village were overjoyed.

1ST WOMAN: At last we have a fine bridge to span the wild waters. Never will we fear the river again.

2ND WOMAN: And now we can buy fine cloth for new kimonos.

GRANDFATHER: The bridge shall bring prosperity to the villages on both sides of the river—and we shall name the bridge for you.

CARPENTER (*Shaking his head*): No, that is not fitting. Just call it the Bridge of the Red Ogre. (TWO WOMEN, GRANDFATHER, *and* CARPENTER *return to their chairs.*)

STORYTELLER: And so it was. The bridge stood sturdy and

firm for many, many suns, bringing fame to a Japanese carpenter who, by guessing a name, removed the small fly in the large ointment of a small village in Japan. (STAGEHAND *strikes gong, and the entire cast comes forward and bows.*) Sayonara! (*Curtain closes.*)

THE END

The Peach Tree Kingdom

A Japanese folk tale

by Rosemary G. Musil

Characters

TASHARI
PRINCESS YOSHIKO
LADY PURPLE STREAM

PRINCE FUJIOKA
LORD HIGH ARRANGER
TWO STORYTELLERS

TIME: *Long ago in old Japan.*

SETTING: *The royal garden, partially enclosed by wall with a gate. A bench stands at one side, next to a small table.*

AT RISE: *Soft Oriental music is heard.* TWO STORYTELLERS *stand at right. Music becomes loud, and* PRINCESS YOSHIKO *enters, sits on bench, and fans herself. She is obviously very angry. Music stops.*

1ST STORYTELLER: This is the Princess Yoshiko. The Princess Yoshiko is angry. This is not the way a princess should be.

2ND STORYTELLER: And why is the Princess angry, you ask?

1ST STORYTELLER: We did *not* ask.

2ND STORYTELLER: I shall tell you anyhow. The Princess has a guilty secret. Many years ago . . .

1ST STORYTELLER: Eighteen to be exact.

2ND STORYTELLER: Stop interrupting. Eighteen years ago, Princess Yoshiko was born into the royal household at the same time the Princess Tashari was born.

1ST STORYTELLER: And they got mixed in their cradles and everyone thought Yoshiko was Tashari, and Tashari was Yoshiko . . . or was it the other way around?

2ND STORYTELLER: If you would please stop interrupting—

1ST STORYTELLER: But you take too much time. We wish the play to continue. (*Bowing*) Lady Purple Stream, the Lady-in-Waiting to the Empress and mother of Yoshiko —whom you see there (*Points to* YOSHIKO), sitting on the bench . . .

2ND STORYTELLER: Fanning herself . . .

1ST STORYTELLER: Well, Lady Purple Stream did the mixing intentionally, so it is said!

2ND STORYTELLER: Lady Purple Stream wished her baby to be raised as a Princess and inherit The Peach Tree Kingdom. So she substituted her baby, Yoshiko, for Tashari, and thus Tashari became a servant in the palace, and Yoshiko was brought up as the Princess. (1ST STORYTELLER *puts hand over* 2ND STORYTELLER'S *mouth.*)

1ST STORYTELLER (*Continuing with story*): Today is Yoshiko's wedding day. At least, it is the day of the marriage of the Princess of the Peach Tree Kingdom to the Prince of the Green Willow Tree Kingdom. Yoshiko is nervous for fear the Prince will discover that she is the false princess. That is all.

2ND STORYTELLER (*Wriggling free*): It is not! The Prince has heard that Yoshiko is a hateful person, and he will be disguising himself as a gardener in a few moments to see for himself what his bride is like, and then . . . (1ST STORYTELLER *puts hand over* 2ND STORYTELLER'S *mouth and continues.*)

1ST STORYTELLER: And now the play will begin. (*They go*

out. Soft music is heard, as TASHARI *enters with water-ing can and trowel. She walks daintily to* YOSHIKO, *then stops and bows.*)

YOSHIKO: Humph! (*Tosses her head haughtily and fans an-grily.*) Humph! (TASHARI *goes to shrine where she kneels and begins to weed flower bed.*)

LADY PURPLE STREAM (*From offstage, calling*): Tashari! Tashari! You stupid dolt! Where are you hiding? Ta-shari! (*Music ends abruptly, as* LADY PURPLE STREAM *enters angrily.*)

TASHARI (*Rising and bowing humbly*): I am here in the garden, Lady Purple Stream.

LADY PURPLE STREAM: And so you are, when you should be inside the palace making wedding preparations! And you, Yoshiko, sit here fanning yourself as though you had not a care in the world!

YOSHIKO (*Rising and pacing back and forth nervously*): I'm too nervous to do anything! (*Stops and throws her-self at* LADY PURPLE STREAM) Oh, what if Prince Fu-jioka does not like me! (*Cries loudly*) Then he won't marry me!

LADY PURPLE STREAM (*Shoving her aside*): Oh, yes, he will. The wedding plans were made at your birth while the two of you were still in your cradles. (*Reciting*) "The Princess Yoshiko of the Peach Tree Kingdom and the Prince Fujioka of the Green Willow Tree Kingdom are to be wed on their eighteenth birthdays. This edict can-not be altered."

YOSHIKO: Does that mean he *must* marry me?

LADY PURPLE STREAM: You have nothing to worry about. The poor boy has no choice in the matter at all.

YOSHIKO: Oh, how wonderful! (*Gives a big sigh and sinks down on bench, fanning herself happily*)

LADY PURPLE STREAM (*Turning to shrine*): Tashari, why do you spend your time staring at those bushes?

TASHARI: The bushes are all covered with insects, dear Lady Purple Stream. I fear the insects will eat the flowers before the wedding takes place.

LADY PURPLE STREAM: Nonsense! (*Bends over to examine leaf*) Insects wouldn't dare to eat the palace garden. Ouch! (*Slaps her wrist*) This is terrible! You must get rid of them at once!

TASHARI: I have tried, Lady Purple Stream, but to no avail.

LADY PURPLE STREAM: Well, you haven't tried hard enough. Don't you realize that the wedding will take place shortly?

TASHARI (*Sighing*): Alas, yes!

LADY PURPLE STREAM: "Alas, yes"! What do you mean, "Alas, yes"?

YOSHIKO: I'll tell you what she means. Tashari is in love with the Prince. I have seen her mooning over his picture many times.

LADY PURPLE STREAM (*Sharply*): His picture? What picture?

YOSHIKO (*Shrugging*): I don't know. Some picture she has.

LADY PURPLE STREAM: There is no such picture. (*To TASHARI*) If you have a picture of the Prince, you must bring it to me at once.

TASHARI: But the insects, Your Ladyship.

LADY PURPLE STREAM: Yes, of course. Well, call in a new gardener.

TASHARI: I have already called upon all of our gardeners. They cannot get rid of the insects.

LADY PURPLE STREAM: Call in a gardener from the royal gardens of the Green Willow Tree Kingdom, then. They have no insects on their flowers. I just visited there.

TASHARI: Yes, Your Ladyship. (*Bows*) Indeed, Honorable One, I sent word to the gardener of the Prince's palace just this morning.

LADY PURPLE STREAM: Very well, then. Continue to tend the flowers until he arrives. Come, Yoshiko, your wedding dress is ready. (YOSHIKO *and* LADY PURPLE STREAM *exit.* TASHARI *kneels and works at shrine.* PRINCE FUJIOKA, *wearing an elegant kimono, peers over wall. He does not see* TASHARI. *He jumps over wall, looks around and listens. Then he pulls a long mustache out of his pocket and fastens it to his upper lip. He quickly unties a bundle he has brought with him and pulls out a shabby, cotton kimono.* TASHARI *rises, takes a few steps backwards and looks at plant she is tending.* TASHARI *and* FUJIOKA *bump into each other, jump apart, then stand and stare at each other for a moment.*)

TASHARI (*Suddenly worried*): Oh, dear! You have stumbled into the private garden of the Princess. Quickly, let me lead you to safety before you are discovered. (*She holds her hand out to him. He stands still, continuing to look at her with interest.*)

FUJIOKA: What a sweet, gentle creature you are . . . and so kind!

TASHARI: I do not understand.

FUJIOKA: I know you. You are the Princess. I would know you anywhere.

TASHARI: The Princess!

FUJIOKA: Yes. I have a picture of you as a baby. You still look like the picture.

TASHARI: You must have hurt your head when you came over the garden wall. I am Tashari, a servant girl. If anyone heard you calling me a princess, I would be in fearful trouble, even as you will be if anyone finds you here. No man is permitted here in the garden except by appointment of her ladyship.

FUJIOKA: Beautiful, beautiful, just as I knew you would be.

TASHARI: Oh, dear, I hate to have to call for help. Ouch! (*Slaps her wrist*)

FUJIOKA: What is it?

TASHARI: A hateful insect that is attacking the plants. Oh! (*Suddenly getting an idea*) You are the gardener, aren't you?

FUJIOKA: The gardener?

TASHARI: Yes, from Green Willow Tree Kingdom. You *are* from Green Willow Tree Kingdom, are you not?

FUJIOKA: Yes, yes, of course I am from Green Willow Tree Kingdom, but I am *not* the gardener. I am . . . (*Stops, suddenly remembering his mustache*) Oh, I forgot what I was . . . I mean . . . where . . .

TASHARI (*Laughing*): Simple one! Come, I shall show you the insects. (*Leads him to plant, while he continues to stare at her*) See, the bush is covered with insects. Nothing is pretty here any more!

FUJIOKA: Oh, yes, it is, it is!

TASHARI (*Angrily*): Stop staring at me that way, and get busy. The wedding is this afternoon.

FUJIOKA: They said that you were shrewish and nagging, but you are not. You are kind and sweet and lovely.

TASHARI: Stop it. Do you wish to have me thrown in the dungeon?

FUJIOKA: Tell me the truth: You *are* the Princess, aren't you? You are just disguised as a servant. You did it to see what the Prince was like when he came today. You knew that he would disguise himself and try to see you.

TASHARI: I am Tashari, Lady-in-Waiting to the Princess Yoshiko, and if I hear another word out of you about my being the Princess, I shall call the guards and have you thrown out.

FUJIOKA: Are you sure you are not the Princess?

TASHARI: I am sure.

FUJIOKA: Too bad. Too, too bad. (*Shakes his head mournfully*)

TASHARI: If you say one thing more about my being a princess . . .

FUJIOKA: Oh, I won't! (*Hastily looking at plant*) I mean, it's too bad about the insects. Tsk! Tsk! Slugs in the agapanthus.

TASHARI (*Frowning*): What?

FUJIOKA: Bugs on the lilies.

TASHARI: Oh, yes. I'm very glad you are here. Perhaps you can save the garden. I shall tell Lady Purple Stream you have come. (*He grabs her arm.*)

FUJIOKA: Wait. Tell me, what is the Princess like? If *you* are not the Princess. . . . (*She draws back, and he quickly continues.*) What is she really like?

TASHARI: The Princess? (*He nods.*) Well, she is pretty. She is pretty, and she is . . . (*Trying desperately to think of something else nice*) She is . . . well, *very* pretty.

FUJIOKA (*Dropping her hand and turning away sorrowfully*): I know. I've heard about her. Her disposition is awful, and she hasn't a brain in her head! Oh, why couldn't *you* be the Princess? (*Goes to her and takes her hands.* TASHARI *does not pull away.*) You look exactly as I think a princess should look, and you are kind and gentle and lovely . . . very, very lovely. (*They stand holding hands and looking at each other.*)

LADY PURPLE STREAM (*From offstage*): Tashari! Tashari! Come here at once. At once, do you hear? The Princess needs you! Where are you?

TASHARI (*To* FUJIOKA): Oh, dear . . . tend the flowers, quickly. No! Hide behind the shrine! Lady Purple Stream is coming here.

FUJIOKA: Now, which do you want me to do? I can't do both.

TASHARI: Hide until she is in a better mood. First, she should be told you are here.

FUJIOKA: A prince hides from no one!

TASHARI (*Dryly*): Perhaps not, but a gardener had better. Oh, go! (*Stamps foot*) Do you want to get the both of us in trouble? (*Starts to cry*)

FUJIOKA: Please don't cry. I can't bear it. I'll hide! (*Hides behind shrine*)

LADY PURPLE STREAM (*From offstage*): Tashari! Come here and hold the umbrella over the Princess! (*Appearing at entrance with* YOSHIKO) We are practicing the wedding ceremony, and you are to hold the umbrella. (TASHARI *goes to them, takes the umbrella, and walks forward.* LADY PURPLE STREAM *taps her angrily with fan.*) Hold the umbrella over her, stupid one, not in front of her. The Prince might like to see the face of his bride. (PRINCE *peers out from behind shrine to watch.*)

TASHARI: I am sorry. Forgive me, Lady Purple Stream. (*As* TASHARI *turns to bow to* LADY PURPLE STREAM, *she knocks umbrella against* YOSHIKO, *who goes sprawling on the ground. She glares at* TASHARI *angrily.*)

YOSHIKO: She did it on purpose. She would like to do it to me again when the Prince comes to the wedding.

TASHARI: No, no. I wouldn't. I couldn't! (*She helps* YOSHIKO *up.*)

LADY PURPLE STREAM (*Brushing off* YOSHIKO's *gown*): Now, now, Yoshiko. Even as stupid a person as Tashari would know better than that! (*To* TASHARI) Clumsy one!

YOSHIKO (*Going to bench, sitting and rubbing her leg*): She is in love with the Prince herself and is angry because *I* am marrying him. (*Smoothing skirt*) How she can be so awkward is beyond me. (*Preening*) It is almost amusing to think how graceful and beautiful I am, and how foolish and awkward she is. (FUJIOKA *reaches out from behind shrine and pushes her off bench onto ground, then hides behind shrine again.*)

YOSHIKO (*Furiously*): She did it again! (*Gets up and brushes herself off*)

TASHARI: But I was not near you!

LADY PURPLE STREAM: Come, come, Yoshiko. The bench is slippery; that is all. Tashari, put a pillow on it. (*TA-SHARI picks up pillow, but it slips from her hand just as YOSHIKO backs up to bench. LADY PURPLE STREAM hits TASHARI with her fan.*) Stupid dolt!

FUJIOKA (*Coming out of hiding*): Stop that! (*LADY PURPLE STREAM and YOSHIKO huddle together, frightened. TA-SHARI wrings her hands.*)

LADY PURPLE STREAM: An intruder, an intruder in the garden! Guards!

TASHARI (*Running to PRINCE and throwing out her hands to protect him*): No, no, Lady Purple Stream. He is the gardener from Green Willow Tree Kingdom.

LADY PURPLE STREAM (*Inspecting him*): You are sure of this?

TASHARI: Yes, yes. I have spoken with him.

LADY PURPLE STREAM: But he was hiding there behind the shrine.

TASHARI: No, no. He was examining the insects on the flowers.

FUJIOKA (*Aside, to TASHARI*): How very kind you are.

TASHARI (*Shaking her head at him nervously*): No, no!

LADY PURPLE STREAM: "No, no"? Well, which is it? Is he the gardener, or is he not?

TASHARI: He is the gardener. He really is!

LADY PURPLE STREAM (*Inspecting him suspiciously*): He doesn't look very bright. (*To FUJIOKA*) Well, young man, what would you do for slugs?

FUJIOKA: If I wanted slugs, I would come to the Princess' garden. She has slugs to spare!

LADY PURPLE STREAM: You don't look like much of a gardener to me!

YOSHIKO: Oh, bother, Mother—er—I mean, Lady Purple Stream. (PRINCE *and* TASHARI *look at her suspiciously.*) We must rehearse the wedding. Let the stupid gardener attend the flowers.

LADY PURPLE STREAM (*Pointedly*): Yes, yes, of course, Your Highness! (FUJIOKA *goes back to flowers, but he watches what is going on.*) Tashari, go to the kitchen and see if the wedding feast is properly prepared. Then see if the Lord High Marriage Arranger has come to perform the ceremony.

TASHARI: Yes, Your Ladyship.

YOSHIKO: And when the Prince comes, keep your silly sheep's eyes off him. He is marrying me, you know, not you! (TASHARI *bows meekly and goes.*) Now, Mother. . . .

LADY PURPLE STREAM (*Hitting her with fan*): Do not call me that!

YOSHIKO: But we are alone.

LADY PURPLE STREAM: The silly gardener is here.

YOSHIKO: What can he do? What can anyone do after I am married to the Prince . . . which I shall be in just a very short time! Now, tell me exactly how the wedding will take place so I may be as composed and gracious as I really am.

LADY PURPLE STREAM: Yes. (*She pulls a scroll out of her sleeve and consults it.*) This is the manner in which all princesses of the Peach Tree Kingdom have been married. You shall come out of the palace with Tashari. She will be holding the royal umbrella over you. The Prince will follow behind you, and the Lord High Arranger behind him. I shall bring up the rear. Yes. Now we take our places in the garden—you there, on the bench (*Points*), and see that you do not fall off it. The Prince sits beside you. (*Points*) The Lord High Arranger sits there, and I sit there. Tashari holds the umbrella over both of you. Then the Lord High Arranger reads the wedding ceremony. It goes like this. (*Opens scroll and reads.*) "Whereas the Prince of the Green Willow Tree Kingdom and the Princess of the Peach Tree Kingdom have been betrothed since infancy, we are met together today to unite the happy couple in marriage . . ." and so forth and so forth and so forth. (*Puts scroll down on bench*)

YOSHIKO: What does *that* mean?

LADY PURPLE STREAM: Nothing. It is simply my way of saying that the ceremony is too long. Let us go to the palace and get ready to receive the Prince. He should be arriving any moment now.

YOSHIKO (*Rising*): Oh, I am so nervous! (*They do not see* PRINCE *pick up scroll. He goes back to work on flowers.*)

LADY PURPLE STREAM: Well, don't be. Nothing can happen now!

YOSHIKO: But what if the Prince should find out *before* the wedding that I am *not* the Princess, but that Tashari is really the Princess?

LADY PURPLE STREAM (*Hitting her with fan*): Will you stop your foolish worrying? You are making *me* nervous. Nothing can happen now, I tell you. The ceremony is due to take place in a few moments. Now, come! (*They go off, and* FUJIOKA *moves back to bench, holding scroll.*)

FUJIOKA (*Looking after them, angrily*): Horrid, conniving women! I knew Tashari was my Princess. I knew it the moment I laid eyes on her. But who will believe me without proof? (*Opens scroll and looks at it*) If there were something here that would put the two of them to the test to find out which girl was a princess. . . . (*Snaps his fingers*) I have it! I'll put in an impossible task for the bride to perform in the ceremony. When Yoshiko cannot perform the task, they will not go on with the ceremony. This will give me time to find evidence of Tashari's royal birth. (*He sits on bench, picks up a stick, and, using berries for "ink," dips point and writes on the scroll. Music is heard.* FUJIOKA *rolls up scroll and places it on the ground. He takes off his mustache and cotton kimono and reveals his elaborately decorated kimono underneath.* TASHARI *rushes into garden and sees* PRINCE. *Music stops.*)

TASHARI: Prince Fujioka! (*Bows low*) Your Highness.

FUJIOKA (*Going to her and helping her up*): Do not bow before me, Princess!

TASHARI (*Rising in alarm*): I know your voice. You are the gardener!

FUJIOKA: Yes, we are the same. I came in disguise to see if the Princess Yoshiko was as mean and shrewish as men say she is . . . then I found you, and immediately knew that you were the Princess, the *real* Princess.

TASHARI: No, no, I am a poor servant, born in the palace. I am maid to the Princess Yoshiko.

FUJIOKA: You are the daughter of the Empress. Yoshiko is Lady Purple Stream's daughter. Lady Purple Stream exchanged her child and you when you were babies in your cradles. The Empress never knew of this, and since she and the Emperor died when you were small, the terrible Lady Purple Stream's secret was safe . . . until today when I heard Yoshiko call Lady Purple Stream "Mother."

TASHARI: No, no, this cannot be true!

FUJIOKA: It *is* true. I heard the two of them admit it. But, alas, I have no real proof, and without that, no one would believe us.

TASHARI: What can we do?

FUJIOKA: I have added an impossible task to the wedding ceremony. Yoshiko must perform it, or the ceremony will not go on. That will give us time to find proof.

TASHARI: I had a picture, a picture that seemed to bring back some memory, but Lady Purple Stream took it from me! Now there is no time to do anything.

FUJIOKA: There will be time. Leave it in my hands. You are my Princess, and I shall be your Prince. (LADY PURPLE STREAM *runs on.*)

LADY PURPLE STREAM: Tashari, you stupid dolt, did you find the scroll with the marriage ceremony? (*Sees* FUJIOKA *and makes a quick bow*) Oh—Your Highness!

FUJIOKA (*Returning bow*): Lady Purple Stream.

LADY PURPLE STREAM: But how did you get out here to the garden?

FUJIOKA (*Ignoring her question*): Is this the document you seek? (*Picks up scroll*)

LADY PURPLE STREAM: Oh, yes. This is the marriage scroll. I must have dropped it. It is time for the wedding. The Arranger is here. He will be so relieved to know you are also ready. Quick, Tashari, get the umbrella. Wait here, Prince, I mean, Your Highness, please wait a moment while I . . . Oh, dear . . . Yoshiko . . . Lord High Arranger. (YOSHIKO *and* LORD HIGH ARRANGER *enter.*)

YOSHIKO: The Prince is here? Oh, my! Your Highness. (*Bows, fusses at hair, smiles.*)

LORD HIGH ARRANGER: So, the eager bridegroom came to the scene of the crime . . . I mean . . . came to the wedding before it happened. I mean . . . Your Highness. (*Bows stiffly over hand of* PRINCE) Well, now. Come, come. Prince, you sit here on the bench. Princess, you sit beside him. (PRINCE *sits.* YOSHIKO *trips over her gown and falls against* PRINCE, *straightens up, laughs nervously, then sits next to him on bench.* LORD HIGH ARRANGER *clears his throat, puts on spectacles that hang around his neck attached to a ribbon, and reaches out his hand.*) The marriage ceremony, please. (LADY PURPLE STREAM *smiles and hands scroll to him nervously. He reads.*) "Whereas the Prince of the Green Willow Tree Kingdom and . . ."

FUJIOKA (*Rising*): Wait. I cannot go on with this ceremony. I do not love this woman. It is Tashari that I love. (*Takes* TASHARI's *hand*) She is the true Princess, don't you see? Not this Yoshiko. Cannot all of you see Tashari's beauty, her gentle ways? She is the Princess. The other one is false! I shall not marry her.

YOSHIKO (*Rising and wailing to* LADY PURPLE STREAM): He has to marry me! You said he did!

LADY PURPLE STREAM: Of course he must! The marriage document is signed. It is legal and unbreakable. The Princess of the Peach Tree Kingdom must marry the Prince of the Green Willow Tree Kingdom. It is all down there in black and white.

LORD HIGH ARRANGER (*Squinting at document*): Yes, indeed, young man. It is a pity. I see what you mean. Tashari is . . . that is . . . (*As* LADY PURPLE STREAM *glares*) I mean . . the Princess must marry the Prince, and Tashari is only a servant.

FUJIOKA: But suppose she is not?

LORD HIGH ARRANGER: Not what?

FUJIOKA: A servant. Suppose Tashari is the real Princess. Suppose Tashari and Yoshiko were mixed in their cradles when they were babies. They were born on the same day, right here in the palace, you know.

LORD HIGH ARRANGER: Dear me, that would be something now, wouldn't it? Now, just imagine that!

LADY PURPLE STREAM (*Indignantly*): I never heard of such

a ridiculous idea. There is nothing to prove it. Get on with the ceremony. The hour grows late.

FUJIOKA: But Tashari is the one I love. I cannot marry someone I do not love.

LADY PURPLE STREAM: Nonsense. People marry without love all the time.

FUJIOKA: But I shall not. I shall marry only my Princess.

LADY PURPLE STREAM: But the Princess is Yoshiko. Lord High Arranger, continue. The poor boy does not know what he is saying. All bridegrooms are nervous at their weddings. Think nothing of it.

LORD HIGH ARRANGER: Sit down, young man. I must proceed.

FUJIOKA: Does the bride have to conform to everything that is in the marriage document?

LORD HIGH ARRANGER: Oh, yes, indeed. Why do you ask?

FUJIOKA: Then let her pass the peach tree test.

LADY PURPLE STREAM: What is that?

YOSHIKO: The peach tree test? What do you mean?

FUJIOKA: She must take a peach seed and plant it. If a peach tree in full bloom springs up from the planting, she is the true Princess, and I shall marry her. It is right there in the document.

LADY PURPLE STREAM: What foolishness is this? (*Snatches the document from the* LORD HIGH ARRANGER)

LORD HIGH ARRANGER: Dear me. I do not remember that.

FUJIOKA: But it is here. I read it just now. (*Takes scroll from* LADY PURPLE STREAM *and hands it to* LORD HIGH ARRANGER, *who reads it carefully.*)

LORD HIGH ARRANGER: You are right. Quite, quite right, young man. Well, where is the peach seed? (FUJIOKA *takes a peach from bowl on table beside bench, opens it, hands pit to the* LORD HIGH ARRANGER *who immediately hands it with a flourish to* YOSHIKO, *along with a trowel left by* TASHARI. *He bows and points toward earth in front of* YOSHIKO.) Plant the seed, my dear, and let us see this great miracle performed.

YOSHIKO (*Looking at trowel and peach pit, bursts into tears*): I can't do it. No one can do it!

FUJIOKA: Then I suggest that the wedding be stopped at once . . . for we must obey the law. Is it not so, Lord High Arranger?

LORD HIGH ARRANGER: Oh, my, yes. Yes, indeed, indeed! Either she plants the seed, or she cannot marry the Prince.

LADY PURPLE STREAM (*Menacingly, to* YOSHIKO): Plant the seed!

YOSHIKO: But nothing will grow.

LADY PURPLE STREAM: Plant it! (YOSHIKO, *looking very unhappy, stoops down, and "plants" peach pit. All stand back to watch, but nothing happens.* YOSHIKO *bursts into tears.*)

YOSHIKO: I told you that nothing would happen.

LADY PURPLE STREAM: Now let Tashari plant it.

FUJIOKA: Why?

LADY PURPLE STREAM: You wish to marry Tashari? Well, you may marry only the real Princess. Is that not so, Lord High Arranger?

LORD HIGH ARRANGER (*Scanning scroll*): Yes, yes, that is so.

LADY PURPLE STREAM (*Handing peach pit and trowel to* TASHARI): Now plant it! Plant it at once!

FUJIOKA: No! No! (*Takes trowel and peach pit from* TASHARI) I wrote it in the marriage document. No one can make such a thing happen. I overheard Yoshiko call Lady Purple Stream "Mother," and I knew she was not the real Princess. That is why I invented this ruse. It won't work!

LADY PURPLE STREAM: It is written in the marriage contract, is it not, Lord High Arranger?

Lord High Arranger: Yes, indeed. (*Looking at scroll*) Right here in black and . . . well, in a sort of crushed berry red, and white.

Lady Purple Stream: Then the one he marries will have to perform such a feat. Is it not so?

Lord High Arranger: Oh, yes. Yes, indeed. The one he marries must be able to show us a peach tree in full bloom after the seed is planted.

Fujioka: What is that? Read it again.

Lord High Arranger: It says that the princess who marries the Prince must plant a seed, then show the Prince a peach tree in full bloom after the seed is planted.

Fujioka (*Handing* Tashari *back the trowel and peach pit*): Then plant it. Plant the seed, my Princess.

Tashari: But . . . but—

Fujioka: You trust me, do you not, dear Princess?

Tashari (*Looking at him lovingly*): Yes, yes, of course I do.

Fujioka: Then plant the seed. (*She stoops and "plants" the seed, as* Yoshiko *did. Immediately* Prince Fujioka *pulls a small ornamental peach tree up from a pot beside the bench and places it over the peach pit. All stare at it in astonishment.*)

Lady Purple Stream: The tree did not grow from the seed.

Yoshiko: It certainly did not. I saw him take the tree and put it there.

Fujioka (*Ignoring them and speaking to* Tashari): Show it to me, Tashari. Pick up the tree and show it to me. (Tashari *obeys, holding tree out to him. He takes it, puts it aside, and holds her hand as he faces* Lord High Arranger.) And so she has obeyed the law. Marry us.

Yoshiko: No, no! The tree did not grow from the seed.

Lord High Arranger: That is true.

FUJIOKA: But it says nothing of *growing* from the seed, does it?

LORD HIGH ARRANGER (*Scanning scroll*): The Princess plants the seed, then shows a tree to her Prince. Yes, yes, that is what it says. It says . . . (*He looks up and sees* LADY PURPLE STREAM *and* YOSHIKO *running out.*) Dear me! Where are they going? Lady Purple Stream, Princess, come back here! There is to be a wedding! Oh, dear . . . Lady Purple Stream. (*Looks after them*)

TASHARI: Oh, dear, they are running away!

FUJIOKA: Let them go, my Princess. We have better things to do. A marriage must be performed. Remember? (*Japanese music is heard, as the curtain falls.*)

THE END

The Great Samurai Sword

A *Kabuki*-style play based on a Japanese folk tale

by Barbara Winther

AUTHOR'S NOTES ON THE KABUKI THEATER

The word "Kabuki" denotes a highly stylized form of drama native to Japan. Originally, the Japanese borrowed a Chinese word compound, *kabu* (*ka,* song; *bu,* dance), and, in the late 16th century used the word *Kabuki* to name a type of dance. The idea developed into musical dramas which are still performed regularly in Japan today. Plays are chosen from a standard list, and are acted, danced, and sung by men in a classic, stylized manner. The costumes and make-up are very elaborate.

THE GREAT SAMURAI SWORD is not from the standard list. However, it is based on a Japanese folk tale, such tales being the source of many *Kabuki* plays. The themes of the faithful wife and the man seeking honor are common in *Kabuki*.

Japanese actors spend years learning the true *Kabuki* style of acting, but a feeling for it can be developed in a short time. A few hints are: Exaggerate gestures; make the movements and speeches definite and related; hold a pose after the more important speeches.

Characters

NAOTO, *a young Samurai warrior*
SUDO, *his father*
SAGAMI, *his mother*
GRANDMOTHER
COUSIN
OSADA, *a lovely lady*
KASAI, *her father*
KANAMI, *her mother*
FOUR SINGERS
MUSICIANS

SETTING: *A large Japanese screen stands, up center, covered with a painting of a lake, Mount Fuji, and houses to right and left of lake. In front of the screen is a long, narrow platform. Down left are four large pillows arranged in a row.*

AT RISE: FOUR SINGERS *enter right, moving stiffly, and cross to pillows. They sit cross-legged, staring straight ahead.* MUSICIANS *enter left in a similar manner, carrying their instruments, and sit cross-legged on the platform. Music begins.*

SINGERS: In the days of the third shogun* lived Naoto, a young Samurai.

1ST SINGER: For ten generations,

2ND SINGER: His people taught the sword.

SINGERS: Most honorable family of Sendai City. (SUDO, SAGAMI, GRANDMOTHER *and* COUSIN *enter and kneel in a half circle.*)

SUDO: Our son, Naoto, has proven himself an excellent warrior. (*Folds arms proudly*)

---

* 1623–1651 (shoguns were military rulers of Japan).

GRANDMOTHER (*Nodding sleepily*): True.

COUSIN: He now teaches the art of fencing with the sword. (*Pulls out sword*)

GRANDMOTHER (*Nodding*): True.

SUDO: His annual income is three thousand bushels of rice. (*Pantomimes eating with chopsticks*)

GRANDMOTHER: True.

SAGAMI (*Wiggling fingers, moving hands back and forth*): But, have you not noticed restlessness in our son?

GRANDMOTHER: True.

SUDO: Naoto needs a wife. (*Slaps one hand on floor*) That would settle him down. (*Slaps other hand on floor*)

GRANDMOTHER: True.

SUDO: Honorable Grandmother has only one word. (*Holds one finger up*) Either she needs dictionary or long nap.

GRANDMOTHER (*Still nodding*): True. (*Falls asleep, snoring*)

SUDO (*Looking upward*): Ah, so! Grandmother sleeps like owl. (*Spreads arms*) Rest of family must think like fox.

SAGAMI (*Rising*): There is a lovely daughter of the Tokugawa house. (*Dances*)

COUSIN (*Jumping up to join her*): Ah, she is charming. Osada is her name.

SAGAMI: Her mind (*Points to head*) works well. She is quick (*Raises one hand*) and clever (*Raises other hand*) in everything she does.

COUSIN (*Leaping around*): Her brothers have taught her the use of the sword and spear. (*Fences imaginary enemy, grunting and leaping wildly*)

GRANDMOTHER (*Waking suddenly*): The enemy attacks! (*Looks at* COUSIN) What is the matter, Cousin? Do you have fleas?

SUDO: Hm-m-m. (*Scratches chin*) I did not call meeting for purpose of cousin-leaping about or owl-snoring and making bad jokes.

COUSIN (*Quickly returning to kneeling position*): Oh, so sorry!

SUDO (*Rising*): I shall go to House of Tokugawa and look at this young lady called Osada. If she is all you say, then perhaps a marriage can be arranged. (*Exits left, followed by* SAGAMI, COUSIN, *and* GRANDMOTHER)

SINGERS: The next afternoon in the hour of the Ram. (MUSICIAN *strikes gong twice.*)

OSADA (*Entering right with dainty, shuffling steps, smiling*): I am Osada. My elders have told me that I will soon marry the handsome Naoto. (*Raises hands to cheeks*) It makes my face feel as warm as the burning incense. (*Puts hands on heart*) It makes my heart beat as the dragonfly's wings. I shall go to our garden and dance about the plum trees, for I am filled with joy. (*Exits right, dancing*)

NAOTO (*Entering left with large strides, frowning*): I am Naoto. My elders have told me that I will soon marry the lovely Osada. (*Points to feet*) It makes my feet feel cold as an icicle. (*Points to hair*) It makes my hair stand up as the porcupine quills. I shall go to the teahouses to play and throw my money about, for I do not wish to settle down.

SINGERS: Away went Naoto, tossing his money, forgetting his sword. (NAOTO *leaps around, tossing arms in air, then exits left.*)

1ST SINGER: Alas, how his relatives worried! (SUDO, SAGAMI, COUSIN *and* GRANDMOTHER *enter left, run around in a circle making worried gestures, and exit left.*)

3RD SINGER: How his friends groaned! (*Loud groans from offstage.*)

2ND SINGER: What a great insult to Osada's family! (KASAI *and* KANAMI *enter right, run around in a circle making angry gestures, and exit right.*)

4TH SINGER: Then, as the young silver moon hid behind

the silent pines—(KASAI *and* KANAMI *enter right as* SUDO, SAGAMI, COUSIN *and* GRANDMOTHER *enter left. They bow to each other, then face audience.*)

KASAI: We come to tell you we do not like the life your Naoto lives.

KANAMI: He shows no interest in our daughter, Osada.

KASAI: She sits sadly under our plum trees, her tears flowing waterfalls.

KANAMI: Your son must have butterflies in his head. (*Taps head*)

KASAI: Therefore, we say, unless Naoto changes his ways by the time the next moon touches the sides of Mount Fuji (*Points to mountain on screen*), we cancel agreement of marriage. (*Makes chopping motion*)

SUDO (*Rubbing hands nervously*): Please accept humble apologies.

SAGAMI: Naoto is not very old in his manners.

COUSIN: It is a bad time. Even the spiders are restless these days.

SUDO: We shall speak to our son and correct his fluttering ways.

GRANDMOTHER (*Aside to* SUDO): What has Naoto done?

SUDO *and* SAGAMI (*Putting fingers to lips*): Sh-h-h!

GRANDMOTHER (*Aside*): Sh-h-h, yourselves. Where is respect for ancient grandmother? (*Points to self*) I might as well sleep.

SUDO (*Touching forehead, bowing to* GRANDMOTHER): Honorable Grandmother, we are trying to get son married, but son would rather be butterfly.

GRANDMOTHER (*Shrugging*): Butterfly? Ah, so! (*All bow to each other, then* KASAI *and* KANAMI *exit right.*)

SUDO (*Loudly*): Cousin, bring Naoto here.

COUSIN (*Speaking quickly and dancing around*): This is greatly disturbing. I have not been able to eat my noodles. My bird's nest soup tastes like straw, and my shark fins have lost their flavor. Naoto must be punished for his idleness. He does not practice his sword anymore. He thinks because of his money and good name that he is a great man. Oh, the sadness of—

SUDO (*Interrupting*): I did not ask for speech from Honorable Cousin. Where is my son?

COUSIN (*Bowing*): Oh, please excuse. (*Exits left, re-entering with* NAOTO, *who bows to* SUDO.)

SUDO (*Loudly*): Naoto, open your eyes and see what you do. (*Points to* NAOTO'S *feet*) You set your sandals in the mud. (*Waving arms*) You play all day and all night without a serious thought. You bring ruin upon our good name. (*Shakes his fist*) You disgrace your forefathers.

GRANDMOTHER (*Shaking her finger at* NAOTO): Shame on you, butterfly!

SUDO: Naoto, we beg you, give up your childish actions, marry the lovely Osada, and become a fine husband (*Gestures widely*), bringing honor to your family.

GRANDMOTHER (*Shaking her finger*): Butterflies do not live long lives.

NAOTO (*Humbly*): Forgive me for the unhappiness I have caused you. Oh, Father, you fill me with shame.

GRANDMOTHER (*Shaking her finger*): Butterflies may be pretty, but they come from *worms!*

SUDO: Honorable Grandmother, now is not time for butterfly lessons. Naoto, we forgive you.

NAOTO: I swear by my great ancestors that I shall follow wiser paths. (*Points left, then exits with great strides.* SUDO, SAGAMI, COUSIN *and* GRANDMOTHER *clasp their hands, sigh with relief, and exit left.*)

SINGERS: Naoto *did* change his life . . . (*Pause*) for awhile.

1ST SINGER: Blow, blow the winter winds.

2ND SINGER: The nightingale has gone away.

3RD SINGER: The temple wears a cap of snow.

4TH SINGER: Beside the fire, Osada waits for spring. (OSADA *enters right and dances as if moving around fire, warming hands.* KASAI *and* KANAMI *enter right.*)

KANAMI: The marriage gifts have been exchanged. (*Spreads arms*)

KASAI: In the time of the cherry blossoms (*Makes tree shape*), our daughter, Osada (*Points to her*), marries the young Samurai (*Draws imaginary sword*), Naoto.

SINGERS: From the tall bamboo the cuckoo calls,

1ST SINGER: To tell us spring is here.

2ND SINGER: And by the lake the cherry trees

SINGERS: Are bursting clouds of pink.

KASAI: Go to your husband's house, Osada. (*Points off left*)

OSADA (*Bowing*): My heart is full of gladness. My feet will fly on the wings of the hummingbird. (*Exits left, running lightly.* KASAI *and* KANAMI *exit right.*)

1ST SINGER: The summer locusts came to sing their song.

2ND SINGER: Poppies lit the fields with glowing light.

3RD SINGER: Then autumn winds gave color to the leaves,

4TH SINGER: Waving their arms through fields of yellow rice.

OSADA (*Entering left, shuffling sadly*): Oya-oya! My husband has returned to his unhealthy ways. (*Stands at center*)

NAOTO (*Entering left, cheerfully leaping about*): I have forgotten what my family told me. It is fun to lose my money here and there. I waste my time, singing in the streets. Ho, what a jolly time I have. (*Continues leaping*)

OSADA (*With her arms outstretched*): Dear husband, will you not come home and stop your running?

NAOTO: All of my money is gone. I shall mortgage my rice income for a half year in advance. (*Continues leaping*)

OSADA (*With arms outstretched*): Dear husband, will you not come home?

NAOTO: I need more money. I shall sell our furniture. (*Continues leaping*)

OSADA: Dear husband! (*Puts her hands over her face.*)

NAOTO: Osada, give me your wedding robes and your jewels. I must sell them to pay these debts. (*Continues leaping*)

OSADA: Oya-oya! (*Sinks to her knees*)

NAOTO: Osada, go to your father and ask him for a loan of two hundred yen. Do not tell him why you need this money. My luck will soon change. I shall pay him back before the year is gone.

OSADA: I go, but it does not make me happy to do so. (*Exits right, shuffling sadly.* NAOTO *exits left, leaping gaily.*)

SINGERS: The House of Tokugawa heard many rumors. (KASAI *and* KANAMI *enter right, with hands to ears, shake heads sadly, and exit right.*)

1ST SINGER: Yet, Osada's father trusted his daughter's wisdom.

2ND SINGER: He asked no questions.

3RD SINGER: But he wondered much.

KASAI (*Entering right, stroking beard*): My daughter has come to visit. (*Gestures for her to enter*)

OSADA (*Entering right and falling to her knees before him*): Oh, Honorable Parent, I come to ask a great favor.

KASAI: Speak, little flower.

OSADA: I know of a Samurai sword (*Draws imaginary sword*) which you have locked up (*Twists fingers as if locking*) in a special room. It was worn by your grandfather.

KASAI: Indeed, it is my dearest treasure. (*Puts hands on chest*)

OSADA (*Holding out arms to him*): Give me that great

sword, Father. (KASAI *strokes his beard, walks away, returns, and strokes his beard again*)

KASAI: I shall give it to you, daughter. (*Exits right, followed by* OSADA)

SINGERS: How beautiful was the sword!

3RD SINGER: A long, curved blade with sharpest edge.

4TH SINGER: A handle carved and set with precious stones.

SINGERS: The Great Samurai Sword! The Great Samurai Sword! (NAOTO *enters left and* OSADA *enters right, carrying sword*)

NAOTO: Where is the money, Osada?

OSADA: I was too full of shame to ask for it without a reason, so instead I asked my father for this valuable sword. I told him that I wanted it to practice fencing with you, as I once did with my brothers.

NAOTO (*Looking at sword*): I can see that this sword is worth much. It should bring a good price.

OSADA: You shall have it, dear husband. However, there is a condition. I may give the sword only to one who defeats me fairly with it.

NAOTO (*Smiling*): Ho, ho! Let us put on fencing gear, and I will show you my fine skill as a swordsman.

OSADA: My skill is only that of a woman, but my brothers taught me something. For the sake of honor, I must fence my best.

NAOTO (*Laughing*): Of course! Quickly now, for I wish to sell the sword tonight. (*He exits left, and* OSADA *exits right. They re-enter wearing masks and chest armor, carrying swords. They fence in a stylized, dancing manner. Finally, with a blow,* OSADA *knocks the sword from* NAOTO's *hand.* NAOTO *is shocked and shamed. In a rage, he picks up his sword and exits left, slashing the air, groaning, and making faces.* OSADA *removes her mask, smiles, and exits right in a dainty, shuffling manner.*)

SINGERS: For five days Naoto lived in the teahouses,

1ST SINGER: Trying to forget his shameful defeat.

2ND SINGER: At last he gathered himself up,

SINGERS: To take a serious look at his life.

NAOTO (*Entering left sadly, then facing audience*): Oh, what a fool I am. Before you stands a bold, brave Samurai, who receives three thousand bushels of rice each year. My father, my father's father, and my many, many, fathers' fathers were excellent swordsmen. I, too, was once good. But, look at me. I have wasted away my money and lost my skill at fencing. My own wife defeated me. (*Groans and makes a face*) I shall go away to the greatest fencing master in the city of Tokyo, and there I shall labor hard and learn much. (*Points right and exits with great energy.*)

OSADA (*Entering right, looking back and pointing*): There goes my husband. While he is gone, I shall live simply and help pay back his debts. (*Exits left*)

SINGERS: Naoto studied hard for five years.

1ST SINGER: He no longer played in teahouses.

2ND SINGER: He no longer threw out his money.

3RD SINGER: He listened to the wisdom of great men.

4TH SINGER: He practiced with his sword every day.

NAOTO (*Entering right*): Ho, Osada, my little wife, I have returned.

OSADA (*Entering left, carrying sword in both hands, and bowing to* NAOTO): Welcome home, Naoto. I have missed you. Time has crawled on the snail's back.

NAOTO: Forgive me, Osada. I have not treated you well. I believe that now you will find me a different man. Shall we have another fencing match for your father's sword?

OSADA (*Kneeling, holding sword out*): Never again, my husband, for now I *know* you would win. The sword is yours. Sell it if you wish.

NAOTO (*Taking sword*): Rise, my wise little wife. Return this great sword to your father and tell him that it has served its purpose and is no longer needed.

OSADA (*Rising and smiling, taking sword*): Most excellent husband, I shall always obey your commands. (*Exits right.* NAOTO *exits left.*)

1ST SINGER: Come to the celebration.

2ND SINGER: A thousand lanterns light the gardens.

3RD SINGER: All night long the temple bells ring. (MUSICIAN *rings bells.*)

SINGERS: Naoto, Naoto, Naoto returns with honor. (KASAI *and* KANAMI *enter right and* SUDO, SAGAMI, COUSIN *and* GRANDMOTHER *enter left. All bow to each other and face audience.* NAOTO *enters left, and* OSADA *enters right. They meet in center between the others, bow to each other, and face audience.*)

ALL: May the fireflies light your way to good fortune. (SINGERS *sing a Japanese or other suitable song; others dance. All bow.* SUDO, SAGAMI, COUSIN *and* GRAND-MOTHER *exit left, as* KASAI *and* KANAMI *exit right.* NAOTO *and* OSADA *circle the stage and exit left.* SINGERS *and* MUSICIANS *exit left. Curtain.*)

THE END

A Spouse for Susie Mouse

A Korean folk tale

by Faye E. Head

Characters

JUNIOR MOUSE	SUN
MAMA MOUSE	CLOUD
PAPA MOUSE	WIND
SUSIE MOUSE	STATUE

SETTING: *An open field near a small park. A large rock is at left, and a screen at right conceals Statue.*

AT RISE: JUNIOR MOUSE *enters and speaks to audience.*

JUNIOR: Hi! I'm a mouse. Junior Mouse. Really, my name is Jonathan Henry Jones Mouse, but everyone calls me Junior. That's because it's a short name and I'm a short mouse.

MAMA (*Offstage, calling*): Junior, Junior, where are you?

JUNIOR: Sh-h-h-h! That's my mother. Don't tell her I'm here. She's always calling me to do something, and then when I don't come she gets my sister to come and look for me. I hate sisters! I don't really—but *my* sister is so silly. She wants to get married. She's always combing her whiskers and putting ribbons on her ears—

MAMA (*Offstage*): Junior! Don't you hear me calling you?

317

JUNIOR: Uh-oh. I'd better hide. (*He ducks behind rock.* MAMA *and* PAPA MOUSE *enter, dressed for a journey.*)

PAPA: Junior, don't you hear your mother? Come here this instant.

MAMA: Where can he be? That mouse is never around when you want him.

PAPA: We can't wait much longer. If we are going to make the journey today we must leave soon. (SUSIE MOUSE *enters.*) Susie, there you are. Did you find your brother?

SUSIE: No, Papa. I looked in the tall grass and in the farmer's corn shed, but I didn't find him.

PAPA: Then we'll just have to go without him.

MAMA: I can't do that. (*Looks around*) I'll worry about him. (*Seeing* JUNIOR *behind rock*) Junior, you naughty mouse. Come here. How long have you been hiding there?

JUNIOR: Only a minute or two, honest.

PAPA: Well, there isn't time to punish him now. We must hurry.

SUSIE: Papa, why do we have to make the trip today, on my birthday?

PAPA: Because it *is* your birthday.

MAMA: It is time we found you a proper husband.

SUSIE: But I don't want a proper husband. I mean—

JUNIOR (*Chanting*): Susie has a mouse friend. Susie has a mouse friend!

SUSIE: You stop that.

JUNIOR: Susie loves Walter Mouse! Susie loves Walter Mouse!

MAMA: Junior, don't tease your sister.

PAPA: Quiet, Junior. I don't intend for my daughter to marry a common, ordinary mouse. When you were born, Susie, I vowed that one day you would have the most powerful husband in the world. Now it is time to go find him.

SUSIE: But, Papa—

MAMA: Susie, don't argue with your father. Whatever he says is right.

SUSIE: But, Mama—

MAMA: Sh-h-h-h-h.

JUNIOR: Where do we go first, Papa?

PAPA: To see the Sun.

JUNIOR: The real Sun?

PAPA: Yes, the real Sun.

SUSIE: But, why?

PAPA: The Sun shines and makes things grow, so I'm sure he must be the most powerful thing in the world. Come, let us walk this way. (*They begin to walk around stage. As time passes, their steps become slower.*)

SUSIE: I'm tired, Papa.

JUNIOR: And it's hot.

PAPA: Naturally it is hot. We are near the castle of the Sun.

MAMA: Can't we rest a bit?

PAPA: We had better not. We will be there soon. (*Pointing off*) Look!

MAMA: What is it? (SUN *enters.*)

PAPA: It is the Sun.

SUSIE: He's so bright!

JUNIOR: He hurts my eyes!

MAMA: Don't look directly at him. (*All shade their eyes.*)

PAPA: Bow before him. (*All bow.*)

SUN: What is this? Who are you?

PAPA: We are mice from down in the valley.

SUN: What are you doing in my kingdom?

PAPA: Pardon us for intruding, Mr. Sun. You see, our daughter has grown up and it is time she was married. We are looking for the most powerful person in the world to ask him to be her husband.

SUN: I don't understand.

PAPA: I vowed that she would marry the most powerful person in the world. By your high position and great power you would seem to be the most powerful of all. So we have come to invite you to be her bridegroom.

SUN: That is a great honor. It may seem to you that I am the most powerful, but, alas, it is not so. Mr. Cloud is more powerful than I, for he can cover me and keep my light from shining. I thank you for the honor of your request, but I recommend you ask Mr. Cloud.

PAPA: Oh. Well, thank you, Mr. Sun.

SUN: No trouble at all. Now I must go and shine on the other side of the world. It is almost morning there. Goodbye. (*Exits*)

ALL: Goodbye.

MAMA: Do you think he is right?

PAPA: I don't know.

SUSIE: I certainly couldn't marry him. He's too bright.

JUNIOR: And too hot!

PAPA: Come, let us go on. We will go to see Mr. Cloud. (*They begin to walk around stage. It begins to get dark.*)

MAMA: It's getting dark.

SUSIE: I'm frightened.

JUNIOR: You're a scaredy mouse!

SUSIE: I am not—

MAMA: Now, children. (CLOUD *enters.*)

JUNIOR: What's that?

PAPA: What?

SUSIE: I see it! That dark shape!

PAPA: Why, it's Mr. Cloud.

CLOUD: Who is calling my name?

PAPA: It is I. Mr. Mouse.

CLOUD: What do you want in my kingdom?

PAPA: Well, Mr. Cloud, our daughter has grown up and it is time she was married. We wish to invite you, the most powerful person in the world, to be her husband, for you can cover the face of the Sun and keep him from shining.

CLOUD: Yes, I can cover the face of the Sun, yet I am not the most powerful. Mr. Wind blows me away whether I wish to go or not. He is far more powerful than I. I recommend him to you.

MAMA: Are you sure? She's a lovely mouse.

CLOUD: I'm sure she is, and I thank you, but you want Mr. Wind.

PAPA: Very well. Where can we find him?

CLOUD: I don't know. At the—(*Suddenly staggers backward as if being blown away.*) Help! Here he comes. (*To* WIND, *who has just entered.*) I wish you wouldn't do that—(*He is blown offstage.*)

WIND (*Laughing*): You should be used to it by now. Whew! Who are you? (*Each time he begins a sentence,* WIND *almost blows mouse family down.*)

PAPA: I'm Mr. Mouse, and these are my wife and my son and my daughter.

MAMA: And we were looking for you.

WIND: Well— what—

JUNIOR (*Backing away as if blown*): Help!

SUSIE: Here, Junior, give me your hand.

WIND: I'm sorry. I forget my own strength. I'll try not to blow so hard. I can't help it, I'm so powerful.

PAPA: That's what we came to see you about.

WIND: What? (*They almost fall.*) I forgot. (*Whispering*) What do you mean?

PAPA: Our daughter has grown up and it is time she was married. We wish to invite the most powerful person in the world to be her husband, so we have come to welcome you as her bridegroom, for you can blow Mr. Cloud away whether he wishes to go or not.

JUNIOR: And us, too.

WIND: I appreciate your kind offer. I am indeed very

powerful, but there is one more powerful than I. It is the stone statue in the park. However hard I blow I cannot blow him away. I cannot even blow his hat off his head. He is more powerful than my strongest puff. I recommend him to you.

PAPA: Thank you. We will try.

WIND: Good. And goodbye! (*Almost blowing them down*) You'd better go now. I'm afraid I will blow you right off the mountain. Wait! Do you know where the statue is?

PAPA: Yes.

MAMA: It's a long walk down to the park in the valley.

JUNIOR: I'm tired.

WIND: All right. If you will hold hands very tightly, I will blow you down the mountain into the valley.

SUSIE: I'm afraid.

JUNIOR: I'm not.

WIND: I will be careful.

PAPA: We trust you. Everyone hold tightly. (*They hold hands*) All right, blow, Mr. Wind. (*He puffs and all run quickly with eyes closed and land with a bump. WIND exits. Meanwhile, a stagehand removes screen at right, revealing STATUE.*)

SUSIE: Oh-h-h-h!

MAMA: Oh, dear!

JUNIOR: That was fun. Look, what's that? (*Points to STATUE*)

PAPA: That is the great statue.

MAMA: He is very big, isn't he?

PAPA: Yes, I think you're right. I'm sure the statue must be the most powerful husband for you.

SUSIE (*Muttering*): Well, I still like Walter better.

MAMA: Now, Susie, you must obey your father.

PAPA: Come, let us bow before he gets angry. (*All bow.*)

STATUE: What do you want here in my park?

PAPA: Excuse us for disturbing you. My daughter is old enough to marry and we invite you to be her bridegroom since you are the most powerful of all.

STATUE: I see. I thank you for your kind offer. But there is one yet more powerful than I.

MAMA: There can't be!

SUSIE: We went to the Sun—the Cloud—

JUNIOR: And the Wind—

PAPA: Who can be more powerful than the all-powerful statue in the park?

STATUE: Who can be more powerful than the all-powerful statue in the park? The mice who live beneath my feet.

ALL: What?

STATUE: Yes. They keep nibbling at the dirt under my feet; one day they will undermine me completely and I will fall.

MAMA: The mice are more powerful?

STATUE: Yes, Mrs. Mouse. I am at the mercy of the mice. Find a good young mouse and let your daughter marry him.

SUSIE: Walter is a very strong good mouse!

PAPA: Thank you, Mr. Statue. We will take your advice. Come—let us go home.

MAMA: I'd never thought of it like that. Walter is very nice.

PAPA: If all these powerful people recommend him, Susie, then we must let you marry him.

SUSIE: Thank you, Papa. (*She exits with* MAMA *and* PAPA.)

JUNIOR (*To audience*): Sometimes your family can really get on your nerves! (*Curtain.*)

THE END

Pepe and the Cornfield Bandit

A fable of old Mexico

by Claire Boiko

Characters

SEÑOR GRANJERO   SAPO, *the toad*
JUAN   IXLANDA, *the enchanted bird*
PEDRO   CHORUS, *six boys and girls*
PEPE   DANCERS

TIME: *Many years ago.*

SETTING: *A hacienda in Mexico.*

BEFORE RISE: CHORUS, *wearing Mexican costumes, enter in front of curtains. The boys carry bongo drums, the girls, maracas.*

CHORUS: Olé! Olé! Olé! (*They beat the drums and shake the maracas. Girls sit down right, on the apron. Boys kneel behind them.*)
Many, many years ago in Old Mexico,
Where the mountains are taller than anywhere else,
And the skies are bluer than anywhere else . . .

1ST BOY (*Fanning himself*): And the sun is hotter than anywhere else . . .

CHORUS: There was a rich farmer.

*   *   *

AT RISE: *The curtains open, disclosing a backdrop of purple mountains, cactus, and a straw-thatched cottage. Down center is a well, behind which hides* SAPO, *the toad. Down left are three rows of corn. Only two rows have tassels. The three brothers are in front of the cottage.* JUAN, *the eldest brother, sits with his sombrero pulled down over his eyes.* PEDRO *stands next to him, combing his drooping mustache as he gazes admiringly at himself in a hand mirror.* PEPE, *the youngest brother, holds a broom.*

SEÑOR GRANJERO (*Entering from up right*): Buenas dias.

CHORUS: This rich farmer was called Señor Granjero.

1ST BOY: Ah, but he was rich.

1ST GIRL: He had two fat oxen.

2ND GIRL: He had a house with a roof.

3RD GIRL: And windows in the front and windows in the back.

2ND BOY: But best of all, he had a cornfield full of corn.

CHORUS: Corn for tortillas. Corn for tostadas. Corn for tamales. Corn for enchiladas. Ah, but he was rich!

3RD BOY: He also had three sons. First, there was Juan Ramon Luiz Estaban.

SEÑOR GRANJERO: Wake up, Juan. (JUAN *pulls sombrero further down.*)

CHORUS: Wake up, Juan. (*He yawns.*)

SEÑOR GRANJERO: He is a little lazy. But he is a good boy.

2ND BOY: Next, there was Pedro Carlo José Francisco.

SEÑOR GRANJERO (*As* PEDRO *continues to admire his mustache*): That's enough, Pedro. You are handsome enough. After all—do you not take after me?

CHORUS: That's enough, Pedro. (PEDRO *continues to stroke his mustache.*)

SEÑOR GRANJERO: He is a little vain. But he is a good boy.

1ST BOY: And then there was Pepe. Just—Pepe.

CHORUS: Ah, Pepe.

SEÑOR GRANJERO: Poor Pepe. I could not think of one more name for Pepe. What can I tell you about my youngest son? He is a very good boy. That's all. (PEPE *sweeps the floor*)

1ST BOY (*As* SEÑOR GRANJERO *crosses down left, examining corn*): One fine Mexican day, Señor Granjero visited his cornfields. The first row of corn was full of fat, waving corn tassels.

SEÑOR GRANJERO: *Magnifico!*

CHORUS: The second row was full of fat, waving corn tassels.

SEÑOR GRANJERO: *Magnifico!*

CHORUS: But the third row had not one single fat, waving corn tassel. Not one.

SEÑOR GRANJERO: Oh! A corn-snatcher! A bandit! (*He runs across stage to his sons.* JUAN *stands up.* PEPE *puts down his broom.*) My sons, listen.

SONS: We hear you, Father.

SEÑOR GRANJERO: A bandit has stolen the corn from the cornfield. You must be good sons and bring me that bandit. Whichever one of you brings me the corn-snatcher—he shall have all my riches.

PEPE (*Eagerly*): I don't want all your riches, my father. But I will go and get the bandit.

JUAN: You? You are only the third son. I am the first son. I will go, my father. Next week. (*He yawns.*)

SEÑOR GRANJERO: Next week there will be no corn at all. You will go tonight.

JUAN: Tomorrow night. (*He yawns again.*)

SEÑOR GRANJERO: Tonight! (*He hands* JUAN *his gun.*)

JUAN: *Si. Si.* Tonight.

CHORUS: When the sun went down behind the mountains, it was night. (SEÑOR GRANJERO *and his sons sit cross-*

legged up center, putting their heads in their hands.)

1ST BOY: It was a wonderful, cool Mexican night.

1ST GIRL: There were more stars crowding the sky than anywhere else. (JUAN *stands, crosses left.*)

3RD BOY: Juan walked a little way. Then he rested. (*He sits.*)

2ND GIRL: He walked a little way more. Then he rested.

JUAN (*Crossing down to well, but sitting on the way*): What a long walk. I'll just rest myself, here by the well. (*He begins to nod.* SAPO, *the toad, hops out from behind well. Short drum roll is heard.*)

SAPO: Wake up! Wake up!

JUAN (*Sitting up*): Ay-yi-yi! An ugly old toad. Vamoose! Get away!

SAPO: Close your eyes if you don't like what you see. But listen. I may be an ugly old toad, but I can help you.

JUAN (*Hitting him with his sombrero*): Go away. Go back in the well where nobody can see you. Vamoose!

SAPO: Very well. But you are making a big mistake. (*He hops back behind well.* JUAN *lies down and sleeps.*)

2ND BOY: When the sun came up from behind the mountains, it was another fine Mexican day. Who should visit the well but Juan's father, and Juan's brothers. (SEÑOR GRANJERO, PEDRO *and* PEPE *cross to well, standing with arms folded, shaking their heads at* JUAN.)

ALL THREE: Wake up, Juan.

CHORUS: Wake up, Juan. (JUAN *wakes with a start, looking foolish.*)

JUAN: *Buenas dias,* my father. *Buenas dias,* my brothers.

SEÑOR GRANJERO: Did you catch the bandit?

JUAN: The bandit? Ah—he was quick as a jaguar and clever as a monkey. How I wrestled with him! But, alas, I did not catch him.

PEDRO: Ha! All Juan has caught is forty winks.

PEPE: Please, my father, let me try this time.

PEDRO: You? Keep your place, little brother. You know very well it is my turn. (*To* JUAN) Give me the gun, you bandit-bumbler. (JUAN *gives him the gun.*)

SEÑOR GRANJERO: Good luck, my son.

PEDRO: I do not need luck, my father. I have brains. Brains will catch the thief. (SEÑOR GRANJERO, JUAN *and* PEPE *return upstage. They again seat themselves, putting their heads on their arms.*)

CHORUS: Again, the sun went down behind the mountain. It was a more beautiful night than the last. That is the way it is—in Mexico! (PEDRO, *pointing his gun here and there, nervously, guards the corn.*)

PEDRO: Nothing here. Nothing there. Well, I'm thirsty. I'll have a drink. (*He bends over the well, scooping with his hand.* SAPO *pops up on the other side of the well. Short drum roll is heard.*)

SAPO: Good evening, friend.

PEDRO: Ugh! A toad. An ugly old toad.

SAPO: I was afraid you'd say that. Well, as I always say, if you don't like what you see, close your eyes. But listen to me. I can help you.

PEDRO: Ha! You don't fool me. I have too many brains. I know that toads don't talk.

SAPO: They don't? Then who is speaking to you, may I ask?

PEDRO: Nobody. It's all in my mind. Go away now, and don't pretend to talk to me.

SAPO: Very well. But you are making a big mistake. (*He hops behind well.* PEDRO, *with his gun ready, crosses to cornfield. He kneels, then cocks his ear. Sound of maracas, shaken softly, is heard.*)

PEDRO: I hear wings. What can it be? (IXLANDA, *dressed as an enchanted bird, dances in from down left. She flutters back and forth.*) A bird! More beautiful than the

quetzal. (IXLANDA *takes an ear of corn*.) Oh, no you
don't. Beautiful or not—I'll shoot you. (*He takes aim,
and fires. Sound of drum beat is heard.* IXLANDA *laughs,
and tosses him a feather, fluttering off left.* PEDRO *runs
upstage to show his father and brothers*.) The bandit!
I've shot the bandit! (*All wake up*.)

SEÑOR GRANJERO: Where is the bandit? Show me!

PEDRO: Here. (*He holds out feather*.)

JUAN: That's not a bandit. That's a feather.

SEÑOR GRANJERO: Is this all you have to show for yourself?

PEDRO (*Sulking*): Isn't it enough? I risked my very life for
this feather. The bandit was an eagle—tall as a yucca
tree. He sounded like thunder as he beat his wings.

SEÑOR GRANJERO: Why, the bandit won't even miss that
feather. He will come back again and again, unless someone catches him.

PEPE: Please, my father, let me go. It is my turn now.

JUAN: You? You are too little. What could you do?

PEDRO: You? You have no brains. I'll bet you even think
toads can talk, eh Juan?

JUAN: Toads talk? Never.

BOTH: Never.

SEÑOR GRANJERO: Very well, little Pepe. Go and try your
luck. (PEDRO *gives the gun to* PEPE. SEÑOR GRANJERO
*joins them as they cross upstage, sitting down with their
heads on their arms as before.* PEPE *crosses to the well*.)

CHORUS: Once again, the sun went down behind the mountains.

2ND GIRL: It was night. The third night.

3RD GIRL: The third night is always the magical night.

2ND BOY: Especially in Mexico.

PEPE: Ah, the old well. It is as good a place as any to eat
my tortilla. (*He takes a tortilla from inside his sombrero.
Sound of short drum roll.* SAPO *hops out from behind
well*.)

SAPO: Good evening, friend.

PEPE (*Politely*): Good evening, Señor Toad.

SAPO: Señor Toad? How polite. Aren't you going to tell me how ugly I am, as your brothers did?

PEPE (*Looking closely*): I don't think you're ugly. You should see some of the lizards I've caught.

SAPO: Really? How kind. You're much kinder than your brothers.

PEPE: Would you like to share my tortilla, Señor—

SAPO: Señor Sapo. Nobody ever asked my name before. Yes, I'll have a bite of your tortilla. (*He munches.*) Do you believe I can talk?

PEPE: Of course. I hear you with my ears.

SAPO: Quite right. What would you say if I offered to help you catch the bandit?

PEPE: I'd say, *si, si*. You can't have too much help.

SAPO: Wise boy. Now, do as I ask you. Bend over the well.

PEPE (*Leaning over well*): Like this?

SAPO: Quite right. What do you see?

PEPE: The stars in the sky reflected in the well.

SAPO: What else?

PEPE: A gleaming white stone far beneath the water.

SAPO: That white stone is magic. It will give you three wishes.

PEPE: Three wishes? Why not? Wish number one. I wish that I may catch the bandit who carries off the corn each night. Wish number two. I wish that I may marry a beautiful wife. Wish number three. I've never seen a real fiesta. I wish that I might see a fiesta when I return home.

SAPO: Let's be off now. To the cornfield! (*They cross down left.* PEPE *keeps his gun ready. Sound of maracas shaken softly is heard.*)

PEPE: Listen. I hear wings. (IXLANDA *enters down left. She flutters beside a cornstalk.* PEPE *raises his gun.*)

SAPO: No—no. Don't shoot. Don't shoot or you will lose your first two wishes. (PEPE *puts his gun down.* SAPO *begins to croak.*) Ker-rivet. Ker-rivet. Enchanted bird who comes in the night. Stop, I pray you. Stop in your flight. (IXLANDA *remains motionless, arms outstretched.*)

PEPE: I've caught the bandit bird. My first wish came true.

SAPO: Of course. Now for wish number two. (*He croaks again.*) Ker-rivet. Ker-rivet. Enchanted bird, who comes from afar. Show us, I pray, who you really are. (*Sound of maracas being shaken.* IXLANDA *takes off her helmet. She shakes out her long hair.*)

PEPE: A bird with long hair! (IXLANDA *takes off her feathered cloak. She is dressed in the costume of an Aztec princess.*) Why—there is a girl inside that bird.

IXLANDA: I am Ixlanda. A thousand years ago, a wicked sorcerer changed me into a bird. Please forgive me. I only took your corn because I was starving. (*She hands* PEPE *the ear of corn.*)

PEPE: No, no. Please. You take it, Señorita Princess.

SAPO: Here. I'll take it. (*He takes corn.*) Well, go on— ask her to marry you. After all, she is your second wish come true.

PEPE: But I didn't expect her so soon. (*He puts his head down.*) I'm too bashful.

SAPO: Jumping iguanas! After a thousand years the poor princess has no one but you. Ask her.

PEPE: Señorita Princess, if you have nothing better to do—

SAPO (*Holding his head*): Popocatepetl! Must I be a match-maker, too? My dear princess, what this stammering boy means is—his heart is on fire with your beauty. His mind is aflame with your charm. Will you do him the great honor of becoming his wife?

IXLANDA (*Lowering her eyes*): It's the least I can do.

SAPO: Quivering quetzals! What the poor princess means

is—you are her knight in shining armor, her noble defender. She begs you to accept her as your wife. Now—
for once and for all—will you marry each other?

BOTH (*Hands on their hearts*): We will.

CHORUS: And they did.

2ND BOY: Together they set out for the hacienda of Señor
Granjero.

1ST GIRL: What rejoicing there was then!

2ND GIRL: Even Juan woke up, at last.

JUAN (*Wide-eyed*): *Qué?* Pepe has caught the bandit?
Little Pepe?

PEDRO: Pepe has brought home a wife? Little Pepe?

BOTH: Well done, little brother.

SEÑOR GRANJERO: Well done, my son. Ah—there is too
much happiness for one small hacienda. We must invite
all Mexico to share this day. I declare—a fiesta!

PEPE: A fiesta! Why—that's my third wish.

CHORUS (*Beating the bongos and shaking the maracas*):
Fiesta! Fiesta! Come from the hills and the valleys of
Mexico.

2ND BOY: Come from the Baja and Chihuahua, and Cam-
peche.

1ST BOY: Come from Hidalgo and Jalisco and Guerrero.

1ST GIRL: Come from Tabasco and Durango and Sonora.

CHORUS: Fiesta! (DANCERS *enter from up right and left,
and down right and left. They stand in two groups on
each side of the well, down center. A Mexican folk song
may be sung, after which* DANCERS *form a circle around
the well.* SAPO *sits on a box in the middle of the well,
a large sombrero on his head.* PEPE *and* IXLANDA *stand
down right.* SEÑOR GRANJERO, JUAN *and* PEDRO *cross
down left.* DANCERS *perform Mexican Hat Dance. At
the conclusion, as curtains close,* SAPO *hops out of the
well, still wearing the sombrero. He hops on the apron*

of the stage as the curtains close.) And that is the story of Pepe and the cornfield bandit.

2ND GIRL: It was told to us by a very old silvermaker in Taxco.

1ST BOY: He heard it from a very old fisherman in Veracruz.

1ST GIRL: And he heard it from a grandmother in Oaxaca.

CHORUS: And she heard it from . . .

SAPO: Why—from me, of course. Who else? (*He tips his hat to the audience and hops off right*) Ker-rivet! Ker-rivet!

THE END

The King Who Was Bored

A Mexican folk tale

by Adele Thane

Characters

PANCHO ⎫ *soldiers*
PEDRO ⎭

GENERALE LOPEZ

JOSÉ

PRINCESS ROSITA

KING CHIHUAHUA

SIX MARKET VENDORS

SETTING: *The plaza of a Mexican village. At rear there is a jail with its door wide open and the padlock dangling. Several market stalls stand left and right, covered with brightly colored awnings.*

AT RISE: *It is noon—siesta time. In front of the jail two Mexican soldiers, wearing sombreros and serapes, are asleep and snoring.* PANCHO *is curled up on the bench,* PEDRO *is seated on the ground under the window.* GENERALE LOPEZ *enters briskly, blowing a tin horn.*

LOPEZ: Wake up! Wake up! No siesta today! King's orders! (*He goes to jail and blows his horn again.*) Pancho! Pedro! Stand up and salute! (*They get to their feet.*) Are you not the King's army? Am I not your Generale?

PANCHO *and* PEDRO (*Saluting sleepily*): *Si,* Generale.

LOPEZ: Then pay attention to what I have to say. (*He whips a document out of his pocket.*) This is a late bulletin from the palace. (*Reading with dramatic emphasis*) *The King—is—bored!*

PANCHO *and* PEDRO (*Looking at each other and nodding*): The King is bored.

LOPEZ: Bored to tears!

PANCHO *and* PEDRO: Bored to tears. (*They burst into mock sobs.*)

LOPEZ (*Speaking louder and louder*): From head to foot, and front to back, completely, utterly *bored!* (*He rolls up the document.*) You know what *that* means.

PANCHO *and* PEDRO (*Blowing their noses in bandannas*): *Si,* Generale.

LOPEZ: It means that His Majesty will order a prisoner to be shot.

PANCHO: But, Generale, there *aren't* any prisoners. We're clean out of them.

LOPEZ: What! Not even *one?*

PANCHO (*Sadly shaking his head*): The last one escaped a month ago.

LOPEZ (*Pacing about in agitation*) : *Caramba!* This is terrible! A national catastrophe! What good is a jail without prisoners? If the King hears of this, he'll have *you* shot—*both* of you!

PANCHO: But then His Majesty wouldn't have an army.

LOPEZ: Hm-m-m, that's so. Well, get busy and arrest someone—*anyone!* We *must* have a prisoner! (*He exits left.*)

PEDRO: What shall we do, Pancho? Desert? Run away?

PANCHO (*Lazily fanning himself with his sombrero*): It's too hot to run away. Let's finish our siesta. (*He is about to lie down again on the bench when the sound of some-*

one whistling a merry tune is heard from the rear of the auditorium.)

PEDRO: Wait! I hear whistling. Look there! (*He points out front.*) A man is coming down the road. (JOSÉ *walks down the aisle, whistling.*)

PANCHO (*Peering out front*): Anybody we know?

PEDRO: I don't think so. I've never seen him before.

PANCHO: Good! We're in luck. (JOSÉ *comes up onstage and cheerfully greets soldiers as he starts to cross.*)

JOSÉ: *Buenos dias!*

PANCHO: Hold on there! (JOSÉ *stops.*) What's your name?

JOSÉ: José Francisco Tabasco Salvador.

PEDRO: Where are you going?

JOSÉ: Nowhere in particular. I just follow my nose. *Adios!*

PANCHO: *Adios,* nothing! You come along with us. (*They grab him by the arms.*)

JOSÉ (*Pleasantly*): Certainly. Where to?

PANCHO: We're taking you to jail.

JOSÉ (*Aghast*): To jail! What for?

PANCHO *and* PEDRO: We arrest you in the name of the King!

JOSÉ: What King?

PANCHO *and* PEDRO: King Chihuahua.

JOSÉ: Never heard of him. (*Freeing his arms*) You let go of me! I haven't done anything wrong. Why should you arrest me?

PANCHO: Because you look like a thief.

JOSÉ: Well, I'm *not* a thief!

PEDRO: Besides, we need prisoners to build the roads.

JOSÉ: I don't see why I should work on the roads if I don't want to, especially if I'm not paid for it.

PEDRO: Prisoners don't get paid.

JOSÉ: It's not fair to make people work and not pay for it. I won't do it.

PANCHO: Very well. If you won't work, you'll go to jail.

And another thing—if you don't work, you don't eat.

JOSÉ (*Objecting*): But I'll die of hunger!

PANCHO: Oh, no, you won't. You'll be shot first.

JOSÉ: Shot! You must be joking!

PANCHO: It's no joke. It's the King's orders.

JOSÉ (*Angrily*): What right has this King What's-his-name to give such an order—to have an innocent person shot for no reason at all?

PANCHO: Oh, *he* has a reason.

JOSÉ (*Sarcastically*): I'm *dying* to hear it!

PANCHO: Well—he's bored.

PEDRO: Bored to tears!

PEDRO *and* PANCHO: From head to foot, and front to back, completely, utterly *bored!*

JOSÉ (*Impatiently*): How can a King get so bored? Surely he has enough to do to keep him busy. Why, just to run the government alone should keep him hopping from morning till night.

PANCHO: Well, you see, King Chihuahua likes to guess riddles and listen to stories.

PEDRO: But now he knows all the riddles and stories and he's tired of them.

PANCHO: And that makes him cranky.

PEDRO: And when he's cranky, he always has somebody shot to liven things up.

PANCHO (*Profoundly, shaking his head*): That's the way it is with Kings, you know.

JOSÉ (*Stubbornly*): Well, he's not going to shoot *me!* He's not my King. I come from the Queen's country across the river.

PANCHO: That makes no difference. (PANCHO *and* PEDRO march JOSÉ off to jail, singing.)

PEDRO *and* PANCHO (*Singing, to the tune of "London Bridge"*):
　　Off to prison you must go,

You must go,
You must go,
Off to prison you must go,
Señor José!

JOSÉ (*At the window, shouting through the grating*): Let me out!

PANCHO: I'll go and tell the Generale we have a prisoner —(*As* JOSÉ *continues to shout*) a noisy prisoner! (*He exits down left.*)

PEDRO (*To* JOSÉ): Be quiet, or I'll stuff your mouth with this! (*He flourishes his bandanna.*)

JOSÉ: It would be more to my liking if you'd stuff my mouth with food. I'm starved.

PEDRO: No work, no food. (*From offstage the voices of several* VENDORS *are heard calling their wares.*)

JOSÉ: Who's coming? Is it the King?

PEDRO: Not yet. Those are the market vendors coming back from having a siesta. (*The* VENDORS, *men and women, enter left and right, carrying baskets of fruit and vegetables.*)

VENDORS (*As they enter*): Buy, come, buy! Fruit and vegetables for sale! See what your pesos will buy! (*They dispose themselves about the stage, sitting cross-legged on floor under the awnings, and spread their produce before them.*)

1ST VENDOR: White onions! Sweet white onions! White as the snows of the Sierras!

2ND VENDOR: Peppers! Red peppers! Hot, hot, for your enchiladas!

3RD VENDOR: Oranges! Bananas! Spicy, juicy mangoes!

4TH VENDOR: Tomatoes! Ripe tomatoes, picked at dawn!

5TH VENDOR: Lima beans, fresh from the vines!

6TH VENDOR: Tortillas! Golden brown and tasty! Who'll buy my tortillas?

José (*Thrusting a coin between the bars*): I will! Here is a peso!

Pedro (*Snatching it*): Gracias, señor. I will buy a tortilla and eat it myself.

José: That's not your money! Give it back!

Pedro (*Laughing*): A man about to die has no use for money. (*He goes to buy a tortilla and stands chatting with the* Vendors *while he eats it.* Princess Rosita *enters down left, dressed as a peasant. No one recognizes her.*)

1st Vendor (*Calling to* Pedro): Hey, Pedro! Where's Pancho?

Pedro: Gone to tell the Generale we have a prisoner.

2nd Vendor: At last, after all these weeks!

3rd Vendor: A lucky thing, too. I hear the King woke up this morning feeling extremely bored.

4th Vendor: Is that true, Pedro?

Pedro: Si, si. (Vendors *gather around him for further details and talk in pantomime, then go to stalls.* Princess Rosita *makes her way to the jail and speaks to* José.)

Rosita: Why are you in jail? Have you done a bad thing?

José: You might say my timing is bad.

Rosita: Your timing? I don't understand.

José: Well, I had the misfortune to come along here at a time when the King is bored and the jail, empty. That's what I call bad timing.

Rosita: Oh, I see. What is your name?

José: José Francisco Tabasco Salvador.

Rosita: Such an impressive name! I must find some way to help you.

José: You might begin by getting me something to eat. I'm ravenous.

Rosita: What would you like?

José: *Muchos tortillas*—and a mango. (Vendors *are now*

back at their stalls and Rosita *buys fruit and tortillas which she carries to* José, *passing it to him through the bars.* Pedro, *who is eating a banana downstage, turns and sees what she is doing. He rushes up to stop her.*)

Pedro: Señorita, no, no! We do not feed prisoners who refuse to work! You are breaking the law!

Rosita (*Drawing herself up imperiously*): How dare you accuse the King's daughter of breaking the law?

Pedro (*Recognizing her*): Princess Rosita! (*He yanks off his sombrero and bows in confusion.*) Forgive me—I did not know—that dress—and no crown—

Rosita: You will answer to the King for your rudeness. (Generale Lopez *enters hurriedly, blowing his horn, followed by* Pancho.)

Lopez (*Flapping his hands at the* Vendors): Back, good people! Clear the way for King Chihuahua! (Vendors *group themselves right and left stage.*) Pancho, set the bench here! (*Indicating center stage*) Pedro, bring out the prisoner! (Pedro *does so and* Lopez *blows another blast on his horn.* King *enters down left. He is small and fidgety.* Rosita *goes to meet him and escorts him to the bench where they both sit.* Generale *stands left of the bench.* Pancho *and* Pedro *bring* José *to right.*)

King: Is this the prisoner?

Lopez: It is, Your Majesty.

King: Prisoner, stand forth! (José *steps forward.*) What is your name?

José: José Francisco Tabasco Salvador.

King: What is your crime?

José: My crime is that I wanted to see the world and I got as far as your country where I was thrown into jail.

King: Ah, ha! You are a bandito?

José: No, I am a tourist.

King (*Puzzled*): A tourist! Generale, have we ever had a tourist in our jail before?

Lopez: I don't know, Your Majesty. Pancho? Pedro? Have we? (*While they confer together,* Rosita *speaks in an aside to* José.)

Rosita: Don't worry, José. I'll find a way to save you. Do you know any riddles?

José: A few—if I can remember them.

Rosita: Think hard! Your life depends on it. (*She turns to the* King.) Papa, if José asks you a riddle that you cannot guess, will you spare his life?

King: Just *one* riddle? No, he must ask me *three*—and, in addition, tell me a story that has no end.

Rosita: Oh, Papa, don't be so greedy!

King (*Petulantly*): But it's been such a long time since I've heard anything *new!* I've had to listen to the same old riddles and stories day in and day out. I want to have some *fun!* So if your young man, Rosita, can amuse me with three new riddles and a story without an end, he can go on living and marry you into the bargain. Well, José, is it a deal?

José: Not quite. I can be greedy, too. The King must promise one thing more—never again to have a prisoner shot simply because he is bored. Do you agree, Your Majesty?

Rosita (*As the* King *hesitates*): That's fair, Papa.

King: All right, I agree. Now let's hear the first riddle.

José: Here it is. There was a rooster who crowed in a place where all the world heard him. The whole world, mind you! Where was that place?

King (*Eagerly*): May I have three guesses?

José: If you can think of three.

King: It wouldn't be the royal hen house, would it?

Rosita (*Laughing*): Oh, Papa, the whole world wouldn't hear a rooster if he crowed there!

King: On top of a mountain? (José *shakes his head.*) In heaven?

JOSÉ: Heaven is not the world, Your Majesty.

KING: I give up. Where was that rooster when he crowed?

JOSÉ: Where else but in Noah's Ark?

CROWD (*Ad lib*): José is clever! . . . How smart he is!

JOSÉ: Now, King Chihuahua, have you ever looked for any-thing?

KING: Of course, many times.

JOSÉ: And do you find it?

KING: Sometimes.

JOSÉ: Well, when you *do* find it, why is it always in the last place you look?

KING: The *last* place, you say—not the first or the second? Hm-m-m-m. (*Pauses, while he thinks.*) Well, why *is* it in the last place?

JOSÉ: Because you always stop looking when you find it.

ROSITA: That makes two riddles you couldn't guess, Papa.

KING (*Elated*): Isn't it wonderful? They're *brand new!* Go ahead, José.

JOSÉ: This is the third riddle. How long is a string?

KING: Which string?

JOSÉ: Any string.

KING: But there are so many kinds of strings! There's a kite string, and a bow string, and a violin string, and the string you tie around your finger to remind you of something.

JOSÉ: Answer the question. How long is a string?

KING (*Pouting*): I can't answer the question unless I know what the string is used for.

JOSÉ: That has no bearing on the case. *How long is a string?*

KING (*Crossly*): Oh, I don't know! How long is it?

JOSÉ: A string—listen carefully—a string is *twice* as long as *half* its length.

CROWD (*Shouting*): Bravo! Olé!

KING (*Pleadingly*): Tell me one more riddle—*please!* I'm having *so* much fun!

JOSÉ: Very well. What is the question to which the answer is always "Yes"?

KING: No matter who asks it or answers it?

JOSÉ: That's right. I'll ask you that question now and you will positively answer "Yes".

KING: What if I answer "No"?

JOSÉ: You'll be a dunce if you do.

KING: What's the question?

JOSÉ: What does y-e-s spell?

KING: It spells—(*He stops, realizing he is caught.*)

ALL: *Yes!* (KING *grins sheepishly.*)

JOSÉ: Shall we go on to the story, Your Majesty?

KING (*Cheering up*): By all means. You know, I'm crazy about stories—crazier than I am about riddles. The more I hear, the more I want to hear. Some of the stories that have been told me have lasted a week; others, a month, and one lasted for *six* months. But even that one finally came to an end. Can you tell a story that will last forever?

JOSÉ: I believe I can. This is a story my grandmother told me, and her grandmother told it to her. And my grandmother's grandmother heard it from *her* grandmother—

KING (*Impatiently*): Never mind all that! Get on with the story.

JOSÉ: Once upon a time there was a farmer who wanted to become a millionaire. But instead of hoarding gold, he hoarded corn.

KING: What a stupid man! Why did he do that?

JOSÉ: He said corn was the *color* of gold and that was all that mattered. Every year he harvested all the corn in the countryside and put it in a storehouse as high as a mountain. He did this year after year, until the storehouse was filled to the top.

KING: Did that make him rich? Did he sell the corn at a profit?

ROSITA: Sh-h-h, Papa! Don't interrupt.

JOSÉ (*Continuing*): One day the ants found a little hole at the bottom of the storehouse. It was just big enough for an ant to go through. One ant went in and carried off a grain of corn. Then another ant went in and carried off another grain of corn. Then another ant went in and carried off another grain of corn—

KING: Yes, yes! You don't have to repeat it. I heard you the first time. What comes next?

JOSÉ: Next another ant went in and carried off—

KING:—*another grain of corn!* I understand that! Go on with the story.

JOSÉ: This *is* the story, Your Majesty. Then another ant went in—

KING: Oh, I'm tired of your ants! How long will it take them to carry away all that corn?

ROSITA: Remember, Papa, that the hole was large enough for only one ant to pass through at a time.

KING: But how long will it take, I say?

JOSÉ (*Shrugging*): Who knows? Perhaps a thousand years —perhaps ten thousand. Then another ant went in—

KING (*Rising with his hands over his ears*): Stop, stop! I can't stand this! Marry my daughter, live happily, take half my kingdom if you wish! Anything to stop those ants!

JOSÉ (*Smiling*): Perhaps now Your Majesty understands why a story must have an end. If it did not, another story could never begin. Isn't that so?

KING: José, you have a wise head on your shoulders. You've shown me what a fool I've been. Let us change places. You be the King and I'll be the tourist. I'll travel about the world and learn all the riddles. Then I'll come back

here and ask you to answer them. And I promise you
that I will never be bored again!

ALL: Hooray for King Chihuahua! Hooray for King José!
José Francisco Tabasco Salvador! (*All cheer. Curtain.*)

THE END

The Sleeping Mountains

A Mexican folk tale

by Barbara Winther

Characters

KING PAPANTCO (*Pah-pahn'-ko*)
PRINCESS, *his daughter*
HIGH PRIEST
JAGUAR, *his son*
TWO GUARDS
KING IXTLI (*Eest'-lee*)
PRINCE, *his son*
SERVANT GIRL
TERANA, *attendant*
OLD WOMAN OF THE MOUNTAINS

SCENE 1

TIME: *A day when the world was young.*

SETTING: *The Courtyard of the Sun in the palace of King Papantco in the Valley of Mexico. There is a stone bench to the right of a well at center. To the left is a throne.*

AT RISE: SERVANT GIRL *is playing a gay tune on the flute.* GUARD *stands behind throne keeping time to the music by waving a large fan. In his belt is a sword.* TERANA

enters right, ushering PRINCESS *to bench.* SERVANT GIRL
bows and exits left. GUARD *stands at attention.*

PRINCESS: Where is my father, Terana?

TERANA (*Nervously*): The King and the High Priest have
been holding a secret meeting all morning, my princess.

PRINCESS (*Shivering*): I do not trust the High Priest.

TERANA: Sh-h, Princess. It is not wise to speak against him.

PRINCESS: He holds too much influence over my father.
And I do not like the High Priest's son, Jaguar! Every
time I look at him, I am chilled all over. (*Sounds of drum
roll and horn blast are heard offstage.*)

GUARD (*Shouting*): To the Courtyard of the Sun comes
King Papantco, the great Toltec ruler over all rich and
green valley lands on the southern side of the mountains.
(GUARD *and* TERANA *prostrate themselves.* PRINCESS *rises
and bows.*)

PAPANTCO (*Entering right, followed by* HIGH PRIEST): A
beautiful day! Rise, everyone. My daughter, you are as
lovely as the feathers of the quetzal [*ket'-sahl*] bird. (*He
sits on throne.* PRINCESS *sits on bench.* GUARD *waves fan
over* PAPANTCO, *and* TERANA *stands behind bench.*) High
Priest, bring your son, Jaguar, before me.

HIGH PRIEST: At once! (*Claps hands and makes magical
gesture*) Itza! (JAGUAR *enters at once.*)

JAGUAR: Yes, Father!

PAPANTCO: Jaguar, we have been discussing you.

JAGUAR (*With a bow*): Oh, Magnificent King, I am honored that you would bring my name to your lips.

PAPANTCO (*To* HIGH PRIEST): He speaks well.

HIGH PRIEST: Of course.

PAPANTCO: His appearance is not the best I have seen.

HIGH PRIEST (*Quickly*): But, he is very loyal to you. I am
teaching him many spells and potions. He will be a
powerful friend for your empire.

PAPANTCO: Your words are convincing. (*Rises thoughtfully and crosses to* PRINCESS) Little flower, the time has come for you to be married.

PRINCESS (*Gasping*): To Jaguar?

PAPANTCO: The son of the most expert magician in my land would make an excellent husband for you.

PRINCESS (*Shocked*): Surely you would not wish me to marry one to whom I am so unsuited!

PAPANTCO: It is said that the mother corn will survive even on the desert. So you too can adjust. (*Crosses to sit on throne*)

PRINCESS (*Reaching for arm of* TERANA, *who comforts her*): But, Father—

PAPANTCO: Tomorrow your feathered wedding robe will be started. (*Sounds of drum roll and horn blast are heard.* 2ND GUARD *enters.*)

2ND GUARD (*Shouting*): To the Courtyard of the Sun comes King Ixtli, the poor Chichimec [*Chee-chee-mek'*] ruler over all lean brown mountain lands to the north.

PAPANTCO (*Leaping up angrily*): Cactus spines!

2ND GUARD (*Continuing*): King Ixtli's son accompanies him.

PAPANTCO: This is even more disgraceful. Two enemies in my palace.

HIGH PRIEST: By the tongue of the great feathered serpent, why are they here?

IXTLI (*Entering left, followed by* PRINCE): I will be quick, for I find your land overrun with poisonous vines.

PAPANTCO: Since you prefer your rocky wasteland, I can see no reason for you to enter my fertile valley.

IXTLI: Your subjects are using my streams for fishing.

PAPANTCO: That is not true!

IXTLI: It *is* true!

PAPANTCO: You whine like a scrawny coyote.

IXTLI: My country is poor, but my people are proud. I will not take your insults.

PAPANTCO: Depart at once, or I will have you hanged on the tallest pyramid. (GUARDS *draw swords.*)

IXTLI: You would not dare. That would mean war.

PRINCE: Please, Father. You are pale. Let me handle this.

IXTLI: Handle it, then. I despise every moment I spend in this overgrown, foul-smelling land. (*Exits left*)

PAPANTCO (*Shouting after him*): Your land is full of prickly pears and rattlesnakes.

PRINCESS (*Crosses to him*): Please, Father. You are flushed. Let me handle this.

PAPANTCO: Gladly! (*Crosses right*) Guard, if the Chichimec Prince does the least thing to threaten the Princess, throw him into the well. (*Exits right, followed by* HIGH PRIEST *and* JAGUAR.)

PRINCESS (*To* TERANA): Wait for me in the Room of Seven Paintings.

TERANA: But, it is not proper—

PRINCESS (*Gently waving her away*): Do not worry. I shall be careful. (TERANA *exits right.*) Guards, put your swords away and stand back. I do not need your protection. (GUARDS *frown at* PRINCE, *and stand at rear.*)

PRINCE (*To* PRINCESS): I am sorry. It is not a pleasant way to meet.

PRINCESS: I understand. Our fathers have always been angry with each other.

PRINCE: Long ago they had a quarrel, and our two tribes fought. The reason for the quarrel is forgotten, but the bitterness remains.

PRINCESS: It is too bad. Our tribes should unite and be friends.

PRINCE: I am certain that if my people could see the lovely Toltec Princess, they would forgive anything. I know I do.

PRINCESS (*Blushing, looking away*): The Chichimec Prince

is flattering, but he does not know me. (*Smiles shyly and indicates her robe*) You judge by my outward appearance.

PRINCE: A woman is only beautiful if she reflects goodness inside. I have met many women with perfect features whose faces became ugly with their thoughts. In your face I see kindness, gentleness, and honesty.

PRINCESS: I see goodness in yours. (*They stare at each other, then laugh in embarrassment, and look down.*)

PRINCE: Will you let me see you again? (JAGUAR *re-enters stealthily, unseen by them, and hides behind well.*)

PRINCESS: I would like to see you very much, but my father has chosen Jaguar, a nobleman of my tribe, to be husband to me.

PRINCE: Do you care for him?

PRINCESS: No! I do not even like Jaguar.

PRINCE: Then, meet me in the forest tomorrow.

PRINCESS (*Crossing right, thinking, and crossing back to* PRINCE): If I should decide to meet you, where would it be?

PRINCE: Do you know the hut where the Old Woman of the Mountains lives?

PRINCESS: Yes. It is near the border which divides our kingdoms.

PRINCE: Meet me at the giant palm beside that hut.

TERANA (*Calling from off right*): Come, Princess, you take too much time.

PRINCESS (*Calling back to her*): I will be there. (*To* PRINCE) When the sun is rising. (*Loudly, to* GUARDS) Show the Chichimec Prince out of the palace.

PRINCE (*Bowing*): Princess, your courtesy is greatly appreciated. (*Exits left, followed by* GUARDS)

TERANA (*Re-entering*): Ah, he has left.

PRINCESS (*Running to her*): I have much to tell you. First, you must promise, by all of the gods we worship, to keep my secret.

TERANA: What is this? (PRINCESS *grabs her arm and pulls her along toward right*)

PRINCESS: Do you promise?

TERANA: Of course, but I am disturbed by this excitement of yours. (*They exit.*)

JAGUAR (*Coming out of hiding*): My pride is deeply stabbed. This enemy comes into our land and tries to steal that which belongs to me. So, the Princess does not wish to marry Jaguar! She will be sorry. (*Spits out words*) I shall make certain that evil overcomes them *both*. (*Curtain closes as* JAGUAR *exits right.*)

* * *

SCENE 2

TIME: *That evening.*

SETTING: *The Courtyard, the same as Scene 1.*

AT RISE: *The* PRINCESS *and* TERANA *are sitting on the bench.*

TERANA: This is a terrible thing you are going to do.

PRINCESS: Why is it so terrible to meet someone?

TERANA: If your father knew, he would have the Prince killed.

PRINCESS: My father has little understanding of the heart of his daughter. (*Rises and starts to exit right*)

TERANA: My child, perhaps you will change your mind by morning.

PRINCESS (*Determinedly*): I will *not* change my mind. (*Runs back to sit by* TERANA) Come with me to the forest. It will give me more courage. I am not as brave as I wish I were.

TERANA (*Throwing up her hands in dismay*): Come with you? If I were caught, it would be the end of me.

PRINCESS: You are right. Forget what I have said. (*Rises*)

TERANA (*Rising*): Wait! I carried you on my back when you first visited the sacred well. I stayed beside you every moment you lay sick with the jungle fever. I will not let you go alone to the forest now.

PRINCESS: Thank you, dear Terana. I know I am asking much of you.

TERANA (*Patting her cheek*): Go to sleep now. I will awaken you before dawn. (PRINCESS *exits right.* TERANA *sighs and starts to exit left.* JAGUAR's *voice is heard from off right. She pauses.*)

JAGUAR (*From offstage*): The Princess meets the Chichimec Prince tonight. (TERANA *quickly crosses to hide behind well, as* HIGH PRIEST *and* JAGUAR *enter.*)

HIGH PRIEST: We must change our plans.

JAGUAR: You are right. She does not wish to marry me, and I believe she will find a way to change the King's mind. How can I become head of the kingdom now?

HIGH PRIEST: A bit of underhanded magic is necessary. (*Pauses*) If something should happen to detain the Princess tonight, then King Papantco would do anything to bring her back. (*Smiles maliciously*) It might be amusing to change the Princess and Prince into two stones for awhile.

JAGUAR: You run the risk of angering the gods.

HIGH PRIEST: Why should they care? The gods have never bothered me before. (*Pompously*) I think they are afraid of my powers.

JAGUAR: Perhaps you will become one of the gods, and people will worship you.

HIGH PRIEST: Perhaps! Come with me now. We shall mix a powder. You will take it to the meeting place and sprinkle it over the Princess and Prince. (*They exit left.*)

TERANA (*Running right, calling softly*): Princess! Princess! (*She exits. There is a moment's pause. She screams from offstage*) Princess, where are you?

1ST GUARD (*Entering left, running, sword raised*): What is wrong?

TERANA (*Re-entering, motioning for him to go away*): Nothing! Nothing! Return to your post. I had a bad dream.

PAPANTCO (*Entering right*): I heard a scream. What is wrong?

TERANA: It is nothing. I was dreaming—that is all.

PAPANTCO: But you are fully clothed. Guard, is the Princess safe? (1ST GUARD *starts to exit right.* TERANA *moves in front of him, blocking his way.*)

TERANA: She is fine. Do not disturb her sleep. Everything is well.

PAPANTCO: This woman is acting strangely. (*To* 1ST GUARD) See to the Princess. (1ST GUARD *exits. Nervously,* TERANA *begins to back away in the opposite direction.*)

1ST GUARD (*Shouting, from offstage*): The Princess is gone! (TERANA *turns and runs out.*)

PAPANTCO: Guard! (1ST GUARD *re-enters.*) Bring back the attendant, Terana. (*He points offstage.* GUARD *runs off. Offstage,* TERANA *screams, then* GUARD *re-enters dragging the struggling* TERANA.)

TERANA: Let me go! Let me go!

PAPANTCO: Where is the Princess?

TERANA: I cannot tell. (*Sinks to knees, sobbing*) I am sworn to secrecy. I promised the Princess I would not tell.

PAPANTCO: You dare refuse the request of your King?

TERANA: Oh, please, please, forgive me. The Princess is in danger. I must warn her. Let me go.

PAPANTCO: You will go nowhere until you tell me everything.

HIGH PRIEST (*Entering left, followed by* JAGUAR): What is the matter with the woman?

PAPANTCO: She tells me the Princess is in danger, but she will not tell me where she is. (TERANA *rises and shrieks, pointing at* HIGH PRIEST.)

TERANA: He knows where the Princess is. Ask him!

HIGH PRIEST: The woman has lost her senses. I know nothing.

TERANA: You are evil. (*Whirls back to* PAPANTCO) All right. I will tell you where she is. She has gone to— (HIGH PRIEST *raises hands in a magic gesture, and* TERANA *gasps and sinks to floor.*)

PAPANTCO: She has fainted.

HIGH PRIEST: I will take care of her.

PAPANTCO: Guard, send a detachment of warriors to search the surrounding area. (1ST GUARD *exits left.*)

HIGH PRIEST: I suggest, King Papantco, that you try to rest. I am certain that by tomorrow this woman will give me the information we need.

PAPANTCO: This is most upsetting. (*Crossing right*) What could have happened to my daughter? (*Turns back*) If you find out anything, call me at once. (*Exits*)

HIGH PRIEST (*To* JAGUAR): Take this powder and go quickly. (*Gives pouch to* JAGUAR *who holds it at arm's length and smiles*) Quickly! (JAGUAR *stealthily exits left, and* HIGH PRIEST *kneels beside* TERANA *as curtains slowly close.*)

*　　*　　*

Scene 3

BEFORE RISE: *Dawn.* PRINCE *enters left, before curtain, gazes right, and kneels to wait.* OLD WOMAN *enters right.*

PRINCE: Good morning, Old Woman of the Mountains. (*Rises*)

OLD WOMAN: Ah, Prince, what brings you to this side of the border?

PRINCE: The Toltec Princess.

OLD WOMAN: I can see by the radiance of your face that you would go anywhere to meet her.

PRINCE: You are right, Old Woman.

OLD WOMAN: It is dangerous. (*Shakes her head.*)

PRINCE: I know. Our fathers are always on the verge of war.

OLD WOMAN: A pity! Lines are drawn, insults and spears are hurled. It appears very difficult to love outside of one's tribe. (PRINCESS *enters right, sees* OLD WOMAN, *and stops.*) It is all right, Princess. I wish you both well. (*Exits left*)

PRINCE (*Crossing to* PRINCESS): I was afraid you would not come.

PRINCESS: There were times when my courage left me.

PRINCE (*Looking around*): You came alone?

PRINCESS: I did not wish to endanger anyone else's life.

PRINCE: You are braver than you realize. All night I have been awake, wondering what I should do. I want to ask for your hand in marriage.

PRINCESS: My father would never consent.

PRINCE: But, I cannot let you marry Jaguar.

PRINCESS: I will go with you to *your* father.

PRINCE (*Shaking his head*): My father would never accept you.

PRINCESS: Is there nothing we can do?

PRINCE: We could run away and leave both kingdoms. It would be difficult.

PRINCESS: If you will stay beside me, I am willing to go.

PRINCE: I will always stay beside you. (JAGUAR *sneaks in, and* PRINCE *sees him.*) Halt! Who are you? (PRINCESS *whirls around, gasps, and hides behind* PRINCE.)

PRINCESS: It is Jaguar!

PRINCE (*Drawing his sword*): Stand back.

JAGUAR: Your sword will be of no use to you, Chichimec Prince. (*Opens pouch and scatters powder over them.* PRINCE *and* PRINCESS *freeze, and* JAGUAR *laughs gleefully.*) I shall return for you, Princess. You will not *dare* refuse to marry me. Until our marriage takes place, the Prince will remain locked in his stone cage. (*Blackout.*)

*   *   *

TIME: *Later that day.*

SETTING: *The palace courtyard.*

AT RISE: KING PAPANTCO *is seated on his throne.* 1ST GUARD *stands behind him.* JAGUAR *sits on bench.* TERANA *kneels, bound and gagged, and* HIGH PRIEST *is speaking to* KING.

HIGH PRIEST: Terana has revealed everything, King Papantco. The Princess has run away to marry the Chichimec Prince.

PAPANTCO: What? (*Rises; furiously*) We shall march against the Chichimec kingdom. (*Sounds of drum roll and horn blast are heard.* 2ND GUARD *enters.*)

2ND GUARD (*Shouting*): To the Courtyard of the Sun comes King Ixtli, the poor Chichimec ruler over all—

PAPANTCO (*Interrupting*): He dares to return?

KING IXTLI (*Entering left; angrily*): Where is my son?

PAPANTCO: He kidnapped my daughter.

IXTLI: That is a lie. My son would not stoop to such a thing.

PAPANTCO: Stoop! Your son is a cucaracha.

IXTLI (*Sputtering*): I demand an apology!

PAPANTCO: Bah!

HIGH PRIEST (*Crossing between them and raising arms*): O kings of the northern and southern lands, I have a solution to this problem. My son, Jaguar, has courageously offered to find the Princess and Prince.

JAGUAR (*Rising*): King Papantco, I will bring your daughter back by nightfall, if you will consent to our marriage this evening.

PAPANTCO: What makes you so certain that you can bring her back?

JAGUAR: My father has given me special magical powers. And, if I should not succeed, you may sacrifice me to the gods! You see, I am most certain of my success.

PAPANTCO: Go, then! (*Sits on throne*) The wedding shall take place on your return.

IXTLI: What about my son?

JAGUAR: Later this evening he will be returned to your kingdom.

IXTLI: If he does not come back as you say, I promise to have every man in my kingdom armed with a club and on the march by morning.

SERVANT (*Entering right, excitedly*): There is a strange old woman here. The guards do not know how she managed to enter the palace.

PAPANTCO (*Rising*): Who is she? (OLD WOMAN *enters.*)

ALL (*In surprise; ad lib*): Who is it? How did she enter? (*Etc.*)

OLD WOMAN: Ah! Again the two enemy kings have met to snarl at each other.

IXTLI: Who are you?

OLD WOMAN: I am the Old Woman of the Mountains.

Your son knows me well. I have lived long, longer than all of your lives together. (*Crosses to* HIGH PRIEST, *who backs away.*)

HIGH PRIEST: Go away! You are not wanted here.

OLD WOMAN: Is that so, High Priest? Are you in charge of the world? Ah! (*Pointing at him*) Your magical powers have grown too large for your little mind.

HIGH PRIEST: How dare you speak to me in this manner! Away with you! (*Claps his hands and raises arms in magical gestures*) Itza! (OLD WOMAN *cackles, unaffected by magic.*)

OLD WOMAN (*In a loud, shrill voice*): The gods have grown angry with you, High Priest. You and your son have brought evil to this land. (*Moves toward them as they back up*) Like scavengers you sneak around and wait for the weak to fall. Henceforth, you are banished from the human race. You shall become animals, confined to the deserts and jungles, always hiding, always waiting, always living in the shadows.

HIGH PRIEST: No! No! (*Turns and runs off left, followed by* JAGUAR. *Loud howling and roaring of wild animals are heard from off left. Others gasp and move away from* OLD WOMAN, *watching as she unties* TERANA *and bids her rise.*)

PAPANTCO (*Cautiously stepping forward*): Old Woman of the Mountains, your powers are greater than ours. Bring my daughter back to me!

IXTLI (*Stepping forward*): Bring my son back to me!

OLD WOMAN: No! I do not choose to bring either of them back.

PAPANTCO: But, the Princess must not marry the son of my enemy.

IXTLI: I cannot allow the Prince to marry my enemy's daughter.

OLD WOMAN: How silly you both are! (*Crosses to bench*)

You are so wrapped up in bitterness that you do not really care about the dreams of your children. I have taken them to a place where they will always be together.

KINGS: Where?

OLD WOMAN (*Standing on bench and gesturing out over audience*): Look there. See those two beautiful mountains rising high above this valley? (*All stare in fear and wonder.*) Their names shall be Ixtlaccihuatl and Popocatepetl. The tops of the mountains are covered with a soft cloak of pure, white snow. Side by side these mountains will live while kingdoms below rise and fall. Some day, when there is less hate, the Princess and Prince will awaken and return to be happily married. Until then, they will sleep. And, when smoke rises from the mountains, it is to remind you that the Princess and Prince are indeed sleeping there. (KINGS *glower at each other and turn away, folding arms.* TERANA *weeps quietly, and* SERVANT *begins to play melancholy flute music, as* OLD WOMAN *looks about, shaking her head sadly, steps down, and slowly exits. Stage lights fade off as curtain slowly closes and music fades out.*)

THE END

The Olive Jar

A Persian tale

by Ethel McFarlan

Characters

MUSTAPHA, *a merchant of old Baghdad*
AMINA, *his wife*
JEDAH, *their young servant girl*
AHMED, *a water boy*
HASAN, *his uncle*
CALIPH, *Prince of Baghdad*
JAFAAR, *the Caliph's minister*

SCENE 1

TIME: *Early morning in eighth century Baghdad.*
SETTING: *Mustapha's courtyard. Against the wall are a bench and a gnarled tree.*
AT RISE: JEDAH *is sweeping the courtyard. From the street come the sounds of camel bells, donkey bells, and the boisterous shouts and laughter of the water boys.*

AMINA (*Entering right*): Oh, that dreadful racket!
JEDAH: The water boys have come, my lady.
AMINA: Jedah, go tell them to move off. Your master will

be angry if they block the passage. Quick! (JEDAH *runs out center. From offstage* MUSTAPHA *bellows angrily and boys laugh.*) Too late. He has told them himself.

JEDAH (*Entering center*): They are going now, all but a little one who is flat on the ground.

AMINA: Pray Allah, he isn't hurt. Where is Mustapha?

JEDAH: He went back into the warehouse. You should see his face, as red as fire.

AMINA: Now he is upset again and you know your master when he is upset. He must eat and drink himself out of his bad humor. Have you brewed the coffee? Is the tray ready? Go serve him in the warehouse—no, I'll fetch the tray. Go see if the boy needs help. (JEDAH *runs out center.* AMINA *hurries off right and returns with tray of food and a cloth.* JEDAH *re-enters, with* AHMED.)

JEDAH: His name is Ahmed, and he is not hurt.

AMINA: You little rascal! Mustapha must not find you here. It is not permitted. Now run along. Here's a coin for you. (*Puts tray on bench; gives him money*)

AHMED: I thank you, my lady.

AMINA (*Giving him another coin*): And one for your mother.

AHMED: I have no mother.

AMINA: Then give it to your father.

AHMED: My father is also dead . . . but I have an uncle.

AMINA: Very well, then, your uncle.

AHMED: My uncle will heap his blessings on you, lady.

AMINA: Tell your uncle I wish him health and long life. Now go.

AHMED: I'll tell him—when I see him. My Uncle Hasan went on a pilgrimage seven years ago and he hasn't come back yet.

AMINA: Surely you are not alone in the world.

AHMED: Oh, no, I live with Zeki.

AMINA: And who is Zeki?

AHMED: My donkey. (*Bells are heard from offstage.*) He carries the water skins. Everyone says Uncle Hasan is dead, but I know better. He will come back this year, the seventh year of his journey. Seven is my mystic number. It always brings me luck.

AMINA: I do hope so. When you have news of this uncle, send me word. Now go. See that he has sesame cakes, Jedah, seven of them for luck. (JEDAH *gives* AHMED *cakes. As he is tucking them in his sash* MUSTAPHA *enters left.* AHMED *runs out center.* AMINA *claps hands, and* JEDAH *spreads cloth on ground.* MUSTAPHA *claps hands and* AMINA *sits beside cloth.* MUSTAPHA *sits opposite her.* JEDAH *places tray on cloth, gets urn and cups off right, and serves coffee.*)

MUSTAPHA: Wife, you have had a street urchin in this court.

AMINA (*Trying to seem lighthearted*): Yes, a remarkable little fellow. I wish to speak of him—

MUSTAPHA: And I do not. He is filthy.

AMINA: Alas, and why not!

MUSTAPHA: Enough! Please eat in silence. . . . Where are the sesame cakes? (*Stares accusingly at women*) Well, does no one have a tongue?

AMINA (*Mumbling*): A few cakes for the boy. Does it matter?

MUSTAPHA: Ah, that boy!

AMINA: We have so much and he has so little.

MUSTAPHA (*Yelling*): And so I am robbed!

AMINA: The dates are good, Mustapha, very good. Try them.

MUSTAPHA: I have no stomach for dates. Where are the olives?

AMINA (*Exasperated*): O my husband, have you forgotten you do not like olives?

MUSTAPHA: When did I say that? Who heard me say I do not like olives?

AMINA (*Rising*): Jedah, take this coin and go buy some olives.

MUSTAPHA (*Furious*): What! You have none in the house? In every house in Baghdad there are olives, but my shiftless wife cannot provide for me. (AMINA, *pretending to cry, sniffles*) I, Mustapha, have been neglected. (AMINA *wails*.) Oh, stop crying. Stop it! I have just remembered a jar of olives in the warehouse. No more tears, no wailing. I cannot stand it. (*Goes out left.*)

AMINA: Now do as I tell you, Jedah. Go buy olives and sesame cakes, too. This must not happen again. (JEDAH *goes out center.* MUSTAPHA *enters left with jar.*)

MUSTAPHA (*Blowing dust off jar*): There, a whole jar of olives.

AMINA: Where did you get it? Look at the cobwebs.

MUSTAPHA: Naturally there are cobwebs. Hasan-al-Ahir left it with me for safekeeping seven years ago.

AMINA: Who?

MUSTAPHA: Hasan, the silver merchant. He went on a pilgrimage to the Holy City and never came back.

AMINA (*Aside*): Ahmed's Uncle Hasan? (*To* MUSTAPHA) But, Mustapha, it is his.

MUSTAPHA: I tell you the man is dead. One can travel to Mecca and back in one year. Hasan has not lived to claim his jar.

AMINA: Pray Allah, it isn't true.

MUSTAPHA: Stop gabbling and eat. Did you not ask for olives?

AMINA: I? It was you, Mustapha.

MUSTAPHA: O exasperating woman, must I show you how to eat an olive? (*Bites an olive and exclaims in disgust.*)

AMINA (*Tasting an olive, and making a face*): They are spoiled. What a pity!

MUSTAPHA: Throw them out, the whole lot. Hand me a bowl. (AMINA *holds bowl.* MUSTAPHA *scoops olives from jar into bowl. Suddenly he stops with hands in jar.*)

AMINA: What is the matter?

MUSTAPHA: Nothing, nothing. Take them away. Leave me in peace. (AMINA *goes out with bowl.* MUSTAPHA *takes coins from jar and fingers them greedily.*) Hundreds of golden dinars! Hasan, you sly fox, you never told me this. All this gold. Whose jar is this now? Who knows about it? Nobody but Mustapha. (*Hurriedly transfers gold to his money belt under his sash*)

AMINA (*Entering right with bowl*): Here are fresh olives, Mustapha.

MUSTAPHA (*Quickly*): Put them into the jar.

AMINA: The jar? (MUSTAPHA *snatches bowl, pours olives into jar.*) Oh my husband, is it ever possible to please you? The olives are for you, not the jar.

MUSTAPHA (*Replacing lid*): Forget the jar. Never speak of it again. (*Carries jar off left.* AMINA *sits on bench, bangs bowl in frustration.*)

JEDAH (*At right*): Did you call me, my lady? The bowl is empty. Where are the olives? Surely the master didn't eat them all.

AMINA: Forget the olives, my little dove. Never speak of them again. (*Curtain.*)

* * *

SCENE 2

TIME: *Late afternoon, several days later.*

SETTING: *The same as Scene 1.*

AT RISE: JEDAH *is carrying loaves of bread, and does not see* AHMED *and* HASAN, *who enter center.* HASAN *sits on bench.* AHMED *sneaks up behind* JEDAH *and shouts. She drops bread.*

JEDAH (*Picking up loaves*): Ahmed, you've frightened me! (*Sees* HASAN) Who is that old man? He can't sit here. My master does not permit strangers in the courtyard. Who is he, Ahmed? Did he come with you? Ahmed, he's your uncle, your Uncle Hasan! (AHMED *nods, grinning*)

HASAN: So you have heard of me. Who are you, child? I know you not.

JEDAH: Jedah, Mustapha's slave. I'll tell my lady the good news. She will be so pleased that you are back.

AHMED: And tell Mustapha that his old friend, Hasan, wants to see him.

HASAN: No, Jedah, tell him only that a visitor wishes to speak to him. I wonder if Mustapha will recognize me. They tell me I have aged. (JEDAH *goes out right*) I am neither as old nor as poor as I look. True, I lost all my possessions when bandits attacked the caravan, but I will have money again after I talk with Mustapha.

AHMED (*Incredulous*): He will give it to you?

HASAN: No, it is mine. He has been guarding my savings for me, a thousand dinars.

AHMED: A thousand!

HASAN: Yes, too great a sum to carry on a dangerous journey.

MUSTAPHA (*Entering right*): Who seeks Mustapha?

HASAN (*With outstretched arms*): Peace and blessings on you, friend.

MUSTAPHA (*Coldly*): And on you. "Friend," you say?

HASAN: We met last in this very courtyard. Don't you remember?

MUSTAPHA: Impossible, since I have never seen you before.

HASAN (*Disturbed*): Mustapha, look at me. Have I changed so much? Have seven years done this to me?

MUSTAPHA (*Shocked*): Hasan! Seven years is a long time to travel to Mecca and back. You told me you would be gone but one.

HASAN: I did, but after visiting the Holy City I traveled into foreign lands. At last I longed for my native city. Here are my friends, or so I thought. It was a sad homecoming. (*Arm about* AHMED) I found my dear nephew, Ahmed, selling water in the street to earn a living. His parents had both died while I was gone.

MUSTAPHA: Humph!

HASAN: Well, I must not detain you. As you may have guessed, I wish to claim my jar. You remember the jar?

MUSTAPHA: You shall have it immediately. (*Goes into warehouse*)

AHMED: What's the matter with the old bedbug, uncle?

HASAN: Mustapha always had his moods. One must be patient with him.

MUSTAPHA (*Returns with jar, places it on ground*): I have always wondered why I should stand guard over a jar of olives.

HASAN: Naturally. Now you deserve to share the secret.

MUSTAPHA: No, take it away. No need to explain.

HASAN: Oh, but you must know that my request was not a whim. (*Removing olives.*) Hidden under the olives . . . (*Tosses out olives frantically*) Gone, gone! My treasure, stolen!

MUSTAPHA: Treasure? What nonsense is this?

HASAN: At the bottom of the jar there was money, a thousand dinars.

MUSTAPHA: What an amazing fantasy! When you left the jar with me you did not tell me it contained a treasure.

HASAN: I told no one. Where is my money, Mustapha? If you borrowed it for a business use I shall not complain. You may pay me back a little at a time. But please understand that without those dinars I am in dire need. I have nothing. I am a pauper.

MUSTAPHA: Borrow? You mean steal. Would I, Mustapha, steal a miserable handful of dinars?

AHMED: Well, Mustapha, did you?

MUSTAPHA (*Brushing* AHMED *aside*): Listen to me, Hasan. If there was money in that jar, I know nothing of it. You placed a jar of olives in my warehouse and a jar of olives has been returned to you. Will nothing satisfy you? Must you ask for gold? Why not rubies as big as hens' eggs?

AHMED: You haven't answered, Mustapha. Did you steal his money?

MUSTAPHA (*Aiming blow at* AHMED, *who ducks*): Dog of a donkey boy!

AHMED: Uncle, let us go to the cadi and accuse this Mustapha of lying.

MUSTAPHA: Go to the cadi. I fear no lawsuit. I am known throughout Baghdad as an honest merchant. Go! Take this tiresome jar and go! (*Tosses a few olives into jar and strides out right.*)

HASAN (*Sinking to ground*): All is lost. I cannot prove he is a thief. The cadi would not believe me.

AHMED: Then petition the Caliph of Baghdad.

HASAN: What a child you are. The Caliph, too, would ask for proof.

AHMED: He would look at you and see that you are honest.

HASAN: The Caliph, seeing me, would ask, "Who is that shabby wretch?"

AHMED: And then he would say, "Bring him to me that I may hear his plea."

HASAN: Indeed he would say, "Cast that beggar from my sight." (*Head on knees*)

AHMED: No, no, he wouldn't. The Caliph of Baghdad is called Haroun the Just. People say that sometimes at

night he and his vizier walk in disguise through the
streets of the city. Everywhere he goes he drops coins into beggars' bowls. He is kind to the poor. He will see
that you get justice. . . . Uncle, are you listening?
(HASAN, *in a trance, stares into space*) What's the matter?
Are you sick? (*Shakes* HASAN, *raises his arm and lets it
fall limp*) O hateful Mustapha, see what you have done
to him. (*Sits beside* HASAN, *puts his arm around him.
Lights dim. Curtain.*)

*   *   *

SCENE 3

TIME: *That night.*
SETTING: *The same as Scene 2.*
AT RISE: AHMED *is asleep.* HASAN'S *eyes are open, his position unchanged. The* CALIPH *and* JAFAAR *enter center
stealthily.*

CALIPH: Who are these wretched ones? Jafaar, this man
does not sleep. His eyes are open and yet there is no
spirit in his body.

JAFAAR: My Prince, let us leave this place. It has an air
of misery and evil.

CALIPH: First I must have the answer to this mystery. Why
was the donkey abandoned in the street? Whose court is
this?

JAFAAR: It is not safe to linger here. We will be discovered.
Listen . . . Someone is stirring. Quick! Into the shadows. (CALIPH *and* JAFAAR *move upstage, fold burnooses
about them, stand against the wall.* JEDAH *enters right,
peers at* HASAN *and* AHMED, *takes fistful of olives, nibbles them absentmindedly.*)

JEDAH (*Softly*): Ahmed . . . Ahmed.

AHMED (*Waking suddenly, sits up*): Oh, it's you, Jedah.

JEDAH: Sh-h-h, they do not know I am here. They are both asleep. You should hear Mustapha snore. He's buzzing like a thousand horseflies. What is the matter with your uncle?

AHMED: He is brooding and doesn't hear or see.

JEDAH: Ahmed, what happened? Why was Mustapha shouting? I couldn't understand a word he said.

AHMED: A girl wouldn't understand these things. What are you eating?

JEDAH: Olives, from the jar. Is it your uncle's jar?

AHMED: Yes, but you are welcome to them. Eat them all. Who wants olives?

JEDAH: One day not so long ago Mustapha made an awful fuss because we had no olives. My lady sent me into the street to buy some and when I brought them back they disappeared.

AHMED: Disappeared? What do you mean?

JEDAH: I never saw them again. They just vanished.

AHMED: Down Mustapha's gullet.

JEDAH: A large bowl of olives? He couldn't eat that many at once. Besides . . .

AHMED: Wait! I am thinking. (*Jumps up, eats olive*) Jedah, I see it all now! I know what happened. There are your olives—in the jar! (*Raising voice*) That's what he did— put them into my uncle's jar and that's the proof!

JEDAH: Quiet! Mustapha will beat me if he wakes. (*Runs out right*)

AHMED (*Shouting*): Let him wake! Who's afraid of Mustapha? Not me! Can you hear me, man? (HASAN *raises head*)

MUSTAPHA (*Offstage*): Miserable donkey boy! Get out or I'll call the police!

AHMED (*Taunting* MUSTAPHA): Help! Police! (*Shakes* HASAN) Get up, uncle. We are going to be arrested.

MUSTAPHA (*Entering right, enraged*): Get out! Get out!
(*Tries to grab* AHMED, *who eludes him, laughing.*
MUSTAPHA *lunges for him, slips and falls; gets up
awkwardly*)

HASAN (*Standing, with dignity*): O my child, do not tor-
ment him. I am reconciled to my fate. My gold is lost
forever. Allah has so willed it. Let us leave this place of
bad memories. Come.

CALIPH (*Moving down*): No, stay. This quarrel must be
settled now.

MUSTAPHA: Trespassers! How dare you. . . .

JAFAAR: Make yourself known, O Prince, or harm might
come to you. (CALIPH *removes burnoose, revealing court
garments*)

MUSTAPHA: The Prince of Baghdad! (*Drops to knees*)

AHMED: The Caliph!

HASAN: Defender of the Faith. (HASAN *and* AHMED *kneel*)

CALIPH: Rise. Quickly, let us settle this argument. I, as
Prince and Caliph, have the authority to hear the case
and pass judgment. I command each side to give testi-
mony. All witnesses must speak the truth, for unless
there is truth there can be no justice. Now, who is the
accuser? He must speak first.

HASAN: I am he, Hasan-al-Ahir.

CALIPH: What is your complaint?

HASAN: I have been robbed, my Prince. Seven years ago
I set out on a pilgrimage to the Holy City. Before I went
away I placed a jar in this man's warehouse for safekeeping. He was my friend. The jar contained olives under
which I had hidden a thousand dinars. Now the money
is gone.

AHMED (*Placing jar before* CALIPH): This is the jar.

MUSTAPHA: I beg for justice, O my Prince! Can you, in
your great wisdom, believe that I, a merchant of renown,
would stoop to petty crime?

CALIPH: I ask the questions, merchant. (*To* HASAN) *Do* you accuse this man, your one-time friend, of stealing your money?

HASAN: I do.

CALIPH: Did you get from him a receipt for your money?

HASAN: No, my Prince, I told him nothing of the gold. Mustapha was known as an honorable man. I did not expect him to meddle with the jar.

CALIPH (*Lifting lid*): Did you tell him there were olives in the jar?

HASAN: No, the jar was covered and I told him nothing.

CALIPH: Can you produce a witness who saw you put the money into the jar?

HASAN: No, my Prince.

CALIPH: Then you can show no proof that the money was there. Does not the Koran teach us thus: Procure a receipt in writing and two witnesses to every transaction?

HASAN: It does. I have been extremely foolish.

CALIPH: Mustapha, did you remove a sum of money from this jar?

MUSTAPHA: I? Indeed not. Not once did I lay a finger on this jar.

CALIPH: Did you never wonder why Hasan placed great value on an ordinary jar?

MUSTAPHA: At first, and then I forgot to wonder. My Prince, I am a businessman with great affairs to occupy my mind—the loading and unloading of camels, the checking of goods—

CALIPH: Yes, yes, I accept your word that you are important.

MUSTAPHA: I had almost forgotten Hasan.

CALIPH: And were you glad to see him when he returned?

MUSTAPHA: Glad? No, distressed.

CALIPH: Distressed!

MUSTAPHA: At his appearance. He was not always as you

see him now, a thin, drab, dirty specter. O my Prince, I believe I know the answer to this riddle.

CALIPH: I am listening.

MUSTAPHA (*Gesturing melodramatically*): My poor friend, Hasan, undertook a difficult journey. Think of the hardships he endured: the fierce sun beating down on him, the thirst, the weariness. Suddenly in the desert he sees a lake and trees beside the lake. O blessed shade and water! But now they are gone. Poor Hasan's mind is playing tricks on him. In his sad state he sees what he wants to see, and so it is with this treasure he talks about. He cannot find it because there never was any gold at the bottom of the jar.

CALIPH: Perhaps you are right.

HASAN: No, no, I never lost my wits!

CALIPH: That, too, may be true. I cannot tell. . . . Even so, it is impossible to charge Mustapha with theft because you cannot prove the gold was ever in the jar.

AHMED: But Mustapha has lied!

CALIPH: I fear, Jafaar, we must let this boy speak. Otherwise he might burst. (*To* AHMED) Come here to me. What is this lie you speak of?

AHMED: Mustapha knew there were olives in the jar. Yet a few minutes ago he said he never touched the jar. Then how did he know?

CALIPH: Well, Mustapha?

MUSTAPHA: I—I—of course I knew. Hasan told me and forgot.

AHMED: There is more, O Prince. (AMINA *enters right*)

CALIPH (*To* AHMED): Go on.

AHMED: Mustapha, did you remove my uncle's olives from this jar?

MUSTAPHA (*Muttering*): Must I pamper this donkey boy!

CALIPH: Answer, Mustapha.

MUSTAPHA: No. Haven't I already said so?

AHMED (*Offering* MUSTAPHA *an olive*): Then taste this olive. Go on, go on, eat it. (MUSTAPHA *nibbles sullenly*) If what you say is true, that olive is seven years old. How does it taste?

CALIPH: That question interests me. (*Tastes an olive*)

AHMED: You see, O Prince, the olives are fresh. The olives my uncle put in the jar would be spoiled. Mustapha has changed the olives in the jar.

MUSTAPHA: What do you know about olives, donkey boy? Who are you to say how they should taste? I tell you I never touched the jar.

AMINA: Oh, no, do not lie!

MUSTAPHA (*Whirling around, speaks in undertone*): Wife, what are you doing here? Go back at once.

AMINA (*Whispering*): I could not sleep. Who are these strangers?

MUSTAPHA: Hush! The Prince of Baghdad. (AMINA *starts to withdraw*)

CALIPH: No, I wish to hear what your lady has to say. Come, do not be frightened. Never fear to speak the truth.

AMINA (*Agitated*): My husband has no reason to lie. What he did was not so dreadful. I do not understand these questions about the olives. Since the olives in the jar were rancid, Mustapha threw them out and put in fresh.

CALIPH (*Furious*): Dog of a merchant, confess!

MUSTAPHA: O, believe me, it was by accident—

CALIPH: Accident! Have you filled my ears with lies by accident? Do you call stealing an accident? Your greed was no accident. When you discovered the gold in the jar, your fingers itched to possess it. Is not that true, Mustapha? (MUSTAPHA *nods.*)

AMINA: Gold!

MUSTAPHA (*At* CALIPH's *feet*): Mercy, O my Prince.

CALIPH: Get up. Get up. (MUSTAPHA *rises to one knee*)

You see, Jafaar, how that money belt weighs him down.
Relieve him of one thousand dinars. (JAFAAR *pulls*
MUSTAPHA *to his feet and collects money.* MUSTAPHA
edges to right) Oh, not so fast, Mustapha. You still must
pay the penalty for your crime, five thousand dinars.

MUSTAPHA: Five thousand! I am fleeced! Not a dinar left!

CALIPH: In your money belt, yes, but upstairs in your
strong box I am sure there are plenty more. See to it
the fine is delivered to me.

MUSTAPHA: O my wife, you have ruined me!

AMINA: I? Was it I who stole the gold? O Mustapha, why
did you? (*Weeps*)

CALIPH: Hasan, it pleases me to restore to you what is
rightfully yours. (*Gives money to* HASAN) Jafaar, do you
not think this boy deserves a reward? (*Gives* AHMED
money)

AMINA (*On knees before* CALIPH): O Defender of the
Faith, I beg you to forgive my husband this one mis-
deed. From this time on, he will be again what he has
always been, an honest man.

CALIPH: I do not doubt it, my lady, and so promise never
to think harshly of him. And you, Hasan, bear him no
grudge. Now, Jafaar, we must go. (JAFAAR *helps* CALIPH
to put on burnoose) Let us all begin the new day with
forgiveness of heart. (CALIPH *and* JAFAAR *move up to
gate where* CALIPH *turns and raises hand.*) The peace of
Allah and His blessings be upon you. (*Curtain.*)

THE END

Peter and the Wolf

A Russian folk tale adapted for musical pantomime

by Sylvia Chermak

EDITOR'S NOTE

A pantomime is a play in which the performers convey the story entirely through action, facial expressions, gestures, and movement. To make the story line clear, it is important for the actors' movements to be precise and clear so that the audience can follow the plot. Pantomime is especially suited to young children, whose spontaneity and love of movement, improvisation, and freedom of action, unhampered by the need to learn lines, enhance their enjoyment. At the same time, they may be successfully taught the basic techniques of acting and creative theatrical improvisation and movement.

This old Russian folk tale was set to music for children by Serge Prokofieff. It is a story in music, and each character in the story has his own musical theme and instrument. Peter is represented by the string quartet; the Bird by the flute; the Duck by the oboe; the Cat by the clarinet in low register; Grandfather by the bassoon; the Wolf by three horns; the Hunters by the kettledrums and bass drums.

It is desirable for a recording of Peter and the Wolf to be used in advance of production so that the children may become familiar with the different musical themes through repeated listening. But for the production of the play in pantomime by children, piano accompaniment may be used for flexibility and adaptability to the onstage action.

Characters

THREE NARRATORS	CAT
PETER	GRANDFATHER
BIRD	WOLF
DUCK	HUNTERS

SETTING: *A meadow. There is a fence at one side of meadow, with a latched gate leading into it. A low stone wall runs along the back and to one side of meadow, behind a tree which stands upstage right. Flowers grow in meadow, and there is a "pond" near rear of stage.*

AT RISE: THREE NARRATORS *sit on stools, downstage right. The* BIRD *is asleep in branches of tree, his head resting under his right wing.*

1ST NARRATOR: Early one morning, Peter opened the gate and went into the big, green meadow. (PETER *dances onto stage, looks around, opens gate, runs into meadow, skips about, stoops to pick flower.*) On the branch of a big tree sat a little bird who was Peter's friend. (BIRD *is asleep, his head resting under a wing.*)

2ND NARRATOR: As Peter continues to dance around in the meadow, he suddenly sees the Bird and stops in front of tree to look at him. (PETER *stares at* BIRD, *who begins to stir, wakens, raises his head, looks about with darting birdlike movements.* BIRD *sees* PETER.)

3RD NARRATOR: When the Bird saw Peter, he chirped at him gaily, "All's quiet here." (PETER *continues to stand in front of tree, gesturing to* BIRD.)

1ST NARRATOR: Soon a Duck came waddling in. (DUCK *waddles in, pauses briefly near gate.*) She was delighted to see that Peter had not closed the gate, and she decided to have a nice swim in the cool, deep pond in the meadow. (DUCK *walks to gate, smiles, waddles through, pauses a moment, then waddles over to edge of pond.*)

2ND NARRATOR: When the little Bird saw the Duck, he flew down, settled himself in the grass beside the Duck, and talked to her. (BIRD *flies to* DUCK.) "What kind of bird are you anyway, if you can't even fly?" asked he. To which the Duck replied, "What kind of bird are *you* if you can't swim?" And the Duck dived into the pond. (DUCK *dives into pond, swims about*) They argued and argued—the Duck swimming in the pond, and the little Bird hopping back and forth along the bank. (*All this time,* PETER *has been watching them with interest from the other side of the meadow.*)

3RD NARRATOR: Suddenly, something caught Peter's eye. It was a Cat, crawling through the grass. (CAT *creeps in stealthily, sneaks along behind fence, comes up behind* BIRD *at edge of pond.*) The Cat said to himself, "Now that the Bird is busy arguing with the Duck, I'll just grab him!" She drew closer to him on her quiet, velvet paws.

2ND NARRATOR: "Look out! Look out!" cried Peter—and the Bird flew quickly up into the tree; while from the middle of the pond the Duck quacked angrily at the Cat. (CAT *lunges at* BIRD *and misses him, then follows him over to tree.*) The Cat walked menacingly round and round the tree, and he thought, "Is it worth climbing there to try to catch him? By the time I get up there, the Bird will have flown away." (CAT *continues to prowl about, looking longingly at* BIRD *in tree.*)

3RD NARRATOR: All at once, Grandfather appears, angry because Peter had gone into the meadow. (GRANDFATHER *enters, leaning on his cane, his knees bent, walking slowly but firmly over to fence.*) "The meadow is a dangerous place," he cried to Peter. "What if a wolf should come out of the forest? What would you do then?" (GRANDFATHER *shakes his fist angrily at* PETER.)

But Peter paid no attention to Grandfather. Boys like Peter are not afraid of wolves. (PETER *dances away from* GRANDFATHER, *impudently and defiantly.*) But Grandpapa took Peter by the hand, led him home and locked the gate. (GRANDFATHER *takes* PETER *very firmly by the hand, drags him through the gate, locks it, and goes out.* PETER *hangs back, but is dragged along, offstage.*)

1ST NARRATOR: No sooner had Peter gone than a big gray wolf *did* come out of the forest. (WOLF *slinks onto stage, looks around menacingly.*) In a twinkling, the Cat sprang up into the tree. (CAT *jumps up onto tree branch.*) The Duck quacked in great excitement (DUCK *begins to quack loudly and flap her wings in panic.*), but in her excitable state, she jumped out of the pond. (DUCK *begins to waddle about awkwardly, as* WOLF *first circles around her and then begins to chase her, in smaller and smaller circles.*) The Wolf is getting nearer and nearer and nearer—closer and closer, so there seems to be no escape for the Duck. She makes one last, desperate effort to escape the Wolf and darts off into the forest (DUCK *runs off right*), with the Wolf in hot pursuit. (WOLF *runs off right, and* NARRATOR *looks off after them.*) Poor Duck! She never had a chance! He swallowed her in one gulp. (WOLF *re-enters, looking very pleased, rubbing his stomach and licking his chops. He goes over to the tree, begins to circle tree slowly.*)

3RD NARRATOR: And now this is how things stood: (PETER *enters quietly from left, and stands behind gate, watching.*) The Cat was sitting on one branch up in the tree, the Bird on another—not too close to the Cat. And the Wolf walked round and round the tree, looking at them both with greedy eyes. In the meantime, Peter, without the slightest fear, stood watching all that was going on. (PETER *exits.*) Presently, Peter ran out and returned quickly (PETER *re-enters, carrying rope.*) with a coil of strong rope. He goes over to the low wall which runs behind the tree (PETER *walks to side of tree and stands on wall.*), climbs up on it, and from there climbs over into the tree. (PETER *grabs branch of tree, then pulls himself onto fork of tree.*)

2ND NARRATOR: Peter said to the Bird, "Fly down and circle around the Wolf, but make sure he does not catch you!" (BIRD *flies down and begins to hop around* WOLF. WOLF *sits under tree, looking unconcerned, and occasionally lunges at* BIRD, *as music indicates.*) The Bird gets closer and closer to the Wolf and almost touches the Wolf's head with his wings. The Wolf snaps furiously at the Bird, and the Bird jumps back just in time at every lunge. How that Bird did worry the Wolf! And, oh, how that Wolf tried to catch him! But the Bird was too clever for him, and the Wolf simply couldn't do anything about it.

Meanwhile, Peter had made a lasso (PETER *slowly lets down lasso from his perch in the tree, dangling it near* WOLF's *tail.*) and, carefully letting it down, he caught the Wolf by the tail. (*Lasso drops behind* WOLF, *who, unseen by the audience, fastens it to his tail.* PETER *begins to pull on it, and* WOLF *jumps about wildly, trying to get his tail loose.*) Peter pulls with all his might, and the Wolf, feeling himself trapped, jumps up and tugs and pulls and jumps wildly, trying to get his tail out of the lasso. (HUNTERS' *shots are heard from offstage, then* HUNTERS *enter from forest, right, as their musical motif is heard.*)

1ST NARRATOR: Just then a band of Hunters comes in from the woods, their guns raised as they take aim at the Wolf whose trail they have been pursuing. But Peter, sitting up in the tree, still holding tightly to the rope attached to the Wolf's tail, cries out, "Oh, don't shoot him! Don't shoot! The Bird and I have already caught him." (HUNT-

ERS *lower their guns and look in amazement at* WOLF *held fast in* PETER's *lasso.*) "Just help us take him to the zoo!" The Hunters were only too willing. (PETER *gets down from tree, first lowering his end of rope so that it can be held by one of the* HUNTERS. GRANDFATHER *enters and watches in amazement.* PETER *then takes hold of rope again, and leads procession off, pulling the* WOLF *out.*)

3RD NARRATOR: And there they go! (HUNTERS *follow* PETER *out, and after them go* GRANDFATHER, CAT, *and finally the* BIRD, *who has been twittering about their triumph in catching the* WOLF. BIRD *exits at end of procession.*) Imagine the triumphant procession: Peter at the head—after him the Hunters, leading the Wolf—and winding up the procession, Grandfather and the Cat. Grandfather tossed his head—"This is all very well—but if Peter had not caught the Wolf—what then!" Above them flew the little Bird, merrily chirping, "Aren't we smart, Peter and I? Just see what we have caught!" And if you listened very carefully, you could hear the Duck—quacking away inside the Wolf—because in his haste the Wolf had swallowed her alive! (*Curtain*)

THE END

Stone Soup

A Russian folk tale

by James Buechler

Characters

SERGEANT	DMITRI, *a carpenter*
PETYA	ANNA
SASHA	MARYA
OLGA, *a seamstress*	OTHER VILLAGERS
VERA, *a baker*	

TIME: *Two hundred years ago.*

SETTING: *A village street in old Russia. Three houses stand along the street, and through large windows we see the interior of each house—a carpenter's shop, a bakery, and a seamstress's shop. There is a stream with stones right.*

AT RISE: DMITRI *is at work in the carpenter's shop,* VERA *works in the bakery kitchen, and* OLGA *sits sewing in the seamstress's shop. Three soldiers enter, and walk down the street.* SERGEANT *carries an old-fashioned rifle;* PETYA, *a knapsack;* SASHA, *a large cooking pot.*

SERGEANT (*To soldiers*): Cheer up, you two! We've come through the forest safely. I'm sure the people of this village will share their dinner with us.

SASHA: I hope so. My stomach is empty. It feels like a cave. (SERGEANT *knocks at* OLGA's *door.*)

OLGA (*Calling out of her window*): Who is it?

SERGEANT: Only three loyal soldiers, tramping home across Russia, after fighting for the Czar. Can you spare us some food, good woman?

OLGA: Food! No, I have nothing. Our harvest was bad. You will find nothing here. (*Turns from window*)

PETYA (*Knocking at* VERA's *door*): Hello in there!

VERA (*At window*): What is it you want?

PETYA: Some supper, if you have any. Here are three loyal soldiers tramping home across Russia.

VERA: I am sorry to see you so hungry, but you have come to the wrong shop. It is everyone for himself in these times! (*Turns away*)

SASHA (*Losing his patience*): Let's see if our luck is better here. (*Knocks at* DMITRI's *door.*)

DMITRI (*Angrily*): Who are you, anyway? Sensible men are inside their houses, working.

SASHA: Three soldiers, sir. It would be kind of you to share your dinner with us.

DMITRI: I have just enough dinner for myself. If I share, I eat one quarter of a dinner, and so do you (*Pointing*), and you, and you. We shall all be hungry afterward. What good will that be? No, I do not believe in sharing. It is a very bad idea. (*Turns away*)

PETYA: What selfish people these are!

SASHA (*Decisively*): They do not know how to share.

SERGEANT: Let's teach this fellow a lesson!

PETYA: No, no! We won't rob anyone.

SERGEANT: Of course not, Petya. All I meant was to teach these peasants to make stone soup.

SASHA (*Catching on*): Aha, stone soup!

PETYA (*Laughing*): Just the thing. (*The three huddle to-*

gether, whispering. Meanwhile, DMITRI *comes to window again.*)

DMITRI: Still here, you vagabonds? If you have no food, it's your lookout. Why aren't you on your way?

SERGEANT (*Pretending not to hear*): Firewood, Sasha! Prepare the kettle, Petya. We will build our fire here, on this spot. (SASHA *goes off left;* PETYA *finds two Y-shaped sticks on the ground.*)

PETYA: We can use these to hang the kettle, Sergeant. (*Sets sticks in place*)

SERGEANT: Perfect, Petya. Now for the stones. We must see if they have nourishing stones in this village. Go and find some in that stream over there. (PETYA *takes kettle to right and throws some stones noisily into it.* OLGA *and* VERA *turn to windows, watching him.* SASHA *enters with dead branch.*) Good! That will burn well and heat our soup quickly. (SASHA *lays fire, pretends to light it.*)

SASHA: What kind of stones will we use for our soup tonight?

SERGEANT: What kind do you want?

SASHA: Oh, something filling! Granite is a good stone, now. I always like a granite soup. It has body. It sticks to your ribs! (PETYA *brings kettle to center, rattling stones.* DMITRI, VERA, *and* OLGA *leave houses, come near fire.* ANNA *and* MARYA *enter, followed by* OTHER VILLAGERS.)

DMITRI (*Tugging* SERGEANT's *sleeve*): Excuse me.

SERGEANT: Eh? Oh, it is you, my friend.

DMITRI: I do not understand. What did you say you are cooking here?

SERGEANT (*In an offhand manner*): Just a stone soup. (*With sudden friendliness*) Tell me, what kind of stone do you like yourself? You might help us choose.

DMITRI: I! Why, I never heard of making soup from stones!

SASHA: Never heard of Stone Soup?

PETYA: I don't believe it.

SERGEANT (*To* DMITRI): Come, sir. If you are not joking, you must dine with us. (PETYA *rattles kettle.*) Have you some good stones there, Petya? Let Sasha choose tonight.

SASHA (*Examining stones*): Hm-m! This chunky one—it will be good! Washed down from the mountains, it has a flavor of snow on it. Ugh! Throw that one away. A flat stone, a flat taste.

PETYA: How about the red one?

SERGEANT: No, no, that is only an old fireplace brick—it will have a smoky taste. Nothing but fresh stones tonight. We shall have a guest.

SASHA: Fill the kettle, Petya. My fire is ready. (PETYA *dips water from well into kettle and hangs kettle over fire.*)

SERGEANT (*To* DMITRI): Have you a spoon? We soldiers often make do with a stick. But for a guest, the soup will need proper stirring and tasting.

DMITRI: I have just the thing—it has a nice long handle. It is in perfect condition. I have not had guests in five years.

SERGEANT (*Clapping him on back*): Splendid, you generous man! (DMITRI *goes inside for spoon.*)

ANNA (*To* MARYA): What's this? The soldiers are making a soup from stones?

MARYA (*Nodding*): Stones from our own brook. That soldier put them in. I saw him myself.

SASHA (*Sniffing*): Oh, it makes me hungry!

DMITRI (*Returning with spoon*): Here you are. Please be careful.

SERGEANT: Sir, you shall be served first. (*Stirs, tastes.*)

MARYA: I am more hungry than usual. It must be the smell of this soup they are cooking.

ANNA: I must have a cold, for I can smell nothing.

MARYA (*Sniffing*): Yes, I am very hungry, indeed. I have worked in the fields since morning, with no lunch, either. What good soup! (SERGEANT, SASHA, *and* PETYA *each taste by turns, and smack lips.*)

OLGA: Is it good?

PETYA: Good.

DMITRI: Good? (*Reaches for spoon*)

SASHA (*Keeping spoon away from him*): Oh, so good!

SERGEANT: It might stand an onion, though. Onion is very good for pulling the flavor from a stone.

OLGA: You know, I might find an onion in my house.

1ST VILLAGER: Hurry then, Olga. Get some. (OLGA *exits.*)

SASHA (*Tasting*): A whiff of carrot, Sergeant? (VILLAGERS *look at each other.*)

VERA: Perhaps I could fetch some carrots for this soup.

SERGEANT: That is gracious of you. And will you bring a bowl for yourself, as well? You must dine with us. (VERA *goes inside as* OLGA *returns with onions.*)

OLGA: Use what you like. I should like to learn to make this soup. (SERGEANT *adds onions, tastes.* PETYA *tastes also.*)

PETYA: Just a bit of potato, perhaps? I cannot say that stone soup is ever quite right without a potato or two.

OLGA: That is true. A stone is certainly nothing without a potato! (VERA *returns with carrots and bowl.* SERGEANT *adds carrots.*)

MARYA (*To* VILLAGERS): Vera was invited, did you hear? How can we be invited as well? (*They whisper together.* ANNA *goes off right.* MARYA *calls out*) If you need some potatoes for that soup of yours, I have a sack in my cottage! (ANNA *appears with sack. Both give it to* SERGEANT.)

SERGEANT: Many thanks. Please stay for dinner. And now, Sasha, to business! (*Tasting*) Add a potato. . . . an-

other. . . . another. (SASHA *is already ahead of* SER-
GEANT's *count.*) No, stop, Sasha. Stop!

DMITRI: What is the matter, Sergeant?

SERGEANT: Too many potatoes! The potatoes have ab-
sorbed the flavor of the stones.

VILLAGERS (*Ad lib*): Oh, too bad! What a shame! (*Etc.*)

MARYA: Is there nothing we can do?

PETYA: I have a suggestion. Meat and potatoes go well
together. Let's add some meat.

DMITRI: I have a ham that will do the trick. Wait here.
(*Goes inside*)

SERGEANT: It might work, at that. (DMITRI *returns with
ham.*)

2ND VILLAGER: Good for you, Dmitri!

1ST VILLAGER: Quick thinking!

ALL (*Applauding*): Hurrah, hurrah! (SERGEANT *adds ham.*)

MARYA: Can anyone make this stone soup?

PETYA: Oh, yes. All you need are stones, fire, water—and
hungry people.

ANNA (*Impatiently*): Well, how is it now, soldier? It smells
delicious.

SERGEANT (*Tasting*): Hm. Some stones, as you may know,
contain salt in them. These from your brook do not
seem to be that kind. (OLGA *goes inside.*)

OLGA (*Returning*): Here is your salt. (SERGEANT *adds salt,
with flourish.*)

SERGEANT: Friends, I know this will be a very good soup.
You have fine stones in this village, no doubt of that!
Stay and eat with us, one and all. (VILLAGERS *cheer and
mill about.* 1ST VILLAGER *goes offstage, returns at once
with bowls.* SERGEANT *fills them and all taste soup.*)

DMITRI: Truly a delicious soup, soldiers!

ANNA: A hearty flavor!

MARYA: It fills you up!

DMITRI: And to think, neighbors, it's made only of stones! (SOLDIERS *now advance to stage front and hold out their bowls of soup.*)

SOLDIERS (*To audience*): Yes, think! It's made only of stones! (*Curtain.*)

THE END

Fish in the Forest

A Russian folk tale

by Hazel W. Corson

Characters

IVAN, *a poor peasant*

OLGA, *his wife*

ANNA
SONIA } *friends of Olga*

COUNT

COUNTESS

SOFIA, *her maid*

COURT OFFICIAL

TWO PAGES

TWO GUARDS

OFFICER POPOFF

PEASANTS

SERVANTS

SCENE 1

TIME: *Long ago in old Russia.*

SETTING: *A small clearing in the forest. There is a tall, hollow stump up right. A small tree stands up left, and a large rock up center. The area is enclosed by a background (backdrop) of trees.*

AT RISE: IVAN *and* OLGA *enter left carrying baskets filled with mushrooms.* IVAN *carries fishing line and a snare, which he places on the ground.*

OLGA: We were lucky to find so many mushrooms, Ivan. Now we can have good mushroom soup to go with our black bread.

IVAN: This was a good idea of yours, Olga.

OLGA (*Pointing off right*): Do you think there may be fish in that little pond?

IVAN: I'm sure there are some. I'll set some lines. (*He takes fishing lines and throws them off right, as if into pond, then ties his end to stump.*) I'll set a snare by this old stump. If I can catch a rabbit, we will have some meat.

OLGA: Do you think you should do that, Ivan?

IVAN: Why not? Surely we need meat, and we have no money to buy any.

OLGA: You know how angry the Count gets if he hears that someone has been hunting in the forest.

IVAN: The Count is always angry. Besides, what the Count doesn't know won't hurt him. Just this once, don't tell anyone, that's all. (IVAN *sets snare, then looks closely into stump.*) What is this? Something is hidden in this hollow stump. (*He pulls out an old leather bag.* OLGA *goes over to see what* IVAN *has found.*)

OLGA: It must have been in this stump for many years. See how old and moldy the leather is! What is in it? (IVAN *shakes bag and a rattling sound is heard. He reaches into bag and takes out some coins, then lets them drop slowly, one by one, back into bag, making a clinking sound.*)

IVAN: Gold! We are rich! What a wonderful thing! We are rich! We are rich! (IVAN *and* OLGA *join hands and do a clumsy little dance.*)

OLGA: Now I can have a new skirt, a new shawl, and some new shoes, and maybe even a ring to wear on my finger, like the Count's wife. (*She struts back and forth, as if showing off new clothes, and holds out her left hand as if admiring a ring.*) I cannot wait to tell Anna!

IVAN (*Angrily*): Not so fast, wife! Not so fast! We must not speak of this to anyone!

OLGA: Why not? Surely our friends would rejoice in our good fortune.

IVAN: Indeed, they would. And they would talk about it to everyone.

OLGA: And what of that?

IVAN (*In exasperation*): Why, sooner or later, the Count would hear of it.

OLGA: Ha! I will tell him myself. And at the same time I will tell him that we do not need to slave for him any longer.

IVAN: No, Olga! It is not as simple as all that. The Count will say that the forest is his, and that anything found in the forest is his. He will have his soldiers take the money from us. No, we must not speak of this to anyone.

OLGA: Can't I just whisper it to Anna and Sonia, and maybe to Sofia?

IVAN (*Sternly*): No, Olga! You must not whisper it to anyone! I forbid it!

OLGA: But all our friends are as poor as we are. What can I tell them when they ask how I can have a new skirt and new shoes, and a new shawl, and new dishes and new . . .

IVAN (*Interrupting*): Enough, Olga! We cannot have new things. We must hide the treasure. We must live as we have been living. Otherwise, the Count will suspect something.

OLGA: If we can't spend any of the treasure, what good is it? Why not give it to the Count? He might give us a reward, and we could spend that.

IVAN: The Count is a rich man. He does not need the money, and he would never use it to help anyone. If we hide the treasure and say nothing about it, we can use it, little by little, to help the poor.

OLGA: So we can help the poor! And who is any poorer than we are, I'd like to know?

IVAN: We can use a little now and then, but we must not buy so many things that we will seem richer than our friends. (*Looking around*) Now, help me plan where to hide the treasure.

OLGA: Why not hide it in our house, under the hearth? Surely it will be safe there, and we will be able to keep an eye on it.

IVAN: That *is* a good plan. We will bury it tonight, when no one is about. Remember, I forbid you to speak of this!

OLGA: All right! All right! But I see no harm in whispering it to Anna.

IVAN (*Frustratedly*): Olga! Must I beat you?

OLGA: Oh, all right! All right! (*They pick up baskets and bag of coins, and exit left as the curtain falls.*)

*   *   *

SCENE 2

TIME: *A few days later.*

BEFORE RISE: OLGA *enters left in front of the curtain as* ANNA *enters from right. They meet at center.*

ANNA: Hello, Olga!

OLGA: Hello, Anna!

ANNA: Where have you been? I have not seen you all this week.

OLGA: Oh, Ivan has been keeping me busy helping him. But I know it is not so much help he wants.

ANNA: Ivan has always been a good husband. Does he now make you work hard?

OLGA: He doesn't make me work hard. He just doesn't want me out of his sight, because he thinks I can't keep a secret.

ANNA (*Eagerly*): Oh! So you and Ivan have a secret?

OLGA: Whatever made you think that?

ANNA: You must know something Ivan doesn't want you to tell. Surely you can whisper it to your old friend, Anna!

OLGA: He thinks if I say anything about what we found, the Count will hear of it. So I will not breathe a word of it.

ANNA: But I am your good friend! You can tell me your secret.

OLGA: I mustn't. Ivan will beat me.

ANNA (*Shrugging her shoulders*): All right, Olga, whatever you say. I must be going now. See you later.

OLGA: Goodbye, Anna. (ANNA *exits left, as* SONIA *enters right.*)

SONIA: Good morning, Olga.

OLGA: Good morning, Sonia. Isn't that a new skirt?

SONIA: Yes. Stefan brought it to me from the fair. Do you like it? (*She turns around, spreading out skirt.*)

OLGA: It is beautiful. I might have many new things if Ivan were not so afraid of the Count.

SONIA: What has the Count to do with a new skirt?

OLGA: Oh, Ivan is so foolish. He says it might make the Count think we had found something valuable, and he would dig under the hearth and take it away from us.

SONIA (*Eagerly*): So you found something valuable? What is it? Where did you find it?

OLGA: How do you find out these things? I will not say another word. (OLGA *puts her hand over her mouth and runs off right.* SOFIA *enters left, and* SONIA *runs up to her.*)

SONIA: Have you heard the news, Sofia? Ivan and Olga Petrovich have found a fabulous treasure, and they are as rich as the Czar!

SOFIA (*Excitedly*): Really? That's marvelous news. (*Hesi-*

tating) But, it would be most unfortunate for Ivan if the Count should hear of this.

SONIA: Ah, yes, but I know you will not tell.

SOFIA: Nothing could drag it from me.

SONIA: You are a good friend. I must go home to my husband. He will be waiting. (*She starts off left.*)

SOFIA: I must be off, too. The Countess gets very angry if I am not there when she wants me. Goodbye, Sonia. (SONIA *exits left, as* SOFIA *starts off right, meeting* COUNTESS *just as she is entering right.* COUNTESS *carries hand mirror and comb.*)

COUNTESS: Here you are at last, Sofia. I have been looking for you to fix my hair. (*They both move center, and* COUNTESS *sits on rock. She hands comb to* SOFIA, *who starts combing* COUNTESS' *hair.* COUNTESS *admires herself in mirror.*)

SOFIA: All the servants are buzzing this morning, Your Ladyship.

COUNTESS: The servants are always buzzing. What is it this time?

SOFIA: It seems that someone in the village has found a fabulous treasure . . . gold, silver, jewels . . . who knows what? Enough for a Czar's ransom.

COUNTESS: I am sure it is. (*Hands mirror to* SOFIA, *then stands up*) You may go now, Sofia, and lay out my riding clothes. I shall take a ride this morning. I'll be along soon.

SOFIA: Yes, Countess. (SOFIA *exits right, as* COUNT *enters left.*)

COUNT: Oh, here you are, my dear.

COUNTESS: Good morning, dear husband. Have you heard the news?

COUNT: News? What news?

COUNTESS: There is news from the village that someone has found a fabulous treasure.

COUNT: That is most interesting! And who is the lucky person?

COUNTESS: No one knows, of course.

COUNT: Hm-m-m. Why don't you ride into the village, and do a little talking among the women?

COUNTESS: That is what I plan to do. I think I'll start with Olga Petrovich. She never can keep a secret. She has given me much information from time to time.

COUNT: Well, you have a way of finding out things from the women that I can't get from the men. Just bring me the name of that scoundrel. I'll make such an example of him that no one else will dare to hide anything. (*They both walk off right. The curtain rises.*)

*   *   *

SETTING: *The same as Scene 1.*

AT RISE: IVAN *enters left, carrying a spade and a basket containing leather bag, fish, and small cakes. He looks all around, as if to be sure that no one is watching, then goes up to rock and sets basket down on ground.*

IVAN: I'll have to hurry. I don't have much time before Olga arrives. First, I'll bury the treasure under this big rock. (*He starts to dig hole under rock, and after a moment, he takes leather bag from basket and hides it in hole.*) Now I'll put these fresh fish along the path. (*He takes fish from basket and lays them along path.*) Now, if these cakes will just stay on the tree! (*He takes small cakes from basket and puts them on branches of tree.*) Now, where did I set that snare? (*He goes toward stump, then stops.*) Ah, here it is with a nice fat rabbit in it! (*He bends over snare, then holds up stuffed rabbit.*) Now, suppose I attach the rabbit to the fish hook and throw it into the pond. (*He pulls in fishing line attached*

*to stump and fastens rabbit to end of it. Then, he throws
line off right, as if into pond, takes empty basket and
moves toward center.*) Well, I'm finished. I am afraid
that Olga's talking has made enough trouble in the past.
Maybe no one will pay much attention to her stories
after this. (*He looks off left.*) She should be here by now.
(*After a moment,* OLGA *enters left, carrying her basket.*)

OLGA (*Going to* IVAN): Hello, Ivan. Why did you want me
to meet you in the forest? Do you think we'll find more
treasure?

IVAN: Stop talking about the treasure, Olga. It will only
get us into trouble. There was a heavy rain last night.
We might find anything. Just keep your eyes open.

OLGA (*Noticing the fish in the path*): Oh, look, Ivan! A
fine fat fish! Imagine finding fish in the middle of the
forest!

IVAN: Have you never heard that one often finds fish in the
forest after a heavy rain?

OLGA (*Excitedly*): No, I never have! But it must be so.
(*Noticing the other fish and pointing to them*) Here is
another, and another. (*She puts fish into basket*) Into my
basket you go, my pretty fish. Why haven't we done this
before, Ivan?

IVAN: Well . . . one doesn't always find them. One has to
come at just the right time, or the forest animals will
have eaten them up. (*He turns aside to muffle laugh.*)

OLGA (*Going to tree and looking at the cakes*): Oh, Ivan!
Look! There are cakes on this little tree! Fresh cakes!
Now who put them there, do you suppose?

IVAN (*Stifling a laugh and following* OLGA): It rained quite
hard last night. Perhaps there were cakes on the ground
as well as in the tree. Animals probably ate them up.

OLGA (*Incredulously*): But I never knew it could rain
cakes! How wonderful!

IVAN: It doesn't happen everywhere, so it isn't a thing one

talks about. Otherwise, all the world would rush to the spot, and no one would have anything.

OLGA: How fortunate we are!

IVAN: Let's see if I caught anything on the lines I set. (*He goes to stump and pulls in line with rabbit on it.*)

OLGA: How strange! A rabbit in the pond!

IVAN (*Nonchalantly*): I do not think it strange. Have you not heard that rabbits, as well as fish, may be found in water?

OLGA: No, indeed! I knew it not!

IVAN: Well, you have seen it with your own eyes. And as for us, we have food fit for the Count himself.

OLGA: Yes, we have. Let's go home and cook it. (*They walk off left, as the curtain falls.*)

*   *   *

SCENE 3

TIME: *A few days later.*

SETTING: *The Count's palace. Two chairs representing thrones stand up center.*

AT RISE: COUNT *and* COUNTESS *sit on thrones.* COURT OFFICIAL *stands directly at left of* COUNT. TWO PAGES *stand behind* COUNT *and* COUNTESS. PEASANTS *and* SERVANTS, *including* ANNA, SONIA *and* SOFIA, *sit at either side of the stage.*

COURT OFFICIAL (*Loudly*): His Lordship has something to say to you.

COUNT: I have called you all here today because there is something I wish you to see and hear. Some of my people are not here because they could not be spared from their work, but every family is represented. (*He signals to* COURT OFFICIAL.)

COURT OFFICIAL (*Loudly*): Soldiers of the guard, with Ivan Petrovich and his wife, Olga. (Two GUARDS *come in left, shoving* IVAN *and* OLGA *in front of thrones. They are forced to kneel.* SERVANTS *whisper to one another, nervously.*)

COUNT (*Sternly*): Do you have anything to tell me, Ivan?

IVAN: What should I tell you, sir?

COUNT: Did you not find a great treasure in my forest? Do you not have it buried under your hearth?

IVAN: A great treasure under my hearth? Your Lordship knows that I am a poor man. Surely you jest, sir.

COUNT (*Furiously*): I never jest! It is only fair to tell you that I know all about it. News of this reached the Countess. She visited Olga. (*Loudly, to* COUNTESS) Tell this rascal what you discovered by this visit, my dear.

COUNTESS: Olga hinted that she and Ivan found treasure in the forest, and that it was buried under their hearth.

OLGA (*Indignantly*): But, Your Ladyship! This was a secret between women. I did not think that you would tell the Count.

COUNT: Silence, Olga! This secret between women is now a question for men to settle.

COURT OFFICER: You know that what is found in the Count's forest belongs to him. You should have come to him at once with the treasure. Doubtless he would have given you a reward.

COUNT: True! However, I may not punish you too severely if you tell me about the treasure at once.

IVAN: But, sir, there is no treasure under my hearth.

COUNT (*Sternly*): Do not lie to me, Ivan, or it will go hard with you. Do not forget that I can put you in the dungeon.

IVAN: But Your Lordship can send soldiers to my house to dig under the hearth.

COUNT: I have already done that, Ivan. They should be

here soon with the treasure. Now do you wish to change your story?

IVAN: Would that I could, my lord! (OFFICER POPOFF *enters.*)

COURT OFFICER (*Loudly*): Officer Popoff of the palace guard, to report to the Count!

COUNT: Good! Let him come forward.

OFFICER POPOFF (*Stepping forward and saluting* COUNT *and* COUNTESS): I took four soldiers to the house of Ivan Petrovich, Your Lordship. I had them dig under the hearth, and under the whole house. There was no treasure, sir.

COUNT (*In amazement*): No treasure?

COUNTESS (*Questioningly*): No treasure?

IVAN (*Pleadingly*): I beg of you, Your Lordship, do not be hard on poor Olga. I see I can no longer hide the truth. Some days Olga is quite all right. Other days she imagines things and does not know what she is saying. She does not mean to lie. She just imagines things at times.

OLGA (*Indignantly*): I do not imagine things! It is the truth! You did find treasure in the forest, and you did bury it under the hearth!

IVAN (*Gently*): Olga, when did I find treasure in the forest?

OLGA: Now let me see. Why, it was a few days before we went into the forest and found the fish.

COUNT (*Surprised*): You found fish in the forest? (PEASANTS *and* SERVANTS *look at each other in amazement.*)

OLGA: Yes, Your Lordship—a fine lot of plump, fresh fish. We gathered a basketful of them along the path. Then Ivan fished in the pond and caught a fat rabbit. I shall never forget that day! (*To* COUNTESS) Perhaps you will remember that day, Your Ladyship. It rained cakes the night before.

COUNTESS (*Dumbfounded*): It . . . rained . . . cakes?

COUNT (*To* COUNTESS): So this is where you get your information! Ha! I fear you are not a good judge of brains.

COUNTESS: I am amazed!

COUNT (*To* GUARDS): Show these two out. They are wasting my time. (GUARDS *help* IVAN *to his feet.*)

OLGA: Are you going to make Ivan give up the treasure, Your Lordship? We might as well give it up. Ivan won't give me any of it to spend.

COUNT: No, Olga. Ivan may keep this treasure, along with any fish he may find in my forest! (*Curtain*)

THE END

Quick-Witted Jack

A Scandinavian folk tale

by Jean Feather

Characters

JACK	PRINCESS
TOM, *his brother*	CHANCELLOR
MOTHER	JEWELLER
ANT KING	GARDENER
BEETLE KING	FORESTER
OLD WOMAN	FOUR ANTS
TWO GUARDS	TWELVE RABBITS
KING	LADIES-IN-WAITING
QUEEN	COURTIERS

SCENE 1

TIME: *Long ago.*

SETTING: *Jack's family's cottage, at the edge of the village green.*

AT RISE: JACK *sits near door of cottage, left, mending net. He looks up as* TOM *enters, right, an empty knapsack on his back.*

JACK: Tom! (*Shouting through door*) Mother, Tom is coming. (*Going to meet* TOM) How was your trip, Tom? Did you see the Princess?

Tom: No, I didn't. A long walk to the palace and a long walk back, for nothing.

Jack: But you carried twelve perfect pearls. That's the gift the King's proclamation asked for. Why didn't they let you marry the Princess?

Tom: Marry her? I'm lucky I wasn't flogged. (Mother enters.)

Mother: What happened, Tom?

Tom: You won't believe this, Mother, but when I opened the bag to show the pearls to the King, all I had were twelve lumps of coal.

Mother: Lumps of coal?

Tom: That's right. Look. (He takes leather bag from pocket and opens it. Mother takes out a small black lump.)

Mother: It's impossible. You started out from here with twelve perfect pearls. I know. I picked each of them out of an oyster myself.

Tom: That's right, Mother. Jack and I helped you.

Jack: And we still have a dozen pearls saved.

Mother: Tom, did you fall asleep on the road?

Tom: No.

Mother: Did anyone have a chance to take your bag and put another in its place?

Tom: No, Mother. It never left my pocket till I took it out to show the pearls to the King. (Bitterly) And I showed him lumps of coal.

Mother: Was he very angry?

Tom: Furious! I thought he'd have me beheaded on the spot. But the Princess started to laugh, and that made everyone laugh.

Jack: She must be very kind. (Tom snorts.) Mother, may I try my luck now?

Mother: Jack, I know I promised the next twelve pearls

to you. But what's the use if they turn to coal at the palace?

JACK: I'd like to try, please, Mother.

MOTHER: Oh, very well. Give me the knapsack. (TOM *hands it to her.*) I'll pack you a lunch. You bring the bag for the pearls. (TOM *hands bag to* JACK. MOTHER *and* JACK *go into cottage.*)

TOM (*To himself*): I can't understand it, unless that old woman I met really was a witch. "What are you carrying?" she asked me. (*Angrily*) What business was that of hers? So I answered, "Lumps of coal, you old hag," never dreaming that my beautiful pearls would change to lumps of coal in my pocket. (JACK *and* MOTHER *reenter.* JACK *carries knapsack.*) You're going? It's a waste of time, you know.

JACK: Perhaps, but all the same I mean to try. Goodbye, Tom. Goodbye, Mother.

TOM: Goodbye, Jack. (JACK *starts off, knapsack on back.*)

MOTHER: Now, Jack, remember your manners and be polite to all you meet, great or small. (*The* ANT KING *enters upstage behind his anthill.*)

JACK: I will, Mother. Goodbye. (JACK *waves and walks toward center.* MOTHER *and* TOM *exit into house.* ANT KING *steps out from behind anthill.*)

ANT KING (*To* JACK): Help, kind sir. Please stop and help.

JACK: Hello. Who are you?

ANT KING: I am King of the ant colony whose home you see here. (*Indicates anthill*)

JACK: What help do you need?

ANT KING: Why, the King of the Beetles claims that all this land is his. Yesterday we had a terrible battle. Nearly half my soldiers were killed. I'm afraid that today will see the end of my people.

JACK: Could you not leave here?

ANT KING: Yes, if the Beetle King would give us time to prepare a new home and move our eggs. But, no. He says we must leave immediately or be killed.

JACK: That seems quite harsh to me. I'll help you, and gladly. Where can I find this Beetle King?

ANT KING: He'll be here any minute.

JACK: I'm on my way to the palace to win the Princess. I don't want to wait long.

ANT KING: Here he comes. (BEETLE KING *enters*.)

BEETLE KING: Well, leader of this miserable little ant colony on my land, have you decided to move?

ANT KING: No. But I have found a champion.

JACK (*To* BEETLE KING): I say that all this land belongs to the ants. Their home is here and they must not be disturbed. You move away and leave them alone.

BEETLE KING: And if we refuse?

JACK: Call your army and see how quickly I'll squash them under my feet.

BEETLE KING: Well, I'm smart enough to know when the odds are too great, so I should be smart enough to find a piece of land just as good as this. (*Exits*.)

ANT KING: He's gone! He's leaving us in peace.

JACK: That's right. No more problems, little friend.

ANT KING: How can I thank you?

JACK: There's no need.

ANT KING: But there is. Some day you will have a task that you cannot do. Just call me. My people and I will help you as you have helped us.

JACK: Thank you. Now I must be on my way. (ANT KING *exits.* JACK *walks along.* OLD WOMAN *enters.*)

OLD WOMAN: Good day, young man.

JACK: Good day to you, ma'am.

OLD WOMAN: Where are you going, and what are you carrying?

JACK: I am going to the palace to win the hand of the Princess with a dozen of the finest pearls.

OLD WOMAN: May I see them?

JACK: Of course. (*Takes out leather bag*) Here they are. (*Shows pearls to* OLD WOMAN)

OLD WOMAN: They are fine enough for a princess, indeed. But you'll have to perform some hard tasks, too, to win the Princess.

JACK: I'll trust to luck when the time comes.

OLD WOMAN: And what have you in the knapsack?

JACK: My lunch. But I'm not hungry. Are you?

OLD WOMAN: Yes, I am, rather.

JACK: Here, then. You have the lunch. (*Takes food from knapsack and gives it to her.*)

OLD WOMAN: Why, thank you, young man. And, in return, here's a magic whistle. Anything you want will come back to you if you blow it.

JACK: Thank you. Thank you very much! Goodbye. (JACK *walks off toward right as the curtain falls.*)

*   *   *

SCENE 2

SETTING: *The palace courtyard, surrounded by a high stone wall, at rear. At right is the palace, with a door leading into the royal apartments, and another door to the store-rooms. An archway in the wall leads to the street.*

AT RISE: TWO GUARDS *stand outside the palace door as* JACK *enters through archway and goes up to them.*

1ST GUARD: State your business at the palace.

JACK: I have brought twelve perfect pearls for the Princess. (*He starts toward door.*)

1ST GUARD: Not so fast, there. Not everyone gets into the palace. We'll send to see if His Majesty is willing to listen to you.

2ND GUARD: Wait here. (2ND GUARD *exits into palace.*)

JACK: Have there been many here before me?

1ST GUARD: Hundreds, my boy, hundreds. Some of them brought the cheapest-looking pearls you could imagine. One fellow even brought lumps of coal. (*Laughs loudly*)

JACK (*Not laughing*): Pretty funny, eh?

1ST GUARD: But that's not the funniest. No, the best part is when they start trying to do the tasks the King sets after he accepts their pearls. (*Laughs*)

2ND GUARD (*Entering from palace*): Make way for Their Majesties, the King and Queen. (1ST GUARD *motions* JACK *back. He runs over and waits beside archway, bowing as* KING *and* QUEEN *enter, followed by the* PRINCESS, LADIES-IN-WAITING, COURTIERS, CHANCELLOR, JEWELLER, GARDENER, *and* FORESTER.)

1ST GUARD (*To* KING): Here is the young man, Your Majesty. (*Pushes* JACK *forward*)

KING: You have some pearls for us?

JACK (*Going down on one knee*): Yes, Your Majesty. Here they are. (*Hands him bag of pearls*)

KING: My Lord Chancellor, you and the Royal Jeweller will examine this gift.

CHANCELLOR: Yes, Your Majesty. (*He takes the bag, and he and the* JEWELLER *examine the pearls.*)

KING: Who are you, young man?

JACK: I am a poor fisherman, Your Majesty. My name is Jack.

KING: Poor! Then how came you by pearls good enough for royalty?

JACK: I found them in an oyster bed near our home, Sire.

KING: I see. And they are perfect?

JACK: I thought they were, Your Majesty, till I saw the Princess. (*Bows to her*) Nothing could be perfect enough for her.

KING (*With a slight snort*): Pretty speeches won't bring you success.

PRINCESS (*Smiling*): But pretty speeches do no harm.

JEWELLER (*Coming to the* KING *with the pearls*): The pearls are perfect.

KING: Are you sure?

JEWELLER: Not a single flaw, Your Majesty. The best I've ever seen.

KING (*Turning to* JACK): Young man, we shall accept your gift. (JEWELLER *steps back, carrying pearls.*)

JACK: Thank you, Your Majesty!

KING: Now for the reward. It is well known that a man may have permission to marry the Princess if, in addition to presenting twelve perfect pearls, he can perform certain tasks. Do you wish to try?

JACK: Yes, please, Sire.

KING: Gardener, bring me the sack of seeds.

GARDENER (*Coming forward, carrying sack of seeds*): Yes, Your Majesty. (*Hands sack to* KING)

KING (*To* JACK): Here is a sack of mixed seeds—barley, rye, oats and wheat. Within an hour you must sort these seeds into four separate sacks. If just one seed is in the wrong sack, your chance of marrying my daughter is gone. (*Calling*) Where are the four sacks?

GARDENER: Right here, Your Majesty. (*He takes four sacks from nearby* COURTIER, *and puts them on ground beside sack of seeds.*)

KING: We shall leave this young man to his task. (KING *leads all into palace.*)

JACK (*Opening sack*): In one hour. An impossible task. It would take an army to do that. Hmm . . . an army! The Ant King had an army. I'll call him. (*Calls softly,*

close to the ground) Ant King! Ant King! I need help.
Jack in the palace courtyard needs help! (*Straightens up*)
I suppose that was a silly thing to do.

ANT KING (*Entering*): You called, my friend?

JACK (*Surprised*): You came! Yes, I did call. See this sack of
seeds? There are four kinds. I have to sort them into four
separate sacks, within the hour.

ANT KING: Put the sack outside the gate where the ground
is softer. I'll call my soldiers. (ANT KING *exits, and* JACK
*follows him, carrying sack of seeds. He re-enters and
stands where he can look off.*)

JACK: What an army of ants! It won't take them long. (*Calling off*) Every seed must be in the right sack. No mistakes allowed.

ANT KING (*From offstage*): Don't worry.

JACK: But I do worry. I want to marry the Princess! (FOUR
ANTS *enter, each carrying a full sack, followed by the*
ANT KING, *carrying the large empty sack.*)

ANT KING: All correct, friend.

JACK: You mean it? Oh, how can I ever thank you?

ANT KING: It's our pleasure to repay our debt to you.
Goodbye. (ANTS *exit.*)

JACK (*Calling after them*): Goodbye, and thank you.
(*Knocks on palace door.* 1ST GUARD *opens it.*) Tell His
Majesty the task is finished.

1ST GUARD: Already? You're joking.

JACK: No. It's finished. Please inform His Majesty. (GUARD
exits.) That's one task done. I wonder what the next will
be. (KING *enters, followed by the court members, as before.*)

KING: Am I informed correctly? Is the task finished?

JACK: Yes, Your Majesty.

KING: The seeds are sorted into four separate sacks already?
It's impossible.

JACK: Perhaps if you would have them examined, sire.

KING: Gardener!

GARDENER: Yes, Your Majesty, we'll take them into the storeroom. (*He picks up bags, helped by* GUARDS, *and they exit.*)

KING: Meanwhile, we shall tell you the next task. Twelve wild rabbits will be turned into the courtyard here. At sunset we will check. All twelve rabbits must be present. Forester, as soon as we leave, let the rabbits in. Come, everyone. (*All but* FORESTER *and* JACK *exit.*)

FORESTER: Ready for your rabbits?

JACK: As ready as I'll ever be, but I don't know how I'll catch them.

FORESTER: I'll let them in them. (*He exits. After a pause,* TWELVE RABBITS *run in, jumping around* JACK, *then running off through archway.* FORESTER *watches from doorway.*)

JACK: Here, rabbits, come here. Come back, little rabbits. (*Sadly*) It's no use. They're going to the green woods outside. If only I had something to give them. (*Puts hands in pockets, then brings them out, holding whistle.*) The whistle! The Old Woman said it was magic. Whatever you want will come back to you, she said. Well, I want those rabbits, every one of them. (*Blows whistle. Immediately the* TWELVE RABBITS *hop in and sit in a circle around* JACK.)

FORESTER (*Aside*): I don't believe it! I must tell the King. (*Exits*)

JACK (*To* RABBITS): Well, my little beauties, are you all here? (*Counts*) One, two, four, eight, twelve! Yes, all here. And here you'll stay till sunset. Now, there's bound to be a third task. The Ant King helped me, and the Old Woman helped me. I wonder. . . . I hope I haven't come to the end of my good luck. (*Sees* PRINCESS *dressed as a peasant in ragged clothes, entering timidly.*) Why, who can this be? She looks just like the Princess.

PRINCESS (*Crossing to* JACK): Good day, sir. You have lots of rabbits, haven't you?

JACK: Yes, Miss. Twelve in all, I hope.

PRINCESS: Will you please give one to me? My mother is a poor woman, and we have nothing to eat.

JACK: I'm sorry, but I must have all twelve of them here at sunset.

PRINCESS: Nonsense. The King won't count them.

JACK: The King?

PRINCESS: Yes. Didn't you say the King wanted them here?

JACK: No, I didn't. But seeing you want one so much, I'll give you one in exchange for a kiss.

PRINCESS: Oh, no, I couldn't.

JACK: You're really not hungry, are you?

PRINCESS: Oh, yes, I am!

JACK: All right. A kiss in exchange for a rabbit.

PRINCESS: Very well. If I must. (*Kisses* JACK *on cheek*) Now, which rabbit may I have?

JACK: Any one you like.

PRINCESS: I'll take this one. (*Holds a* RABBIT *by shoulders*) Come on, little rabbit. (*They walk off.*)

JACK: That was a clever trick, little Princess, but not clever enough. (*Blows whistle and* RABBIT *comes back and sits down.*) How nice to have you back where you belong! (QUEEN *enters, dressed shabbily. To himself*) The Queen herself, I believe.

QUEEN (*Crossing to* JACK): Good day, young man. You have more rabbits than you need, I see. Could you spare one for a poor old woman who expects travelers at her home, and hasn't a bite to set before them?

JACK: You, ma'am?

QUEEN: Indeed, yes, young man. Take pity on me.

JACK: You cannot have one of my rabbits without paying for it.

QUEEN: I have no money right now. Perhaps . . .

JACK: Oh, I don't want money. But if you will walk around on tiptoe, look up into the sky, and cackle like a hen, I'll let you take a rabbit.

QUEEN: Good gracious! Everyone will think I've gone mad.

JACK: But there's no one here except you and me. And the rabbits, of course.

QUEEN: Oh, very well. (*She walks on tiptoe, looking up. and cackling.* JACK *is amused.*)

JACK (*Pleasantly*): I've heard better cackling from our hens, but you may take a rabbit.

QUEEN (*Taking a* RABBIT *by the neck*): Come on, you, come on. (QUEEN *and* RABBIT *walk off.* JACK *whistles as before and the* RABBIT *returns.*)

JACK: Well, my beauty, you're back. (*Sees* KING, *shabbily dressed, in doorway. To himself*) Why, that's the King!

KING (*Crossing to* JACK): I'd like to buy one of your rabbits.

JACK: I'm sorry, sir. They're not for sale.

KING: Come on, I have plenty of money. Name your price.

JACK: Very well. You must stand on your head, whack your heels together, and shout hurrah!

KING: You must be mad.

JACK: That's my price. Take it or leave it.

KING: Oh, all right. What was it? Stand on my head . . .

JACK: Whack your heels together, and shout hurrah. (KING *tries, but is very awkward.*) Well, you didn't exactly stand on your head, but you tried. Choose your rabbit.

KING (*Taking a* RABBIT): Come on, my fine fellow. (*He exits with* RABBIT. JACK *whistles and it returns.*)

JACK: Welcome back, friend. Well, the sun is setting. Time to report. (*Knocks at palace door.* 2ND GUARD *opens it.*) Please tell the King that the sun is setting, and the rabbits are all here.

2ND GUARD: I'll do that. (*Exits*)

JACK: I wonder what he'll set me to do next? (KING *and the others enter as before.* KING, QUEEN, *and* PRINCESS *have on royal robes over their shabby clothes. The* TWO GUARDS *enter last, carrying a large tub.*)

KING: Are all the rabbits here? Get them out of the way, Forester.

FORESTER: Come, little rabbits. (RABBITS *follow him off.*)

KING: We have one other task for you, young man.

JACK: Yes, Your Majesty?

KING: You are to tell as many undoubted truths as will fill this tub. (GUARDS *bring the tub forward and set it down.*)

JACK: But—pardon me, Your Majesty—but how do we know when the tub is full?

KING: Don't you worry. That's my part of the business.

PRINCESS: Father, that's not fair.

KING: Daughter, be quiet.

JACK: Very well, Your Majesty. Here is the first truth. To-day, in exchange for a kiss, I gave a rabbit to a pretty young girl, and that girl was the Princess.

KING: Daughter! That can't be true!

PRINCESS: It is the undoubted truth.

JACK: Is the tub full, Your Majesty?

KING: Of course not!

JACK: Very well. Today I gave a rabbit to a plump old woman, but first, she had to walk around on tiptoe, look at the sky, and cackle like a hen. And that plump woman was the Queen. Right?

QUEEN: Of course not. How ridiculous!

PRINCESS: But Mother, why do you have on that ragged dress under your royal robes? (QUEEN *tries to hide dress.*) It was you. That's another undoubted truth.

JACK: Is the tub full, Your Majesty?

KING: No, it is not full.

JACK: You are quite sure, sire?

KING: Of course I'm sure.

JACK: Very well. Then there came a fat old fellow and asked me for a rabbit. He got one, but first he had to—

PRINCESS: Wait a minute. Did he wear clothes like Father's? (*She pulls aside* KING's *robe.*)

JACK: Why, I believe he did.

KING: Stop! Not another word! The tub is full.

JACK: Then I may marry the Princess?

KING: You may.

JACK: At once?

KING: At once. Perhaps it will be a good thing to have a clever son-in-law to help me rule the kingdom. (PRINCESS *and* JACK *join hands as* KING *leads others off.*) Come, we must prepare for the wedding! (*Curtain.*)

THE END

Simple Olaf

A Scandinavian folk tale

by Mary Nygaard Peterson

Characters

SIMPLE OLAF	1ST ATTENDANT
PEASANT	2ND ATTENDANT
1ST GUARD	COURTIERS
2ND GUARD	STAGEHANDS
KING	

TIME: *A sunny morning, long, long ago.*

SETTING: *A forest path in a mythical Scandinavian kingdom. There is a fallen log at left.*

AT RISE: OLAF *enters jauntily from left, whistling. Over his shoulder he carries a stick with a colored kerchief tied at end.*

OLAF (*Stopping, downstage center, to look about him, pleased with what he sees*): What a beautiful world this is! And it's mine—all mine. I wonder which way I should go now—to the village (*Points toward audience*), to the seashore (*Points right*), or to the mountains? (*Points left*) That mountain road looks interesting. (*He peers upstage left, shading his eyes with his hand.*) I believe there's a mansion up there—a castle, perhaps.

(OLAF *tilts his head to the side and listens intently.*) It sounds as if someone is coming. I wonder who it could be, on this lonely path? (*Cups hand behind ear, listening*) I think I'll just sit down on this fallen log and see who it is. Maybe we can walk along together. (*He sits, puts his stick and kerchief on ground, and looks about him with interest. He begins whistling softly.* PEASANT *enters, carrying an unwieldy box with obvious difficulty, and looking hot and irritable.* OLAF *gets up and goes toward* PEASANT *in a friendly manner.*) Good morning, sir. (PEASANT *ignores him and continues walking.*) May I help you, sir? I would be glad to carry your box for you. What is in it?

PEASANT (*Glaring at* OLAF *and speaking gruffly*): Nothing for you.

OLAF: I'm sorry, sir. I didn't mean to be inquisitive. (PEASANT *walks around* OLAF *and continues left.* OLAF *looks after him, shaking his head regretfully. Absent-mindedly he begins jingling coins in his pocket, then turns and starts toward right exit.* PEASANT *pauses, puts down box, and walks toward* OLAF.)

PEASANT (*Suddenly friendly*): Wait, wait, my boy!

OLAF (*Stopping and turning toward* PEASANT; *politely*): You called me, sir?

PEASANT: Did I hear money jingling in your pocket?

OLAF (*Still speaking politely*): I don't know whether you did or not, sir.

PEASANT (*Impatiently*): Don't be impertinent, lad. Do you have money in your pocket?

OLAF (*Surprised*): Why, yes, sir. I do. (*He takes out a handful of coins and holds them out in his open palm.*) See?

PEASANT (*With surprised whistle*): I should say you have! (*Then, suspiciously*) Who are you, lad?

OLAF: My name is Olaf, sir.

PEASANT: Olaf. Is that all they call you?

OLAF: Well, my brothers call me *Simple* Olaf. But that's not really my name, you know.

PEASANT: Simple Olaf, eh? Hm-m-m. Where'd you get all that money, Simple Olaf?

OLAF (*Replacing the money in his pocket*): My brothers gave it to me—just this morning. "Here, Simple Olaf," they said, "Here's your share of the money. Why don't you go and seek your fortune? The world is yours." (OLAF *looks about him appreciatively*) A very nice world it is, too, don't you think?

PEASANT (*With a quick look*): Oh, yes. Beyond a doubt. Beyond a doubt. (*Then he looks again at* OLAF) But this money, now. If you were to see something you really liked, you would buy it, with your money, wouldn't you?

OLAF (*Thoughtfully*): I suppose I would, sir.

PEASANT (*Going to his box and lifting it up*): Now, in this box I have something very nice. I should like you to see it. (*He carries it toward* OLAF *and tries to open lid with his free hand.* OLAF *goes to help him, peeks into box, whistles appreciatively.*) What did I tell you? Mighty fine, isn't it?

OLAF: Mighty fine, indeed. I don't believe I've ever seen a finer goose.

PEASANT: I know you haven't. There couldn't be a finer goose than this. I have cared for it since it was an egg. Fed it from my own table, I did.

OLAF (*Admiringly*): It's a mighty fine goose, sir. You must be proud to be the owner of it.

PEASANT: I am. But, since you like it so much, I might be willing to trade it for the money you have in your pocket.

OLAF: That is fair enough. After all, I can't eat money. (OLAF *hands the* PEASANT *his money. Then he starts to exit right, and* PEASANT *left.*)

PEASANT (*Barely concealing his glee*): *Simple* Olaf is right!

(OLAF *is almost at right exit and* PEASANT *at left, when* OLAF *stops, as if struck by a sudden thought. He turns and calls to* PEASANT.)

OLAF (*Calling*): Oh, sir! (PEASANT *ignores him and keeps walking left.* OLAF *calls more insistently.*) Sir, please wait a moment!

PEASANT (*Stopping reluctantly*): Oh, no, my lad! You can't change your mind now. A trade's a trade! (*He turns back again and starts to exit, as* OLAF *calls more insistently.*)

OLAF: Please wait, kind sir. I don't want to change my mind.

PEASANT (*Pausing, suspiciously*): What do you want, then?

OLAF (*Pointing left*): I just wondered, sir, what is that building on the hillside yonder?

PEASANT (*Looking briefly off left and speaking scornfully*): That's the castle, of course.

OLAF: A castle. Who lives in it?

PEASANT: Why, the king, of course. You don't know much, do you, Simple Olaf?

OLAF (*Thoughtfully*): The king. Think of that! I believe I'll go to the castle and give my goose to the king. It is a goose fit for a king. Don't you think? (*He looks questioningly at* PEASANT.)

PEASANT: Beyond a doubt. Beyond a doubt. (OLAF *exits right.* PEASANT *looks after him, shrugs his shoulders and makes a twirling motion with his finger at his head.*) A fool and his money are soon parted. (*He jingles coins in his pocket, as he exits left. After a brief pause,* 1ST GUARD *enters and takes his position at right.* 2ND GUARD *enters and takes his position between center and left.* OLAF *enters right, carrying box and whistling. He starts to pass* 1ST GUARD, *but* GUARD *steps in front of* OLAF, *halting him.*)

1ST GUARD: Where do you think you're going?

OLAF: Why, I'm going to see the king.

1st Guard: Oho! You think anyone who wants to can just walk right in and see the king? What do you want with him?

Olaf: Why, I just want to give him a gift.

1st Guard: Now, that's different. Why didn't you say so in the first place? I must tell you, though, that half of every gift that is brought to the king belongs to me. As soon as you have given me my half, you may go on.

Olaf (*Doubtfully*): I don't know about this. You see, my gift is a goose. I don't think it would look right to give the king half a goose. Do you think it would?

1st Guard (*Scratching his head*): Maybe not. (*Thinking for a moment*) Tell you what we'll do. You take that goose to the king. When the king gives you a present in return, you must give half of it to me. Is that agreed?

Olaf (*Doubtfully*): I suppose so, sir.

1st Guard: Very well, then. You may go on. But remember, I'll be waiting right here when you return, and you'd better not try any tricks on me. (1st Guard *steps back to his position and motions to* Olaf *to proceed left.* Olaf *walks left again, until he reaches* 2nd Guard.)

2nd Guard: Halt! Where do you think you are going?

Olaf: Why, I am going into the castle to give this present to the king.

2nd Guard: Oho! And do you think just anyone can go in to see the king whenever he feels like it?

Olaf: The guard at the gate said I could enter.

2nd Guard: He said you could enter the *gate*. *I* am the one who guards the door, and whoever brings a gift to the king must give half of it to me, or he does not enter.

Olaf: That doesn't seem fair. Anyway, my gift is a goose. I don't think it would look right to give half a goose to the king. Do you think it would?

2nd Guard (*Rubbing his chin reflectively*): Probably not. The king might begin wondering what happened to the other half. (*He rubs his chin again.*) I'll tell you what we can do. You give your goose to the king. He will offer you something in return. Whatever it is, you must promise to give me half. Is that agreed?

OLAF (*Reluctantly*): I suppose so.

2ND GUARD: Then you may enter. But, remember! (OLAF *passes* 2ND GUARD.)

OLAF (*To himself*): Half to the first guard, half to the second guard! What does that leave for me? (OLAF *and* GUARDS *exit, left, and* STAGEHANDS *enter right to set up throne.* OLAF *and the* GUARDS *re-enter, left, and stand close together as fanfare and shouting are heard from off right.*)

COURTIERS (*Offstage*): The King! Long live the King! Make way for His Majesty. (KING *enters, followed by his retinue. He seats himself on throne, and* COURTIERS *line up at his left and at his right. An* ATTENDANT *stands on either side of throne.*)

ALL (*Together*): Long live the King!

1ST ATTENDANT (*Stepping forward*): His Gracious Majesty, our King, is ready to receive petitions from his people. (*There is a pause, and no one moves or speaks.*) Isn't there anyone here this morning who wishes to speak to the king? (1ST *and* 2ND GUARDS *begin to push* OLAF *forward.*)

1ST GUARD (*Pushing* OLAF *toward* KING): Ask for gold!

2ND GUARD (*Pushing* OLAF *from other side*): Ask for diamonds! (COURTIERS, ATTENDANTS, *and* KING *look curiously toward* GUARDS *and* OLAF *as he is pushed forward, toward throne.*)

1ST ATTENDANT: Did you wish to see the king, lad?

OLAF (*Going forward, uneasily*): Yes, sir. I have a gift here I should like to give to the king.

1ST ATTENDANT (*Looking into the box*): You may present it to the king, lad. It is very nice. (OLAF *goes to throne, kneels, and holds out box to* KING. 2ND ATTENDANT *takes box and opens it for* KING.)

KING (*Looking into box*): What a fine goose! It is many a year since I have seen such a fine goose as that. I shall look forward to having it for my dinner. (*To* 2ND ATTENDANT) See that the cook receives it at once.

2ND ATTENDANT: Yes, Your Majesty. (*He bows low to* KING, *hands the box to* COURTIER, *who then exits, right, with box.*)

KING (*Turning to* OLAF): Now, my fine lad, I should like to reward you for your thoughtfulness. What may I give you that will please you most? (OLAF, *still kneeling, glances over his shoulder at* GUARDS.)

OLAF: Your Majesty, I find it hard to speak.

KING (*Impatiently*): Come, now. Surely, there must be many things a lad like you would want. Gold, perhaps? (1ST GUARD *looks delighted.*) Or jewels? (2ND GUARD *looks pleased.*)

OLAF: If it is all the same to you, Your Majesty, I wouldn't care for either gold or jewels. (GUARDS *look angry.*)

KING (*Mildly*): It is many a day since anyone refused a gift of gold or jewels from the king. Are you quite sure you don't want them?

OLAF: Quite sure, Your Majesty. If it is all the same to you, Sire, I should like to have only a good beating. (*This astounds everyone, and there is murmur of disbelief among those near throne.* GUARDS *look enraged.*)

KING (*In astonishment*): Did I hear you correctly, my lad? You want only a good beating?

OLAF: That is correct, Your Majesty. A good beating is all I ask.

KING: A most unusual request, I must say. I do not like to grant your wish, but since you insist, it shall be as you say. (*To* ATTENDANTS) Take this lad out and give him ten good strokes. (ATTENDANTS *seize* OLAF *and start to hurry him toward exit.*)

OLAF (*Protesting*): Wait! Wait. (ATTENDANTS *ignore him, and he calls to* KING *over his shoulder.*) Your Majesty! Your Majesty!

KING (*Sternly*): Wait! (ATTENDANTS *halt.*) Bring the lad back here. (*They do so.* OLAF *again kneels at* KING'S *feet.*) I must warn you, lad. I do not like to have my time wasted by foolishness such as this. What is it, now? Have you changed your mind about the reward? Let us have no more nonsense.

OLAF: Forgive me, Your Majesty. Forgive me. I have not changed my mind about the reward, but it is not right that I should take it for myself.

KING (*Coldly*): You had better explain yourself. I do not understand such foolishness.

OLAF: You see, Your Majesty, the reward does not belong to me. I have promised it to someone else. Before the guard at the gate would let me enter the palace grounds, he made me promise that half of any reward I might receive should go to him.

KING (*Glancing at* 1ST GUARD *and speaking thoughtfully*): Hm-m-m. I see. (1ST GUARD *looks frightened.*)

OLAF: Then, before I was allowed to enter the castle, I had to promise to give the other half of anything I might receive to the guard at the door. (KING *looks at* GUARDS.) So, you see, Your Majesty, the reward does not rightly belong to me. I do not feel as though I should accept it.

KING: I see what you mean—and I agree with you heartily. (*He speaks to his* ATTENDANTS) Take the two guards out and divide this lad's beating between them. (ATTENDANTS *grab protesting* GUARDS *and hurry them off.* KING *speaks kindly to* OLAF, *who is still kneeling.*) What is your name, my lad?

OLAF: Olaf, Your Majesty.

KING: Olaf? Is that all they call you?

OLAF: Well, my brothers call me *Simple* Olaf, but that is not rightfully my name, Your Majesty.

KING: I should say not, Olaf, for if you are simple, I only wish we had a great many more simple people just like you. You are just the kind of person I need to help me rule my kingdom. Will you stay with me, and be my adviser? I need your help so badly!

OLAF: I would gladly serve you with my life, Your Majesty.

KING: Then that is settled. Now, I think the first thing we shall do is to change your name. No more shall you be called *Simple Olaf,* but *Olaf, the Wise. (He touches* OLAF *on both shoulders with his scepter, as he pronounces the new name.)* Come. You shall sit beside me on my throne, so I may turn to you for advice whenever I need it. (OLAF *rises and seats himself beside* KING.)

ALL (*Together*): Long live the King! Long live *Olaf, the Wise! (Curtain)*

THE END

The Builder of the Wall

A Norse folk tale

by Helen Roberts

Characters

FRIGG, *the chief goddess, wife of Odin*
FREYA, *the goddess of love and spring*
FULLA, *favorite servant of Frigg*
HEIMDAL, *Keeper of the Bridge of the Gods*
ODIN, *chief god*
THOR, *god of thunder*
LOKI, *the sly god of mischief*
STRANGER, *giant in disguise*
SVADILFARE, *his horse*

SCENE 1

SETTING: *Asgard, home of the gods.*

AT RISE: HEIMDAL *is keeping watch at the end of the rain-bow bridge.* FRIGG *walks in the garden of Asgard, with* FULLA *and* FREYA. FREYA *is carrying a flower basket and scissors.*

FRIGG: Aren't you proud of our gardens here in Asgard, Freya?

FREYA (*Setting down her basket*): Indeed, I am. You know

how much I love flowers and eternal spring. (*Picks flowers*)

FULLA: See! The rainbow bridge is newly finished, too. How it gleams! I hope it won't ever grow dim.

FRIGG (*Touching bridge*): Such lovely colors in it! The gods will always enjoy it.

FULLA: Not only the gods. Even the poorest man on earth can see this rainbow after a gentle rain.

FREYA: I am pleased with my castle and its many rooms. I want to fill each one with flowers.

FRIGG: I am happy with my new home too. The gods have done well with all their building.

FULLA (*Shielding her eyes to look beyond the bridge*): Do you see the blue mountains—far away in the distance?

FRIGG: Yes, my dear, but that's where the giants live—in Jotunheim. I don't like to think of them. It is much pleasanter to think of our own home in Asgard.

FREYA: I'm like you, Frigg. The very thought of the Frost Giants makes me shiver.

FULLA: But they are so far away. Forget about them!

FREYA (*Smiling*): That's good advice. There's our wise Heimdal, keeping watch by the rainbow bridge.

FRIGG: He's the most faithful god in Asgard!

FULLA: He hardly sleeps—day or night—keeping watch over the safety of our kingdom.

FRIGG: I wonder if *he* ever sees anything to worry him?

FULLA: Of course not. Not here in Asgard.

FREYA: We might learn something worthwhile—if we listen to him. (*They cross to* HEIMDAL, *who rises to greet them.*)

FRIGG: Good morning, Heimdal.

HEIMDAL: Good morning, fair ladies. You are up early for your stroll.

FREYA: The garden is more beautiful in the morning. (*Puts flower into his buttonhole*)

HEIMDAL (*Admiring it*): Thank you, Freya.

FULLA: The air is clearer, too. We can see farther.

HEIMDAL: That's very true. But surely three such lovely ladies should not try to look far away into the distance.

FRIGG: Why not, Heimdal?

HEIMDAL: Because that is my job.

FREYA: Your voice sounds anxious, Heimdal. Is there anything you see in the distance—that distresses you?

HEIMDAL: I have no desire to worry you.

FREYA: What is it, Heimdal?

HEIMDAL: My eyes are accustomed to looking far away. I see the Frost Giants busily at work in Jotunheim.

FREYA: Oh dear! I'm so afraid of those giants.

FRIGG (*Putting an arm around her*): Nonsense, Freya. They're too far away to bother us.

HEIMDAL: I wish I were as sure of that as you are, Frigg. Wherever there are plotting giants, there's sure to be trouble.

FREYA (*Shivering*): We mustn't let the Frost Giants gain a foothold in Asgard. (*Holds her flowers close*) My poor flowers! I'll protect you from the cruel Frost Giants!

FRIGG: Come, Freya. We must tell Odin that Heimdal thinks they plan mischief. (*They start off.* FULLA *remains.*)

FULLA: Do you think they will try to enter Asgard soon?

HEIMDAL: No, Fulla. Maybe not for years. But you know that the giants are the natural enemies of the gods.

FULLA: And they are jealous of our power in the world.

HEIMDAL: I don't wish to alarm my brothers—but I think we should make plans to defend ourselves. (ODIN, THOR, *and* LOKI *enter.*)

ODIN: Why have you been frightening the ladies with talk of dangerous giants?

HEIMDAL: I'm sorry, Odin, if they were alarmed.

FULLA: Excuse me. I'll join my mistress. (*Exits*)

THOR (*Thunderously*): We know you are far-sighted, but what is this danger you suspect?

HEIMDAL: I think we should be prepared for any sort of invasion, now or in the future.

ODIN: We have just finished building our castles and bridges. Isn't that enough?

HEIMDAL: But what is to prevent the giants from attacking us?

THOR (*Blustering*): They wouldn't dare. They wouldn't dare!

HEIMDAL: I'm not so sure. They are making many preparations in Jotunheim.

ODIN: What do you suggest, Heimdal? I respect your counsel.

HEIMDAL (*Going over to far end of bridge*): I think we should build a solid stone wall, so tall and so strong that it would keep out all the giants.

THOR: Where would you build it?

HEIMDAL: At this end of the Bridge of the Gods. (*Shows them*) From here—to here.

LOKI: *I* think it's a lot of nonsense.

ODIN: Perhaps Heimdal is right.

THOR: But, Odin! We are not wall-builders.

LOKI: We can do graceful things like the rainbow—but a stone wall is quite different.

ODIN (*Thoughtfully*): It would be such a long, heavy task.

HEIMDAL: I thought you should know my opinion, at least. (*They return to sit at end of rainbow.*)

LOKI (*Disagreeably*): I'm *sure* I don't want to help build it. I was planning to make a trip to Midgard this week to see how our mortal neighbors are getting along.

THOR: You always plan a trip when there's work to do.

LOKI: I don't notice *you're* such a willing worker yourself, Thor.

ODIN: Please, don't start quarreling. That won't help. (*A

very tall, poorly dressed STRANGER *enters, and knocks loudly at end of rainbow.*)

HEIMDAL: Whoever is that? I've never seen him before. (*Gets up*)

ODIN: He's a stranger to me. And I don't like his looks.

HEIMDAL: Well, I must be polite to any stranger who knocks at my gate.

LOKI: Don't be too polite. Get rid of him as quickly as you can.

HEIMDAL (*Going over to man*): Who are you and what do you want?

STRANGER: I have no name. Just call me Stranger.

HEIMDAL: Very well, then, Stranger. Are you looking for food?

STRANGER (*Angrily*): Indeed not! I came to do the gods a favor.

HEIMDAL: A favor? What could you do for us?

ODIN (*To other two*): He's a big fellow, isn't he?

THOR: I believe he's almost as big as *I* am.

LOKI: Bigger, if you ask me.

STRANGER (*Boldly*): I am a mighty builder. I came here to build a wall for you at the rainbow's end.

HEIMDAL: Surely one person could not build a wall!

STRANGER: Not one ordinary person. I am an expert. Building is my business.

HEIMDAL: It would take you hundreds of years to build it.

STRANGER: That's where you're wrong. I can build it in three years.

HEIMDAL: Three years!

STRANGER: In three years it will be finished. A strong wall —along here. (*Paces along site of wall*)

HEIMDAL (*Suspiciously*): What is your price?

STRANGER: If I finish it in three years, I demand the sun, the moon, and the goddess Freya. If I don't finish it you pay nothing.

HEIMDAL: You must be mad to think we would make such a bargain.

STRANGER: Tell the others my terms! I'll wait here. (*Sits down*)

HEIMDAL (*Returning to others*): Did you hear what the stranger said?

ODIN: That he could build the wall in three years.

THOR: It's impossible. It would take many times that long.

HEIMDAL: He said if he didn't finish on time he would make no charge for his labor.

ODIN: Yes—but if he *did* finish on time, he demanded the sun, the moon—and the goddess Freya.

HEIMDAL: We couldn't take such a risk.

THOR: Of course we know he couldn't finish it in three years.

LOKI: And we do need the stone wall.

HEIMDAL: The price he asks is too great—

THOR: Only if he finishes on time.

LOKI: Make it harder for him. Tell him he must finish it in *one* season—this winter.

HEIMDAL: He wouldn't consent to that.

ODIN: Try him.

HEIMDAL: I can ask. (*Goes to* STRANGER) We can't accept your terms.

STRANGER: You'll be sorry!

HEIMDAL: We will give you *one* season to complete the wall.

STRANGER (*Laughing*): Now you're making fun of a poor man.

HEIMDAL: No, we're serious. You may begin now—but you must finish by the first day of summer.

STRANGER: I'll do it, on one condition.

HEIMDAL: What's that? We don't usually grant special terms.

STRANGER: That I can have the help of my horse, Svadil-fare.

HEIMDAL: I don't know if the others will consent. Wait here a moment. (*Goes back to them*)

ODIN: Did he accept our terms?

HEIMDAL: He agreed to do it if he could have the help of his horse, Svadilfare.

THOR: His horse!

LOKI (*Laughing loudly*): You mean he agreed to finish it in one season with just a horse to help him?

HEIMDAL: Yes, he did. But don't forget what he demands if he finishes it on time.

ODIN: We can't risk our lovely Freya—or the sun—or the moon.

LOKI (*Irritably*): Don't be childish! You know as well as I do that he couldn't finish it in one season or even twenty. We'll have a good wall—that won't cost us a thing.

HEIMDAL: I'm afraid of cheap bargains. They cost too much in the end.

LOKI: Now, look here! We must have the wall. Let's get it done while we can. I'll take the responsibility.

ODIN (*Weakening*): Maybe we should!

THOR: Perhaps—

HEIMDAL: I don't think so. Really I don't. You'd better stop to consider further.

LOKI: Let's tell him to start now. (*Starts toward* STRANGER)

ODIN: I'll tell him. I am Odin, the father of all.

STRANGER (*Standing and bowing mockingly*): Ah! The council of the gods! What is your decision?

ODIN: We agree that if you—with the help of your horse —build this wall before the first day of summer—

STRANGER (*Smiling*): That I will receive as payment the sun, the moon, and the goddess Freya.

ODIN: And if it is *not* finished on time, we pay you nothing.

STRANGER: Agreed! (*Smiles*) And of course you have nothing to fear. You surely have the best of the bargain.

LOKI (*Gaily*): You can begin as soon as you wish. (*To others*) We may as well return to our homes and celebrate with a feast. We've made a very good bargain.

HEIMDAL (*As they start off*): I wish I were sure of it. (HEIMDAL, LOKI, THOR *and* ODIN *exit.*)

STRANGER: Svadilfare! Svadilfare! (*Whistles for his horse.*)

SVADILFARE (*Entering, walking upright, carrying a load of cardboard blocks*): Here I am, Master. There are other piles of stone ready—right over there. (*Points offstage.*)

STRANGER: Good! You see, I promised to complete the wall by the first day of summer.

SVADILFARE (*Unloading*): I thought you planned on *three* years.

STRANGER (*Beginning construction of wall*): They refused that. We'll have to work night and day to finish on time.

SVADILFARE: And they don't know who you are?

STRANGER: No! I am just a stranger to them.

SVADILFARE: Won't they be furious when you take away their sun and moon?

STRANGER: And Freya, too. She's most precious of all. Oh hurry, hurry! We have no time to lose. (*They work very fast, as curtains close.*)

*   *   *

SCENE 2

TIME: *The day before the first day of summer.*

SETTING: *Asgard, as in Scene 1.*

AT RISE: *The wall has been almost entirely erected. One small space remains unfinished.* SVADILFARE *and* STRANGER *stand looking at wall.*

SVADILFARE (*Laughing noisily*): We need a few more loads of stone. Then the wall will be finished!

STRANGER: It will be done in plenty of time. This wall is strong enough to last forever. I'm proud of our work.

SVADILFARE: When it's finished, the wedding bells will ring for you and the fair Freya.

STRANGER: You're right! We must hurry. I'll go with you to the quarry for more rocks.

SVADILFARE: Off to the quarry we go! (*They both exit. After a moment,* FRIGG *enters with* FREYA *and* FULLA.)

FRIGG: We haven't been here for a walk since the wall was started.

FREYA: Fancy the stranger thinking he could build it in time! Why, it's—— (*Seeing wall*)

FRIGG: Oh, it's almost done!

FULLA: We must do something right away. If it isn't already too late.

FREYA: They have pledged *me* if he finishes on time. (*Runs off crying*) I can't do it! I won't do it!

FRIGG: Poor Freya!

ODIN (*Entering with* FREYA, *followed by* THOR, HEIMDAL, *and* LOKI): You say the wall is almost done?

FREYA (*Weeping*): Another few loads of rock will finish it! Oh, help me, Odin! Dear friend, help me!

THOR: But the stranger's time will soon be up.

HEIMDAL: They work very fast. I fear they'll finish on time.

ODIN: And we pledged you, our beloved Freya.

FREYA: Don't forget you'll also lose the sun and the moon. Ugh! You'll have darkness and cold forever in Asgard!

FRIGG: But we'd miss *you* most of all, Freya.

THOR: How did we ever agree to such terms?

HEIMDAL: It was the sly Loki who persuaded you to let the stranger use his horse. That horse does twice as much work as his master.

ODIN (*As* LOKI *tries to slink away*): Stop, Loki! Come back here!

LOKI (*Crossly*): What do you want?

ODIN (*Severely*): *You* are responsible for this madness.

THOR (*Taking* LOKI *by the shoulder*): What shall I do with him? He has always been a mischief-maker among us.

LOKI (*Pleading*): Don't hurt me! Please don't hurt me. I'll do anything you say.

ODIN: Then find some way to prevent the stranger from finishing by morning. If you don't, we'll punish you severely.

FREYA: You must use your wits this time, Loki.

LOKI: Oh, I will! My cunning has never failed me.

FRIGG: Listen! Are not the horse and the stranger approaching?

HEIMDAL: They mustn't find us here. Quick! To our homes! (*They all exit.*)

STRANGER (*Entering with* SVADILFARE *and a load of rock*): I'll be glad when our task is finished.

SVADILFARE: So will I! I'm getting tired.

STRANGER: I could never have done it without you. Hurry with these blocks, Svadilfare.

SVADILFARE: One more load should finish it. (*They work on wall.*)

STRANGER (*Laughing gleefully*): And finish those proud gods, too. What a surprise they'll have! (*As they work,* LOKI *slips in quietly, carrying a horse's head, which he puts on. Then he neighs gently, and hides.*)

SVADILFARE (*Looking in* LOKI's *direction*): What was that?

STRANGER: I didn't hear anything.

LOKI (*Hidden; neighing again*): Mhmhmhm!

SVADILFARE: There it goes again.

STRANGER (*Irritably*): For goodness' sake, Svadilfare! What's the matter with you? Get to work!

LOKI (*Neighing again*): Hmmhmhmhm! (*Comes out of hiding and starts to gallop near the Rainbow Bridge.*)

SVADILFARE: I can't stand it! I'll have to find out what that is! (*Prances after* LOKI, *who turns as* SVADILFARE *pursues him and gallops offstage, whinnying. Both exit.*)

STRANGER (*Not noticing*): Hand me the next block, Svadilfare! (*There is no answer*) Svadilfare! (*Looks up*) Where could that miserable beast have gone? (*Looks around the wall*) I'll have to look for him to help with the next load! (*He goes off, calling to his horse as he goes.*)

ODIN (*Entering cautiously, followed by* THOR *and* HEIMDAL): I don't see the stranger here now!

THOR: Where have they gone? They can't be far away.

HEIMDAL: I was watching them from a distance, and do you know, it was the strangest thing . . .

ODIN: What was? What do you mean?

HEIMDAL: They were working at top speed, when the horse Svadilfare began to act up.

THOR: What caused it?

HEIMDAL: I heard a horse neighing in the distance.

ODIN: A horse! In Asgard? Are you sure?

HEIMDAL: Very sure. The stranger's horse, Svadilfare, deserted his work and started to follow the other horse.

ODIN: Hm! So Svadilfare was lured away by the strange horse!

THOR: What of the stranger?

HEIMDAL: At first he didn't notice it! When he did, he was furious and went off to look for his helper.

ODIN: And the wall—is it finished?

HEIMDAL: I don't see how it could be yet. They worked only a few moments before they left.

THOR: We can examine it. There's no one here to see us. (*They go over to look at the wall.*)

ODIN (*Shouting happily*): Look! It isn't finished!

HEIMDAL: It's all done but the gate!

THOR: How wonderful! We can finish that ourselves.

ODIN: Without paying the penalty.

FREYA (*Entering, followed by* FRIGG *and* FULLA): Have you heard any news?

FRIGG: Not a word, dear Freya. But the gods have not been home to tell us.

FULLA: There they are—over by the wall!

FRIGG: So they are!

FREYA (*Calling*): Odin! What of the wall?

ODIN: Come over here and see for yourselves. (*Women go over to wall.*) See what protection we have here!

FREYA (*Not understanding*): Don't—don't tell me it's all finished!

THOR: Look here, dear Freya! See the gate! See here!

FRIGG (*Joyfully*): Don't you see? It's not finished!

FREYA: Oh, thank goodness! My heart almost stopped beating when I thought the wall was completed.

FULLA: Someone is coming! I hear footsteps.

ODIN: It must be the stranger. Hush!

STRANGER (*Entering slowly, with his head down*): I can't finish it alone.

HEIMDAL (*Sharply*): No you can't. And your time is up.

STRANGER: I would have finished—in plenty of time, if—

ODIN: Of course. You have to think of *some* excuse.

STRANGER: My horse was coaxed away. I can't understand it.

ODIN (*With sarcasm*): How unfortunate!

STRANGER (*With fury*): Don't use that tone with me! Look! (*He takes off his cloak, revealing he is a Frost Giant.*)

THOR: Why—why, you're a Frost Giant!

OTHERS (*Terrified*): A Frost Giant! A Frost Giant!

STRANGER (*With a snarl*): Yes, I am. A mighty Frost Giant! (*Clutches* FREYA) And I almost won the fairest goddess!

FREYA: Don't touch me! How dare you? Get your frosty hands off my arm. You're freezing my flesh. (*She breaks away.*)

THOR (*Stepping forward*): We made a bargain with you.

ODIN (*With sarcasm*): Thanks for such a safe wall to protect us from all your brother giants.

HEIMDAL: You won't bother us any more now.

FREYA: Go home to your frost castles!

FRIGG (*Smiling*): We don't need your help now.

STRANGER (*Snarling*): I'm tired out! Surely I deserve some reward. Give me the moon, at least.

THOR: We kept our bargain. Now, go home!

STRANGER: But I have lost my precious horse, my Svadilfare.

LOKI (*Entering in horse disguise and neighing*): Hmhm-hmhmhm!

STRANGER: There's the villainous creature that lured my Svadilfare away from his work. (*Approaches* LOKI *threateningly*) I'll soon cut off *his* head.

ODIN: Indeed you won't! He must not be harmed.

LOKI (*Taking off his horse's head and bowing deeply*): Yours truly, O Frost Giant!

ALL (*In surprise*): Loki! Loki!

STRANGER: Loki! I should have known! Where's my horse?

LOKI (*Pointing*): He's galloping like the wind—on his way home to Jotunheim—

ODIN (*Threateningly*): Where you had better follow, wicked Frost Giant—if you know what is good for you! (*Curtain*)

THE END

The Magic Cloak

A Scandinavian fairy tale

by Virginia Payne Whitworth

Characters

Peasant Girl	Princess Adele
Jon, *a soldier*	Princess Babette
Herald	Princess Charlotte
Old Woman	Lady Kay
Prince Donald	Lords
Duke Frederick	Ladies
King	Three Dancing Partners

Scene 1

Setting: *A path in the forest, with a wooden bench at one side.*

At Rise: Herald *enters from left, holding a scroll, from which he reads. He walks to center.*

Herald (*Reading*): Hear ye! Hear ye! Today is your last chance to win the hand of a Princess. For further details, present yourself to the King. (*Rolls up scroll and goes off right.* Peasant Girl *enters from left, carrying bundle of sticks. She limps over to bench, sits down and takes off shoes, and shakes out some stones.*)

435

PEASANT GIRL: No wonder my feet hurt. (*She sticks her finger through hole in sole of shoe.*) A fine thing! I'm as bad off as the Princesses, but they have more shoes and wear them out faster. (*Pauses*) I wonder how they do it. (*Whistling heard off left.*) Now, who can that be? (JON *enters, wearing a shabby uniform and carrying a worn knapsack.*)

JON: Hello! (*Looks at her bare feet.*) Are you having some trouble?

GIRL: Yes, I am. (*Hangs a shoe on each hand by sticking a finger through hole.*) This is the only pair I have.

JON (*Opening knapsack*): Let me see them. (GIRL *hands shoes to* JON. *He puts them on rock, takes two pieces of cloth out of knapsack and puts one piece into each shoe.*) Here you are. (*Hands shoes to her*) I'm always happy to help a pretty girl in distress.

GIRL: Thank you, soldier. (*Puts shoes on and gets up.*)

JON: That will get you home, anyway.

GIRL: Are you just back from the wars?

JON: Yes, I am.

GIRL: Then you may not have heard of the King's newest proclamation. He has a big problem and he's offering a reward to anyone who can solve it. Whoever does, will win the hand of a Princess. If you are interested, you must present yourself to the King for the details.

JON: The hand of the Princess? That is a rich reward.

GIRL (*Picking up bundle of wood*): Well, I must get home with my firewood. Goodbye, goodbye, soldier. And thank you, again.

JON: You're very welcome. Goodbye. (GIRL *exits left.* JON *sits down on bench, deep in thought for a moment.*) Hm-m. . . . I wonder . . . (OLD WOMAN *enters, carrying sack.*)

OLD WOMAN: Good day, soldier.

JON: Good day, old woman. Won't you sit down? Here, let me help you. (*Helps her to sit.*)

OLD WOMAN (*Sitting*): Thank you. You are a kind young man. Where are you heading?

JON: I'm off to seek my fortune. I have no real home, but I like this country. I heard of the King's proclamation, and I would like to try to win the hand of the Princess. What is the Princess like?

OLD WOMAN: Princesses. They are three very beautiful but spoiled young women who are causing their father, the King, great worry and expense. It seems that they wear out a pair of shoes every night, but he can't seem to find out how they do it.

JON: Three pairs a night! Goodness!

OLD WOMAN: So he's offered the hand of one of the Princesses in marriage to any suitor who can find the answer. Hundreds of Dukes, Princes, and Earls have come from many countries to try their luck. But so far all have failed.

JON (*Thoughtfully*): I wonder if I might have any luck.

OLD WOMAN: Why don't you try? You have been kind to me, and I may be able to help you. (*Looks at JON carefully.*) First, brush your clothes off, or they'll never let you into the Palace. (JON *brushes off sleeves of uniform with his hand.*) Then I'll lend you this cloak. (*Takes gray cloak out of sack.*) Although it looks very plain, it has magic powers. (OLD WOMAN *slips on cloak and skips about, making herself "invisible" to* JON.)

JON: Where have you gone?

OLD WOMAN: I'm over here. (JON *looks from side to side.*)

JON: Where? Come back! (*Looks around, and* OLD WOMAN *laughs.*) I can hear you, but I can't see you.

OLD WOMAN (*Slipping off cloak*): Here I am. You see? (JON *turns and sees her.*) I will lend you my Cloak of

Invisibility. Its magic will last for only twenty-four hours, so you must make the time count. (*Hands cloak to* Jon)

Jon: How will I know when to use it?

Old Woman (*Mysteriously*): You'll have to use your own judgment. One more warning. If the Princesses offer you refreshments, you must *not* eat or drink anything.

Jon: I shall remember. And thank you for your help.

Old Woman: Goodbye . . . and don't forget my warnings! (*She exits left.* Jon *rolls up cloak and puts it in knapsack.* Prince Donald *and* Duke Frederick *enter right.*)

Jon: Good day to you, Your Highnesses—Your Graces—or Your Excellencies. (*Pauses*) Which *are* you?

Prince Donald (*Dejectedly*): Oh, we're just two defeated suitors. I am Prince Donald, and this is Duke Frederick. (*Nods toward* Frederick)

Jon: I'm Jon, a soldier of the realm. What was the trouble? Didn't you like the Princesses?

Donald: Oh, I liked them all right. Especially that charming little Adele. But they just slipped away somehow while I blinked my eyes. The next thing I knew, it was morning, and each Princess had worn out another pair of shoes. (*Sighs*) And I thought Adele rather liked me.

Jon (*To* Frederick): Why are you leaving, Duke Frederick?

Frederick: Yesterday, when it was my turn to solve the problem, pretty little Princess Babette seemed quite friendly toward me. We were all having a lovely time, drinking punch and playing Blindman's Bluff. I thought I had caught Babette, but when I took off the blindfold, I had only her velvet cape in my hand, and all three Princesses had disappeared. I was so unhappy that I fell down on a bench and went to sleep. Today the three came into the court with their shoes worn out, as usual. (*Sadly*) We're going home.

JON: That's very mysterious. I think I'd like to try my luck.

DONALD: You! But does the King know you?

JON (*Hesitantly*): Well . . . not exactly.

FREDERICK: I'm afraid the guards won't even let you in.

JON: I have an excellent idea! Why don't you go back to the palace and help me get in.

FREDERICK (*Pausing*): I *would* like to talk to Babette once more.

DONALD: And I could see Adele again!

JON: Good! Let's be on our way. (*They exit right, as curtain falls.*)

* * *

SCENE 2

TIME: *Later that day.*

SETTING: *The King's Palace.*

AT RISE: KING *is sitting on his throne at center,* LADY KAY *and other* LORDS *and* LADIES *are standing at each side, chatting quietly. A bench stands down left.* HERALD *is looking off left.*

KING (*Unhappily*): Where are my daughters? They're always late.

HERALD: Your Majesty, the Princesses are coming. (*He announces them as they enter left.*) Princess Adele . . . Princess Babette . . . Princess Charlotte. (*All but* KING *bow as* PRINCESSES *sit on bench.*)

KING: My daughters, have you mended your ways?

ADELE (*Giggling*): Mend, Father?

BABETTE: We never do any mending.

CHARLOTTE (*Innocently*): Our ladies-in-waiting do that for us.

KING (*Annoyed*): Don't be silly. Let me see your shoes. (PRINCESSES *stick their feet out and show shiny shoes.*)

ADELE: These are our very newest shoes, Father.

BABETTE: All the others are worn out.

KING: What! Even the new ones you wore yesterday?

CHARLOTTE: Yes, Father. Quite full of holes. (PRINCESSES *giggle.*)

KING: But that makes ninety pairs in just one month! The keeper of the gold cannot stand it. And neither can I. (*Shakes his head sadly*)

ADELE: We just can't seem to help it. (PRINCESSES *nod in agreement.*) And we'll need more shoes tomorrow, or we'll have to appear in our bedroom slippers!

BABETTE: Or our tennis shoes!

CHARLOTTE: Or our snow boots! (PRINCESSES *laugh.*)

KING (*Angrily*): Stop! Stop laughing this instant! Oh, this is terrible . . . just terrible. Herald! Read the proclamation! (KING *holds hand to his head.*)

HERALD (*Unrolling scroll and reading*): "Hear ye! If any man present will attempt to win the hand of a lovely Princess, let him come forth." (*Members of the court shake heads and begin to murmur.*)

KING: No one? (*Groans*) What am I to do?

LADY KAY (*Looking off right*): One moment, Your Majesty. There is someone at the gate. (DONALD *and* FREDERICK *enter right, with* JON *walking between them.*)

KING: Who's this?

CHARLOTTE: Oh, Father, we've seen these two young men before. They both failed.

DONALD: Your Highness, we'd like to recommend our friend, Jon. (JON *steps forward.*)

ADELE: What? That common soldier?

BABETTE: How dare he?

FREDERICK: I assure you, he's a very brave young man.

CHARLOTTE (*With interest*): He is?

JON: I heard of your proclamation from someone I met in the forest, and I would like to try my fortune.

KING (*Frowning*): Who are you? And where are you from?

JON: I am called Jon, and I'm a soldier from a faraway part of your kingdom.

KING: I meant to invite only noblemen, worthy of the hand of a princess.

JON: But the proclamation did not say so, Your Majesty!

KING: Yes, I know, I know. Oh, dear, this is most unusual. Are there no other applicants?

HERALD: Not one, Your Majesty.

KING (*Hesitantly*): Well, if you can find the answer to my problem and rid me of—er—that is, prove that you deserve one of my daughters, then I suppose I must allow you to try.

JON (*Bowing*): Thank you, Your Majesty.

KING (*Sadly*): He's our last chance.

ADELE (*Aside*): And a pretty sorry chance, at that.

KING: Court is dismissed. (*Stands up*) Come, Prince Donald and Duke Frederick. We'll pass the time together while my daughters get acquainted with the soldier. (*To* PRINCESSES) Girls, mind your manners.

HERALD (*Going toward exit*): Make way for the King! Make way for the King! (HERALD, KING, DONALD, FREDERICK, *and other* LORDS *and* LADIES *exit.* LADY KAY *stands at right of stage.* JON *takes cloak out of knapsack.*)

ADELE (*Going to* JON): Well, Jon. Tell us about yourself.

BABETTE: Won't you be seated? (*She leads him to bench.*)

JON: Thank you. (*He sits.*) You're very kind.

CHARLOTTE: Lady Kay, will you bring us some refreshments? (LADY KAY *goes out briefly and returns carrying tray with glasses and pitcher, which she sets on end of bench.*)

ADELE: Let me pour you some punch. (*She turns toward audience and drops a large pill into a glass.*) Here. (*Pours punch into glass and hands it to* JON.)

JON: Thank you. (*He pretends to take sip. When no one is looking, he pours punch into large plant near him.*) Ah . . . delicious! (*Sets glass on tray*)

CHARLOTTE: Won't you sit down? You must be very tired.

ADELE (*To* LADY KAY): You may go now.

BABETTE: And take the tray with you, please. (LADY KAY *exits with tray.*)

JON (*Yawning*): Ho-hum! I am a bit weary. It's been a long day.

CHARLOTTE: Feel free to stretch out and rest. We'll try to be quiet and not disturb you. (PRINCESSES *watch him as he stretches out, yawns, and pretends to sleep.*)

ADELE (*Calling softly*): Soldier! Jon! (*To sisters*) He's off in a deep sleep. (*Music is heard from offstage.*)

BABETTE: Come on! Let's hurry. (BABETTE *and* ADELE *exit left.*)

CHARLOTTE (*Looking at* JON): I did rather hope . . . oh, well. On to the enchanted forest. (*Exits left.*)

JON: The enchanted forest? (*He sits up.*) I mustn't lose them! Where is my cloak? (*Puts it on.*) Oh, those mischievous girls! (*Exits. Quick curtain*)

*   *   *

A few moments later. Offstage music is heard. PRINCESSES *dance across stage in front of curtain with* DANCING PARTNERS. JON, *carrying a silver branch with silver leaves, enters behind them and watches as they dance offstage.*

JON: So this is what's been going on! Each night the Princesses sneak away to the enchanted forest and dance till their shoes are in shreds. (*Looks off*) I suppose they will keep dancing until dawn and wear out three more pairs of shoes. Well, I may as well go back to the Palace and get a good night's sleep. (*Holding up branch*) I have this silver branch from the enchanted forest to prove that I've been here. That should convince the King. (*Exits*)

*   *   *

SCENE 3

TIME: *The next morning.*

SETTING: *The same as Scene 2.*

AT RISE: JON *is lying asleep on the bench wrapped in the "invisible" cloak. A trumpet sounds.* HERALD *enters right, followed by* KING, LORDS *and* LADIES, LADY KAY, PRINCE DONALD *and* DUKE FREDERICK. JON *is "invisible" to all.*

HERALD: Hear ye! Hear ye! Let the King's court assemble. (KING *sits on throne. All bow.*)

KING: Where are my daughters? Why are they always late?

LADY KAY: Your Majesty, I believe they are looking for some shoes to wear. (KING *scowls; others snicker*)

HERALD: Make way for the Princesses! (PRINCESSES *enter.* ADELE *wears large bedroom slippers;* BABETTE, *over-sized tennis shoes;* CHARLOTTE, *flapping boots. All but* KING *laugh as* PRINCESSES *curtsy to* KING)

KING: Oh, dear, don't tell me you've worn out your last pairs of shoes!

ADELE: Alas, Father, I'm afraid we have. (PRINCESSES *go to bench where* JON *is lying. Just before they sit down,* JON *rolls onto floor with thud.*)

BABETTE: What was that?

CHARLOTTE (*Looking behind her*): I heard a thump. (JON

gets up, still in cloak, and tiptoes across stage. He stands just behind DONALD *and* FREDERICK. PRINCESSES *yawn.*)

KING: I didn't hear a thing. Now then, where is the soldier? I fear we have another failure on our hands.

ADELE: He's not only a failure, he's a coward. He must be afraid to show himself.

BABETTE: Maybe he's still asleep somewhere. (ADELE *and* BABETTE *giggle.*)

FREDERICK: He must be around somewhere. (JON *takes off cloak and, keeping silver branch hidden, pushes in between* DONALD *and* FREDERICK.)

JON: Here I am, Your Majesty. (*Bows*)

KING (*Annoyed*): Young man, you can see that my daughters have worn out their shoes again. (JON *looks toward* PRINCESSES.) I was *so* hoping you'd be able to prevent this.

JON: I couldn't prevent it until I found out how it happened. (*Pauses*) And I am now prepared to reveal the answer.

KING (*Leaning forward eagerly*): You are? Tell us!

ADELE (*To* JON): This is nonsense. You slept through the whole evening.

BABETTE: We tried to wake you, but you wouldn't budge.

CHARLOTTE: You were asleep on this very bench.

JON: I was on the bench, but I wasn't asleep. (*To* KING) Your Majesty, these young ladies have been a little dance-mad lately. No young man could discover this because the Princesses gave a sleeping potion to everyone who tried to solve the mystery.

ADELE: Well!

BABETTE: How silly! You haven't proved a thing.

JON: Oh, no? (*To* KING) After their victim is asleep, your daughters run to the enchanted forest, where dancing partners await them. Then they dance all night until their shoes are worn out. At dawn they return to the

Palace and sleep all day. (PRINCESSES *look surprised; others murmur.*)

KING: Astonishing! Go on.

JON: I didn't drink the punch that the Princesses offered me, and I only pretended to be asleep.

ADELE (*Interrupting*): You didn't even take a sip?

BABETTE: Very clever, but what does it prove?

JON: Then I followed you, although you couldn't see me. (*He puts on cloak and moves about them, as if invisible.*)

ADELE (*To* BABETTE): Where is he?

DONALD (*Looking around*): He isn't here.

BABETTE: Oh, let him go.

CHARLOTTE: No, he mustn't get away! (*Pauses*) I mean—er—he hasn't really proved anything yet.

JON (*Taking off cloak*): Here I am. I wore this Cloak of Invisibility and followed you through the enchanted forest. Here is proof. (*Holds up silver branch*) A branch from the forest.

KING (*Rising*): Young man, I believe you have come up with the answer. (*To* PRINCESSES) Is that right, girls?

ADELE (*Unhappily*): Yes, I suppose so.

BABETTE (*Pouting*): I never thought *he'd* guess it.

CHARLOTTE (*To sisters*): We have to admit he's clever.

KING (*Sitting*): And now, Jon, you may choose your bride. (*Hopefully*) Does one of the Princesses appeal to you?

JON (*Pausing*): Why, let me see . . . I think perhaps I could . . . find it agreeable to . . . (*Strolls back and forth before* PRINCESSES) offer my hand, heart, and humble fortune to . . . Charlotte! (*Kneels beside her and takes her hand*)

KING (*Excitedly*): Good! (*Pauses*) Charlotte, you are very fortunate. Jon, step forward. (JON *rises and kneels before* KING.) I dub thee Count Jon of the Faraway Lands. (*To* DONALD) Prince Donald, I gather that you might find a second choice agreeable?

DONALD (*Going to* ADELE): Your Majesty, Adele is my *first* choice. That is, if she will have me. (ADELE *nods eagerly as* DONALD *takes her hand.*)

KING: And Duke Frederick, would you settle for the last of my daughters?

FREDERICK: I would settle for no other, Your Majesty. (*Takes* BABETTE's *hand*)

CHARLOTTE: Just one more thing, Jon. I don't quite like the idea of your having a Cloak of Invisibility. What if I can't find you because you are wearing it?

JON: Don't worry. Its magic power is nearly gone. (OLD WOMAN *enters.*)

OLD WOMAN: That is right. I've come to collect my cloak.

JON: I'm glad to see you, madam. Thank you again for your help. (*Hands cloak to her*)

KING: And *I* thank you, old woman. (OLD WOMAN *takes off shawl and scarf, revealing her royal dress.*)

HERALD: It's the Duchess of Greenaway!

KING (*Rising in surprise*): Dear Duchess, it *is* you!

OLD WOMAN: Yes, Your Majesty. I couldn't bear to see your plight, and I resolved to help you out. Jon seemed a likely young man, so I lent him my magic cloak.

KING: This is a very happy day for all of us! (*All nod, as curtain closes.*)

THE END

King Horn

A Scottish tale

by Margaret C. Hall

Characters

KING HORN, *ruler of Scotland*
LADY MARGARET, *his betrothed*
GWYNETH ⎫
ISABEL ⎭ *ladies-in-waiting*
CHAMBERLAIN
DICKON, *a servant*

SCENE 1

TIME: *Long, long ago in Scotland.*
SETTING: *The throne room of King Horn's castle.*
AT RISE: LADY MARGARET, ISABEL, *and* GWYNETH *are
seated before tall embroidery frames, sewing.* GWYNETH
is humming a tune.

MARGARET (*With a gracious smile*): You sing as happily as
a lark today, Gwyneth. Has some particular good fortune
come to you, that you are so lighthearted?
GWYNETH: Indeed, Lady Margaret, everyone in the castle
is happy these days, preparing for your marriage. I am
so excited, I cannot help singing.

MARGARET: Why, how kind you are, Gwyneth, to be so happy for my sake.

ISABEL: The whole Scottish realm is rejoicing in your coming wedding, Lady Margaret. There is great joy that our brave King Horn, beloved of his people, is about to wed his cousin, the fair Margaret. That is what I hear everyone say, from the lords in the manor houses to the children in the streets.

GWYNETH: It's true, my lady. They all say, "With a king so true and noble and a queen so gentle and fair, Scotland shall be doubly blest."

MARGARET: How touched and grateful I am that we have such loyal and devoted subjects. And to think 'tis only a week till our wedding day.

ISABEL: We still have much to do before the bridal gown is ready. There are many pearls to sew in place, and all the rooms to prepare for the wedding guests.

GWYNETH: I know someone who is not happy about the wedding.

MARGARET: Why, who is that?

GWYNETH (*Looking around furtively and lowering her voice*): The Lord Chamberlain. He goes about the palace scowling at everyone in sight, and he gives King Horn threatening looks and shakes his fist behind his back.

ISABEL: That is right. I have seen him do that, too.

MARGARET: I am distressed that our Chamberlain is taking the news with such poor grace. He has declared his love for me and sought my hand for several years, but I could not love him. I tried to refuse him without hurting his feelings too much, and I thought he was resigned to my betrothal to King Horn. I must confess I am just a little afraid of him. It gives me an uneasy feeling to be around him.

GWYNETH: King Horn will surely dismiss anyone in the

court who annoys your ladyship. (DICKON *enters right.*)

DICKON: Lady Margaret, King Horn is just outside and desires to speak alone with you. He seems to be in a great hurry and says he has only a few minutes.

MARGARET: Only a few minutes? I wonder if something is the matter. Thank you, Dickon. I will see the King. Isabel, Gwyneth, I will call you back later. (ISABEL *and* GWYNETH *rise, curtsy and exit right, followed by* DICKON. KING HORN *enters left. He is in battle dress and looks worried.*)

KING: Good morning, my dear. (*Kisses her hand.*)

MARGARET (*Smiling*): Good morning and welcome, my love. Dickon frightened me just now when he told me you had only a few minutes to spare. I hope nothing is wrong.

KING (*Greatly troubled*): Something *is* wrong, I fear. I wish I could spare you this sad news, Margaret.

MARGARET: Sad news? What has happened, my love?

KING: A message has just reached me, calling me to France, and I must leave at once.

MARGARET: Must leave at once? For France? But why? It is only a week to our wedding day.

KING: France is at war, and I must help France's king fight against the heathen.

MARGARET: Oh, my lord, do not go, I pray you! Let the French king fight his own battles. Stay home safe in Scotland.

KING: No, I cannot do that. It is not only my brother in France who calls me, but my own honor. Would you have me shamed?

MARGARET: No, my lord, of course I would not. You must go forth and conquer. But I tremble to know that you are in danger—and it is so near our marriage day. (*Weeps*)

KING: Do not grieve, my love. I shall soon come back.

Come, dry your eyes and give me a token to carry with
me.

MARGARET (*Trying to smile bravely as she takes a jeweled
ring from her finger*): I want you to have this ring as a
token. It is a magic ring that was given to me by my
mother, who received it from a great wizard. The magic
lies in the seven diamonds it bears. Read what is written
within.

KING (*Taking ring and looking inside, then reading
aloud*): "When these stones grow dim and wan, you may
know by it my love is gone." Ah, my lady, I know your
true heart too well. These stones will never grow dim.

MARGARET: Of course they will not, my love. (CHAMBER-
LAIN *enters right. He gives* KING HORN *a look of hate,
then quickly becomes smiling and servile when he
speaks. He bows low to* MARGARET. *She looks at him
haughtily.*)

CHAMBERLAIN: Greetings, my lady. Sire, your ship awaits
you with all your knights already on board. They sent a
message to tell you to make all possible speed.

KING: Thank you. You may tell them I shall be with them
in a moment's time.

CHAMBERLAIN: Yes, my lord. (CHAMBERLAIN *goes out right
door, pulling it nearly shut, then pauses to eavesdrop.*)

KING: Margaret, in my absence you must rule as Scotland's
Queen. If I fall in battle, you will become Queen in
truth, for you are the next heir to the throne. I leave
you my golden scepter. Rule my people with gentle
justice till I come again. (*He hands her his scepter.*)

MARGARET: I shall do everything you say, but it terrifies
me to think of your falling in battle.

KING: We must both have courage. I leave you also the
seven laverock birds in their golden cage which now
hangs in my own room. These birds are sweet singers.
As long as they greet the morning with song, you may

be sure all is well with me. But should they droop and
be silent, you will know that I am slain and will return
to my land and my bride no more. Guard the bonny
birds well, and pray for my safe return.

MARGARET (*Concealing her emotion*): I shall strive to be
as brave as you and your good knights, my lord, and do
my duty here as faithfully as you will do yours in France.
(KING HORN *exits left.* CHAMBERLAIN, *at right door, gives
a self-satisfied nod and exits. Curtain closes.*)

*   *   *

SCENE 2

TIME: A year later.

SETTING: *The throne room, as in Scene 1.*

AT RISE: DICKON *is polishing candlesticks.* KING HORN *enters left, dressed in beggar's clothes.* DICKON *does not
recognize him.*)

KING (*Aside*): It hardly seems a full year since I last saw
my dear native land. How I bless the kind fortune that
has scattered the heathen and allows me to return to my
own people. (*Seeing* DICKON) Why, isn't that my faithful Dickon? Come greet me, Dickon! Have you forgotten
your king?

DICKON (*Dropping the candles*): King Horn!

KING: Did I take you by surprise, Dickon? Your manner
seems so strange. Everyone I have passed in the courtyard acts strangely. They seem to be celebrating something, but they look unhappy. What is the news of the
country? What news of the Queen? Hasten and tell me.

DICKON: Alas, my lord, I hate to be the one to tell you.
My news brings joy to no true Scottish hearts. The
Queen weds today.

KING (*In disbelief*): Queen Margaret—weds—today? But she was promised to me! The diamonds in my magic ring have remained bright through all the time I was away. (*He raises his hand to look at the ring and staggers back in dismay.*) No, no, it cannot be! My eyes deceive me! There is no longer a single gleam from the magic gems. Every stone is as dull as a wayside pebble! The Queen has not been true to me!

DICKON: Yes, sire, the Queen was true to you, but it is now a year since you sailed away with your gallant company to the wars in France. Since then nothing has been heard of you, and the wily Chamberlain has convinced the Lady Margaret that you and all your knights are dead.

KING: The Chamberlain? What is it to him?

DICKON: It is he who weds the Queen today. I have always believed he lied, to gain the Queen and the throne. The common people believe King Horn will come again to claim his own. You have not returned an hour too soon. You must prevent this sad marriage, and you will find every true Scottish blade ready to cut a way for you to your rightful throne.

KING: Your assurance of love and loyalty touches me deeply. May the day soon dawn that will restore the King to his people. Do not doubt that when the time comes, he will know how to reward his faithful friends, as well as how to punish traitors.

DICKON: I am sorry I did not know you, sire, but you are dressed like a beggar.

KING: Yes, the brave array I wore a year ago was destroyed long ago. We all came home in rags. But that is well, for I want to be unrecognized for a time. Tell me, what words shall I speak if I try to pass as a beggar?

DICKON: Say, "Give alms, I pray, for the sake of King

Horn." There is no name dearer to Scottish hearts than that of our good King. It never fails to fetch a gift.

KING: Thank you, Dickon. I think I see one of the ladies-in-waiting approaching now. I shall try the power of your plea. (GWYNETH *enters and* DICKON *returns to polishing candlesticks.* KING HORN *bows humbly before* GWYNETH.) Alms, I pray, my fair maid.

GWYNETH: Out of the way, old man! Do you think we have time to waste on beggars, in the midst of preparing for the Queen's wedding? Dickon, why did you allow this man to enter the palace?

KING: But I beg alms in the name of King Horn.

GWYNETH (*Kindly*): Come with me to the kitchen, good man. For our dear King's sake, who was always good to the needy, you shall have your fill today. No servant in this castle can refuse anything asked in King Horn's name.

KING: Then in the name of King Horn, I beg you to ask the Queen to come here. Tell her it may be the last time anyone shall ask a favor of her in the name of King Horn.

GWYNETH: I shall ask her, but I know not if she will come.

KING: Not come? Has the Queen already forgotten King Horn? Does he live only in the memory of beggars and servants?

GWYNETH: You wrong our Queen. It is the Chamberlain who is forcing her into this marriage. Wait here, and I will carry the message to her. (GWYNETH *exits. After a pause,* MARGARET *enters. Her face is pale and she looks about to weep. At the sight of her,* KING HORN *steps forward and tries to bow but he is overcome with emotion.*)

KING: Lady Margaret!

MARGARET: Poor man! He is faint with hunger and weariness. Dickon, run and bring a cup of wine. (DICKON

runs off and returns at once with a large wine goblet.
MARGARET *takes it from him and holds it out to the*
KING.) Drink this wine, and you will regain your
strength. (KING HORN *drinks the wine and then drops
the magic ring into the cup. He returns the cup to* MAR-
GARET *and speaks in a disguised voice.*)

KING: A wedding gift, oh Queen!

MARGARET (*Glancing at the cup*): The ring! Where did
you get this ring, beggarman? Did you steal it? Did you
find it on my dead lord's hand? Oh, speak to me!

KING: I stole it not. Neither did I find it on any man's
hand. It was given to me.

MARGARET: It cannot be true. I do not believe that King
Horn would give this ring to any man. It was too precious in his eyes.

KING (*Meaningly*): Madam, he no longer valued it after
the stones turned dull.

MARGARET: But they were never dull on his hand! They
were bright and beautiful as long as he lived. It was but
yesterday I promised to wed the Lord Chamberlain, and
King Horn died ten long weary months ago.

KING: How do you know this, my lady?

MARGARET: Oh, I know by a certain sign. When my lord
left, he gave me seven birds in a golden cage. He told
me that as long as they sang and were happy, I might
know he was safe; but if they drooped their heads and
were silent, I might know surely that he was slain. I
guarded my birds so carefully, but scarcely a month after
he left, I found them all dead in their cage. And so I
knew my dear king was no more. (CHAMBERLAIN *enters
proudly, dressed in kingly robes.*)

CHAMBERLAIN: Why all this crowd, and why are there tears
in your eyes, my Queen?

MARGARET: This is a beggar who bears news of King Horn.
I have not yet heard his tale. Wait and hear it with me.

CHAMBERLAIN (*Frightened*): King Horn! (*He recovers himself and takes* MARGARET'S *hand to draw her away.*) Come away. Do not listen to him. Doubtless he brings us a lying tale. Who heeds the words of a wandering beggar?

KING (*Stepping forth boldly*): But you shall heed the words of me, your rightful king!

CHAMBERLAIN (*Gasping and falling back*): King Horn! Oh, no!

MARGARET: King Horn! Is it really my own dear cousin? I must be in a dream. Is it a phantom?

DICKON: This is really King Horn, my lady. He has come home. (GWYNETH *and* ISABEL *rush in and see* KING.)

ISABEL (*Astonished*): It is King Horn, come home again!

GWYNETH: King Horn? And I did not know him! I took him for a beggar. Oh, pray forgive me for speaking so harshly to you, sire. (*Both ladies kneel to him.*)

MARGARET: I didn't know him either, Gwyneth. But, Sire, I thought you were dead, and I had given up all hope. (CHAMBERLAIN *is trying to sneak out, but* KING HORN *spies him.*)

KING: I believe I know the reason everyone has been deceived. Chamberlain, I want a word with you. (CHAMBERLAIN *shamefacedly turns around and comes back. He stands with bowed head.*) Speak up, sir, and tell me what you have done to convince the Queen and my people of my death.

CHAMBERLAIN (*Whining*): I had nothing to do with the rumor, sire. Why do you try to blame me?

ISABEL: That is not true! You swore to all of us that our King had fallen in battle.

GWYNETH (*Putting her arm around* MARGARET, *who is weeping*): I saw the Chamberlain eavesdropping the day King Horn went away.

KING: Explain, villain!

CHAMBERLAIN (*Falling on his knees*): I will confess everything. I have always longed for power. On the day that you left for France I heard what you told the Queen about the birds, and I saw a chance to gain the throne. I carried the birds to my own room and put seven dead birds into the golden cage.

MARGARET: That is what convinced me of your death, sire.

KING: What did you do then?

CHAMBERLAIN: After long urging I persuaded the Queen to marry me, telling her that the people wanted a king to lead them in battle and to rule over them. Once married to the Queen and sitting on the throne, I thought I could defy you if you returned, because you yourself had given her the golden scepter.

ISABEL: Then the seven birds have been alive all this time in your room.

CHAMBERLAIN: Yes, I have spoken the truth. Now deal with me as I deserve, for I am indeed a traitor.

KING: My Queen, you still hold the scepter of our land. Therefore the duty of judging this man falls on you. What is your will regarding him?

MARGARET: Chamberlain, when the King gave the scepter into my hand, he urged me to rule with gentle justice. I therefore grant you your life, but I decree that you shall leave this court and this country forever.

CHAMBERLAIN (*Rising*): Thank you, my lady.

KING: Not one more word shall you utter in the Queen's presence. I command you to go. (*The* CHAMBERLAIN *slinks offstage.*)

ISABEL: The Queen has been too merciful! Someone should go after him.

DICKON: Sire, is that villain to remain unpunished? He should not escape—slay him!

KING: No, Dickon, let him go. I came back in time to

prevent this unhappy marriage, and I freely forgive him. You will, too, Margaret, will you not?

MARGARET: Surely I can be merciful if he who so nearly lost his throne can forgive his enemy.

GWYNETH: You are splendid, Lady Margaret!

KING: King Horn can never lose his throne while he reigns in the hearts of his loyal people and his Queen! And now, friends, let us proceed to the marriage.

ISABEL: The wedding veil is all ready. (ISABEL *and* GWYNETH *run to a large wooden chest and lift out a magnificent bridal veil.*)

GWYNETH: This is the happiest day in the lives of the Scottish people. After all his trials and dangers, King Horn has arrived in time to marry the beautiful Queen Margaret. (*As curtain falls,* ISABEL *and* GWYNETH *place veil on* MARGARET'*s head.* DICKON *and* KING HORN *watch proudly.*)

THE END

Pedro and the Burro

An old tale of Argentina

by Mary Nygaard Peterson

Characters

PEDRO	MARIA
FERNANDO, *his friend*	PEPITA
SEÑOR LUIS, *a fat neighbor*	BARBARA
MANUEL, *Luis' servant*	DOLORES
PÁJARO, *Luis' burro*	OTHER GIRLS

SCENE 1

SETTING: *A mountainside clearing in Argentina.*

AT RISE: PEDRO *runs on, calling out excitedly. He carries box of small wooden figures, which he sets on ground.*

PEDRO: Here, Bonita! Come back, my little burro! (*He looks around stage, behind bushes, etc.*) Here, Bonita, my pretty little burro. See what I have for you—some sweet sugar cane. (*He searches pockets, finds sugar cane. He looks offstage, beckons.*) Come, Bonita, it's good. Come, my pretty burro. (*He holds out candy, with no success, then walks back to boulder, sits down on it, and tastes sugar cane himself.*)

FERNANDO (*Entering*): Good morning, Pedro.

458

PEDRO (*Sadly*): Good morning, Fernando.

FERNANDO: What is wrong, Pedro? You are not happy?

PEDRO: I was happy (*Shrugs his shoulders*), but now everything is wrong.

FERNANDO: That is too bad. I thought you would be all
excited about going to market. Did you finish your wood
carvings of the Holy Family? (*He picks up figures one
at a time and admires them.*)

PEDRO (*Discouraged*): They are ready. I worked on the
little lamb last night until I could no longer see. This
morning I polished him some more.

FERNANDO: I don't see how you did it, Pedro, but each one
is just the way he should be. The Child is so peaceful,
and so calm, and beautiful. (*He picks it up while speaking about it.*) And the Mother looks so proud and happy.

PEDRO: It's hard to believe, Fernando, but the figurines
seemed to make themselves. All I had to do was hold
the knife.

FERNANDO: Just look at Joseph. He seems so dependable.
Mother and Child are safe with him.

PEDRO: Yes, I felt that, too.

FERNANDO: I like the burro, too. He is such a patient beast,
and strong.

PEDRO (*Bitterly*): My own burro is not so patient, nor so
dependable.

FERNANDO (*In surprise*): Bonita? I thought your sun rose
and set on that little burro of yours, Pedro.

PEDRO: The sun will probably rise and set many times
before I see her again.

FERNANDO: What happened? Did she run away?

PEDRO (*Gloomily*): Yes, she did, just before you came.

FERNANDO: Do you think maybe something frightened her?

PEDRO (*Shrugging*): Who knows? If she wanted to go, it
would not take much to frighten her—her shadow, the

shadow of a rabbit on the path, an acorn dropping from a tree—a leaf falling. (*He shrugs again and spreads his hands.*) Anyway, she is gone. That is all I know.

FERNANDO (*Sympathetically*): I am sorry, my friend. And you so especially wanted to go to market this time.

PEDRO: Yes. It is Mama's birthday tomorrow. I promised her a surprise—a big surprise that would make her very glad.

FERNANDO (*Leaning forward with interest*): What did you plan to buy for her, Pedro?

PEDRO: A fine, new fiesta dress. She has wanted one such a long time, and the fiesta is next week.

FERNANDO (*Impressed*): A fiesta dress! But they cost so much money!

PEDRO: Yes, I know they do. Yet Father Sebastian said he was sure I would be able to get enough money for my figurines. He said they were the best he had ever seen.

FERNANDO: Really, Pedro? He said they are worth so much? (PEDRO *nods.*) Then you must take care of them, Pedro, and not let them get scratched up. Here, let me help you. (*He begins to wrap each in paper or scraps of cloth. He puts them into his shoulder bag.*) I will help you carry them home.

PEDRO: Thank you, Fernando. I am going to polish the lamb some more. He is a little rough yet under the chin. (*They sit on boulder.* PEDRO *polishes lamb. After a moment of silence, a group of* GIRLS *enter, talking and laughing. They carry market baskets.*)

MARIA: Good morning, Pedro and Fernando.

PEDRO *and* FERNANDO (*Sadly*): Good morning.

PEPITA: Why are you so sad? It's market day, and you always like to go to market.

PEDRO: My donkey ran away, and now I can't go. I wanted to buy Mama a new fiesta dress for her birthday.

GIRLS (*Ad lib*): That's too bad. Poor Pedro! (*Etc.*)

BARBARA: How terrible! We're just on our way to market, and I'm going to get a new blouse to wear to the fiesta next week.

DOLORES: We're going to dance together at the fiesta. Here, let us do our dance for you. Maybe that will cheer you up a little.

PEDRO: Maybe so, but I think only my burro could cheer me up right now. (*Girls do a typical South American dance. If desired, some may sing and clap, while others dance.*)

FERNANDO: That's very nice.

PEDRO: You'll look pretty at the fiesta. I just wish Mama could have her new dress, so she'd look pretty, too.

MARIA: We have to go now, or we'll be late. See, we have many baskets of fruit to sell at market. Goodbye. (*She exits, followed by other girls.*)

FERNANDO: If my burro, Diablo, weren't so mean, we could ride double. But he would never carry the two of us, and he wouldn't let you ride him alone, Pedro. He's a mean one, that burro of mine.

PEDRO: I know better than to try to ride him, Fernando. I remember the last time he pitched me off. It took a week to pull all the thorns out.

FERNANDO: Yet with me he is gentle as a kitten. You know, Pedro, I can even *see* Bonita up there. (*He waves his hand up left.*) Don't you suppose she'll come down pretty soon?

PEDRO (*Bitterly*): I doubt it. She is trying to tease me. We could never catch her, either. The minute we'd try, she would be gone.

FERNANDO (*Sighing and shaking his head*): It's too bad. I don't know what we can do.

PEDRO: I suppose I could walk.

FERNANDO: Fifteen miles?

PEDRO (*Insisting*): Downhill, I could walk fifteen miles easily. But uphill, fifteen miles—I wouldn't get there before evening.

FERNANDO (*Looking offstage*): I think someone's coming up the hill, Pedro.

PEDRO (*Craning his neck*): Probably our neighbor, Señor Luis.

FERNANDO: Do you think he's coming just to visit with you? He must like you.

PEDRO: He says he does, but more likely he wants me to do something for him.

FERNANDO: Is that the way he is?

PEDRO: I guess he is not so bad. Sometimes I even feel sorry for him. He says his heart is empty. He has no children, no relatives. He calls me his nephew.

FERNANDO: Hm-m-m. I don't know if I'd like that.

PEDRO: He means no harm, I suppose.

LUIS (*Puffing as he enters*): If it isn't my dear nephew, Pedro. How are you, lad? (*He laboriously seats himself on a boulder.*)

PEDRO (*Unenthusiastically*): I'm fine, Señor Luis, thank you. How are you and the Señora?

LUIS (*Heartily*): Fine, lad. Fine. But call me *Uncle* Luis, won't you, please? My heart is so empty.

PEDRO: I'll try to remember, if it will please you. Did you want something special, Uncle Luis?

LUIS: Why, no, Pedro. Can't a lonesome old man climb the mountainside—at risk of life and limb, I might add —to pass the time of day with his favorite nephew without wanting something?

PEDRO: I just wondered. It's a pretty steep climb.

LUIS: No, I didn't want anything except to see you. But since you ask, I wonder if you are planning to go to market today?

PEDRO: Aren't *you* going, yourself, Señor—I mean, *Uncle* Luis?

LUIS: No. The fact is, Pedro, your Aunt Emilia is not well, not well enough to go.

PEDRO: That is too bad. I had planned to go, Uncle Luis, but now I don't think I'll be able to go, either.

LUIS (*Disappointed*): You don't think so? And here I climbed—I mean, you always go to market, Pedro. I thought you might bring back some soap for us. You know, the perfumed kind your Aunt Emilia likes so well for her bath.

PEDRO: I'd be glad to, Uncle Luis, only I'm quite sure now that I won't be going.

LUIS (*Rising*): All right, if you don't want to put yourself out for us, we understand. We love you just the same. Our hearts are empty. That is why we chose you to be our nephew.

PEDRO: It isn't that I don't *want* to go, Uncle Luis. I'd help you if I could, but I can't. My burro just ran away into the hills and she probably won't come back for a week.

LUIS (*Relieved*): Oh, is that all? In that case, you just use my little burro, my Pájaro. She will have you to market and back in no time.

PEDRO (*Excited and happy*): You mean it, Uncle Luis? I may take your burro to market?

LUIS: Why, of course. You will probably want to give a little present of some kind to your Aunt Emilia for the use of her burro, if you decide to use it—but that won't cost much. She loves her little Pájaro, you know. It is a valuable beast, too, and not to be trusted with just any-one. But, of course, she would trust it with you, Pedro. She loves you very much.

PEDRO (*Flatly*): How much do you want for the use of your burro, Uncle Luis?

LUIS (*In hurt tone*): Why, Pedro! You talk as if I were

charging you money. You know I wouldn't charge you for the use of the burro. Why, you are a member of the family. We chose you to be our *favorite* nephew. I just thought you might want to give a little present to your Aunt Emilia, that is all. If you don't want to, why, that is all right. Think nothing of it.

PEDRO: What kind of present did you have in mind, Uncle Luis?

LUIS (*Craftily*): What did you intend to sell at the market, Pedro?

PEDRO: My wood carvings. That's all I have to sell.

LUIS: The Holy Family?

PEDRO: They're all I have, Uncle Luis.

LUIS: Well, they're very nice carvings, Pedro. Of course, you realize you're just an amateur—a beginner. The figurines will probably not sell for much.

FERNANDO (*Hotly*): Pedro's figurines are beautiful. Father Sebastian said they are the best he's ever seen. He says Pedro is a real artist and may someday be famous. His carvings are worth a lot of money.

LUIS: That may be. That may be. I think you'll find, though, Pedro, that the figurines will not be easy to sell. Your Aunt Emilia is very fond of the carvings. She often speaks about them. It would be a nice little surprise for her if you would give her three or four of them for the use of her burro.

PEDRO: Three or four! There are only five in all, and they belong together. I never meant to sell them separately.

LUIS: Is that all? Then, let's just say three of the figurines, Pedro. We don't want to be greedy.

PEDRO: Two, maybe, at the most. Perhaps I could let you have the little lamb, and maybe the burro. But the Child belongs with His Mother and Joseph. I wouldn't separate the family.

LUIS: Is that the little lamb?

PEDRO: Yes. (LUIS *reaches over and takes it out of* PEDRO'S *hand*.)

LUIS (*Turning lamb over in his hand and looking at it*): Very nice, Pedro. Made of ebony, isn't it?

PEDRO (*Proudly*): The best ebony I could find. The burro is mahogany; the Holy Family is rosewood. All are from good wood—the best I could find.

LUIS (*Slipping the figurine into his pocket*): Then it is settled. You will use my burro. When you come for him you will bring me two more figurines as a present for your Aunt Emilia. She really loves you, Pedro, and will take wonderful care of the figurines.

PEDRO: No, Señor, Uncle Luis, wait! (LUIS *has started to walk off right. He speaks over his shoulder*.)

LUIS: My little burro will be waiting for you, Pedro. Don't forget to bring the figurines with you. (*Exits*)

FERNANDO (*At last*): How do you like that? He looks out for Señor Luis, doesn't he?

PEDRO (*Bitterly*): I knew he wanted something when I saw him coming. He always does. But I never thought he would take my figurine.

FERNANDO: It's a shame to break up your Holy Family, Pedro.

PEDRO: Yes. They belong together. Mary and Joseph, the Child and the lamb. They need the burro, too. The Mother needs him to ride on when she is tired. (*They sit looking glumly into space*.)

FERNANDO (*Suddenly*): Why, Pedro, isn't that your burro? (*He points left*.) She's come down here.

PEDRO (*Leaping up*): Yes, it is. (*Calling off*) Bonita, oh, my pretty Bonita, you've come back—just in time. (*He exits left, calling back*.) I'll tie her to a bush this time. (FERNANDO *watches. In a moment*, PEDRO *returns*.)

FERNANDO: Now you won't have to use Señor Luis' old burro. Let's go and get your lamb figurine back, before he gives it to your *dear Aunt Emilia*.

PEDRO (*Glumly*): He'll never give it back to me. I just know he won't.

FERNANDO (*Shocked*): You mean he'll keep it, even when you don't use his burro?

PEDRO (*Bitterly*): That's my *Uncle* Luis. He'll find some reason for keeping the lamb.

FERNANDO: He wouldn't do that to me. I know that much.

PEDRO: How would you stop him?

FERNANDO (*Jumping up and pacing about, in deep thought*): There must be some way. (*Suddenly, he snaps his fingers.*) I have it!

PEDRO: What?

FERNANDO: I'll explain. Come with me. I'll tell you on the way. First, we have to go to your house and borrow your mother's measuring line. (*Rubs hands together*) Then we'll pay a visit to Señor Luis.

PEDRO: But why? What?

FERNANDO: Come on, Pedro. Don't just stand there. It's getting late. We have lots to do before dark. Or do you *want* to give three of your Holy Family to "dear Aunt Emilia who loves you so"?

PEDRO (*Emphatically*): No, I don't.

FERNANDO: Come on, then. (*They exit, as curtain falls.*)

*   *   *

SCENE 2

TIME: *A few minutes later.*

SETTING: *The patio of Señor Luis' home.*

AT RISE: LUIS *is sprawled in a comfortable chair, holding*

a glass of lemonade. MANUEL *is fanning him.* PEDRO *and* FERNANDO *enter right.*)

LUIS (*Raising himself up out of the chair*): My dear boy. How nice of you to come and see your old uncle! Did you bring the figurines?
PEDRO: No—yes—but—
LUIS: Now, now. What kind of an answer is that?
PEDRO: What I mean is, Señor—Uncle Luis, I must see the burro right away.
LUIS: See the burro? But you have seen the burro many times. You know he is a good little beast, swift as a bird. You will think you are flying when you ride him.
PEDRO: Yes, I know, Uncle, but I must measure him. (LUIS *sees for the first time the tape measure dangling from* PEDRO's *hand.*)
LUIS: What is this, Pedro, a joke?
PEDRO: No, it is no joke. You see, I must measure the burro to see how big he is.
LUIS (*Laughing indulgently*): Oh, very well. You may measure him. Manuel, please get Pájaro. You may bring him right in here. He is a good little beast. (MANUEL *bows slightly and exits.*) Why do you want to measure my little burro, Pedro?
PEDRO: You see, my whole family wants to go to market. I must see if your burro is long enough to carry them on his back.
LUIS (*Sputtering*): The whole family! But they can't all ride.
PEDRO: They wouldn't think of *walking* that far, Uncle Luis. It's fifteen miles each way, you know. (MANUEL *enters with* PÁJARO. PEDRO *and* FERNANDO *go over and begin measuring burro with tape, disregarding the protesting* LUIS. PÁJARO *cavorts about a bit from time to time.*)

FERNANDO (*Eyeing the beast skeptically*): This is the burro that can fly? Are you sure you have the right one?

PEDRO: This is Pájaro. Uncle Luis says he goes like a bird.

FERNANDO: That I should like to see.

PEDRO: We'd better get on with the measuring. Let's see, there is my father. He will take at least sixteen inches. (*He measures length of tape on* PÁJARO's *back.* PÁJARO *acts skittish.*)

FERNANDO: This burro is frisky. Maybe he's speedier than he looks.

PEDRO: Could be.

FERNANDO: Now, your mother—

LUIS (*Shouting*): Your mama!

PEDRO: Yes, Mama has to go to buy cloth for a new fiesta dress. She does not like the dresses that are ready-made. How much room do *you* think she would take, Fernando?

FERNANDO (*Thoughtfully*): Let's see (*Measures imaginary distances with his hands*) . . . at least eighteen inches.

PEDRO (*Measuring*): Eighteen inches, and sixteen for my father.

LUIS (*Protesting*): Look here, boys, you can't—my burro can't—they're too heavy, Pedro. Fifteen miles, each way! Thirty miles!

PEDRO (*Disregarding him*): Then there's cousin Felipe. Felipe said not to forget him. He wants to sell his gourds and buy a pig. He'll be taking the pig back.

FERNANDO: Felipe will need at least twelve inches. Don't you think so?

PEDRO: At least. (*He measures.*) Twelve inches, and eighteen for my mother, and sixteen for my father. We'd better hang baskets on the side for the twins; there's not much more room. What do you think?

LUIS (*Holding his head*): You can't, Pedro. All those people would kill my little burro. I forbid—

FERNANDO: I suppose you're taking the Cid?

PEDRO: Of course. I forgot about him.

LUIS: The Cid? Who is that? Is he in the family?

PEDRO: The fighting cock. He'll have to go for the fights.
Papa never goes without him. Of course, he won't take
up any room. Papa will hold him.

FERNANDO: Where are you going to put Teresa?

LUIS (*Wailing*): My burro *can't* hold all those people. He
can't carry a whole family.

PEDRO: Don't worry, Uncle Luis. Pájaro is a good little
beast. He is strong. See? (*He hits burro with a resound-
ing slap.* PÁJARO *jumps and prances about.*)

LUIS (*Walking about distracted, holding his head*): My
poor burro. They will kill you, Pájaro. They will wear
your feet off at the knees.

FERNANDO: Can't Teresa sit up here between the ears? The
animal is quite wide, and Teresa is not very big.

PEDRO: Yes, she can. I would never have thought of that.
Let's see, now. Where will I sit?

LUIS (*Groaning*): My little burro can't carry so many.

PEDRO (*Coldly*): He can try, Señor—Uncle Luis. He will
have to try, for we all intend to go.

FERNANDO: Looks as if you'll have to sit back here by the
tail. Think you can stay on?

PEDRO: If I hold on. (*He gives a tentative jerk and flip to
the tail.*)

LUIS (*Screaming*): You will not put so many on my little
burro. I will not let you have him. Never. Never. I will
not even let you touch him. Go away. Go away.

PEDRO: But Uncle Luis, a bargain is a bargain. You have
my little lamb. You wouldn't cheat a relative, would
you?

LUIS: The bargain is off. You can't have my burro, I tell
you. (*He screams at* MANUEL.) Get that little lamb figure.
Quick! Quick! (MANUEL *darts off right.*) I will get him

myself. (*He runs clumsily off after* MANUEL. PEDRO *and* FERNANDO *double up with laughter.*)

PEDRO: It worked. Fernando, it worked. (*Jubilantly, he grabs* FERNANDO *and twirls him about.*)

FERNANDO (*Sobering*): Hush. Here he comes. Straighten up, Pedro. (PEDRO *and* FERNANDO *pretend to be measuring.*)

LUIS (*Entering, out of breath*): Here's your lamb, Pedro. Take him. Take him. (*He thrusts the figurine upon* PEDRO.)

PEDRO (*Appearing to take it reluctantly*): Well, all right, uncle, but a bargain's a bargain, and should be kept. But since you are in the family—

LUIS: Yes. Yes. I break the bargain. But we are not really in the family, not really. Now, goodbye, boys. I don't feel so well any more. (*Claps hand to brow*) Manuel! Manuel! (*He sprawls in chair and claps his hands.*) Manuel!

MANUEL (*Entering*): Si, Señor.

LUIS: Bring another lemonade, and the fan. Quick. Goodbye, boys. Goodbye. Goodbye. (*He waves them off.*)

PEDRO: Goodbye, Señor Luis. I hope you will feel better soon. I will bring you some soap from the market.

FERNANDO: When your heart feels empty, I will be your nephew, too. (PEDRO *carries lamb figurine proudly, polishing it on his sleeve, as he exits, followed by* FERNANDO. MANUEL *fans* LUIS, *as curtain falls.*)

THE END

The Baker's Neighbor

A Peruvian folk tale

Adapted by *Adele Thane*

Characters

MANUEL GONZALES, *a baker* JUDGE
PABLO PEREZ, *his neighbor* THREE WOMEN
CARLOS, *a boy* VILLAGERS
RAMONA ⎫
INEZ ⎬ *his sisters*
ISABEL ⎭

SETTING: *A street in an old town in Peru. Manuel's Bakery is at right. There is an outdoor counter with shelves for the display of pastries in front of the bakery, and a wooden table and stool near the counter. Across the street, at left, is the patio of Pablo's house, with a bench and chairs on it. At the rear of the stage, there is a flowering tree with a circular seat around the trunk.*

AT RISE: *It is early morning. MANUEL comes out of bakery with a tray of pies which he carries to counter. As he is putting the pies on a shelf, PABLO steps out onto his patio, sniffs the air and smiles with delight.*

PABLO: Good morning, Baker Manuel. Your pies smell especially delicious this morning. How many did you bake last night?

MANUEL (*Sullenly*): What's it to you, Pablo? You never buy any; you just smell them. Every day you stand there and fill your nostrils with the fragrance of my pastries. It's a miracle there's any flavor left in them when my customers come to buy.

PABLO: But it makes me happy to smell your pastries. You are the best baker in Peru. Everyone says so.

MANUEL: Well, why don't you buy a pie or a cake and take it home? Then you could smell it all you want.

PABLO: Oh, but if I bought it and ate it, I couldn't smell it any more.

MANUEL (*Snorting in disgust*): Bah! (*When he finishes setting out the pies he goes into the bakery with the empty tray.* PABLO *crosses to the counter and inhales deeply, closing his eyes in delight.* MANUEL *returns with tray of cakes and cash box. He pushes* PABLO *away from counter.*) Hey! Take your big nose away from there! I can't sell those pies if you sniff them all over! (PABLO *saunters back to his patio.* MANUEL *places tray of cakes on counter, then carries cash box to table and sits down.*)

PABLO: Are you going to count your money, Manuel? (MANUEL *ignores* PABLO *but empties coins from cash box onto table.* PABLO *then sits in a chair and watches* MANUEL *with an amused smile.*) How much did you take in yesterday?

MANUEL: None of your business! (*He inspects each coin carefully, then writes in a small notebook, adds figures, scowling and mumbling to himself.* CARLOS *and his sisters enter left. They stop when they see* MANUEL *counting his money and talk quietly together.*)

RAMONA: Gracious, what a lot of money!

CARLOS: Papa says the bakery has made Manuel the richest man in town.

INEZ: If he's that rich, why doesn't he smile? He looks so cross and unfriendly.

CARLOS: That's because he's a miser. A miser doesn't like people—only money. The more money he has, the more he wants. And he keeps it all to himself—he never shares it with anyone.

ISABEL (*Catching sight of* PABLO): There's Pablo!

CARLOS *and* GIRLS (*Enthusiastically; ad lib*): Hello, Pablo! How are you? Good to see you! (*Etc.*)

PABLO (*Beaming at them as he gets up*): Hello, my young friends, hello! You're up bright and early.

ISABEL: We're going to the bakery.

RAMONA: Carlos is going to treat us.

CARLOS: I helped Papa pick beans and he gave me this. (*He holds up a silver coin.*)

PABLO: You're a good boy, Carlos.

INEZ (*Starting across to the bakery*): Come on! Let's see what there is. (*Children crowd around the counter.*)

RAMONA: Look at those coconut patties!

ISABEL: And the jelly roll! Yummy!

INEZ: Carlos, why don't you buy a pie and cut it into quarters? Then we'd each have a piece.

CARLOS: I don't know. I'd sort of like a cake.

MANUEL (*Impatiently*): Well, young fellow, what do you want? (*To* INEZ) Keep your fingers off that pie!

INEZ (*Indignantly*): I didn't touch it!

MANUEL: Come now, hurry up and decide. This isn't a waiting room. I have to make a living. What with rent and taxes, it's as much as I can do.

CARLOS: How much is that cake with the pink frosting?

MANUEL: You can't afford that. How much money do you have? (CARLOS *holds out his hand to show him.*) Not enough. That cake costs three times what you can pay.

CARLOS: What *can* I buy with my money? I want something for all of us.

MANUEL: You can have four tapioca tarts—and I'm giving them away at that price. (*He hands tarts to* CARLOS.)

Here you are. Now take your tarts over to Pablo and let him smell them. (*He puts* CARLOS's *coin with others on table, sits down and makes entry in his notebook.* CARLOS *passes out tarts to his sisters as they cross to the patio.*)

CARLOS (*Offering tart to* PABLO): Have a bite?

PABLO: No, thank you, Carlos. You earned it—you eat it.

ISABEL: Pablo, why did Manuel say we should let you smell our tarts?

PABLO: Oh, he's annoyed, because every morning I stand here and enjoy the smell of his freshly-baked pies and cakes when they are right out of the oven. Ah, what fragrance! It's as if the bakery has burst into bloom.

RAMONA: If you could be a beautiful smell, Pablo, instead of a man—would you like to be a beautiful bakery smell?

PABLO (*Laughing*): Well, that's a new one on me! If I were a *smell* instead of a man? Of all the comical ideas!

INEZ (*Explaining*): It's a game we play among ourselves. We ask each other what thing we'd like to be if we weren't a person—what color, what sight, what sound—

RAMONA: What sound would *you* like to be, Pablo, if you weren't a person?

PABLO: This minute?

RAMONA: Any minute.

PABLO: Let me think. (*Suddenly he slaps his knee*) I have it! If I were a sound instead of a man, I'd choose to be a song! A happy little song in children's hearts. Or turning up in a boy's whistle—like this! (*He whistles a merry tune.*)

ISABEL: What sound do you think Manuel would like to be?

CARLOS: That's easy. He'd be the sound of gold pieces jingling in his own pocket.

ISABEL: I'm going to ask him. (*She goes to the table where* MANUEL *is putting his money back into cash box.*) Manuel, may I ask you a question?

MANUEL (*Scowling*): What is it?

ISABEL: If you were a sound instead of a baker, what sound in the whole wide world would you choose to be?

MANUEL: Well, of all the idiotic nonsense! Clear out of here and stop bothering me! I have better things to do than to answer stupid questions. (ISABEL *returns to patio, and* PABLO *goes center.*)

PABLO: It has taken you a long time to count your money, Manuel.

MANUEL (*Sneering*): It wouldn't take *you* long to count yours.

PABLO: That's right. I don't care much for money.

MANUEL: You're too lazy to earn it.

PABLO (*Good-naturedly*): Oh, I work when I have to. But I'd rather sit in the sun and take advantage of all the small, everyday pleasures that life has to offer.

MANUEL: Like smelling my pastries, I suppose—without charge?

PABLO (*Shrugging*): The air is free.

MANUEL: It's not as free as you think.

PABLO: What do you mean?

MANUEL: I'm going to make you pay for all the pastry smells I've supplied you with for many years.

PABLO (*Smiling in disbelief*): You can't mean that!

MANUEL: But I do! You stand outside my bakery every day and smell my pies and cakes. To my mind, that is the same as taking them without paying for them. You are no better than a thief, Pablo Perez!

PABLO (*Mildly*): I never took anything that didn't belong to me, and you know it. What's more, I haven't done your business any harm. Why, I've even helped it. People often stop when they see me standing here and go in to buy something. (*Children giggle, then begin to taunt* MANUEL *and run around him, sniffing.*)

ISABEL: I smell raisins!

RAMONA: I smell spice!

INEZ: How much does it cost to smell the flour on your apron?

CARLOS: May I smell your cap for a penny? (*He snatches baker's cap from* MANUEL'S *head and sniffs it, laughing.*)

MANUEL (*Angrily, snatching it back*): You'll laugh on the other side of your face when I get the Judge!

PABLO: When you get *who*?

MANUEL: The Judge. I'm going to tell him the whole story. I'll show you I'm not joking. The Judge will make you pay me. (*He grabs his cash box from table and exits left as* THREE WOMEN *enter right. They come downstage and question the children.*)

1ST WOMAN: What's the matter with Manuel?

2ND WOMAN: Will he be back soon? I want to buy a cake.

3RD WOMAN: So do I. What happened?

1ST WOMAN: He looked so angry. Where's he gone?

GIRLS (*Excitedly, ad lib*): He's gone to get the Judge! He is angry! He is furious! (*Etc.*)

1ST WOMAN: The Judge! What for?

CARLOS: He says Pablo will have to pay for smelling his cakes and pies.

2ND WOMAN (*To* PABLO): He wants you to pay him for doing *that*?

3RD WOMAN: He can't be serious!

PABLO: Oh, yes, he is! But I think it's very funny. (*He laughs, and the* WOMEN *join in.*)

1ST WOMAN: It's ridiculous! Everyone who goes by the shop smells his pastry.

2ND WOMAN: Is he going to take everyone in town to court?

(*They are all in gales of laughter when* MANUEL *returns with* JUDGE, *followed by several* VILLAGERS.)

MANUEL (*To* JUDGE): There he is! (*Points to* PABLO) There's the thief!

JUDGE: Calm yourself, Manuel. It has not yet been proved that Pablo is a thief. First he must have a fair trial. (*He sits down at table and motions for two chairs to be placed facing him.* VILLAGERS *and* THREE WOMEN *gather under tree and on patio with children. They whisper and talk together as they seat themselves.*)

1ST VILLAGER: In all my days, I've never heard of a case like this before.

2ND VILLAGER: How can a man steal the *smell* of anything?

3RD VILLAGER: I'm surprised the Judge would even listen to the baker's story. Money for smelling his cakes! How absurd!

2ND WOMAN: He sells as much bread and pastry as he can bake. What more does he want?

3RD VILLAGER: Manuel loves money and he figures this is a way to get more of it.

JUDGE (*Rapping table with his gavel*): Quiet, everyone! Court is in session. I am ready to hear Manuel Gonzales, baker, against Pablo Perez, neighbor. I will hear the baker first. Manuel, tell your story.

MANUEL (*Rising*): This man, Pablo Perez, comes and stands outside my bakery every day.

JUDGE: Does he block the way?

MANUEL: Not exactly.

JUDGE: Does he keep other people from going into your bakery?

MANUEL: No, sir, but—

JUDGE: Then what *does* he do?

MANUEL: He stands there, looking at my pies and cakes *and smelling them.*

JUDGE: That pleases you, doesn't it?

MANUEL: Pleases me! Far from it! Look here, your honor
—every night I mix the flour and knead the dough and
slave over a hot oven while that shiftless, good-for-noth-
ing Pablo sleeps. Then he gets up in the morning, fresh
as a daisy, and comes out here to smell the fine sweet
pastry I've baked. He takes full value of this free, daily
luxury. He acts as if it's his privilege. Now I ask you,
Judge—is it right that I should work so hard to provide
him with this luxury, without charge? No! He should
pay for it!

JUDGE: I see. You may sit down, Manuel. Now, Pablo Perez,
it is your turn. (PABLO *stands*.) Is it true that you stand
in front of Manuel's bakery and smell his cakes and pies?

PABLO: I can't help smelling them, your honor. Their
spicy fragrance fills the air.

JUDGE: Would you say you *enjoy* it?

PABLO: Oh, yes, sir. I am a man of simple pleasures. Just
the smell of a bakery makes me happy.

JUDGE: But did you ever pay the baker for this pleasure?

PABLO: Well, no, sir. It never occurred to me that I had to
pay him.

JUDGE: Pablo Perez, you will now put ten gold pieces on
this table—for Manuel Gonzales. (VILLAGERS *gasp*.
MANUEL *looks surprised and delighted*.)

PABLO (*Stunned*): Ten gold pieces! For smelling the air
near my own house?

JUDGE: Do you have that amount?

PABLO: I—I guess so, but it's my life's savings.

JUDGE: Where is it?

PABLO: In my house.

JUDGE: Get it and bring it here. (*Slowly* PABLO *crosses
patio and exits left.* VILLAGERS *talk to each other disap-
provingly*.)

1ST VILLAGER: The Judge shouldn't make Pablo pay.

1ST WOMAN: Pablo is an honest man.

2ND VILLAGER: I don't see how the Judge could rule in the baker's favor.

3RD VILLAGER: Why, he's richer than the Judge himself.

2ND WOMAN: And now he's going to get poor Pablo's savings.

3RD WOMAN: It's not fair!

JUDGE (*Rapping with his gavel*): Silence in the court! (PABLO *returns sadly with purse, puts it on table before* JUDGE. MANUEL, *elated, rubs his hands together greedily.*)

MANUEL (*To* JUDGE): I knew your honor would do the right thing by me. Thank you, Judge. (*He picks up purse and starts to put it into his cash box.*)

JUDGE (*Rising*): Not so fast, Manuel! Empty that purse on the table and count the gold pieces, one by one.

MANUEL (*Grinning craftily*): Ah, yes, your honor. I must make sure I haven't been cheated. How kind of you to remind me! (*He empties purse and begins to count, excitedly.* JUDGE *watches* MANUEL *as he lovingly fingers each coin.*)

JUDGE: It gives you great pleasure to touch that gold, doesn't it, Manuel? You *enjoy* it.

MANUEL: Oh, I do, I do! . . . Eight . . . nine . . . ten. It's all here, your honor, and none of it false.

JUDGE: Please put it back in the purse. (MANUEL *does so.*) Now return it to Pablo.

MANUEL (*In disbelief*): *Return* it! But—but you just told Pablo to pay it to me.

JUDGE: No, I did not tell him to pay it to you. I told him to put it on this table. Then I instructed you to count the money, which you did. In doing so, you enjoyed Pablo's money the way he has enjoyed your cakes and pies. In other words, he has smelled your pastry and you have touched his gold. Therefore, I hereby declare that the

case is now settled. (*He raps twice with his gavel.* MAN-
UEL *shamefacedly shoves purse across table to* PABLO
and turns to leave. JUDGE *stops him.*) Just a moment,
Manuel! I hope this has been a lesson to you. In the
future, think less about making money and more about
making friends. Good friends and neighbors are better
than gold. And now, if you please—my fee!

MANUEL: Yes, your honor. (*He opens his cash box willingly
but* JUDGE *closes the lid.*)

JUDGE: Put away your money. There's been enough fuss
over money already today. The fee I am asking is this
—pies and cakes for everyone here—free of charge!
(MANUEL *nods his head vigorously in assent.* VILLAGERS
*and children cheer, then they rush to pastry counter and
help themselves.* MANUEL *goes into bakery and reap-
pears with more pastry piled high on tray.* PABLO *and*
JUDGE *hold a whole pie between them and start to eat
from opposite edges toward the center of pie, as the curtain closes.*)

THE END

Dame Fortune and Don Money

A Spanish folk tale

by Hazel W. Corson

Characters

DAME FORTUNE	SHERIFF
DON MONEY	JUDGE
DON JOSÉ, *a rich man*	TWO WOMEN
MANUEL, *a poor peasant*	BANKER
ROSA, *the baker's wife*	LAWYER
MARIA, *the cloth merchant*	VILLAGERS
TWO THIEVES	

SCENE 1

SETTING: *The marketplace in a Spanish village. At rear, there are two cutaway stores—Maria's cloth store and Rosa's bakery. There are benches right and left.*

AT RISE: DON JOSÉ *is sitting on bench down right, reading document.* ROSA *and* MARIA *are busy in their stores at back.* DON MONEY *enters right, carrying a newspaper, and* DAME FORTUNE *follows, carrying knitting. They sit on bench down left.*

DON MONEY: I tell you, Dame Fortune, I am more powerful than you.

481

DAME FORTUNE: And I tell you, Don Money, you are not. (*She knits.*) Money isn't everything. Good fortune is important, too.

DON MONEY: I never said that money was everything, but I do say, you won't get far without it.

DAME FORTUNE: Oh, I wouldn't say that. Money by itself is nothing. It is what a fortunate man does with his money that makes it worth having.

DON MONEY: You are always saying that. What do you mean when you say a man is fortunate?

DAME FORTUNE: Well, even when a fortunate man does something very foolish, things will turn out happily in the end. And I think that is better than just having money. Now, look at Don José there. He's the richest man in town; does his money bring him happiness? (MANUEL *enters left. He stands looking at* DON JOSÉ *for a minute.*)

DON MONEY: And that poor peasant there who works for Don José? He doesn't have a cent to his name, but he is not happy. (DAME FORTUNE *and* DON MONEY *watch as* MANUEL *approaches* DON JOSÉ.)

MANUEL: Good morning, Don José.

DON JOSÉ (*Looking up*): So it's you again, Manuel. Is anything wrong at the hacienda?

MANUEL: No, Don José.

DON JOSÉ (*Crossly*): Don't tell me something good has happened for a change. Perhaps someone wants to pay a good price for the wool from the sheep?

MANUEL: No, Don José.

DON JOSÉ (*Coldly*): Then I cannot imagine why you need to speak to me.

MANUEL: It's about my family, sir. My little ones are crying for bread. I have no money, and no way of getting any bread. I work hard for you, day after day. Can you not give me some of my pay now?

DON JOSÉ: Pay! What pay? You have already eaten up your pay for some time to come. I told you the last time you asked for money not to bother me again.

MANUEL: But my children, Don José!

DON JOSÉ: It is not my fault that you have more children than you can feed. I'm concerned with greater sums of money than your pay! Why, only today I'm investing two thousand dollars in a trading ship bound for India. Your pay indeed! Do not speak to me again unless you have something important to say. (*Rolls up his document and exits right.* MANUEL *sinks down on the seat and puts his head in his hands.*)

DON MONEY: Here is a man who is very poor, and very unfortunate. You watch and see how happy I can make him, just by giving him a little money.

DAME FORTUNE: Very well! And when *you* have failed to help him, I will see what *I* can do, just by making him more fortunate.

DON MONEY: Agreed! (*Goes over to* MANUEL.) Good day to you.

MANUEL (*Looking up*): Good day to you, good sir.

DON MONEY: What is your name, my good man?

MANUEL: My name is Manuel, sir.

DON MONEY: And do you know who I am, Manuel?

MANUEL: I have never seen you before in my whole life, sir.

DON MONEY: I am Don Money, Manuel. Tell me, does anything at all belong to you?

MANUEL: Yes, indeed, sir. I have a wife and six sons, all of them ragged and hungry. No matter how much I borrow or beg, they never have enough to eat.

DON MONEY: Borrow! Beg! Have you never thought of working?

MANUEL: Indeed, I do work, sir. But still I never seem to have enough money.

Don Money: Why is that?

Manuel: Truly, I don't know. On payday I must give all my pay to my master, Don José, for the hut he lets me live in, and there is no money left to buy food. When I try to borrow from Don José, he always says that I owe him too much already. I cannot read the accounts, so I must take his word for it.

Don Money: Well, Manuel, let me improve your lot. (*Hands him money*) Here is a dollar. May it bring you a new start in life.

Manuel: Oh, thank you, gracious sir! A thousand blessings on you! I will go and buy bread at once. (*Neither notices that the bill falls to ground by bench rather than into his pocket.*) How my wife and children will rejoice. Thank you! (*Runs to* Rosa's *bakery.* Don Money *returns to* Dame Fortune.)

Dame Fortune: Do you think that little bit of money will help him?

Don Money: It doesn't take much money to improve one's lot in life.

Dame Fortune: We shall see. (*They sit on bench.* Dame Fortune *knits.* Don Money *reads newspaper.*)

Manuel (*To* Rosa): What good fortune! I can hardly believe it. Give me two huge loaves of bread, good woman, and a cake, and some of those little pies.

Rosa (*Coldly*): Not so fast! I know you. Before I put so much as a crumb into your hand, I want to see your money.

Manuel: This time I have money, good woman. A kind gentleman just gave me some. Come out, little dollar, and show yourself. (*Reaches into pocket, turns it inside out.*)

Rosa: Ha! I knew you had no money.

Manuel: It must be in my other pocket. (*Finds nothing*) Oh, unlucky me! Holes in both pockets. I must have lost the money on the way. I'll go look for it. My poor children! (*Retraces his steps to* DON MONEY, *looking for money.*)

DON MONEY (*Looking up from paper*): Ah, Manuel! How did your children enjoy the bread you bought?

MANUEL: Alas, I didn't buy any.

DON MONEY: Oh? I suppose you found a good investment for the money?

MANUEL: No, sir. I lost the money before I could spend it.

DON MONEY: I don't understand how anyone can lose money. However, if I am to improve your lot, I can see that I must give you more. Here is a gold piece. (*Hands him money*) Do not lose this.

MANUEL (*Looking at gold piece in amazement*): Never fear! With this much money, I can buy cloth for clothes for my family, and have enough left to buy food, too. Oh, thank you! Thank you! (*Runs to* MARIA's *cloth store*)

DAME FORTUNE: That dollar didn't do much good.

DON MONEY: He seems to be an unlucky man. (*Both follow* MANUEL.)

DAME FORTUNE: But money was supposed to bring him good fortune, according to you.

DON MONEY: Now it will, Dame Fortune. Watch!

MANUEL (*To* MARIA): Good woman, I would like cloth to make clothes. Good sturdy stuff I want, nothing too fine or fancy.

MARIA: You look as if you could use new clothes. But just how are you going to pay for my cloth?

MANUEL: I shall pay for it with this gold piece (*Hands her coin*) and have money left over. Now, let me pick out what I want.

MARIA: Ha! How did a sorry-looking man like you get a gold piece, I'd like to know?

MANUEL: It is mine, and just as good as any other gold piece.

MARIA (*Flinging gold piece on counter*): I doubt that! This coin does not ring true. It is counterfeit. You are trying to cheat me. Do not think you can get cloth from me with it. I will take this coin to the sheriff, and he will arrest you. Out of my shop! (MARIA *chases* MANUEL *off-stage with a broom.*)

DAME FORTUNE: How money has helped poor Manuel! Now he is not only dressed in rags and has no food, but is about to get into trouble with the law.

DON MONEY (*Angrily*): That coin was not counterfeit! The woman is a fool. I *will* improve Manuel's lot. I'll give him a great deal of money. (*Runs off after* MANUEL, *calling*) Wait! Manuel! Wait! (DAME FORTUNE *follows him off.*)

MANUEL (*Re-entering right with both hands full of bills*): What a kind gentleman! Money! Money! Money! I have never seen so much money in my life. I didn't know there was so much money in all the world! (*Sits on bench, looking at the money.*) Ah! What a beautiful sight! (Two THIEVES *enter left, wearing kerchief masks.* 1ST THIEF *sees* MANUEL *and beckons to* 2ND THIEF, *as* DAME FORTUNE *and* DON MONEY *enter right and stand watching.*)

1ST THIEF: Look at him!

2ND THIEF: He's just asking to be robbed.

1ST THIEF: What are we waiting for? (1ST THIEF *pretends to hit* MANUEL *on the head, and he slumps down.* 2ND THIEF *grabs money and both stuff money into a sack.*)

2ND THIEF: He never knew what hit him.

1ST THIEF: Let's get out of here. (*They run off left.* DAME FORTUNE *and* DON MONEY *go to* MANUEL.)

DAME FORTUNE: Is this the happiness your money brings?

(*Kneels by* Manuel) Are you going to help him any
more, Don Money?

Don Money: It is plain to see that Manuel is unlucky.
Nothing can help an unlucky man, not even money.

Dame Fortune: Then you agree that it is now my turn to
see if I can bring him good fortune?

Don Money: Go ahead if you must, but nothing can help
him. You'll find out. (Dame Fortune *takes a fan from
her pocket and fans* Manuel. *He moves and groans.*)

Manuel: Oh, my head! My head! (*Sits up slowly, groaning
with each movement*) What has happened? Oh, unlucky
day! My money! Someone has taken my money!

Dame Fortune: Never mind the money. Take heart,
Manuel; I have a feeling things are going to be better
for you.

Manuel: I hope so. My life could hardly be worse. (*Getting up*) Now I must go home to my hungry wife and
children.

Dame Fortune: Manuel, what is that by the bench?

Manuel (*In surprise*): Why, it is a dollar! (*Picking it up*)
It is the same dollar Don Money gave me this morning!
I remember it because it was torn just so. (*Holds it up*)
At least I can buy some bread for my family now.

Maria (*Entering from left*): Here you are at last! I have
been looking for you everywhere!

Manuel: I wish you had not found me. I have had enough
bad luck for one day.

Maria: My friend, I have done you a great wrong. I took
your gold coin to the sheriff. We found it to be a very
good coin, not counterfeit, so here it is. (*Hands coin to*
Manuel)

Manuel: Then I can pay for some cloth for my family
after all.

Maria: I am ashamed of the way I treated you this morning. Come to my shop with me now and tell me what cloth you want. Perhaps you will pay less for it than you thought! (MANUEL *and* MARIA *go to her shop.*)

DAME FORTUNE: Manuel does not seem so unlucky now. (DAME FORTUNE *and* DON MONEY *sit on bench. She knits.* MANUEL *selects his cloth, pays for it, and goes to the baker's shop, where he buys a long loaf of bread.* TWO WOMEN *enter left.*)

1ST WOMAN (*Excitedly*): I saw it myself. The sheriff has arrested two thieves, and they are to come before the judge here and now!

2ND WOMAN: How exciting! Look, here they come. (*Points right.* SHERIFF *enters right, leading* TWO THIEVES *and carrying their sacks. Some* VILLAGERS *enter behind them and join* TWO WOMEN, *all talking excitedly.* DAME FORTUNE *and* DON MONEY *watch the proceedings with interest.* JUDGE *enters left and sits at his desk.* MANUEL *joins crowd, holding his cloth and bread.* ROSA *and* MARIA *leave their shops and come to watch.*)

JUDGE: Sheriff, how did you catch these men?

SHERIFF: I saw them running along the street, Your Honor. They wore masks, and kept looking back as if they were being followed.

JUDGE: Did you search them?

SHERIFF: We didn't need to, Your Honor. They were carrying sacks on their backs. (*Holds up sacks*) In the first sack, there were some jewels, probably taken from the count's palace. And there was one hundred dollars in the second sack. (*Shows sacks to* JUDGE)

MANUEL (*Excitedly*): Those must be the thieves who robbed me! That is my money!

JUDGE (*Looking at* MANUEL): You were robbed? When was this?

MANUEL (*Stepping forward*): Just today, Your Honor. This kind gentleman (*Points to* DON MONEY), who has been trying to help me, gave me one hundred dollars. While I was sitting over there (*Points to bench*) counting my money, someone jumped at me, and knocked me out. When I revived, my money was gone.

JUDGE: Are these the men?

MANUEL: I didn't see the men, Your Honor, but I did get a good look at the money. It was new, and there were ten beautiful ten-dollar bills.

DON MONEY (*Stepping forward*): That is true, Your Honor. I am Don Money, and I gave Manuel ten new ten-dollar bills today.

JUDGE: How much money did you find, Sheriff?

SHERIFF: One hundred dollars, Your Honor. (*He counts.*) There are ten new ten-dollar bills.

JUDGE: Then the money must belong to Manuel. I see no reason why we should not return it to him at once. (SHERIFF *gives bills to* MANUEL.)

MANUEL: Oh, thank you, Your Honor! This started out to be the worst day of my life. Suddenly, everything has changed. This is the luckiest day of my life! (*Curtain*)

*　　*　　*

SCENE 2

TIME: *A year later.*

SETTING: *The same as Scene 1.*

AT RISE: DON JOSÉ *is sitting on bench, adding up figures in big ledger.* DAME FORTUNE *and* DON MONEY *are sitting on another bench. She is knitting, and he is reading a paper.* BANKER *enters right.*

BANKER: Good morning, Don José. I have good news for you.

DON JOSÉ: Ah, my banker! It's news about money, I hope?

BANKER: What could be better news? It is about the ship we sent out to trade in India last year. It is back after a successful voyage. Your share of the profit is five thousand dollars!

DON JOSÉ: Five thousand dollars? Why, I invested two thousand dollars in that ship, and you dare to return to me a miserable five thousand dollars? Do not think you can cheat Don José so easily!

BANKER (*Coldly*): If that is the way you feel about it, sir, I doubt if we shall care to do business together in the future. (*Exits left. LAWYER enters right.*)

LAWYER: Good morning, Don José. Your clerk said I would find you here.

DON JOSÉ: Ah, my lawyer. You have good news about my father's will, I trust?

LAWYER: I think so. Your brother has agreed to a settlement that is very favorable to you. He will take the house and land, and you will have everything else, about fifty thousand dollars, in all.

DON JOSÉ: And you think that is good? I am the oldest. I should have everything, the land as well as the money.

LAWYER: Your brother could demand much more, but he wants to settle the matter. You must admit that the land has prospered under his management.

DON JOSÉ: Management! His *mismanagement* has kept it from being worth twice as much. Think of what he has spent on the peasants' houses, on giving them gardens of their own, and that silly school for their children. I want you to sue him for wasting so much of my money.

LAWYER: I think you had better get another lawyer, Don José. I will not take a case like that. (*Exits*)

DON JOSÉ (*Shouting after him*): The world is full of thieves and robbers, and you are the worst of the lot! It is impossible for an honest man to make money today! (*Exits*)

DAME FORTUNE: Now there is a man who has plenty of money. You say it should bring him happiness.

DON MONEY: Don't forget that his luck is good, Dame Fortune. Three thousand dollars profit on a ship that could have been lost at sea! His good fortune in business hasn't made him happy, either. (MANUEL *enters left. He is well dressed, and looks happy and prosperous.*)

MANUEL: Good morning, sir, and madam. Do you remember me?

DON MONEY: Ah, Manuel! What a change! I hardly know you.

MANUEL: I well remember your kindness to me, sir. Here is the money you gave to me a year ago. I have been carrying it in this little purse hoping to see you and repay you. (*Gives him purse*)

DON MONEY: Are you sure you do not need it, Manuel?

MANUEL: Truly, I have more than I need. I used some of the money to help a friend who was looking for buried treasure. He found enough to make us both rich. My family and I live in a fine house now, and I have enough to help other people who are as poor as I once was. I have done much with my money, always at great profit to myself.

DAME FORTUNE: So your luck did change, Manuel?

MANUEL: Yes, my lady. I remember the day you said that things would be better for me. You were right, and I have been a happy man ever since. I thank you both. (*Exits left*)

DAME FORTUNE: So you see, Don Money, it is just as I said. All Manuel's money, without his good fortune, would be worthless to him.

DON MONEY: But I gave him the money in the first place.

DAME FORTUNE: And I helped him get it back when he lost it. After you gave him up, I brought him good fortune.

DON MONEY: Here we are with the same old argument. Which is more powerful, money or good fortune? We cannot settle it.

DAME FORTUNE: Don Money, what is the difference between Manuel and Don José?

DON MONEY: The difference of day from night. Manuel is a happy man with many friends, but Don José is miserable, and his misery spreads to all he meets.

DAME FORTUNE: Yet both have made money, and both seem to have good luck. Could it be that there is something more important than luck or money?

DON MONEY: Yes, there is. Don José, with all his huge fortune, will never be as happy as Manuel, who has a good and generous heart. (*Curtain*)

THE END

A Test for William Tell

A Swiss folk tale

by Helen Roberts

Characters

HENRIC, *8-year-old son of William Tell*
PHILIP, *12-year-old nephew of William Tell*
MISTRESS MELCHTHAL
1ST BROTHER OF RÜTLI
THREE OTHER BROTHERS OF RÜTLI, *secret patriotic group, wearing small red feathers in their caps*
WOODCARVER
WOMAN
FOUR SOLDIERS
WILLIAM TELL, *the Crossbowman of Bürglen*
LALOTTE, *Tell's niece, about 14*
TUMBLERS (*or* DANCERS)
GESSLER, *the governor*
VILLAGERS

SETTING: *Marketplace at Altdorf, Switzerland, about 1307.*
AT RISE: WOODCARVER *sits at small stall, whittling wooden figures and whistling.* 1ST BROTHER OF RÜTLI *tends next stand, selling fruit. Toy and candy stand is tended by* MISTRESS MELCHTHAL. *Lunch stall is served by* WOMAN.

VILLAGERS *walk about.* TWO SOLDIERS *stand guard by flagpole, laughing and talking loudly. Unnoticed by* SOLDIERS, PHILIP *and* HENRIC *enter cautiously, look at stalls.*

1ST SOLDIER: Just look at these simple Swiss peasants!

2ND SOLDIER: They must have been surprised when Governor Gessler ordered their senseless flag pulled down from this flagpole.

1ST SOLDIER (*Laughing loudly*): And what a joke it was on them to put this empty Ducal Bonnet in its place!

2ND SOLDIER: They'd better bow low in front of the Ducal Bonnet, if they don't want some help from our spears. Of course, if anyone refuses . . . (*Gestures cutting off his head.*)

1ST SOLDIER (*Confidentially*): You know, I've heard rumors that some of these peasants are a little upset at the notion.

2ND SOLDIER (*Laughing uproariously*): Ha, ha! How I'd like to see one of them with enough gumption to defy the new law! (*They continue conversing in pantomime, while* THREE OTHER BROTHERS OF RÜTLI *enter near fruit stand.*)

1ST BROTHER: Good morning, Brothers. Have you finished your marketing already?

3RD BROTHER: Oh, no! We've been watching the dancing bears in another part of the marketplace.

2ND BROTHER: Tell me, have you seen our friend William Tell this morning? I'm so glad that he agreed to be the leader of our Brothers of Rütli.

3RD BROTHER (*Whispering in alarm*): Hush, Brother! The walls have ears! Those guards may not be as stupid as they look. We must work in secret. (*Louder*) What splendid apples these are!

1ST BROTHER: Indeed they are! I recommend them highly.

(*Whispering*) Aren't those lads yonder the son and the nephew of our brave leader, William Tell? (*They all turn to look.* HENRIC *and* PHILIP *dart behind a stall.*)

3RD BROTHER (*Loudly, to divert* SOLDIERS' *attention*): Wonderful fruit! Give me some of those huge pears! (*Buys them.*)

4TH BROTHER: I'm anxious to try some of Mistress Melchthal's homemade candy! (*They move on to candy stall.* SOLDIERS *notice them.*)

MISTRESS MELCHTHAL: Good morning, friends.

BROTHERS: Good morning, Mistress Melchthal.

4TH BROTHER: Have you some of your famous peppermint drops?

MISTRESS MELCHTHAL: Plenty of them.

4TH BROTHER: Let me have a pound of them, please. (*Puts a kerchief out to hold candy, offers some to others.*)

3RD BROTHER: I ate my breakfast long before daylight and I want some lunch. Come on over to the lunch stand. (*They pass on, and are stopped by the* SOLDIERS.)

1ST SOLDIER: Stop! Pay homage to the Ducal Bonnet!

3RD BROTHER: Oh! (*Hesitating.*) Oh! Of course! (*Bows*)

2ND SOLDIER (*Roughly*): You other two! Follow your friend's example! And see that you bow a little lower, too! Remember, it's the order of your ruler, Governor Gessler.

2ND *and* 4TH BROTHERS: We obey orders. (*They bow, then go to lunch stand and sit down.*)

2ND SOLDIER: Say now! That's an idea! *I'm* hungry, too. Why should these peasants get first choice?

1ST SOLDIER: That's right! Why should they? Our precious Ducal Bonnet can look after itself for a while. *We* need food! (*They strut toward lunch stall, push* BROTHERS *out of way on bench.*)

1ST SOLDIER (*Sitting down and pounding on counter*): Hey, peasant woman! What have you here that's fit to eat?

WOMAN: Here are some oat cakes and fresh buttermilk. And some fine country cheeses.

1ST SOLDIER: Well, give us the best you have, and waste no time about it. (WOMAN *brings food. They begin eating and drinking noisily.*)

WOMAN (*Timidly*): That's fivepence for the cakes and threepence for the milk and cheese.

2ND SOLDIER (*Laughing loudly*): Present the bill to our noble Governor Gessler! Ha, ha! Just try to collect from him! (WOMAN *cringes;* SOLDIERS *continue eating, laughing and slapping each other.* PHILIP *and* HENRIC *come out from behind stall.*)

PHILIP (*Points to Ducal Bonnet*): Look, Henric! Do you see that Bonnet on yonder flagpole?

HENRIC: Yes, Cousin Philip! I see it all right!

PHILIP (*Boasting*): You should have seen it rolling in the mud last night after I knocked it down. The soldiers were standing quite near, but they weren't smart enough to catch me, I can tell you. (HENRIC *lets go of* PHILIP's *hand, picks up stone*)

HENRIC: I believe *I* could hit that funny hat, too.

PHILIP: Henric! Are you crazy? Drop that stone! Those soldiers would just as soon cut off your head with their spears as look at you. (*They go back toward* WOOD-CARVER.)

WOODCARVER (*To* HENRIC): What's your name, child?

HENRIC (*Indignantly*): I'm not a child! I'm a boy. A *big* boy, too. My name's Henric. What's yours?

WOODCARVER (*Laughing*): Everyone calls me Woodcarver Grandfather. See all these fine wooden dolls? (*Shows him dolls*)

HENRIC: *I* don't like dolls! They're for babies!

WOODCARVER: Oh, no, my lad! Not wooden dolls like mine. Here are some splendid soldier dolls. Boys always like soldiers.

HENRIC: No! I'm afraid of soldiers. (*Points toward real* SOLDIERS)

WOODCARVER: But not afraid of *wooden* soldiers. Whenever you're afraid of them, you can snip off their heads with one blow. See? (*He makes gesture of cutting off heads of wooden soldiers.*)

HENRIC: Oh! I'd like that! (*Picks up soldiers, laughing.*)

WOODCARVER (*Gets up, puts an arm around* HENRIC): You don't need to fear those soldiers, either. They're a lot like my wooden soldiers. When they're filling their stomachs, their heads are as empty as—as my pockets. (*Turns pockets inside out, and some coins scatter*)

HENRIC: Ho, ho! Your pockets weren't so empty after all! (*They pick up coins.*)

WOODCARVER (*Surprised*): Three coins. Let's buy some candy!

HENRIC (*Clapping his hands*): Candy! Hooray! I almost never have a coin to spend. (*They go to candy stall.*) I want some candy!

MISTRESS MELCHTHAL: Here's some fine red candy for both of you. (*She comes around the stall, gives each a big candy, takes* WOODCARVER'S *coins, then secretly slips them back into his pocket. Noise is heard offstage.*)

1ST BROTHER: Out of the way, everyone. Here come the tumblers!

WOODCARVER: Hurry, Henric! (*They go back to* PHILIP *and sit down.* TUMBLERS *enter, performing cartwheels and somersaults across stage, while* VILLAGERS *sing and cheer. As* TUMBLERS *go out,* HENRIC *steps forward.*)

HENRIC (*Clapping and shouting*): I think I could do that. (*He starts tumbling and falls down.*)

PHILIP: Henric! You're the worst scamp I know! Haven't you any sense at all? Do you want those soldiers to cut off your head and mine as well?

HENRIC: I'm sorry. (*Suddenly*) Look, Philip. There's father coming into the marketplace. (WILLIAM TELL *enters, carrying his crossbow and a cloth bag.*)

PHILIP (*Whispering*): Now we're in for it, if he as much as sees us. We'll have to keep hidden here by the Woodcarver. (*They hide.*)

TELL (*Stopping at fruit stall and saluting* 1ST BROTHER): Hail, Brother of Rütli!

1ST BROTHER: Hush, Brother. We must be more cautious.

TELL (*Boldly*): There's a time for caution and a time for bravery. Why, what splendid apples these are. I must have some to take home to my dear family. (*He buys some.*) Don't forget our meeting in the glen tonight, Brother. It's high time we took action.

1ST BROTHER (*Frightened*): Hush, William Tell! You're far too bold. (TELL *passes to toy and candy stall.*)

TELL: Good morning, Mistress Melchthal. Is there anything our little band of patriots can do to help you while your husband is imprisoned so unjustly?

MISTRESS (*Wiping her eyes*): No, thanks, Neighbor Tell. But the children all miss their father.

TELL (*Kindly*): Of course they do, dear friend. (*Softly*) The Brothers of Rütli miss him too, and are determined to free him. (*Loudly*) Do you have any more of those toys he made last month? I want some for my lads. They were *so* disappointed not to get to the Fair.

MISTRESS (*Holding up toys*): Here are some! The Fair is no place for children these days. In fact, there's no place now for freedom-loving people to go! (TELL *takes toys.* SOLDIERS *resume their posts at flagpole, in good spirits.*)

HENRIC (*Whispering*): Look, Philip! Look! My father just bought me a fine toy! Oh, I wish I were home again. I wish I were home! Whatever will he do if he finds me at the marketplace?

PHILIP: He'd better *not* find you. We'd be in trouble— and you'd have no toy!

TELL (*Walking toward lunch stall and speaking to* WOMAN, *but ignoring* SOLDIERS): Good morning, my friend. How is your . . .

1ST SOLDIER: Stop!

TELL: How is your lunch business today?

2ND SOLDIER (*Shouting*): Stop, I say!

TELL (*Turning around*): What now? What's the matter?

1ST SOLDIER (*Pointing to Bonnet*): Matter enough! Don't you see this *noble* bonnet?

TELL (*Deliberately*): Yes. I see that *empty* bonnet.

2ND SOLDIER: You insolent peasant. (*Pulls him roughly in front of pole*) Bow down before it!

TELL: Suppose I refuse? (*Crowd edges forward tensely.*)

1ST SOLDIER: What? You'd never dare!

TELL: I would *never* dare bow down before it.

2ND SOLDIER (*Blustering*): But our noble Governor has ordered everyone to bow down before it as a sign of allegiance.

TELL (*Drawing himself to his full height*): I—am loyal to my *own* country—Switzerland.

1ST SOLDIER: You're a traitor. Do you know the penalty for refusal?

TELL (*Vehemently*): I know! And I would rather die as a revolt against such tyranny than bow before that empty symbol. My death might serve to arouse all Switzerland to throw off its burden of unbearable oppression! (LALOTTE *enters timidly, looking for* HENRIC. 3RD *and* 4TH SOLDIERS *enter and stroll across by fruit stand. First two* SOLDIERS *begin to bind* TELL *while others are talking.*)

3RD SOLDIER: Who's this foolish peasant so anxious to die for his country?

4TH SOLDIER: Some half-wit, I suppose. (*Pounds on fruit stall*) Who is he? Do you know him?

2ND BROTHER: He is William Tell, the Crossbowman of Bürglen.

3RD SOLDIER: Tell? Tell? That name sounds familiar to me.

4TH SOLDIER: Of course it does! It was some mischievous relative of his who led a mob of boys to knock down the Ducal Bonnet.

3RD SOLDIER: So it was! (*Looks around*) That's the boy over there. (*Points to* PHILIP.)

4TH SOLDIER: He'll soon regret his folly.

WOODCARVER (*Jumping up*): Run, Philip! Run! The soldiers are after you! (PHILIP *runs out, dodging the crowd, chased by* SOLDIERS.)

HENRIC (*Crying*): Philip! Philip! I want my father!

WOODCARVER: I'll take you to him, Henric. Don't cry, my boy. (*He starts to lead* HENRIC *to* TELL *as* GESSLER *comes in left.*)

GESSLER: So! Someone has dared to defy the edict of his noble Governor! Who is he?

TELL (*Proudly*): I am William Tell.

HENRIC (*Throwing his arms around* TELL's *legs and sobbing*): Oh, Father! Forgive me, Father! Forgive me!

GESSLER (*Roughly shaking the child*): Is this your child, William Tell?

TELL: Harm him not, I beg you! He is my first-born son.

GESSLER (*Pompously*): I would not harm the child. (*Laughs cruelly*) So! You're William Tell, the famous crossbowman, eh? I've always wanted to see a test of your skill! Ha, ha! I'll give you a chance to prove it and save your life at the same time.

TELL: Are you jesting? What are your conditions? (WOODCARVER *returns to his corner, while* LALOTTE *comes nearer.*)

GESSLER: Only this! Today is Altdorf Fair, and I am in-

clined to be generous. Then, too, we would gladly see
some sport.

TELL: Sport? What sport?

GESSLER: Aha! I have it! You shall shoot an apple off this
small boy's head. If you miss the apple or touch the
child, you will surely die! If you hit the apple, your life
is saved.

TELL: Take me away. I would never risk my son's life to
save my own.

GESSLER: Not so fast, bold Tell! If you refuse to shoot,
you'll die, of course, but not before you've seen your
own child shot before your very eyes.

TELL: Then command my bonds to be loosed. I will do
my best.

GESSLER: Release the man! (SOLDIERS *untie him;* LALOTTE
takes HENRIC'S *hand,* 3RD *and* 4TH SOLDIERS *re-enter and
stand at rear.*)

LALOTTE: Where shall I take the lad?

GESSLER: Take him over beyond the fruit stall! One hundred paces. That should make a good test. Place an apple
on his head . . . and we shall see the fun. Bold William
Tell, *you* stand over there! I have no desire to endanger
the lives of my soldiers! (*Points offstage.*)

LALOTTE (*As she leads* HENRIC *right*): Henric, my dear
child, will you stand perfectly still until I call you to
me? (*She takes an apple from the fruit stand, as they
pass it.*)

HENRIC (*Bravely*): Of course, Cousin Lalotte. I'm not
afraid. My father's aim is always true!

TELL (*Taking out two arrows as he goes offstage left*):
God grant it may be true this time! Turn the child's
face away. I cannot shoot with those dear eyes so trust-
ingly upon me.

LALOTTE (*Leading* HENRIC *off right*): Don't forget, Henric.

Stand perfectly still! (*They exit, followed by some of* VILLAGERS.)

HENRIC (*From off right*): I'm ready, Father. (VILLAGERS *are quiet, and all watch off right. Sound of arrow is heard, then loud cheers from crowd.*)

LALOTTE (*Running in, with* HENRIC, *holding apple with an arrow through it*): The apple is pierced in the middle! Good lad, Henric! (TELL *re-enters left, followed by cheering crowd.*)

GESSLER (*Slapping* TELL *on the back good-naturedly*): Well done, William Tell. Well done! You've given us a great exhibition. But tell me, why did you prepare *two* arrows?

TELL (*Bitterly*): Because, *noble* Gessler, if I had missed with the first, I should never have missed with the second. I saved it for your own murderous heart.

GESSLER (*Taken aback*): You're a—a—bold, villainous traitor.

1ST SOLDIER: A dangerous traitor!

GESSLER: I promised you your life. You surely don't deserve it, but Gessler's word is good. For the safety of our country, the rest of your days must be spent in prison. Bind him, soldiers!

HENRIC (*Crying and holding* TELL's *leg*): Father! Father! What are they going to do?

TELL: Henric! You're my oldest son!

HENRIC (*Bravely*): Yes, Father.

TELL: I will be gone a little time. Will you look after your mother and the little ones while I'm gone?

HENRIC: I will, Father. I will.

TELL: Lalotte, take him safely home to his mother. Break the news to her as gently as you can, will you?

LALOTTE (*Weeping quietly*): I will, Uncle. Come, Henric. (*They start off.*)

GESSLER (*To* SOLDIERS): Prepare the boat for the journey!

(*They go off.*) We must put our prisoner in the dungeon of Kussnacht for the safety of our country. Let's go.

TELL (*Calling to* HENRIC, *who looks back*): Henric! My dear son! *Don't ever forget this!* I am leaving you—so that our beloved country may rise against the oppressor and be *forever* a *free* and *happy* people! (*Curtain*)

THE END

The Covetous Councilman

A Turkish folk tale

by J. H. Bealmear

Characters

CARPENTER
CARPENTER'S WIFE
COUNCILMAN
MAYOR'S WIFE

TIME: *Long ago in Turkey.*
SETTING: *Councilman's house, on a street in a small village.*
AT RISE: COUNCILMAN *sits in room, up right. Lights are dim on room, and full on street downstage.* CARPENTER *and* CARPENTER'S WIFE *enter left.* CARPENTER *carries a purse.*

CARPENTER'S WIFE: We'll soon have enough money to go to the city, won't we? It's so exciting I can hardly wait. When do you think we will have saved enough?
CARPENTER: With what we have here, and what we have already left with the Councilman for safekeeping, we will soon have enough. Don't be impatient, wife.
CARPENTER'S WIFE: I, impatient! You are just as excited as I am about going to the city.

CARPENTER: Hurry, wife! (*He looks around.*) We don't want some thief to come along and steal our money. (*She looks around fearfully, and they hurry right. He knocks on* COUNCILMAN'S *door, up right. As* COUNCILMAN *opens door, lights come up.*)

COUNCILMAN: Oh, it's the carpenter again. Come in.

CARPENTER: Thank you, sir. We have saved some more money, and we would like you to put it into your locked box, with our other savings.

COUNCILMAN: I am honored that you should want to leave your money with me for safekeeping. (*He takes money and locks it in safe.*) Now your money is safe. When you have need for it, tell me, and I will get it for you. You can depend upon me. I always keep my word.

CARPENTER: We are sure of that, sir, or we never would have left our money with you. We hope to bring you more money soon to save for us.

COUNCILMAN: Come any time. It is good to see such industrious people. (*As* COUNCILMAN *closes door after them, lights go down in his room. He sits down at table.*)

CARPENTER'S WIFE: Aren't we lucky that you happen to know such a kind and trustworthy man as the Councilman?

CARPENTER: A carpenter meets many important people in his work, wife. You know that.

CARPENTER'S WIFE: I still say we're lucky. It is not everyone who would feel free to go to such a man as the Councilman and ask him to keep his savings.

CARPENTER: Come, wife. We must hurry. I have work to do. (*They exit left.* MAYOR'S WIFE *enters right and knocks on* COUNCILMAN'S *door. As he opens it, the lights come up.*)

COUNCILMAN: Why, it's the Mayor's wife. Come in, madam.

MAYOR'S WIFE: Thank you. I hope I am not disturbing you. Were you busy?

COUNCILMAN: Never too busy for a word with the Mayor's wife.

MAYOR'S WIFE: I came to visit with your wife, but I wanted to be the first to congratulate you on your new appointment. My husband, the Mayor, told me just this morning that he plans to appoint you the head of the exchequer. As you know, that is the most responsible position in our community. You will be in charge of all the public's money.

COUNCILMAN (*Haughtily*): Yes, madam, I realize the importance of being selected as head of the exchequer, and I am deeply grateful for the honor. You may assure your husband that I will honestly care for all moneys entrusted to me. And I thank you, madam, for being so kind to tell me of this great honor.

MAYOR'S WIFE: You are quite welcome. My husband would have come himself, but, as you know, he is busy today.

COUNCILMAN: I quite understand, madam.

MAYOR'S WIFE: You won't say anything about it until the formal appointment is made? The Mayor would be most unhappy if the news should leak out before the appointment ceremony.

COUNCILMAN (*Bowing*): You may trust my discretion, madam.

MAYOR'S WIFE: Then I shall go to visit with your wife.

COUNCILMAN: Thank you again, madam, for your kindness in telling me first. (MAYOR'S WIFE *exits.*) Imagine that! I will be the head of the exchequer. (*Greedily*) I will have all that money in my hands. (*Lights go down in his room as* CARPENTER *and his* WIFE *enter from left.*)

CARPENTER'S WIFE: Hurry, husband. I can hardly wait to get our money so we can go to the city. I know it will be more wonderful than we have ever dreamed. Are you sure we have saved enough?

CARPENTER: Didn't we figure it together and decide that we would have enough, with what I have here and our savings?

CARPENTER'S WIFE: Then let's hurry. What if the Councilman isn't home? (CARPENTER *knocks on door. As* COUNCILMAN *opens it, lights come up.*)

COUNCILMAN: It's the carpenter again. Come in.

CARPENTER: Thank you, sir. We won't take much of your time. You see, sir, we have saved some more money, and with this and the money you've saved for us in your locked box, we can go to the city as we had planned. We're sorry to be such a nuisance, sir, but if you'll just give us our money we'll not trouble you again.

COUNCILMAN (*Slyly*): Money! What money? What are you babbling about? Why would I have your money?

CARPENTER: But we gave it to you to keep for us.

COUNCILMAN: Don't be foolish. Do you expect anyone to believe such an unlikely story—that a carpenter would leave his money with a Councilman for safekeeping? I'm not the head of the exchequer—that is, I'm not yet head of the exchequer. But that is no concern of yours.

CARPENTER: But it's true, sir. Look in your safe. You'll find the money is there.

COUNCILMAN: Of course, there is money in my safe. That is what a safe is for, but it is my money.

CARPENTER: But we gave it to you to keep for us.

COUNCILMAN: Where is your receipt? Show it to me. If you gave me money, you surely have a receipt to show for it. Where is it?

CARPENTER: We don't have a receipt.

COUNCILMAN: Then get out of my house. How dare you come into my home and demand money from me? I could have both of you arrested.

CARPENTER'S WIFE: But it's our money! (COUNCILMAN *pushes them out door. Lights go down in room.*) He can't keep our money. Do something!

CARPENTER: Do what? Who would take my word against that of the Councilman? I am only a carpenter. (*They walk toward bench at left and sit down. MAYOR'S WIFE enters, looking back and forth as she walks toward the bench.*)

MAYOR'S WIFE: I beg your pardon.

CARPENTER (*Standing up*): Why, it's the Mayor's wife.

MAYOR'S WIFE: Didn't you just come out of the Councilman's house? (*They nod.*) I was sure I recognized you. I was waiting for his wife in the next room, and I overheard everything that was said. I recognized your voice, Mr. Carpenter. Remember, you made that beautiful jewel box for me? (*He nods.*) It is my most prized possession. And I remember your telling me that you and your wife were saving your money to make a trip to the city. (*He nods.*) I could hardly believe what I was hearing. To think the Councilman should try to cheat you out of your money!

CARPENTER'S WIFE: Oh, it's terrible, madam. We have worked and scrimped and saved for such a long time, and the Councilman assured us that he would give our money to us whenever we asked for it.

CARPENTER: What could have made him change so suddenly? Always before he has commended us for saving our money.

CARPENTER'S WIFE: And now we have lost all our money. We'll never get to go to the city.

MAYOR'S WIFE: Don't you worry. The Councilman has no right to keep your money. I'll help you get it back. After all, I am the Mayor's wife.

CARPENTER: You, madam? You'd do that for us?

MAYOR'S WIFE: Yes, I'll help you. You are a fine carpenter,

a skilled artisan, and I know you have worked hard for your money. The Councilman has no right to keep it.

CARPENTER'S WIFE: But how can you help, madam?

MAYOR'S WIFE: You'll see. Let me go home for just a moment. You wait here for me. I'll return immediately and we'll get your money for you. (*She exits.*)

CARPENTER'S WIFE: I don't understand how she can help us.

CARPENTER: I don't, either, but she is the Mayor's wife. We'll just have to trust her.

CARPENTER'S WIFE: Imagine knowing the Mayor's wife.

CARPENTER: She's a kind and gracious lady.

CARPENTER'S WIFE: Yes, I could see that she is.

MAYOR'S WIFE (*Entering from left, carrying jewel box*): Now, you must do exactly as I say.

CARPENTER: Yes, madam, anything if we can get our money. (*His WIFE nods.*)

MAYOR'S WIFE: Then this is what I want you to do. I'll go to the house of the Councilman, and keep my face veiled so he will not recognize me. After a few minutes you come in and ask for your savings as though you had not already asked. Explain that you and your wife are going to the city and need your money. Do you understand?

CARPENTER: Yes, but that's what we did before, and he refused.

MAYOR'S WIFE (*Smiling*): But I wasn't helping you then. Come, walk along with me. Remember, wait a few minutes, then come in, and request your money. (*CARPENTER and his WIFE go to bench, as MAYOR'S WIFE pulls veil over her face and knocks. As COUNCILMAN opens door, lights come up.*)

COUNCILMAN: Who is it?

MAYOR'S WIFE: Your humble servant, sir. May I come in for a moment?

COUNCILMAN: Yes, of course. Come in. Won't you be seated?

MAYOR'S WIFE: Thank you, sir. (*They both sit down.*)

COUNCILMAN: I don't believe I know you, madam.

MAYOR'S WIFE: That is not important, sir. I know you.

COUNCILMAN (*Proudly*): Yes, everyone knows me. I am the Councilman and soon to be head of the exchequer.

MAYOR'S WIFE: Oh?

COUNCILMAN: I see you are surprised. But never mind, that is no concern of yours. Everyone will know as soon as the Mayor announces my appointment.

MAYOR'S WIFE: The Mayor is going to appoint you head of the exchequer?

COUNCILMAN: Certainly, madam. Is there a more honorable or trustworthy man in our community? Of course not. I am known everywhere for my honesty and integrity. Just this morning the Mayor's wife was in this very room to congratulate me upon my appointment as head of the exchequer. That has a pleasant ring to it, doesn't it? Head of the exchequer!

MAYOR'S WIFE: I'm sure it's a very great honor, sir.

COUNCILMAN: But nothing to which I am not entitled. In all of my dealings with the public, and there have been many, I have always been fair and honest.

MAYOR'S WIFE: I am sure the Mayor would never select a man who was not fair and honest.

COUNCILMAN: True! But, how may I be of service to you, madam?

MAYOR'S WIFE: I have a favor to ask of you, sir. My husband is away—he has been for many years—and he has sent for me to join him. I am overjoyed at the prospect. You understand, sir?

COUNCILMAN: Yes, of course, you want to join your husband.

MAYOR'S WIFE: You're very understanding, sir.

COUNCILMAN: True! But what has this to do with me, madam?

MAYOR'S WIFE: Everyone knows what a fine, upstanding man you are. You even said so yourself.

COUNCILMAN: True!

MAYOR'S WIFE: It's my jewels, sir. (*She opens jewel box and hands it to him.*) They are very valuable, and I am afraid to take them with me on such a long journey. Knowing that you are a just and honorable man, I thought to ask you to keep them for me while I am away. I do hope that is not too much of an imposition? If you will, sir, you will have my undying gratitude. (*He examines jewels greedily.*)

COUNCILMAN: Beautiful! Lovely! I have never seen such jewels.

MAYOR'S WIFE: Then you'll keep them for me?

COUNCILMAN: I would feel honored to keep them for you, madam. Never in my life have I touched such beauty!

MAYOR'S WIFE: Then you can understand why I worry about taking them with me.

COUNCILMAN: Never fear, madam. Your jewels will be safe with me. No one, I repeat, no one can ever take them away from me.

CARPENTER (*Entering without knocking*): I beg your pardon, sir. We hate to trouble you when you are busy, but my wife and I are going to the city for a holiday. We need our money which we left with you for safekeeping.

COUNCILMAN: Certainly, my good man. I am never too busy to return what rightfully belongs to another. It is no trouble. Let me get it for you. (*To* MAYOR'S WIFE) You see how trustworthy I am? This gentleman left his savings with me for safekeeping without getting a receipt or an acknowledgment of any kind. But it was not necessary. He has asked for his money. That is enough. I will give it to him. (*He puts jewel box on table and takes money from safe and hands it to* CARPENTER.) Here you are. Just as it was when you left it with me. Count it if you like. It is all there.

CARPENTER: Thank you, sir. (*He counts the money.*) You're right. It's all here.

COUNCILMAN: Of course, it is. Am I not the Councilman, soon to be head of the exchequer?

CARPENTER: Thank you, sir. (CARPENTER *rejoins his* WIFE.)

COUNCILMAN: You see what confidence the people have in me? Is it any wonder that the Mayor plans to appoint me head of the exchequer? I am always happy to be of service, and I assure you I will take good care of your jewels. You may depend upon me.

MAYOR'S WIFE: Yes, sir. I am sure you would take good care of my jewels.

COUNCILMAN: You may rest assured that your jewels will be safe with me.

MAYOR'S WIFE: But, on second thought, I believe I won't leave my jewels with you.

COUNCILMAN: I have always been trust— (*Suddenly alarmed*) What's that you said?

MAYOR'S WIFE: I said, I believe I won't leave my jewels with you.

COUNCILMAN: But, madam, you can't change your mind. Why, I have already—

MAYOR'S WIFE: Already what? (*Pulls her veil aside*) Already returned the carpenter's money to him?

COUNCILMAN: What? The Mayor's wife? Why—what—I don't understand—

MAYOR'S WIFE: Don't you? I think it's obvious. And you can be sure I will tell my husband, the Mayor, everything that has happened here today.

COUNCILMAN: But how did you happen to know the carpenter? The Mayor's wife helping the carpenter!

MAYOR'S WIFE: That's not so strange. You see, it was he

who made this beautiful jewel box for me. Isn't it lovely? (*She holds it up.*)

COUNCILMAN: Then this means—

MAYOR'S WIFE: That you will not be appointed head of the exchequer? As you would say—true! And neither will you be the Councilman after today. My husband, the Mayor, will see to that. Good day, sir. (*She walks toward* CARPENTER *and his* WIFE, *who sit on bench, as curtain falls.*)

THE END

Big Paul Bunyan

A tall tale of the American timberlands

by Adele Thane

Characters

NARRATOR, *a lumberjack*
JIM, *a neighbor's boy*
TRAVELING LADY
PAUL BUNYAN
MR. BUNYAN ⎫
⎬ *Paul's parents*
MRS. BUNYAN ⎭
TOWNSPEOPLE
BABE, *the Blue Ox*
BUM ⎫
⎬ *honeybees*
BILL ⎭
JOHN SHEARS, *overseer of Paul's farm*
LITTLE MEERY, *chore boy*
FARMERS
LUMBERJACKS

SCENE 1

BEFORE RISE: *A tree stump is down right in front of the curtain.* NARRATOR, *dressed as a lumberjack and carrying an ax on his shoulder, enters and stops by the stump.*
NARRATOR: Big Paul Bunyan! He swung his ax (NARRATOR

swings *his ax and strikes the stump*)—and he cut a road through the wilderness from Maine to Oregon in three days. Think of it! A mile a minute—faster than a train can cross the continent. (NARRATOR *moves downstage.*) Paul Bunyan is a real American folk hero. The stories about him came out of the Northwest in the pioneer days of our country. In those days, most of America was covered with dense forests. As more and more people settled the land, these forests had to be cleared. The men who cut down the trees were called loggers. All day long they worked hard, but in the evenings, they liked to sit around the camps and tell stories—funny stories and tall tales. And the tallest tales were told about Paul Bunyan, the mightiest man that ever came into the woods, the greatest lumberjack of them all. (NARRATOR *sits on tree stump.*) Paul was born in the state of Maine. But he wasn't like any other baby you have ever seen. He was so big, he had to be wheeled about in a wheelbarrow instead of a baby carriage. And what do you suppose his mother used for buttons on his clothes? Brass doorknobs! They were the only fasteners that would hold his clothes together when he stretched! (*Curtain opens.*)

*   *   *

SETTING: *Maine. Rocky coastline in the background.*
AT RISE: JIM *enters from left, with a wooden whistle. He stops at center and tries it out.* TRAVELING LADY *enters from right, carrying a carpetbag.*

LADY (*To* JIM): Excuse me, young man, but would you direct me to the nearest hotel? I'm a stranger here.
JIM: Sure. (*Pointing off left*) Straight ahead. You can't miss it, ma'am. It's the only hotel in town.

LADY: Thank you. (*She starts left but stops in surprise as* MR. *and* MRS. BUNYAN *enter with a wheelbarrow holding* PAUL. MRS. BUNYAN *is in front, pulling on a rope that is attached to the wheelbarrow, while* MR. BUNYAN *pushes it from behind by the handlebars. Both are panting, exhausted.* PAUL *is seated with his knees drawn up against his chest and covered with a blanket. He wears a baby bonnet and has a thick, black beard.*)

PAUL (*In a booming voice, waving to* JIM): Hullo, Jim! Whatcha whittlin'?

JIM: Oh, just a whistle. (*He toots it at* PAUL *who bounces with delight.*)

PAUL (*Reaching for whistle*): Give it here. (*He blows a continuous blast on it as* MR. *and* MRS. BUNYAN *wheel him across the stage and off right.*)

LADY: Good heavens! *What* was that?

JIM (*Laughing*): That was Paul Bunyan. His parents are taking him out for an airing.

LADY (*Shocked*): He should be ashamed of himself!—a big heavy lummox like that making his poor parents wheel him about! *He* should be giving *them* a ride!

JIM: But he's just a baby, ma'am. He's only three months old.

LADY (*Incredulous*): That—that monstrous boy—with a full-grown beard—is only *three months old?* I don't believe it! Why, he *talks!*

JIM: Oh, Paul can talk like a house-a-fire. He learned his ABCs when he was two weeks old. (MR. *and* MRS. BUNYAN *return without* PAUL *and the wheelbarrow.*)

MRS. BUNYAN: There! We've put Paul in his cradle out in the bay. Jim, will you keep an eye on him?

JIM: Sure, Mrs. Bunyan. (*He exits right.*)

LADY (*Looking off right in horror*): Do you mean to say you've put your baby out there in the Atlantic Ocean? He'll drown!

MR. BUNYAN: Oh, no, he won't, ma'am. I made a cradle for him out of a boat and anchored it close to shore.

MRS. BUNYAN (*Explaining*): He outgrew his cradle at home. And when we put him in a bed, he sawed off the legs and used one of them for a teething ring.

MR. BUNYAN (*Proudly*): I'll bet that boy of ours is going to be a great logger some day. You just wait and see.

JIM (*Running in, greatly excited*): Mr. Bunyan, come quick! Paul is rocking his cradle and making waves a mile high! You have to quiet him down before the whole town is flooded! (JIM *and* MR. BUNYAN *exit as several* TOWNSPEOPLE *race onstage, screaming.*)

TOWNSPEOPLE (*Ad lib*): Head for the hills! . . . Tidal wave coming! . . . Run for your lives! (*They shout at* MRS. BUNYAN.) Get that baby out of here! . . . He's a danger to the whole state! . . . A baby like that is against the Constitution! (*Pandemonium.* MRS. BUNYAN *runs out right, the others, left. Curtain closes.*)

NARRATOR (*Rising and leaning ax against stump*): Well, after that, Paul's parents decided that they had better move away to a place where Paul wouldn't be a public nuisance—where he could play and romp about without endangering others. So they went to Canada and, deep in the woods, they built their new home. (*Walking to center*) Paul grew up helping his father cut down trees. One winter he left his father's logging camp to do some logging on his own. That was the winter of the blue snow. Nothing like it has been seen since—bright blue snow falling from the sky! It kept on falling for a week, and when it stopped, Paul heard a terrific noise outside the cave where he had taken shelter. (NARRATOR *crosses to left, punching the air for emphasis.*) Boom, boom! Crash! (*He sits down left on the floor. Curtain opens.*)

* * *

Scene 2

SETTING: *There is a cave at left, indicated by an opening at center stage. To the right, several blue snowbanks stand in a field. Blue light floods the field. Inside the cave, a campfire burns, with a large cooking kettle hanging over the fire.*

AT RISE: PAUL *is sleeping inside the cave.* BABE, *as a baby ox, hides behind snowbank, right. There is a loud cracking noise, and cut-out of tree falls over onto stage, from offstage right.* PAUL *jumps to his feet, startled, and looks out of cave in amazement.*

PAUL: By the great horned spoon! *Blue* snow! (*The mooing cries of an ox are heard from behind a snow bank up back.* PAUL *listens.*) Some poor critter is lost out there. I'll go and look for it. (*He puts on his snowshoes and walks about the stage, searching among the snow banks. Finally, he notices* BABE's *pointed blue ears sticking out of the bank at rear.*) There's two ears sticking out of the snow. (*He goes and looks.*) Why, it's a baby ox! (*He lifts him up in his arms.*) Poor little thing, he's blue with cold. (PAUL *carries* BABE *inside the cave and lays him down beside the fire. Then he takes off his snowshoes and covers the ox with a blanket.* BABE *moos gratefully.* PAUL *dips a ladle into the kettle on the fire.*) Here, little feller, drink this hot soup. (BABE *drinks noisily from the ladle two or three times, then, sitting up suddenly, he picks up the kettle and drinks down the contents without stopping.* PAUL *slaps his knee, chuckling.*) By jiminy, you feel better, hey? (BABE *winks at him and bites off a piece of kettle rim.* PAUL *doubles up with laughter.*) Oho! What an appetite! (*While he is bent over,* BABE *butts him from behind and knocks him flat.* PAUL *laughs louder than ever.*) You young rascal! You want to play, do you? (BABE *moos and tosses the kettle to* PAUL, *who catches it and gets to his feet. He pats* BABE *affectionately.*) Ah, you're a beautiful blue baby. That's what I'll call you—Babe—the great blue ox. We'll be wonderful friends, hey, Babe? (BABE *nods his head and moos.*) You'll be a giant of an ox and carry trees on your back. I'm tired of lugging logs under my arms. You'll carry them for me, hey, Babe? (BABE *moos and cuts a caper.*) That's the work for you and me, Babe—logging! Together we'll clear the forests and make room for the pioneers to build homes. We'll have logging camps all over America. Yes, sirree, Babe! We'll be the best lumberjacks that ever lived! (*He hugs* BABE, *who moos happily. Curtain closes.*)

NARRATOR (*Standing up*): And everything that Paul said came true. He cut down the trees and Babe hauled the logs to the river to float them down to the mills, where they could be sawed into lumber. (NARRATOR *crosses slowly to the tree stump at right, speaking as he walks.*) Paul's fame as a logger soon spread, and men fell over themselves to work for him. Before long, he had a crew of the best loggers in the country. (NARRATOR *picks up his ax which is leaning against the stump.*) All through the North Woods you'd hear the shout go up (*Raises his ax and brings it down on the stump*)—"T-i-m-b-e-r-r-r!" And then the echo. . . .

OFFSTAGE VOICES (*Repeating, fading away to a whisper*): Timber-r-r! Timber-r-r!

NARRATOR (*Putting down his ax*): Now, Paul had a farm in Smiling River Valley where the food for his loggers was raised. The overseer of Paul's farm was a man named John Shears. John and his farmhands raised so much food that it took ten thousand horse teams to carry it to the loggers up in the woods. So John grew very puffed up. (*Strutting to center*) John Shears, well, he was *some-*

body, to run a farm like that! And he began to think that if he could put an end to Paul's logging business, then all the men would have to become farmers. And if all the men were farmers, they'd make John Shears the big boss instead of that logger Paul Bunyan. (*Walking back to the stump*) One day John called some of the farmers together and told them his plan. (NARRATOR *sits. Curtain opens.*)

*   *   *

SCENE 3

SETTING: *The barnyard of Paul's farm. Babe's stable is at left. A corral-type fence runs across the back of the stage and halfway down each side. Three or four wooden fruit crates are piled center. Up right, outside the fence, there is a large cut-out beehive with a sliding panel in front which is now open. A gate is in the fence opposite the beehive.*

AT RISE: *A loud buzzing sound is heard, and* BILL, *a honeybee, flies out of the beehive, through the gate and into the barnyard, followed by* BUM, *another bee.*

BILL: Buzz-z-z-z! Come on, Bum!

BUM: Coming, Bill! What'z-z-z the hurry?

BILL (*Pointing off right, angrily*): They're cutting down the clover! Buzz-z-z-z!

BUM: They can't do that! We haven't gathered all the honey yet!

BILL: Let'z-z-z go and chase-z-z-z them away!

BUM: Yez-z-z! (*They exit right.* JOHN SHEARS *and three* FARMERS *enter left.* JOHN *is roughly shoving* LITTLE MEERY *ahead of him.* MEERY *is carrying two heavy pails of mash.*)

JOHN: Get a move on, Meery! Carry that mash to the pigs. Then feed the hens.

FARMERS (*Jeering*): Dearie, dearie! Little Meery! Here, piggy-wiggy! Here, chick, chick, chick! (*They grunt like pigs and cluck like hens as* MEERY *goes through the gate and off left behind the stable.*)

JOHN (*Laughing*): Is he gone?

1ST FARMER (*Looking off*): Yup.

JOHN: Sit down, boys. I've something important to tell you. (*They all sit on the crates.* LITTLE MEERY *comes out from behind the stable and listens.*) As you know, I've been trying to think of a plan to do away with logging, so you farmers can be the big shots in this country, instead of the lumberjacks. And, by gravy, last night I hit on a plan!

FARMERS (*Ad lib*): What is it? . . . Tell us! (*Etc.*)

JOHN: The thing to do is to get rid of Babe, the blue ox.

2ND FARMER: Why Babe?

JOHN: Doesn't he haul the logs to the river? Without him, there wouldn't be nary a chance for Paul to carry on at logging!

3RD FARMER: That's true. But Babe's a powerful strong critter. How are you going to get rid of him?

JOHN: Easy. Babe's favorite food is parsnips. Right?

FARMERS: Right!

JOHN: But the crop of parsnips in the North field went bad. They're rotten. Right?

FARMERS: Right!

JOHN: So, we'll feed Babe those rotten parsnips. And *that* will put an end to Babe and the logging business, or I'll eat those parsnips myself.

FARMERS (*Jumping up together*): Hurrah! Three cheers for John Shears! Down with loggers! Up with farmers! Rah, rah, rah!

JOHN (*Pointing off left*): Go dig 'em up, boys! (FARMERS

pick up the crates and exit left. LITTLE MEERY *ducks out of sight behind the stable. Off right the angry buzzing of bees is heard, followed by the shouts of men.*)

FARMERS (*From offstage*): Ouch! Go away! Get out of here! Shoo!

BUM *and* BILL (*From offstage, chanting*): We want honey! We want honey!

JOHN (*Calling*): Meery! Come here!

MEERY (*Entering at left*): Yes, Mr. Shears.

JOHN: Those bees are bothering the mowers in the clover. Shut 'em up in the beehive. (*He exits left.* MEERY *runs off and returns, chasing* BUM *and* BILL *upstage.*)

BUM *and* BILL: We want honey! We want honey! (*They fly into the hive and* MEERY *slams down the sliding panel. The tramp of heavy boots is heard off right, and* PAUL, *leading his crew of* LUMBERJACKS, *enters with* BABE, *now full-grown. As they enter, they are singing.*)

LUMBERJACKS (*To the tune of "Oh, Susannah!"*):

> We are a crew of lumberjacks,
> As jolly as can be;
> No matter where we go, my boys,
> We're always gay and free.
> The boss he is a mighty man,
> Paul Bunyan is his name,
> The hero of a hundred deeds
> That lumberjacks acclaim.
> Big Paul Bunyan!
> And Babe, his ox of blue!
> There's nothing they can't do, my boys,
> And all we say is true. *Hi!*

PAUL: Enjoy yourselves, men! No work for a week! (LUMBERJACKS *cheer and exit left.* PAUL *scratches* BABE'S *ears.*) Are you tired, Babe, old pal? (*Tired moo from*

BABE.) And hungry? (*Hungry moo*) How would you like a bushel of parsnips? (*Enthusiastic moo.*)

MEERY (*Approaching timidly*): Mr. Bunyan—

PAUL: Why, hello, little Meery! Would you get some parsnips for Babe?

MEERY: I—I want to talk to you about the parsnips, Mr. Bunyan. (*He hesitates.*)

PAUL: Yes?

MEERY: The parsnips—they—

JOHN (*Entering suddenly from left*): Meery! What are you doing here? Clear out! You're needed in the kitchen. (MEERY *exits left.*) I didn't expect you, Paul. Have you broken up camp?

PAUL: We've logged off Minnesota and I thought the crew could use a little vacation. Put Babe in his stable, John, and let him have plenty of parsnips.

JOHN: *Yes, sir!* (PAUL *exits left.* JOHN *turns to* BABE, *grinning.*) He wants me to feed you parsnips. By gravy, if that isn't funny! Well, parsnips you'll surely get! (*He opens the stable door,* BABE *enters, and* JOHN *closes it after him.* MERRY *peeks around corner of stable as* 1ST FARMER *leans over left fence and calls softly to* JOHN.)

1ST FARMER: Psst! John! The parsnips are ready.

JOHN: Good! We'll feed 'em to that ox-critter right now and poison him dead as a doornail. (*They leave.*)

MEERY (*Anxiously, coming into barnyard*): What shall I do? I have to save Babe some way. (*Loud buzzing heard from beehive attracts his attention.*) I know! I'll let the bees out. They'll sting Babe and keep him away from the parsnips. (FARMERS *and* JOHN *re-enter as* MEERY *quickly hides behind beehive. They carry crates of parsnips which they dump in center of barnyard. Then* FARMERS *line up right, behind fence.* JOHN *goes to the stable door and opens it. At the same time,* MEERY *creeps out from behind beehive and stands ready to open the sliding panel.* BABE *moos inquisitively and sniffs the air. He sees the parsnips and moos again, delighted. As he gallops toward them,* MEERY *releases* BUM *and* BILL, *and they fly straight for* BABE, *buzzing fiercely. He is infuriated and starts to buck and bellow.* FARMERS *yell and run off.* JOHN, *who is inside the barnyard, tries to climb over the fence, but* BABE *chases him around the pile of parsnips several times.* PAUL *enters left and shouts above the uproar.)*

PAUL: *What's going on here?* (JOHN *makes his escape, with* BUM *and* BILL *in hot pursuit.)* Whoa there, Babe! What's got into you? Quiet down and eat your parsnips.

MEERY (*Quickly*): Don't let Babe eat those parsnips, Mr. Bunyan! They're poison! John Shears dug up a bad crop of parsnips to kill Babe!

PAUL (*Restraining* BABE): Why would he want to kill Babe?

MEERY: He said if Babe was out of the way, there would be no more logging, only farming, and then *he'd* be the big boss instead of you.

PAUL: Oho, so John Shears is getting too big for his britches, hey? Well, we'll see about that. (*He clasps* MEERY *on the shoulder.*) Little Meery, you're a man and a hero! What can I do to reward you for saving Babe's life?

MEERY: Oh, Mr. Bunyan, let me go up in the woods with you and be a lumberjack. I want to do that more than anything else in the world.

PAUL: You're mighty small to be a lumberjack, Little Meery.

MEERY (*Eagerly*): I'll grow, Mr. Bunyan. I'll *make* myself grow! I promise.

PAUL (*Shaking hands with him*): You're hired, my boy! And while we're waiting for you to grow, you can be the little chore boy in the camp, and help take care of Babe. How does that suit you?

MEERY (*Happily*): It suits me fine, Mr. Bunyan—just fine! (*He puts his arm around* BABE's *neck.* BABE *nuzzles him and moos. Curtain closes.*)

NARRATOR (*Rising*): And that's how Babe was saved for logging. (*Walking to center*) Little Meery grew up to be a big lumberjack, just as he promised Paul he would. For years and years, Paul Bunyan and his men cleared the forests of America to make homes for the people. And the name of big Paul Bunyan and Babe, his mighty blue ox, will be remembered in lumber camps as long as men cut down trees. (NARRATOR *returns to stump and picks up ax.*) They say that when the wind is right, they can still hear Paul swinging his ax and shouting (NARRATOR *brings ax down on stump*)—"*T-i-m-b-e-r-r-r!*"

OFFSTAGE VOICES (*Echoing and fading away*): Timber-r-r-r! Timber-r-r-r! (NARRATOR *shoulders his ax and exits.*)

THE END

The Indian Boy without a Name

An American Indian folk tale

by Rod Vahl

Characters

RUNNING DEER ⎫
LITTLE BUFFALO ⎬ *Indian boys*
NO NAME ⎭
SINGING CLOUD ⎫
RED FLOWER ⎬ *Indian girls*
CHIEF BLACKHAWK
BRAVE
SQUAW

TIME: *Many years ago.*
SETTING: *Clearing in front of an Indian village.*
AT RISE: RUNNING DEER, LITTLE BUFFALO, SINGING CLOUD,
   and RED FLOWER *sitting on logs, are talking happily at*
   center. NO NAME *sits beside them, looking very sad.*

RUNNING DEER: Chief Blackhawk told me that I shall be
   named Running Deer because in all the tribe, I am the
   most fleet of foot! (*He jumps up and gives war whoop.*)
SINGING CLOUD: He told me that I shall be called Singing
   Cloud because my voice is like the trill of the morning
   lark and the song of the nightingale.

LITTLE BUFFALO (*Proudly*): The Chief said that I had the power of the buffalo as he charges the prairie wolf which attacks him. So I shall be named Little Buffalo! (*He pretends to charge like a buffalo.*)

RED FLOWER (*Excitedly*): And I shall be known as Red Flower. Chief Blackhawk said that I was as beautiful as the colors of the rainbow after the rains.

RUNNING DEER (*Turning to* NO NAME): What will Chief Blackhawk name you?

NO NAME (*Dejectedly*): Chief Blackhawk did not say a word to me.

LITTLE BUFFALO: Oh, yes, he did!

NO NAME (*Turning away*): No, he did not!

LITTLE BUFFALO: Chief Blackhawk will call you No Name!

RUNNING DEER (*Puzzled*): No Name?

SINGING CLOUD: That is a silly name for a boy!

RED FLOWER: Why will you be known as No Name? (NO NAME *does not reply.*)

LITTLE BUFFALO: He shall be called No Name because he fails in all that he attempts to do.

RED FLOWER (*Turning to* NO NAME): Is this true? (NO NAME *still does not answer.*)

SINGING CLOUD: Are you not a runner?

NO NAME (*Sadly*): No.

RED FLOWER: Can you aim an arrow as the handsome braves do?

NO NAME: Not very well.

RUNNING DEER: Or ride a pony as the warriors in battle?

NO NAME: Not too well.

RED FLOWER (*Giggling*): I know what you could do! You could bake and cook with the women in our village. (*Everyone but* NO NAME *laughs.*)

RUNNING DEER: It is not good to laugh at No Name. It might cause him to weep as the rain falls!

RED FLOWER (*Teasing*): Then Chief Blackhawk could name him Weeping Willow. (*They laugh again.*)

SINGING CLOUD: Or Falling Waters!

LITTLE BUFFALO: Well, Chief Blackhawk will not give us our names until the next full moon. Perhaps No Name can discover a name by that time.

RUNNING DEER: Come, Little Buffalo, let us leave and race as the deer through the woods.

LITTLE BUFFALO: Only if we then wrestle like the braves.

RUNNING DEER: I agree! Let us race, now! (LITTLE BUFFALO *and* RUNNING DEER *run off right.*)

RED FLOWER: No Name! What a silly name!

SINGING CLOUD: Red Flower, let us leave and watch the boys race and wrestle. (*The two girls exit right, leaving* NO NAME *alone. He sits on a nearby log.*)

NO NAME (*Speaking aloud to himself*): No Name! I do not blame them for laughing at me. I would do the same. (*He picks up a stick and draws lines on the ground. After a moment,* CHIEF BLACKHAWK *enters from left.*)

CHIEF BLACKHAWK: You look very sad, young boy.

NO NAME (*Standing and facing* CHIEF BLACKHAWK): Yes, Chief Blackhawk, I am very sad.

CHIEF: What is the cause of such gloom, like that of the dark clouds?

NO NAME: I am sad because I will not receive a good name at the powwow.

CHIEF: But you must show great promise in a skill before you are named by your chief.

NO NAME: I know, Chief Blackhawk. But I am not good at anything. I cannot run well. I cannot aim the arrow straight. I wrestle poorly. That is my problem.

CHIEF (*Sitting on log*): Sit down, my son. (NO NAME *sits down beside him.*) I remember my father as chief of this great tribe before me. And I remember wise words that he said to me when I was but a small boy as you are today.

NO NAME (*Looking at* CHIEF): What were they, Chief Blackhawk?

CHIEF: My father and I were hunting rabbits one afternoon, and I was very sad because I was not very good with the bow and arrow. I thought I could never become chief of the tribe because of that.

NO NAME: I would not believe that the great Chief Blackhawk would ever be sad.

CHIEF: Ah! The Indian's life is like the life of the stars, my boy. At times, the glow of the heavens cannot be seen for the clouds.

NO NAME: What did your father say?

CHIEF: My father told me that each of us has a skill in which we are very good. He said that we must search every path of our lives to discover that part of life which brings us happiness.

NO NAME: That is good advice.

CHIEF (*Arising*): It is many days before the next full moon. Do as the sun—cast aside the clouds and glow upon the tribe with a radiance of warmth and happiness.

NO NAME (*Arising*): Thank you, Chief Blackhawk. (CHIEF BLACKHAWK *pats* NO NAME *on the back, then exits left. NO NAME sits on log again and appears to be thinking very hard. In a moment,* BRAVE *and* SQUAW, *who carries a large rock, enter from right. They are arguing. They stop near* NO NAME.)

BRAVE (*Sternly, to* SQUAW): But I shall not carry your pretty rock through the village.

SQUAW (*Complaining*): But the rock is heavy. It is like carrying the earth. (*She puts rock down.*)

BRAVE: The other braves in the village will laugh. And I do not need laughs from the other braves.

SQUAW: I see no laughs in helping your squaw!

BRAVE (*Arrogantly*): Squaw forgets that brave is head of his family! I say that I will not carry the rock!

SQUAW (*Angrily*): Then you shall go hungry! I will cook no meal as the sun goes down!

BRAVE: My squaw does not understand! The braves would laugh at me! Do you want your brave to lose the respect of all the tribe? Do you forget that I am the strongest of all the braves?

SQUAW: You will not lose respect or pride when you help a weak squaw carry a heavy load!

BRAVE: Squaw is foolish! I will hear no more! Remember, the brave is head of the family. You are to obey your brave, as I obey Chief Blackhawk. I will not carry the rock!

SQUAW (*Determinedly*): Then you are not a good brave!

NO NAME (*Interrupting*): I should not interrupt, but I know a solution to your problem, honored brave. (NO NAME *stands up.*)

BRAVE (*Turning to* NO NAME): Little boys should be silent as the fish in the deep waters!

SQUAW (*Kindly*): What does the little brave want to say?

NO NAME: If I were a brave, I would not want to carry a rock through the village. I would not want the other braves to laugh at me.

BRAVE: See, squaw?

NO NAME: And, if I were a squaw, I would not want to carry a heavy rock too far.

SQUAW: See, brave?

NO NAME: So, if the brave carried the rock under his blanket, none of the braves would see it. Then, both the brave and squaw are happy!

SQUAW: Will the brave try it?

BRAVE (*Hesitating a moment before speaking*): Yes! I shall try it once! (BRAVE, *who wears blanket over his shoul-*

ders, *picks up the rock, puts it under blanket and holds
it with one hand.*) This is a good idea. I will carry the
rock. Come, squaw, we will go to our wigwam. And shall
we have a good meal?

SQUAW: Yes, you shall have a good meal, my honored
brave!

BRAVE (*Turning to* No NAME): You are a wise boy. (BRAVE
and SQUAW *exit left, and* No NAME *sits on log again.
Shortly,* RUNNING DEER *and* LITTLE BUFFALO *enter, arguing loudly.* LITTLE BUFFALO *carries a rope.*)

RUNNING DEER (*Loudly*): But I found the rope, so it is
mine!

LITTLE BUFFALO: The warrior gave it to *me!*

RUNNING DEER: He gave it to *both* of us! (*They stop near*
No NAME.)

LITTLE BUFFALO: Running Deer did not hear my words!
I said the warrior gave it to *me!* He placed the rope in
my hands.

RUNNING DEER (*Angrily*): I ask you, Little Buffalo, who
found the rope?

LITTLE BUFFALO (*Pointing to* RUNNING DEER): You . . .
(*Then pointing to himself*) and me.

RUNNING DEER: No! Only *I* found the rope.

LITTLE BUFFALO: I ask Running Deer, to whom did the
warrior give the rope?

RUNNING DEER (*Pointing to* LITTLE BUFFALO): To you
. . . (*Pointing to himself*) and to me.

LITTLE BUFFALO: No! He gave it only to *me!*

No NAME (*Standing up*): The words I hear are like the
sting of the hornet. What causes such harsh words between two friends?

RUNNING DEER (*To* No NAME): You mean two enemies,
like the wolf and the rabbit.

LITTLE BUFFALO (*To* No NAME): We were in the woods,
running a race, and Running Deer was a little ahead of

me. As we ran, we found a rope. Not far in the distance was a warrior and we learned that it was his rope that we discovered.

RUNNING DEER: I gave it to the warrior, but he said he had no further use for the rope, so he gave it to us.

LITTLE BUFFALO: He gave it to *me!*

RUNNING DEER: But I found it, so I should have it!

LITTLE BUFFALO: But the warrior placed the rope in my hands, so I should own the rope.

NO NAME (*Curiously*): May I see the rope?

LITTLE BUFFALO (*Giving rope to* NO NAME): This is the rope. (NO NAME *takes rope and looks at it carefully.*)

NO NAME: It seems this rope is as long as the mountain trails.

LITTLE BUFFALO: Yes, it is very long.

NO NAME: If this were two ropes instead of one, would each rope be long enough for use?

RUNNING DEER: Yes. The rope is too long for one boy.

NO NAME: Then why not cut this rope in half?

LITTLE BUFFALO (*Surprised*): What?

NO NAME: If you cut this rope evenly into two pieces, then each of you would have a rope.

RUNNING DEER (*Happily*): Little Buffalo, I believe this is a good idea.

LITTLE BUFFALO (*Excitedly*): Yes! Let us go and borrow a knife.

RUNNING DEER: Thank you, No Name! You are wise as the Medicine Man seeking the cause of a disease. (RUNNING DEER *and* LITTLE BUFFALO *run off left. Once again* NO NAME *sits on the log.* SINGING CLOUD *and* RED FLOWER *enter right, arguing.*)

SINGING CLOUD (*Determinedly*): I shall be the one to perform the Sun Dance at the next powwow!

RED FLOWER (*Protesting*): You danced the last time. I should do it the next time!

SINGING CLOUD: You are like the mockingbird, always wanting to do what I do!

RED FLOWER (*Indignantly*): Singing Cloud is wrong! It is you who are the mockingbird.

SINGING CLOUD: Chief Blackhawk shall name me Singing Cloud. The clouds live with the sun in the heavens. It is only fitting that one with a name such as mine perform the Sun Dance.

RED FLOWER: And the Chief shall name me Red Flower. Singing Cloud should remember that the sun only helps to make grass and flowers grow. It is the flower which the tribe admires for all its beauty. So it is only fitting that *I* perform!

NO NAME (*Standing up, interrupting*): I have never heard you girls argue before. It is like seeing the moon and stars in separate skies.

SINGING CLOUD (*To* NO NAME): Red Flower wants to do the Sun Dance at the powwow. And I also want to perform the dance.

RED FLOWER: Singing Cloud did it the last time. Now, it is my turn!

NO NAME: When is the powwow?

SINGING CLOUD: You know when it is! At the next full moon when we receive our names from Chief Blackhawk.

RED FLOWER: And I will do the Sun Dance.

SINGING CLOUD: No, Red Flower. *I* will!

NO NAME: I do not see why you girls have any problem.

RED FLOWER: Your words have little sense.

NO NAME: But I still see no problem.

RED FLOWER: No Name should tell us what his advice would be!

NO NAME: At the powwow two braves will do the Eagle Dance. Right?

SINGING CLOUD: Yes.

NO NAME: And two warriors will do the War Dance?

RED FLOWER: Your words are true.

NO NAME: And two squaws will perform the Harvest Dance?

RED FLOWER: Again your words abound in truth.

NO NAME: Then, two girls could perform the Sun Dance together.

SINGING CLOUD (*Surprised*): Two girls?

NO NAME: Yes! Tell me, why not?

RED FLOWER (*Caught by surprise*): I do not know why not!

NO NAME: Singing Cloud, why not?

SINGING CLOUD: I know not, either.

NO NAME: Then there is no problem. You have many days before the full moon. You could practice together.

RED FLOWER (*Happily*): I believe it is a good idea.

SINGING CLOUD (*Excitedly*): It is not late in the day, Red Flower. Let us go and practice now!

RED FLOWER: Red Flower agrees with Singing Cloud. It will give us much to do. (*Turning to* NO NAME) You should be proud as the soaring eagle, for you are a very wise boy. (SINGING CLOUD *and* RED FLOWER *exit left, and* NO NAME *resumes his sitting position on log.* CHIEF BLACKHAWK *enters left. He stops to speak to* NO NAME.)

CHIEF (*Pleasantly*): Well, I see that you are still in deep thought.

NO NAME (*Surprised*): Oh, I did not see you coming, Chief Blackhawk. (*He rises and faces the* CHIEF.)

CHIEF: A moment ago two girls told me about a wise young boy who brought peace between them.

NO NAME (*Modestly*): Yes. They are happy once again.

CHIEF (*Crossing his arms across his chest*): I also heard that you solved a disagreement over a rope.

NO NAME: It is not good for two friends to argue. It is like the summer storms. All that was needed was for one rope

to become two ropes. It was not difficult to split the
rope. A knife took care of that, Chief Blackhawk.

CHIEF (*Smiling*): Yes, it did! And a young squaw whis-
pered to your chief that a certain young boy settled a
family feud.

NO NAME: It is not good for a man to go without his meal.
The rock could not be seen if the brave carried it under
his blanket.

CHIEF: You have been a very busy young man.

NO NAME (*Puzzled*): I do not know what your words
mean, Chief Blackhawk.

CHIEF: The dark clouds which hung about you have now
disappeared.

NO NAME: I still am not clear in mind as to what you say,
Chief Blackhawk.

CHIEF: Do you know who is the most important man in
our village?

NO NAME: Of course! You are, Chief Blackhawk.

CHIEF (*Smiling*): Your courtesies are most kind, young
boy, but I have in mind someone other than your chief.

NO NAME: The warrior?

CHIEF: The gallant warrior is honorable, but I have not
the warrior in my mind.

NO NAME: The hunter?

CHIEF: Without the hunter, our tribe would soon disappear. But again, I have another in my thoughts.

NO NAME: Then I fear I do not know, Chief Blackhawk.

CHIEF: The best Indian in the village is the one who
brings peace, whether between two friends who argue or
between two tribes who meet upon the fields of war.

NO NAME: I believe I am beginning to understand.

CHIEF: It is the man who can offer wisdom to those who
are not at peace.

NO NAME: I agree with my honored chief.

CHIEF: Then you have earned your good name.

No Name (*Puzzled*): I do not understand.

Chief: Because you have kept peace when others would have fought, I will give you a good name at the next full moon. You will be known as Little Peacemaker.

No Name (*Surprised*): Little Peacemaker?

Chief: Yes! Does that please you?

No Name (*Excited and happy*): Oh, yes, Chief Blackhawk! I hope that I will always be worthy and proud of that name!

Chief: Good! Now, come with your chief. I want to walk awhile by the flowing waters, for I have many problems, and I might need some good advice, Little Peacemaker. (Chief Blackhawk *and* No Name *exit slowly right, as the curtain falls.*)

THE END

A Gift from Johnny Appleseed

The story of an American folk hero

by Helene Whittaker

Characters

JOHNNY APPLESEED
MITTY TREVIS, *about 10 years old*
MR. TREVIS ⎱ *her parents*
MRS. TREVIS ⎰
BETSY TREVIS, *her cousin*
MR. BAILEY
MRS. BAILEY
ROSE BAILEY, *their daughter*
BOY
TOM TREVIS, *Betsy's father (offstage voice)*

TIME: *Early evening in the fall of 1838.*
SETTING: *The yard of the Trevis farmhouse in Licking Creek, Ohio. There are four chairs on porch.*
AT RISE: BETSY *and* MITTY *are sitting on the farmhouse porch steps at left, putting small paper packets tied with string into a large colored handkerchief.* BETSY *suddenly looks up and listens.*

BETSY: Someone's coming! (*Both girls hide packets under their full skirts.*)

MITTY: It's Pa coming up from the barn.

BETSY: I hope he keeps going right into the house.

MITTY: Me, too. (MR. TREVIS *enters from right.*)

MR. TREVIS (*Looking from one girl to the other*): What are you two up to now?

MITTY (*Quickly*): Nothing, Pa.

MR. TREVIS: You're up to something. You have that look.

BETSY: We're excited, Uncle Dan, because the Baileys are bringing Rose over to spend the night here.

MR. TREVIS: Oho, so that's what all the buzzing has been about today. Well, if we're having company, I'd better clean up before they get here. (*He goes into house.*)

MITTY: That was a close one. You thought fast to tell him about Rose.

BETSY (*Taking out packets*): Let's finish these things so we can hide the bundle.

MITTY: Where are you going to hide it, Betsy? If you put it in the house, Ma's likely to find it.

BETSY: I'm going to hide it under the lilac bush. There! (*Ties up bundle*) All done. (*Goes to bush at right and puts bundle behind it*)

MITTY: Rose said she'd try to bring you more food.

BETSY: I hope she can. I'm going to need more than this.

MITTY (*Giggling*): It nearly drove Rose wild when I wouldn't tell her what the food was for.

BETSY: I don't think we should tell her.

MITTY: I had to promise we'd tell her tonight or she wouldn't bring the food.

BETSY: All right, but no one else. Remember that, Mitty.

MITTY (*Looking right*): Here come the Baileys. (*Calls into house*) Ma, the company's here. (ROSE *enters from right with* MR. *and* MRS. BAILEY. MR. *and* MRS. TREVIS *come out of the house.*) Hello, there, Rose.

ROSE: Hello, Mrs. Trevis. (*Turning*) Hello, Betsy—Mitty.

BETSY: Hello, Rose. Come sit here with us. (ROSE *sits.*)

MRS. TREVIS: Hello, folks. Sit here on the porch. I'll bring out a pitcher of cold cider. (BAILEYS *sit on porch chairs*)

MRS. BAILEY: That sounds refreshing. (MRS. TREVIS *goes into house*.) It's warm tonight for September, isn't it?

MR. BAILEY: Too warm. Going to storm, I say.

MR. TREVIS: All your crops in, Will?

MR. BAILEY: All the early ones. Going to be a good harvest this year. (MRS. TREVIS *comes out of house carrying tray with pitcher of cider and glasses on it. She pours cider and hands glasses around*.)

MRS. TREVIS: Cider's good this year, too. Sweet as nectar.

MRS. BAILEY (*Looking at her glass*): I've never seen these glasses before, Mary. They're very pretty.

MRS. TREVIS: They were my mother's. When she came out here to Ohio from New Hampshire, she brought them with her. (*Points to lilac bush while* BETSY *and* MITTY *exchange nervous glances*) She brought that lilac bush, too. It was just a little slip from a bush back home. She said the bush originally came from England. When Betsy goes to Kansas Territory with her pa, I'll give her a slip to take with her.

MRS. BAILEY: When is Betsy's pa coming for her?

MRS. TREVIS: He'll be on the next stage from the East. He's planning to stop off here for a few days before he goes on to Fort Leavenworth to report for his post.

MR. BAILEY: I heard the stage was in Marietta yesterday.

MR. TREVIS: Then it'll be here tomorrow.

MITTY: Oh, Betsy! I can't bear to have you leave!

MRS. TREVIS: Mitty, don't start that again. I've had enough of you and Betsy pouting around. You'll be seeing each other again next summer.

ROSE: Next summer's such a long time off!

MRS. BAILEY: Girls taking it hard, their being separated?

MR. TREVIS: They've been moping around here ever since they heard the news. But I told them, Betsy's place is with her father. She's all he has left and he wants her with him. Can't blame him for that.

MRS. TREVIS: Still, it is hard for them. They've been together since they were babies.

MR. TREVIS (*Firmly*): She's going and that's that! Now let's change the subject. (*To* MR. BAILEY) Will, I heard down at the store that Johnny Appleseed's in the neighborhood.

MR. BAILEY: Johnny Appleseed? He hasn't been around here in years.

MR. TREVIS: He's on his way to the Iowa Territory. Ohio is getting too civilized for his taste. This is in the nature of a farewell visit.

MRS. BAILEY: Good old Johnny Appleseed!

MRS. TREVIS (*Raising her cider glass*): It's thanks to Johnny Appleseed we're enjoying this cider tonight. He brought us our apple trees.

MR. TREVIS: Let's see. (*Thinks*) It was in eighteen hundred and six he first started bringing his bags of seeds. I was just a little tad then.

MRS. TREVIS: I remember him coming to my father's farm. He kept coming back year after year to see if the trees were coming along as they should.

MRS. BAILEY: Remember how he always brought little gifts for us? There would be a pretty hair ribbon for the girls, a willow whistle or some other trifle for the boys. How we loved to see Johnny Appleseed coming down the road!

MITTY: Do you think he'll stop here this time, Ma?

MRS. TREVIS: Probably he will.

MR. TREVIS (*Laughing*): Remember the crazy way he dressed? A burlap sack with holes cut in it for his arms and head?

MR. BAILEY: And an old tin cooking pot on his head for a hat!

MRS. BAILEY: He cooked his corn meal mush in the same pot. He had some odd ideas.

MRS. TREVIS: But he was so kind and gentle that everyone trusted him, even the Indians.

MITTY: Oh, I hope he gets here soon, don't you, Betsy? And not after you've gone away—

BETSY: Sh!

MR. BAILEY (*To* MRS. BAILEY): Let's get back home, Esther. I still think it's going to storm.

MRS. BAILEY (*Standing*): Thanks for the cider, Mary. Be a good girl, Rose, and don't stay up all night talking. Betsy, I'll drop over to see you before you leave. Goodbye.

ALL (*Ad lib*): Come back soon. Goodbye. (MR. *and* MRS. BAILEY *go out right.* MRS. TREVIS *starts picking up the cider glasses.*)

MRS. TREVIS: Well, Betsy, sounds as if your pa'll be here tomorrow, doesn't it?

BETSY (*Unenthusiastically*): Guess so.

MRS. TREVIS: I hope you can summon a little more enthusiasm than that when he comes. It'll hurt him if you aren't glad to see him.

BETSY (*Sadly*): Yes, Aunt Mary.

MR. TREVIS: Think I'll go down to the lower pasture to see how that cow's doing with her new calf. (*He goes off right.*)

MRS. TREVIS: You girls get ready for bed now. I'm going to wash up these glasses. (*Goes into house with tray*)

ROSE: At last they're gone. Now you can tell me the secret!

MITTY: Did you bring the food?

ROSE (*Taking two small packets from her pocket*): Here it is. It's all I could manage to sneak out. My ma has sharp eyes. (BETSY *reaches for them but* ROSE *holds them back.*) Not till you tell me the secret!

BETSY: First, I have to swear you to secrecy. Cross your heart and hope to die?

ROSE (*Crossing her heart*): Cross my heart and hope to die. Now tell!

MITTY: Betsy's not going with her father to Fort Leavenworth. She's going to run away!

ROSE (*Shocked*): Betsy Trevis, you aren't!

BETSY: I certainly am. I'm not going to some old dusty army post way out in Kansas where I don't have anyone to play with.

ROSE: But where will you go?

MITTY: She's going to hide in that old cave down by the creek when her father comes for her.

BETSY: That's why I need the food—so I can stay out of the way till he has to report for duty. Then it'll be too late for me to go with him and I'll be able to stay here with you and Mitty.

ROSE (*Handing food packets to* BETSY): But, Betsy, aren't you scared to stay in that spooky old cave in the nighttime?

BETSY: Oh, nothing can happen. (*She goes to lilac bush, and puts food packets into bundle.*) I left my heavy sweater down there yesterday so I'm all ready.

MITTY: You're going there to hide right now?

BETSY: It's the best time. You go in and get ready for bed and roll up a blanket to put under the covers so Aunt Mary will think I'm asleep.

MITTY: All right, Betsy.

BETSY: 'Bye, Mitty. 'Bye, Rose. When my pa is gone, you can come and get me, but don't come before then. And remember, you promised hope-to-die not to tell a soul where I am.

MITTY: We won't tell.

ROSE: 'Bye, Betsy. (BETSY *hurries off right, carrying bundle.*)

MRS. TREVIS (*Coming out of house*): I thought I told you to get ready for bed. Now scoot! Where's Betsy?

MITTY: She's . . . she's already gone, Ma.

MRS. TREVIS: Well, that's the first time in her life she ever went to bed without an argument. Now, you two do the same.

MITTY: All right. Come on, Rose. (MITTY *and* ROSE *go into house.* MRS. TREVIS *sits in chair as* MR. TREVIS *enters from right.*)

MRS. TREVIS: Calf all right?

MR. TREVIS: Frisky as can be. I'll bring her up to the barn tomorrow. Looks like Will Bailey's storm went north of here. The sky was pretty black up there. (*He sits on porch too.*)

MRS. TREVIS: I suppose Johnny Appleseed's sleeping under a tree somewhere. Remember how we never could get him to sleep in the house?

MR. TREVIS: The only time I ever saw him in the house was when he came in to read to us out of the Bible before we went to bed. (JOHNNY APPLESEED, *with burlap bag over his shoulder, enters quietly from right and stands listening.*)

MRS. TREVIS: He called it "carrying the good news fresh from Heaven."

JOHNNY: So you still remember old Johnny?

MR. *and* MRS. TREVIS (*Jumping to their feet*): Johnny Appleseed!

JOHNNY: It's Dan Trevis and Mary, who used to be little Mary Davis. Am I right?

MRS. TREVIS: Right, Johnny. It's been a long time.

MR. TREVIS: How are you, Johnny?

JOHNNY: Right fine! And still carrying my "good news fresh from Heaven." Only now I'm going to take it further West, into the Iowa lands. There's a lot of new

settlers moving in and they'll need old Johnny Appleseed with his apple trees.

MRS. TREVIS: Tomorrow morning, you must walk through
our orchards. They're a beautiful sight with the branches
hanging heavy with apples. (*Hoofbeats are heard off
right.*)

MR. TREVIS: Who's coming so fast along our road at this
hour? (*Hoofbeats stop and a* BOY *runs in from right.*)

BOY: Mr. Trevis! Mr. Trevis! If you have any stock in your
lower pasture, take it out. There's been a cloudburst up
north and the creek's rising fast. I'm telling everyone on
this road.

MR. TREVIS: Thanks for the warning, son.

BOY: You're welcome, Mr. Trevis. (*Runs off right.*)

MR. TREVIS: Come on, Mary. I have to bring that cow and
her calf up to the barn. You can help me.

JOHNNY: You need me, Dan?

MR. TREVIS: No, thank you, Johnny, you stay here.

MRS. TREVIS: We have three little girls asleep in the house.
You can stay here and keep an eye on them. (MR. *and*
MRS. TREVIS *hurry off right.* JOHNNY *puts his bag down
and sits on porch steps, rubbing his shoulder.* MITTY *and*
ROSE, *in their long nightgowns, come to the doorway.*)

MITTY: I heard someone talking.

ROSE (*Seeing* JOHNNY): Who's that? Look, Mitty, he's
wearing a kettle on his head.

MITTY: Why, it must be Johny Appleseed!

JOHNNY (*Turning and seeing them*): Right, young ladies.
Come on out. Old Johnny's going to look in his bag
and see if he can find a gift for you. (*Girls come out onto
porch while* JOHNNY *takes two hair ribbons from his
bag.*) Here, how's this?

MITTY (*Taking one*): Thank you. It's lovely.

ROSE (*Taking the other*): Thank you.

MITTY: Where are my ma and pa?

JOHNNY: They'll be right back. They went to fetch a cow from the lower pasture. There's been a cloudburst up north and the creek's rising.

MITTY: The creek's rising?

JOHNNY: That's what I said.

ROSE: Mitty, that's where . . .

MITTY: Sh! We promised not to tell.

ROSE: But, Mitty!

JOHNNY: Something bothering you young ladies?

ROSE: Mitty, we'd better tell him.

MITTY: But we crossed our hearts and hoped to die if we told.

ROSE: But this is different. This is real danger.

JOHNNY: Suppose you tell old Johnny all about it. Who's in danger?

MITTY (*Reluctantly*): It's my cousin, Betsy. She's down by the creek in a cave.

JOHNNY: In a cave?

ROSE: She's hiding there so she won't have to go away to Kansas with her father when he comes.

MITTY: The cave's right near the creek. We have to go and find her!

JOHNNY (*Standing*): You stay here. I'll get her. I know where that cave is and I can run faster than you. (*Runs off right*)

MITTY (*Calling after him*): Please hurry!

ROSE: Do you think he'll get there in time?

MITTY: He has to, Rose, he simply has to.

ROSE: Let's go back in the house to wait. If your ma and pa find us out here, we'll have a lot of explaining to do. (ROSE *and* MITTY *go into house. After a moment,* MR. *and* MRS. TREVIS *enter from right*)

MR. TREVIS: Cow and calf are safe in the barn. Let's go inside.

MRS. TREVIS: I wonder where Johnny Appleseed went.

MR. TREVIS: He probably found a likely spot nearby and went to sleep. Don't worry about Johnny. The woods are his home. The only dangerous place is down in the lower pasture near the creek and he knows about that. (*They go into house.* JOHNNY *enters right, leading* BETSY *by the hand.*)

JOHNNY: So you're Sergeant Tom Trevis's little girl?

BETSY: Yes. (MITTY *and* ROSE *run out to meet them.*)

MITTY: I'm so glad Johnny Appleseed found you in time, Betsy. You could have drowned.

JOHNNY: It was a close call. The water was coming up fast when we left. Now, suppose you tell me why you were hiding out in that cave?

BETSY: I was running away.

MITTY: Her pa's coming to take her away to Fort Leavenworth in the Kansas Territory.

JOHNNY: And you don't want to go?

BETSY: No. I'll hate it out there.

JOHNNY: How do you know that? You've never been there.

BETSY: I just know I'll hate it.

JOHNNY: If I were you, I'd jump at a chance like that.

BETSY: You would?

JOHNNY: Do you know that Fort Leavenworth is at the beginning of the Santa Fe Trail and the Oregon Trail, too? Why, Betsy, stop and think of the sights you're going to see. There'll be explorers and trappers, and Indians, and pioneers setting out to settle the great West. You'll see history made right in front of you. You'll be living in the middle of it.

MITTY: Betsy, it does sound grand, the way he tells it.

ROSE: I wish I could go with you. Nothing ever happens around here.

JOHNNY: There's another reason too, Betsy. It's the best reason of all. (*Opens his bag and takes out his Bible as* MR. *and* MRS. TREVIS *come out of the house*)

MR. TREVIS: Here are the girls.

MRS. TREVIS (*Laughing*): Clustered around Johnny Apple-seed just the way my sisters and I used to.

JOHNNY: Betsy has been telling me about her going away.

MRS. TREVIS: She's not very happy about it.

JOHNNY (*Sitting on steps and opening his Bible*): Betsy, I'm going to read a story to you from the Good Book. It applies especially to your case.

ROSE: What's the story, Johnny?

JOHNNY: The story of Ruth and Naomi.

MITTY: We know that story, don't we, Betsy?

BETSY: Yes, but it doesn't apply to me. That story is about a wife and her mother-in-law.

JOHNNY: It's a story about love. That's the most important part.

BETSY (*Slowly*): Yes, I see what you mean. If you *really* love someone, you put that person first, before every-thing else. Oh, Johnny, I'm so glad you saved me from the flood. I might never have had a chance to show my pa how much I do love him.

JOHNNY (*Patting her head*): You're worth saving, Betsy. I'm thankful I got there in time.

MR. TREVIS: What's all this about being saved from the flood?

JOHNNY: I'll tell you later, Dan. Right now, Betsy is wres-tling with something more important.

BETSY: My place is with my pa because I'm his daughter and he needs me. Oh, I wish he were here so I could tell him. (*Hoofbeats are heard again off right.*)

TOM TREVIS (*Calling from offstage*): Anybody home at the Trevis Farm?

MR. TREVIS: It's your pa, Betsy. He must have hired a horse and come ahead of the stage.

BETSY (*Calling*): Pa, Pa, it's Betsy. I'm still up. And I'm ready to go with you. (*Runs off right*)

MITTY: Johnny, aren't you going to give her a gift?

MRS. TREVIS: Johnny already has, Mitty. The best gift Betsy will ever receive.

MITTY (*Puzzled*): I think I like hair ribbons better.

MRS. TREVIS (*Laughing*): You would, Mitty Trevis. But someday when you're older, you'll understand. (*Curtain*)

THE END

Baron Barnaby's Box

A Welsh tale

by J. G. Colson

Characters

WILL GOODWIN

BESS GOODWIN

NICHOLAS NOODLE

THOMAS TINHEAD

MATTIE MEDDLER

BARBARA BUSYBODY

SIMON SNAFFLE

SALLY SNAFFLE

BARON BARNABY

TIME: *Early one summer evening.*

SETTING: *The village green in the tiny village of Barnaby Turf, Wales.*

AT RISE: WILL GOODWIN, *an old man, enters from downstage left, followed by his wife,* BESS, *obviously very tired.*

WILL: Come, Bess, come. Keep a stout heart.

BESS: Stout heart, did you say, Will? My heart's stout enough, Will, but my legs—they just won't go.

WILL: We must go on.

BESS (*Seeing a log and sitting on it*): That's better. It's shady here, and it's so hot on the road.

WILL: The hottest day this summer, I'll be bound. But you

mustn't sit there, old girl. 'Tis evening already, and we've many a mile to walk yet.

BESS: My poor legs! Can't we stay at an inn for the night? There's sure to be one in this village.

WILL: No.

BESS: Why not, Will?

WILL: You know why not. (*He reaches into his pocket and takes out two pennies.*) Look!

BESS: Two pennies—is that all we have?

WILL: That is all. Not enough for a night's lodging. (*He puts pennies back into his pocket.*)

BESS: But my legs will never carry me to Cousin John's. Appleby is miles off yet, on the other side of yonder hills.

WILL: You'll feel better when you've rested. Don't worry.

BESS: But I am worried. We shall have to walk all night. Why didn't we stop that coach when it passed us? Perhaps we could have begged a ride for part of the way.

WILL: A coach! It wouldn't stop for the likes of us. Didn't you notice that fine lord sitting inside?

BESS: He had a kind face. Of course, we look poor.

WILL: We are poor. But cheer up, Bess, there's plenty of work waiting for us at Cousin John's.

BESS: If we get there, Will. Why, oh, why did we leave Wyberton?

WILL: You're tired, Bess. You know in your heart that we would have starved there. No more life left in the ground. Nothing would grow any more.

BESS: Ay, you're a good man, Will. You tried hard.

WILL: And you helped me, Bess.

BESS (*Rising*): Let's move on, Will.

WILL: Lean on my shoulder, Bess old girl. You'll feel better soon.

BESS: Ay, but oh, my legs! (*They start left, as voices are heard from offstage right.*)

WILL: Listen!

BESS: People. They sound upset, too.

WILL: Something's the matter! Look over there! (*He points upstage right.*) Can't you see them?

BESS: Ay, proper excited they are, too.

WILL: They're coming this way. They're coming here! (MATTIE MEDDLER *enters from right, carrying a medium-sized wooden box, which is tied shut. She is followed by* BARBARA BUSYBODY. WILL *and* BESS, *who move upstage, are unobserved by the villagers.*)

MATTIE: I've got it! I've got it! Here it is. (*She puts the box down.*) Come and see!

BARBARA: Just in time, Mattie. That Simon Snaffle would have run off with it.

MATTIE: Ay, Barbara, we got rid of him, we did. (NICHOLAS NOODLE *and* THOMAS TINHEAD, *two old men, enter, followed shortly by* SIMON SNAFFLE *and his wife,* SALLY, *who hurry in.*)

NICHOLAS: What's to do?

THOMAS: What's all this shouting for, Mattie Meddler?

MATTIE: I'll tell ye, Thomas Tinhead, I'll tell ye.

NICHOLAS: Go on, we're waiting.

MATTIE: Barbara Busybody and I saw Simon Snaffle there— (*She points to him.*) —pick up this box on the roadside.

SIMON: I was only going to show it to my wife.

MATTIE: A likely tale that is, Simon Snaffle.

SALLY: Don't you go saying things about my husband, Mattie Meddler, or I'll—

NICHOLAS: Now, now! Don't squabble. This is a fine box, this is. How did it come to be on the side of the road, Simon?

SIMON: I don't know.

THOMAS: Perhaps the fairies brought it, Nicholas.

NICHOLAS: There are no such things, Thomas.

THOMAS: Oh, yes, there are, Nicholas Noodle.

NICHOLAS: Oh, no, there aren't, Thomas Tinhead.

THOMAS: There are!

NICHOLAS: There aren't!

BARBARA (*Breaking in*): Quarreling is no good. Now that we've brought this box to the Village Green, what are we going to do with it?

NICHOLAS: Don't open it.

THOMAS: No, don't. Might be something queer inside.

SALLY: There might be money in it.

SIMON: Ay, money—silver money.

NICHOLAS: Silver! I haven't seen any silver since grandfather showed me his silver fourpenny.

BARBARA: What's to be done with it?

THOMAS: Throw it in the river. Might be spirits inside. (*They all crowd round.*)

SALLY: No. Take it to my house.

NICHOLAS: Have nothing to do with it, I say.

THOMAS: Give me a hand, Nicholas. Let's dump it in the river.

SIMON: No! (*There is a slight scuffle around box.* WILL *and* BESS *move downstage.*)

WILL (*To* BESS): What simple folk!

BESS: Almost stupid.

WILL: We had better go across to them. Perhaps we can help. (WILL *and* BESS *move over to crowd on left.*) Good evening, good people. (*Villagers stare at them.*)

SIMON: Who are you?

BARBARA: What are you a-doing in Barnaby Turf?

SALLY: Where do you come from?

WILL: All in good time. All in good time. I'm Will Goodwin. (*Pointing*) Bess my good wife, here, and I have come from Wyberton.

THOMAS: From Wyberton! All that way!

NICHOLAS: And where be you a-going?

BESS: To Appleby to work with my cousin John.

THOMAS: I've heard tell that folk from Wyberton be wise.

NICHOLAS: Ay, that be true. Wyberton folk be the wisest in the world.

SIMON: Just the chap we need. Tell us what to do with this box?

THOMAS: Ay, what shall we do?

WILL: Let me look at it first.

SIMON: Ay, do, but don't interfere with it.

WILL (*Looking at box*): Lock's broken.

SALLY: Ay, we know that—but the the cord looks strong.

WILL: Carefully knotted.

SIMON: I'll cut it with my knife.

NICHOLAS: No, you won't. Let the wise man decide.

SALLY: Let's take it to my house, stranger. That's what we ought to do.

WILL: All in good time, mistress. I must think. (*He examines box more closely.*) Ha! Now I can see some writing on it.

NICHOLAS: Writing! Writing! What's that?

THOMAS: Letters, you old fathead. Didn't you ever go to school?

NICHOLAS: School! If there's a school in Barnaby Turf, nobody told me about it.

BARBARA: Tell us what those letters say, Master Goodwin.

WILL (*Peering*): It's a long time since I learned my alphabet. Come, Bess, you're cleverer than I am. Read the words for us.

BESS (*Looking at box*): It says "Baron Barnaby, his box."

SIMON: Baron Barnaby!

WILL: Baron Barnaby! Who is he?

BARBARA: The richest man for many a mile.

MATTIE: Owns all the land as far as you can see.

NICHOLAS: Lord of the Manor, he is called.

BESS: Then this must be his chest.

SALLY: It's ours! Simon found it!

SIMON: That's true. I found it. It's mine.

WILL: But it belongs to the Baron.

SALLY: The Baron's rich enough. He won't miss one box.

WILL: Now take my advice, good villagers of Barnaby Turf. Take the box to the Baron.

BARBARA: But it might be full of silver.

NICHOLAS: Silver!

SIMON: I'll take it home.

MATTIE: No you won't! We'll divide the silver among us. Cut that cord with your knife, Simon Snaffle.

SIMON: I'd rather take the box home, but (*Looking at unsympathetic crowd.*) I'll cut the cord.

BESS: But that's stealing!

WILL: Ay, it's wrong to steal.

NICHOLAS: Stealing! What's that? Never heard of it.

THOMAS: But you don't come from Wyberton, do you, Nicholas?

WILL (*Interrupting*): Listen, good folk, this box might be a trap.

NICHOLAS: Ay, it might be, wise man.

WILL: I've heard of queer things before, especially in chests like this. Things that hurt. Harmful things.

SIMON: Have you now! Perhaps I'd better not touch it.

BARBARA: Harmful or not, I'd like to see the inside. Go on, cut that cord, Simon. Baron Barnaby wouldn't put anything dangerous in his own box.

THOMAS: That's true. Perhaps he carried money in it.

NICHOLAS (*To* WILL): Dare you open it, Master Goodwin?

WILL: 'Tis not mine to open. Besides I suspect that someone has set a snare for you. Be careful! I'm sure there's danger in it.

SALLY: Nonsense! We've fooled about long enough.

BARBARA: Ay, open it, Simon. (SIMON *does not move.*)

SALLY: Open it, or upon my word (*Threateningly*)—I'll have something to say—later.

SIMON: Oh, very well—since you all wish it. (*He takes knife from pocket, moves reluctantly to box, cuts cord, and slowly throws back lid, revealing a quantity of golden coins.*)

NICHOLAS: Yellow money!

THOMAS: Yellow coins! Hundreds of 'em. (*Villagers move forward, anxious to handle money. WILL moves forward.*)

WILL: Keep back! Don't touch those coins. (*He waves them away from box.*) They're dangerous. It's a trap!

NICHOLAS: Trap! I can't see any trap. Those coins do be a funny color, though. I've never seen money that color before.

THOMAS: Nor have I.

WILL: Of course they are a peculiar color. That's the trick. I'll show you. Look! (*He pretends to pick one up, then draws his hand back, as he touches it.*) Oh! (*Puts his fingers into his mouth.*)

NICHOLAS: Now what's the matter?

WILL: As I knew. They're hot! Burning hot! Oh, my finger! Those coins are on fire. They're red hot.

THOMAS: What!

WILL: Ay, I only just touched one of them. If I'd picked it up, it would have burned my fingers off. Feel for yourselves. (*Villagers shrink back.*)

THOMAS: Not me.

WILL: You, Simon, come and feel.

SIMON: No—no—I don't want to. I believe you, master.

NICHOLAS: It's a good thing you came along, Master Goodwin.

WILL: Isn't it! I'll close the trap now, while we're all safe and sound. (*He closes lid on box.*) I saw those coins and knew they were burning. That's what made them a golden color. I've seen that sort of red-hot silver before.

THOMAS: I don't want to see it any more. We might have lost our fingers.

WILL: You might, Thomas. Look at mine.

BARBARA: Now we're back where we started.

NICHOLAS: It could have been worse if we'd been burned.

WILL: Good folk, you're disappointed, and I'm sorry for you. But, here, take these. (*He pulls his two pennies out of his pocket.*) Spend them at the inn.

SALLY: Two pennies! (*Villagers crowd round.*)

MATTIE: Ay, we'll spend them, Master Goodwin.

SIMON: Give me them!

MATTIE: No, me!

WILL: Patience! Patience! (*They crowd round him. He throws pennies offstage right. They rush out after coins. THOMAS and NICHOLAS are at rear. NICHOLAS turns as he is about to go off.*)

NICHOLAS: Throwing your money about! Even if you do come from Wyberton, Master Goodwin, you are a fool.

THOMAS (*Calling from offstage right*): Come on, Nicholas —I be thirsty.

NICHOLAS: So be I. Good day to you both. Take care of that box. (*He goes out right.*)

WILL: Poor folk! Poor simple folk!

BESS: You worked that very well, Will. You're cleverer than I expected.

WILL: I had an inspiration. But do you know, Bess, I've never seen so many golden crowns in my life.

BESS: It's a good thing those villagers had never seen any gold. (*She walks across to box.*)

WILL: I felt sure they hadn't.

BESS: Enough here to make us rich for life.

WILL: It's not ours.

BESS: No, we can't have it. And you've thrown away your last pennies.

WILL: No use crying over that, Bess. (*He moves over to box.*) Help me hide this chest. Those villagers might come back. We'll put it behind the bushes over there. (*Points left*)

BESS: You know best, Will.

WILL: Then you sit on that log and rest your legs. Keep an eye on the box while I go off to find this Baron Barnaby. (BARON BARNABY, *a tall, imposing looking, middle-aged man, enters from upstage left.*)

BARNABY: There is no need. He is here.

BESS: You, sir?

BARNABY: I am Baron Barnaby.

WILL: Then you've saved me steps, sir. I was just going to look for you.

BARNABY: I think I know why.

WILL (*Pointing to chest*): Tell me, sir, is that your box?

BARNABY: It is. It fell off my coach.

BESS: Ah, sir, then you must have passed us along the way.

BARNABY: I did. As a matter of fact, I saw you, my good woman, with your good man.

WILL: Those stupid villagers brought your chest here.

BESS: And would have stolen your gold.

BARNABY: I know. But Will, my good fellow, you had an inspiration and saved it. I stood behind those bushes (*He points upstage left*) and heard everything.

WILL: But—

BARNABY: No buts, Will. I was curious, so I didn't interfere. Believe me, I'm grateful. You shall both be rewarded—well rewarded.

BESS: Oh, sir. (BARON BARNABY *moves to the box and takes out some gold coins.*)

BARNABY: Take these. You're welcome to them. (*He gives each a handful of gold coins.*)

BESS: Oh, thank you, sir.

WILL: Thank you, sir.

BARNABY: Don't thank me. It is I who should thank you. Now where are you going?

BESS: To work at Appleby where my Cousin John lives, sir.

BARNABY: Appleby! That's a long way from here. How do you propose to reach there?

BESS: On foot, sir.

BARNABY: Oh, no, you shall not go on foot. You will ride in my coach. It's close by. My coachman shall drive you there.

WILL: You are very kind. You've given us enough gold to start a farm. I don't know how to thank you.

BARNABY: Don't try, Will. You're both honest folk and deserve to be rewarded. (*Curtain.*)

THE END

Production Notes

AFRICAN TRIO

Characters: 6 male; 5 female; 10 male or female, including Storytellers. Stagehand and Property Girl are non-speaking parts.

Playing Time: 15 minutes.

Costumes: The Storytellers and human characters wear the costumes of the tribe of their story. The Princess must have sandals, a headdress, cloak, and jewels, worn over a simple dress. The animals can wear large paper bag or papier-mâché masks.

Properties: African drum, *mbira* or other African harp, yellow pot, red pot, yellow and red cardboard discs, blue crepe paper streamers, cutouts of palm tree, rainbow, and peacock.

Setting: Slides of East Africa, South Africa and West Africa (Liberia) may be projected on the back wall of stage, or on a screen at rear. The three different houses —veld-style, Masai and Vai—may be made of painted cardboard. Masai houses are long, low and plastered, and are entered by crawling. Veld houses vary; some are beehive-shaped, and others have circular walls with thatched roofs. The Vai house is round with a tall, pointed, thatched roof.

Lighting: No special effects.

THE SECRET OF THE WISHING WELL

Characters: 12 male; 7 female; female extras.

Playing Time: 15 minutes.

Costumes: The Elf wears brown, the Miser black, the King and Courtiers, purple, the dancers, ballet costumes. The rest of the characters may wear everyday clothing.

Properties: Leaves, doll, hammer, cakes, books, mouth organ, gold, flower, violin.

Setting: The Wishing Well is at right center. Near it is a tree. (Leaves that can be detached should be pasted on the tree.) Upstage center should be a rise or opening where the Figures of the Future may appear. A back curtain or a screen pulled to one side by two extras could be used if the lighting suggested in the text is not feasible.

Lighting: As noted in the text.

LADY MOON AND THE THIEF

Characters: 6 male; 1 female; 7 boys or girls for fishermen, xylophonist, gong player, property boys; as many actors as desired for Villagers.

Playing Time: 20 minutes.

Costumes: Chinese costumes. Lord Sun wears gold armor, and car-

559

ries a round gold shield. The front of Lady Moon's kimono is silver and the back is black. She carries two fans, silver on one side and black on the other. Bow-Low wears a silk robe, and carries a scroll. Nid-Nod wears a bright kimono, and is made up as an old man. Others wear kimonos or short Chinese jackets, trousers, sandals, and coolie hats. Property Boys are dressed in black.

Properties: Fans for Villagers, fishing poles, cardboard fish, basket containing rice shoots, dark cloak, long-handled fan for Ah Me, fishnet on pole, pillows, gong, xylophone, tea table set with teapot and cups.

Setting: Ting-a-ling, a village in ancient China. A blue pagoda, large enough to hide Lord Sun behind it and with steps to climb it on both sides, is on a platform at center. Day Screens, painted with scenes of trees, sky, clouds, etc., are on either side, and behind them are Night Screens, painted black. A bridge over a pond is at left, and up right is a hill painted to resemble a terraced rice paddy. A twisted pine tree with a tea table set with tea pot and cups is down right. Exits are at right and left, and behind pagoda, if desired.

Lighting: No special effects.

Sound: Gong and xylophone, Oriental music, as indicated in text.

THE TIGER CATCHER

Characters: 4 male; 2 female; 1 boy or girl for Tiger; as many extras as desired for Villagers.

Playing Time: 15 minutes.

Costumes: Appropriate Chinese dress. The Magistrate wears an elaborate robe, with scroll in pocket. Loo Ming has a red cloth wrapped around his head when he first enters. The Widow walks with a staff. The Tiger wears a mask.

Properties: Scroll, rope, toy rabbit, table, chair.

Setting: An open space before the house of the Magistrate in a Chinese village. A gong, suspended from a support, is at right. A mallet is attached to the support. Exits are at right and left.

Lighting: No special effects.

PLUM BLOSSOM AND THE DRAGON

Characters: 2 male; 7 female; the Chorus, the Dragon and the Musicians may be male or female; as many extras for Ladies as desired.

Playing Time: 20 minutes.

Costumes: Mother, Butterfly Fairy, Empress and Ladies wear long Chinese gowns with full sleeves. Plum Blossom, Chorus, Jade Pearl, Poppy Seed, Pear Flower, Ah Fang and Musicians wear long trousers and tunic-length tops. Plum Blossom must have pockets in her costume. Ah Fang wears a belt with a money bag at his waist. Dragon has a yellow costume with a long tail. He has long claws (which may be attached to gloves).

Properties: Instruments for Musicians, bowl for Mother, fans for girls, money for Ah Fang, petals for Butterfly Fairy. The following properties are in the chest: a large paper fish, a large butterfly on a string, a flowering branch, a large fluffy white cap for Ling Po, some colorful necklaces, a large fan, and a scroll that says: THE END.

Setting: The stage is bare except for a large red chest upstage center and some chairs down right.

Lighting: No special effects.

Triumph for Two

Characters: 15 male; 6 female; as many extras for court ladies and gentlemen and villagers as desired.

Playing Time: 25 minutes.

Costumes: Intelligence wears a scholar's cap and gown. Luck wears a top hat with a four-leaf clover on it. Vanek, Vanek's Father, Villagers, Head Gardener and Boris wear peasant clothes. The Headsman wears a black mask that covers his face and head. Others wear appropriate court costumes.

Properties: Book, gardeners' tools, three chairs, pillow, material for chairs, toy dog, bird cage with toy bird in it, blindfold, rope, large cardboard ax with detachable handle.

Setting: Scene 1: The King's garden. There is a stone wall with roses growing over it up center, and plants may be placed about the stage. Scene 2: Execution Hill. There is an execution block midstage. Exits are at right and left.

Lighting: No special effects.

Robin Hood Outwits the Sheriff

Characters: 13 male; 6 female.

Playing Time: 25 minutes.

Costumes: Robin and his men are dressed in Lincoln green. Robin has a small hunting horn attached to his belt. The Sheriff wears a robe of velvet, trimmed with fur or silk. His men wear soldiers' uniforms, with swords, under their monks' robes. Friar Tuck wears long robe; Lady Alice wears a rich, but well-worn dress, and Sir Richard wears shabby knight's costume. Nell, Margot, and Peg wear shawls over their dresses. Marian and Ellen wear simple dresses.

Properties: Baskets, chest, sack, bags of gold, bag filled with stones, meat and other foods for feast, platters, plates, goblets, bows and arrows, quarterstaves, kindling, kettles, pitchers, blindfolds, brocades, velvets, wool cloth, jeweled sword, gilded goblet.

Setting: Robin Hood's den in Sherwood Forest. At center is a table, and several benches are placed about it. A fire and roasting spit are up left. A small table is at right.

Lighting: No special effects.

A Most Special Dragon

Characters: 5 male; 1 female; Mikta may be a boy or girl. The Guard is a non-speaking role.

Playing Time: 10 minutes.

Costumes: Zartoum wears a long black robe with handkerchief in a pocket and wand tucked into the flowing sleeves. He also wears a conical black hat, decorated with cabalistic signs. Redmond wears imitation armor, and a cardboard sword and sheath. Mikta wears a dragon's costume, which may be as elaborate as desired. Eric and Gloriana wear brightly-colored regal clothes; Gloriana may wear a long dress with a small crown, and Eric may wear knickers or short pants, long socks, shoes with buckles and a short cape. The King wears long regal robes, an ornate pendant, a long cape and a crown. The Guard is in a regal uniform.

Properties: Thick book, wand, huge paper flower, handkerchief (which conceals a rubber ball), small cloth bag of "nolorem" on ribbon, scarf, a large feather, cup, cauldron or small kettle, cardboard spear for Guard, and cardboard sword and sheath for Redmond.

Setting: The courtyard of the King's castle. A long bench is at center, covered with a cloth that hangs to the ground. The paper flower is behind the bench in Scene 1. Two chairs are left and right of the bench. The backdrop may depict the castle walls. Exits are left and right.

Lighting: Stage lights off and on.

Sound: Thunder or loud crash offstage, as indicated in text.

THE WISE PEOPLE OF GOTHAM

Characters: 10 male; 6 female.

Playing Time: 15 minutes.

Costumes: Herald and Lord High Chancellor wear appropriate Court costume. The Lord High Chancellor wears a hat. The Stranger wears a cape over his royal robes; he has a royal emblem on his coat. Others wear appropriate peasant costume.

Properties: Wheelbarrow, boxes, pans, butterfly nets, large feather, net, four mirrors, two buckets (one full of water), a large sieve, white rabbit.

Setting: A square in the town of Gotham. There is a small platform or stone at one side of stage, and bench and tree center.

Lighting: No special effects.

THE STOLEN TARTS

Characters: 6 male; 1 female.

Playing Time: 15 minutes.

Costumes: The men wear doublets and hose—the Pages, white and blue; the Knave, red and white; the King, purple and white; The Guards, green and white. The Queen wears a bodiced gown with a long, full skirt of rose and white. All costumes are patterned with hearts of various sizes.

Properties: Huge bowl, large and small spoons, huge baking pan, large jar labeled ROYAL HONEY, sticks of cinnamon (rolled brown paper may be used), large bowl labeled BARLEY FLOUR, jar labeled ROYAL GOOSEBERRY JAM, round package marked GOAT'S MILK CHEESE.

Setting: The royal kitchen. There is a door at right leading into the royal palace, and a door at left leading into the supply pantry. There is a large, low window at back which opens into the royal kitchen garden. An oven, made from a large box covered with wrapping paper, baking utensils, a copper kettle, and a work table with a stool complete the furnishings.

Lighting: No special effects.

KING ARTHUR AND HIS KNIGHTS

Characters: 24 male; 5 female; female extras for Ladies; male extras for Pages, Squires, and Lancelot's Knights. Parts for extras may be doubled, and knights' parts may be doubled also, if desired.

Playing Time: 30 minutes.

Costumes: Medieval court dress. The men wear tunics and hose, long robes, swords, in various colors. Galahad's tunic is red. The women wear long full robes and headdresses. In Scene 6, Guinevere is robed as a nun. Three Queens wear black. For complete details, consult a book on costume. In general, refer to Malory's *Morte d'Arthur*.

Properties: Large book; Arthur's sword Excalibur, heavily encrusted with jewels and gilt; trumpets; baskets of bread; embroidery on frame; small pin or ornament; cross on chain; crown of flowers.

Setting: Scene 1: Outside a cathedral, which may be painted on a flat. Sword in stone and anvil is at center; this may be a simple cardboard mock-up. Scene 2: The throne room, with the Table Round, at Camelot. Only the upper half of the table appears, surrounded by chairs bearing the names of knights. Arthur's seat is at center, and beside it is the covered Siege Perilous, on which is lettered in gold, "THIS IS THE SIEGE OF GALAHAD, THE HIGH PRINCE." Tables and chairs are at left and right for Ladies. The backdrop may indicate a high stone wall, with tapestries or hangings. Scene 3: The same as Scene 2, with a small chair or bench for Guinevere placed at left. Scenes 4 and 5: The same as Scene 2. Scene 6: Outside Lancelot's castle of Joyous Gard. A low wall runs along stage at rear, and there is a parapet, or simple raised platform, at one side. The backdrop shows a lake. Scene 7: The same as Scene 6.

Lighting: A spotlight shines on the Siege Perilous and on wall, as indicated in Scene 4.

Sound: Offstage sounds of clanging, battle, triumphal music and trumpet fanfare, as indicated in text.

PIERRE PATELIN

Characters: 4 male; 1 female.

Playing Time: 30 minutes.

Costumes: Judge may wear long robe; others may wear simple peasant costumes. Tibald carries a shepherd's crook.

Properties: Ragged, patched dress, shoes, broom, lengths of cloth, price tags reading 2 FRANCS and 20 FRANCS, scissors, bench for Judge.

Setting: A street in a small French town. At left is Pierre's house; the front of house is open, re-

vealing small table, stool, and bed. At rise, Pierre's shoes are by the bed, and there is a broom in one corner. A window looks toward draper's house and shop, at right, and door opens into street, center. Inside draper's house, right, is a counter with pieces of cloth and scissors. One piece of cloth has a large price tag reading 2 FRANCS. Behind counter is second tag reading 20 FRANCS.

Lighting: No special effects.

Sound: Appropriate music may be played at beginning, as overture, and at intervals during play.

THE PRICE OF EGGS

Characters: 2 male; 2 female.

Playing Time: 10 minutes.

Costumes: Peasant dress. The women wear white, lacy blouses and long, colorful skirts. The men wear dark-colored knee breeches, white shirts and colorful vests. The Stranger's clothes are very ragged when he appears in Scene 1. In Scene 2 his costume is quite elaborate. He wears a heavy gold watch chain and a blue frock coat.

Properties: Broom, a dozen hardboiled eggs in a kerchief, two bags of gold.

Setting: A French village street. If possible, a backdrop should show several houses. One of these houses should have a door which opens, so that Widow may use it for her exits and entrances. There is a doorstep in front of this door.

Lighting: No special effects.

THE MUSICIANS OF BREMEN TOWN

Characters: 4 male; 1 female; 5 boys or girls for animals and Narrator.

Playing Time: 15 minutes.

Costumes: Animals wear masks; Cat

has a long tail. Robbers wear dark clothes and half-masks. Farmer and Wife are dressed appropriately. Narrator wears everyday dress, and carries a book.

Properties: Hay, large bone, corn, toy mouse, table with food, valuables, and money.

Setting: A bare stage is used throughout. A wooden black box is at right. Exits are at right and left.

MERRY TYLL AND THE THREE ROGUES

Characters: 15 male; 5 female; 5 male or female for Cow and Children; as many extras as desired for Villagers and additional Children.

Playing Time: 30 minutes.

Costumes: Appropriate medieval dress. Tyll is in jester's costume and has a pointed hat with bells. He has a whistle in his pocket. Popinjay wears ornate costume—velvet pants and jacket trimmed with lace. Cow wears appropriate mask or complete animal costume. Men wear bright-colored shirts, dark trousers. Women wear long skirts, shawls, etc. Peter is shabbily dressed.

Properties: Cream puff, two red cardboard hearts joined by an arrow, bouquet of flowers, yardstick for Tyll; bag with coins; knitting; four plates with food; jewelry (rings, watch chain, cuff links, stickpin, etc.), lace.

Setting: The marketplace of a town in Germany in the early 14th century. Five booths are up right and left with vegetables, lace, toys, pies, and trinkets displayed. There is a stool beside Vegetable Woman's booth. Café table and chairs are right center. Up left center is an elevated platform. On the platform is a large

frame with a curtain which opens and closes. A stuffed owl is on top of the frame. Exits are right and left.

Lighting: No special effects.

Sound: Offstage trumpet, music for folk dance as indicated in text. If desired, a recording of "Tyll Eulenspiegel's Merry Pranks" by Richard Strauss may be used as an overture and at intervals throughout play.

KING MIDAS

Characters: 3 male; 1 female; 1 male voice (offstage); offstage voices for Voices of the Reeds.

Playing Time: 30 minutes.

Costumes: Appropriate Greek costume. Cora's dress should be white, and have a satin finish so that it will appear gold under an amber spotlight. Antonius may wear bright clothes. Midas has long page-boy hair. His robe should have a large collar which can hide his donkey's ears at end of play. Bacchus first appears in a ragged cloak, which covers his white tunic.

Properties: Vase, wine goblet, grapes, cheese, knife, comb, scissors, rose (all have duplicates painted gold for the "golden touch"); basket, cape, towel, tray, plates, bag of gold, gold coins, turban.

Setting: A room in the palace of King Midas. Doors at right and left are indicated by framework only. Door at right is the entrance to the palace, and door at left leads to the garden. A few rocks and some tall reeds are visible at one side of the garden. In the palace are a table and two chairs, a large chest, and a small table at one side with wine jug and goblets.

Lighting: An amber spotlight may be used when Cora becomes a golden statue.

Sound: Offstage voices may be amplified, if desired.

ONE WISH TOO MANY

Characters: 2 male; 3 female.

Playing Time: 20 minutes.

Costumes: Traditional Dutch dresses and aprons with white pointed caps for the women; Peter wears breeches and a vest, with a big bow tie for Gretchen to cut; and the Old Man wears a similar outfit that is dusty and patched.

Properties: Lengths of cloth; tablecloth; scissors, curtains. The properties that Gretchen cuts may be made of paper, or she may only pretend to cut.

Setting: Cutaway of sitting rooms of two adjoining houses—Hootson house, left, and Van Hoek house, right. Street runs in front of houses. Exits from each sitting room lead to other rooms of houses. Each room contains table and several chairs.

Lighting: If desired, lights may go up on the house in which the action is taking place.

Sound: Clock striking, as indicated in text.

A GIFT FOR HANS BRINKER

Characters: 8 male; 7 female.

Playing Time: 20 minutes.

Costumes: Appropriate Dutch costumes. Gretel and Hans wear ragged clothes. Gretel wears a wooden necklace and Hans wears a cap. They have wooden skates; other children have regular skates.

Properties: Two pair of wooden skates for Hans and Gretel; skates for other children; boxes containing two pair of skates covered with tin foil or painted silver; coins; small package; Dutch flags; skate strap.

Setting: The bank of a canal near Amsterdam. The bank is separated from the canal by a stone wall, about three feet high, across stage toward back. An opening in the wall at left leads to the canal. Since skaters' feet are hidden by wall, actual skating may be pantomimed. A windmill is in the background. Holders for flags are on the wall. There are several wooden benches in front of the wall. A table for the silver skates is added in Scene 2.

Lighting: No special effects.

THE TIGER, THE BRAHMAN, AND THE JACKAL

Characters: 9 children; all parts may be taken by boys, if desired.

Playing Time: 10 minutes.

Costumes: Everyday dress for Narrator and Children. Others wear appropriate costumes.

Properties: None required.

Setting: The stage is bare, except for a cage at left center which has a door that opens and closes. Exits are at right and left.

Lighting: No special effects.

FINN McCOOL

Characters: 5 male; 6 female.

Playing Time: 15 minutes.

Costumes: Peasant dress. Grannie and ladies wear shawls, and Una wears an apron. Finn puts on a long white nightshirt and ruffled bonnet.

Properties: Basket of laundry, bowl containing dough, small skillets, white stone, "cheese" (a white sponge with water in it), cups and plates, blanket, washtub.

Setting: The interior of Finn Mc-Cool's cabin. A table is at center, with several chairs around it. A bed is at right, and a fireplace and oven are up center. A door at left leads to the outside, and beside it is a window. An exit at right leads to another room.

Lighting: No special effects.

Sound: Loud offstage crashes, as indicated in text.

THE BRIDGE TO KILLYBOG FAIR

Characters: 7 male; 7 female; 2 male or female for pigs.

Playing Time: 20 minutes.

Costumes: Appropriate peasant costumes. Leprechaun and pixie wear green elf costumes. Leprechaun has a beard. Pigs may wear masks.

Properties: Wand, basket, cakes, drums and drumsticks.

Setting: The woods near the hamlet of Killybog, in Ireland. A small wooden bridge stands down right. Two stumps surrounded by bushes and foliage stand up left.

Lighting: No special effects.

THE LEPRECHAUN SHOEMAKERS

Characters: 4 male, 5 female. Three or more girls for Fairy Ladies-in-Waiting.

Playing Time: 15 minutes.

Costumes: Leprechauns wear black or gray suits and pointed red hats; pixies are dressed in green; brownies wear brown. Eileen Elf may be dressed in yellow. Beggar Fairy wears black cape with a hood and is barefoot. Under cape she wears white dress and crown. She may have slippers in pocket of cape, which she puts on as indicated in text. She carries a cane, to which a star may be attached, as indicated, to transform it into a magic wand. Ladies-in-Waiting wear pastel-colored dresses and tiaras.

Properties: A pair of slippers, large needle and thread, shoemakers' tools, shoe measurer, workbasket containing strips of imitation leather or heavy cardboard, sketch of a dancing shoe, and sketch of a woman's shoe, two teacups and saucers, printed sign reading, THE QUEEN'S ROYAL SHOEMAKER.

Setting: A leprechaun shoe shop. Two cobbler's benches with tools stand down right. A workbasket stands between the benches. Small, gaily-painted chairs and tables may be placed about. Door at left leads to the outside; door at right leads to the rest of the shop.

Lighting: No special effects.

THE KING AND THE BEE

Characters: 4 male; 2 female.

Playing Time: 10 minutes.

Costumes: Colorful, Biblical costumes. The men wear long robes with wide belts, heavy necklaces, and turbans. The King has a crown. The Keeper may have a slightly humorous touch, such as a long, curved feather. The Queen may wear full Turkish trousers and a filmy veil or scarf held in place by a small crown or circlet. The Bee may wear a black and yellow tunic, dark stockings, a glittering cap with antennae, and cellophane wings.

Properties: Cardboard stinger, several jars or boxes, a large magnifying glass, blob of putty for King's nose, a pair of tongs or large tweezers, a roll of bandage, a scarf, and two bouquets of artificial flowers.

Setting: The garden of King Solomon. A long, low wall with many brightly colored flowers is in the back. In front of it is a long bench draped with a rich, oriental fabric. There may be trees, shrubs, and ornamental vases at right.

Sound Effects: During the Bee's scenes there should be a continuous low buzzing sound, or the very soft playing of a record, such as "Flight of the Bumblebee." A trumpet or gong may announce the coming of the Queen.

Lighting: No special effects.

THE MAGIC GRAPES

Characters: 6 male; 3 female.

Playing Time: 10 minutes.

Costumes: Pietro, the Farmer, the Woodcutter and the Beggar wear overalls and shirts. The Shepherd Boy wears a gay shepherd's costume, the policeman, a uniform. The female characters wear peasant costumes with full skirts.

Properties: Large bunch of grapes, load of wood, bird and cat, stick.

Setting: A country road. The backdrop may show vineyards and orchards. A grape arbor made of white cardboard and painted with grapes and leaves stands near the road. A few bunches of real grapes should be attached to the arbor. A large stone is near the arbor.

Lighting: No special effects.

THE MAGIC BOX

Characters: 10 male; 4 female.

Playing Time: 25 minutes.

Costumes: Traditional peasant costumes. In Scene 1 Tonio's clothes are very colorful; in Scene 2 he wears a simple shirt and dark trousers. The Old Woman wears a dark blouse, long full skirt, and dark shawl.

Properties: A box, about the size of a shoe box, intricately decorated and fastened with leather bands.

Setting: The main room of a prosperous farm home. There are a chair and desk, upstage left, and a bell rope behind the desk. Down right are some plain chairs and small tables. The door, left, leads to the street; the door at right leads to the rest of the house. There may be paintings and curtains on the walls, and rugs on the floor. Scene 2, Before Rise: at center is a small stack of wood with a light under it, to give the effect of a fire.

Lighting: No special effects.

Sound: Marching music, as indicated in text.

THE OGRE WHO BUILT A BRIDGE

Characters: 3 male; 2 female; 5 male or female for Storyteller, Stagehand, and Children.

Playing Time: 15 minutes.

Costumes: Ogre and Ogre Children wear fierce red masks. Other characters may wear simple Japanese costumes or school clothes.

Properties: Scroll with THE OGRE WHO BUILT A BRIDGE printed vertically in Oriental script, gong, piece of curved cardboard labeled BRIDGE.

Setting: A row of four chairs is up right center with a sign reading SMALL VILLAGE. Down right is a diagonal screen labeled WOODS. Up left center is a screen labeled RIVER, with a roll of blue cloth at its base. At the left of the river is a sign reading TO LARGE VILLAGE. A low stool is down left.

Lighting: No special effects.

THE PEACH TREE KINGDOM

Characters: 3 male; 4 female.

Playing Time: 25 minutes.

Costumes: Traditional Oriental costumes are worn. Yoshiko, Lady Purple Stream, and Prince Fujioka wear elaborately decorated kimonos. The Prince puts on a cotton kimono and a mustache when he assumes his disguise. Yoshiko and Lady Purple Stream carry fans. The Lord High Arranger wears spectacles, which hang around his neck (attached to a ribbon) when he isn't using them.

Properties: Watering can and trowel for Tashari, bundle containing kimono and mustache for Prince Fujioka, Japanese umbrella, scroll for Lady Purple Stream, stick, berries, bowl of "peaches" (one "peach" should be easy to open, and should contain a large pit), small peach tree in pot, pillow.

Setting: The Japanese garden is enclosed by a wall. At one side is a gate in the wall which leads to the palace. The garden contains a shrine (two black wooden poles connected by wooden strips at the top), a bench with some pillows, a small table (on the table is a bowl of "peaches"), and some flowering plants and bushes, including a small ornamental peach tree in a pot.

Lighting: No special effects.

Sound: Oriental music is heard, as indicated in the text.

THE GREAT SAMURAI SWORD

Characters: 4 male; 4 female; Four Singers and Musicians may be either male or female.

Playing Time: 20 minutes.

Costumes: Japanese kimonos, slippers or sandals, sashes and obis, and flowers or ornaments for the women's hair. Osada and Naoto wear armor in the fencing scene, and fencing masks. All characters have heavy powder on their faces, giving a mask-like appearance. The men have heavy eyebrows;

Sudo and Kasai have gray beards and hair. Grandmother has white hair.

Properties: Gong, bells, and as many other instruments as desired for Musicians. Two long, curved swords with highly decorated handles. The Great Samurai Sword has a gold sheath.

Setting: A large folding screen or backdrop, painted to give the effect of a Japanese scene: a lake, Mt. Fuji, and houses to right and left of lake. There is a platform for Musicians, and four brightly colored pillows for the Singers.

Lighting: No special effects.

Sound: The Musicians play whenever no character is speaking. The rhythm, tempo, and instruments used vary with the scene and character. Music is used to accompany movements, create moods, and punctuate lines.

A SPOUSE FOR SUSIE MOUSE

Characters: 6 male; 2 female.

Playing Time: 10 minutes.

Costumes: Mouse Family wear appropriate brown or gray sweaters and tights, whiskers, pointed ears, and tails. Sun wears a suit of yellow crepe paper with a disk at center, and long "rays" projecting from it. Cloud wears a stiff sheet, bunched up at neck and ankles. Wind may wear streamers. Statue may wear an old-fashioned jacket and knee breeches, if desired.

Properties: None required.

Setting: A field near a small park. A large rock is placed at left, and a screen at right conceals the Statue, who may rest behind it until screen is removed.

Sound: No special effects.

Lighting: Lights may dim when Cloud enters, as indicated in text.

PEPE AND THE CORNFIELD BANDIT

Characters: 8 male; 4 female; (Chorus: 3 boys, 3 girls). Sapo may be played by a girl. As many Dancers as desired.

Playing Time: 20 minutes.

Costumes: Señor Granjero, Juan, Pedro, Pepe—loose cotton tunics, cotton trousers, sandals, sarapes, sombreros. Sapo—green tights, flippers, green polo shirt, green gloves with long green fingernails, knobby hood, freckles. Ixlanda—helmet with long peak, trailing multicolored feathers, long cape of many colors resembling feathers. Ixlanda's Aztec costume, short-sleeved blouse, long skirt, many necklaces and large dangling gold earrings. Chorus, Mexican costumes. Dancers, Mexican costumes.

Properties: 3 bongo drums, 3 maracas for Chorus. Comb, hand mirror, broom, rifle, feather, tortilla, extra sombrero (very large).

Setting: Backdrop with mountains, cactus, and a thatched cottage. Well with opening at the back for the toad, placed down center. Three rows of corn placed down left, one without tassels.

Lighting: No special effects.

Music: Mexican folk song; Mexican Hat Dance; as indicated in text.

THE KING WHO WAS BORED

Characters: 8 male; 4 female. Extra Vendors may be added, if desired.

Playing Time: 20 minutes.

Costumes: Traditional Mexican costumes. Soldiers wear *serapes* and *sombreros*. Generale wears a uniform. King wears a small crown. Vendors wear colorful *serapes* and *rebozos*.

Properties: Tin horn, document, baskets of fruit and vegetables, tortillas, coin.

Setting: The plaza of a Mexican village. At the rear there is a jail with its doors wide open and the padlock dangling. A barred window is right of the doors, a bench is left. There are several market stalls left and right, consisting of brightly-colored awnings supported on poles. A cactus tree is up right.

Lighting: No special effects.

THE SLEEPING MOUNTAINS

Characters: 7 male; 4 female.

Playing Time: 25 minutes.

Costumes: All wear simple costumes with an Aztec influence. Old Woman wears black. Prince and guards wear swords.

Properties: Pouch containing white powder, swords, large fan on the end of long stick, rope and handkerchief to bind and gag Terana, flute or recorder.

Setting: The courtyard of the Sun in the palace of King Papantco in the Valley of Mexico. There are a well at center, and a bench at right, both painted to look like stone. Throne is at left, painted gold, and draped with bright cloth. The backdrop is a painting of a dull red-colored plastered wall, with potted tropical plants hanging from it. Actual potted plants may be set upstage to give dimension to the backdrop.

Lighting: Scene 2 is a moonlit evening; Scene 3 is at dawn.

Sound: Horn blast (like a conch shell) and drum roll (played on a tom-tom); snarling wild cat, and howling coyote; flute or recorder music, played live, recorded, or whistled offstage by crew, if desired.

THE OLIVE JAR

Characters: 5 male; 2 female.
Playing Time: 25 minutes.
Costumes: Appropriate Middle Eastern dress. Women wear colorful, long, loose garments, fastened with long sashes in front. Jedah can wear bangles on her ankles; Amina wears necklaces, and a head scarf which she draws across her face in last scene. Jedah's hair is worn long. Mustapha wears long, full skirt, blouse belted with a sash, colorful vest and turban. The Caliph's garment under burnoose is similar to Mustapha's but richer in color and with jewels. The burnoose can be fashioned from a white sheet. Hasan wears an abba (a striped coat with full sleeves) and a cloth headdress. All men wear beards; Hasan's is henna to indicate he has made the pilgrimage. Ahmed is dressed in ragged shirt and short pants.
Properties: Broom, bells, coins, tray with food, cloth, coffee urn, two cups without handles, earthen jar with lid, olives, brass bowl, flat loaves of bread, money pouch.
Setting: The courtyard is surrounded by two-storied buildings. The entrance from the street is an arched, brick passage. To the right is Mustapha's house, to the left, his warehouse. Against the wall are a bench and a gnarled tree.
Lighting: Stage lights dim as indicated in text.
Sound: Donkey bells, camel bells, voices.

PETER AND THE WOLF

Characters: 4 male; 7 male or female. Extras, for additional Hunters, if desired.
Playing Time: 20 minutes.

Costumes: Animals wear appropriate costumes. Peter is dressed in bright shorts, a jacket, and a hat with a long feather. Grandfather wears a tall hat, has a white beard, and carries a cane. Hunters wear bright jackets, caps and carry sticks for guns.
Properties: Rope with a loop in it.
Setting: A meadow. There is a fence at one side, with a latched gate in it. A low stone wall runs along the back and to one side of meadow, behind a tree which stands upstage right. Pond is near rear. Three stools are downstage and at one side for narrators. Tree may be made of stepladder with cardboard cutout in front; pond is blue paper tacked to floor.
Lighting: No special effects.

STONE SOUP

Characters: 4 male, 4 female; male and female Villagers.
Playing Time: 15 minutes.
Costumes: Soldiers wear shabby long shirts, buckled over trousers. Sergeant wears cap. Male peasants wear long men's white overblouses, tied at waists with belts. Women wear blouses and colorful skirts. Anna and Marya wear kerchiefs on heads, babushka-style.
Properties: Three or four stones of various sizes; a large kettle or pot; a long spoon; a knapsack containing three tin cups for soldiers; branch; bowls for peasants; Y-shaped sticks to hang kettle; vegetables; an old-fashioned gun.
Setting: Three houses with large windows and doors stand along rear of stage. Interiors represent carpenter's shop, bakery, and seamstress's shop, and may be painted on backdrop. Windows and doors may be cut out of

cardboard. There are stones in stream at right.
Lighting: No special effects.

FISH IN THE FOREST

Characters: 8 male; 5 female; as many boys and girls as desired for Peasants and Servants.
Playing Time: 20 minutes.
Costumes: Ivan and Olga and other peasants wear shabby country clothes. Sonia wears a brightly colored full skirt. Count and Countess and other members of the court wear appropriate costumes.
Properties: Baskets, fishing lines, snare, old leather bag filled with coins, hand mirror, comb, spade, stuffed fish, stuffed rabbit, small artificial cakes.
Setting: Scenes 1 and 2 are a forest. There is a tall stump up right and a large rock is up center. Up left is a small tree with spaces where the artificial cakes may rest. Mushrooms, flowers and bushes may be scattered about stage. If desired, a backdrop of tree trunks may be used to suggest a forest. Scene 3 is the Count's palace. Two chairs representing thrones are up center.
Lighting: No special effects.

QUICK-WITTED JACK

Characters: 19 male; 12 female. Male and female extras for Ladies-in-Waiting and Courtiers.
Playing Time: 25 minutes.
Costumes: Fairy tale dress. King, Queen and Princess wear royal robes over shabby disguises, and also wear crowns. Jack wears simple breeches or short pants and knee socks; he carries a knapsack and bag of pearls in his pocket. Ants, Beetles, and Rabbits wear simple animal costumes.

Properties: Knapsack, leather bag of coal lumps, pearls, whistle, large tub, sack of seeds, four smaller empty sacks.
Setting: Scene 1: A cottage at the edge of a village green. A door to Jack's house is at left. A path through grassy woodlands runs across the stage. Anthill is at rear. Scene 2: The palace courtyard. Doors at right lead to palace apartments, and to storeroom. A long wall at rear has an arched entry in it, leading to the street.
Lighting: No special effects.

SIMPLE OLAF

Characters: 7 male; as many male and female extras as desired, as Courtiers and Stagehands.
Time: 20 minutes.
Costumes: Simple Olaf and Peasant are dressed in simple clothes. Guards wear colorful jackets with gold epaulets. King wears a long robe and crown. Attendants and Courtiers are dressed in courtly clothes.
Properties: Colorful bandana, stuffed with clothes and tied to the end of a stick; large box; heavy, high-backed chair for throne.
Setting: The stage is bare except for a log.
Lighting: No special effects.

THE BUILDER OF THE WALL

Characters: 6 male; 3 female.
Playing Time: 20 minutes.
Costumes: The men wear simple tunics, helmets with pointed horns, and carry shields. They may wear furs over their shoulders. Stranger wears a cloak with high collar to conceal his silvery costume, and long white beard. Women wear long robes, and helmets similar to those the

men wear. Svadilfare wears a long brown robe and horse's head. Loki also puts on a horse's head later in play.

Properties: Flower basket, scissors, cardboard stones, large cardboard cut-out of high wall made of rough stones, with a gateway half-completed.

Setting: Asgard, the garden of the gods. Rainbow bridge, made of cutout cardboard painted with colors of rainbow, is at center. Flowers, shrubs, rocks, benches are placed about the set.

Lighting: No special effects.

THE MAGIC CLOAK

Characters: 8 male; 6 female; as many extras as desired for Lords and Ladies, and other dancers.

Playing Time: 25 minutes.

Costumes: Traditional peasant and court costumes. Peasant Girl wears shoes with holes in soles. Old Woman wears large dark shawl and scarf. In Scene 3 she takes these off and reveals a royal costume. Jon wears old pants and tunic, and carries a knapsack. Adele wears bedroom slippers, Babette, oversized tennis shoes, and Charlotte, boots.

Properties: Bundle of sticks; knapsack with two pieces of cloth inside; sack with gray cloak; scroll; tray with pitcher and three glasses; large pill; silver branch with silver leaves.

Setting: Scene 1: A path through the forest, a wooden bench along the path. Scenes 2 and 3: The King's palace. A throne is at center and a bench is down left, with a plant nearby. Exits are right and left. If desired, an elaborate ballroom scene, set in the enchanted forest, with other dancers, musicians, etc., may be inserted between Scenes 2 and 3.

Lighting: No special effects.

Sound: Offstage whistling and sound of trumpet, music for dancing, as indicated in text.

KING HORN

Characters: 3 male; 3 female.

Playing Time: 15 minutes.

Costumes: Medieval court clothing. King Horn wears battle dress in Scene 1 and beggar's clothes in Scene 2. Chamberlain wears appropriate court clothing in Scene 1 and royal robes in Scene 2. Isabel and Gwyneth wear long flowing robes and flowers in their hair. Lady Margaret's robes should be richer; she wears a small crown.

Properties: Embroidery frames for Isabel and Gwyneth; scepter for King Horn; embroidery frame, jeweled ring and bridal veil for Margaret; candlesticks, minstrel harp and wine goblet for Dickon.

Setting: Scene 1: The throne room of King Horn's castle. The walls are hung with tapestries. At center is a richly decorated throne, with a scepter on it. At stage left is a chest containing bridal veil and at stage right, a table with candlesticks. Three chairs for Isabel, Gwyneth and Margaret are placed right of center stage. Scene 2: Same as Scene 1, except that chairs have been removed or placed at one side.

Lighting: No special effects.

PEDRO AND THE BURRO

Characters: 4 male; 4 female; 2 male or female for Pájaro; female extras as desired.

Playing Time: 20 minutes.

Costumes: South American peasant costumes. Boys wear sombreros and serapes. Girls wear blouses, full skirts, and shawls. Burro costume for Pájaro.

Setting: Scene 1: A hillside. Upstage are some shrubs, trees, and boulders. Scene 2: Señor Luis' patio. There is a comfortable lawn chair, with a large umbrella or tree over it.

Properties: Figurines, piece of sugar cane, paper or scraps of cloth, market baskets, fan, glass, measuring tape.

Lighting: No special effects.

Sound: South American folk dance recording. If desired, some girls may sing and clap, while others dance.

THE BAKER'S NEIGHBOR

Characters: 4 male; 6 female; as many extras as desired for Villagers.

Playing Time: 15 minutes.

Costumes: Traditional Peruvian village folk costume. Manuel wears an apron and white hat, and Judge wears a long robe.

Properties: Tray of small pies, cash box containing coins, notebook and pencil, small cakes, tarts, cookies, etc., gavel, coin purse containing ten coins, trays.

Setting: A street in an old town in Peru. At right is the bakery, outdoor counter with shelves in front of it. Near bakery are a table and stool. At left is the patio of Pablo's house, with chairs and a bench. At rear is a flowering tree with circular bench around trunk.

Lighting: No special effects.

DAME FORTUNE AND DON MONEY

Characters: 9 male; 5 female; Villagers may be male or female.

Playing Time: 30 minutes.

Costumes: Dame Fortune wears a long skirt and mantilla. Don José and Don Money wear suits, ruffled shirts, and boots. Manuel wears ragged clothes in the first scene, everyday Spanish clothes in the second. Others wear everyday Spanish clothes, suggested by shawls and sombreros.

Properties: Document, newspaper, knitting, play money (dollar bill, gold piece, sack of coins, ten ten-dollar bills), broom, cloth sacks, fan, big ledger, long loaf of bread, pies, cakes, and bolts of cloth.

Setting: The town square of a Spanish village. Stores of baker and clothier at back. A bench is down right, a seat, judge's desk and chair down left. Exits right and left. Tubs of plants and flowers placed here and there.

Lighting: No special effects.

A TEST FOR WILLIAM TELL

Characters: 13 male; 3 females; extras.

Playing Time: 20 minutes.

Costumes: The costumes should be quite simple. The Brothers of Rütli wear a small red feather in their caps. All characters may wear traditional Swiss costumes. The soldiers may carry spears, and William Tell a crossbow.

Properties: A crossbow, boxes, imitation spears, candy, fruit, various foods for lunch stall, wooden soldiers, three coins, cloth bag, a few pieces of cloth to be used as skins, toys for the toy stall, rope for binding. Tell, two arrows, apple with arrow through it.

Setting: Large cardboard boxes may be used for stands on which wares are displayed, according to what each is to sell. A tall flagpole stands in the rear, on top of which is a fancy hat decorated with a plume. There are four stands altogether, two at the center rear of the stage, the lunch stand with a bench in front of it downstage left, and a small one downstage right, for the Woodcarver. Large and small cardboard and wooden boxes may be used for the stands.

Lighting: No special effects.

THE COVETOUS COUNCILMAN

Characters: 2 male; 2 female.

Playing Time: 15 minutes.

Costumes: Carpenter and his Wife wear peasant costumes. Mayor's Wife and Councilman wear appropriate costumes, and Mayor's Wife wears a hat with a veil.

Properties: Purse full of coins, small jewel box.

Setting: Councilman's house is up right, suggested by a low wall or screen. Inside are a table, two chairs, and a safe. The street is downstage, and there is a bench down left. Exits are right and left, to the village, and up right, to the other rooms in the house.

Lighting: Lights on room go up and down, as indicated in text.

BIG PAUL BUNYAN

Characters: 8 male; 2 female; 4 or more male and female extras for Townspeople, Farmers, and Lumberjacks; 3 boys for Babe (non-speaking parts). Paul Bunyan should be played by a tall, husky boy with padded shoulders and platform boots to make him appear even larger. In contrast, everyone else in the cast should be of small or average stature and build. Babe, as a baby ox in Scene 2, is played by a very small child; as a full-grown ox in Scene 3, Babe should be played by two large boys wearing a blue ox costume.

Playing Time: 20 minutes.

Costumes: Paul has a black beard, and wears red plaid shirt with padded shoulders, jeans, and platform boots. He wears baby bonnet in Scene 1. Babe, as a baby ox, is played by one actor in blue sleepers, with an attached hood and pointed ears. As a full-grown ox, Babe is played by two boys wearing a blue ox costume with mask and horns. Traveling Lady and Mrs. Bunyan wear long, old-fashioned dresses. Bum and Bill wear striped shirts, leotards, hoods, and wings on their backs. John Shears, Little Meery and Farmers wear overalls, and Lumberjacks wear plaid shirts, jeans, boots, and knit caps. Some may have beards.

Properties: Toy ax, wooden whistle, carpetbag, wheelbarrow with rope attached, blanket, kettle with papier-mâché rim attached (for Babe to bite), cut-out of tree, snowshoes, ladle, 3 or 4 fruit crates, two pails, parsnips.

Setting: Tree stump stands at left. *Scene 1:* Maine. Backdrop of rocky sea coast. *Scene 2:* Cave at left, with a cut-out opening standing at center. Inside cave campfire burns, and large cooking kettle hangs over fire. At right, blue snowbank cut-outs stand in field. *Scene 3:* Barnyard of Paul's farm. A corral-type fence runs across back of stage and halfway down each side. Up right is a large cut-out of a beehive with sliding panel in front. Gate is in fence opposite beehive. Babe's stable is at left.

Lighting: Blue floodlight in Scene 2.

Sound: Offstage voices (members of cast or crew), as indicated in text.

THE INDIAN BOY WITHOUT A NAME

Characters: 5 male; 3 female.

Playing Time: 15 minutes.

Costumes: Indian costumes. The Chief wears a long feathered headdress. The Brave has a colorful blanket thrown over one shoulder.

Properties: Long rope, large rock.

Setting: Clearing in front of an Indian village. Two or three logs are on ground at center, and two or three wigwams are visible up left. The backdrop is a wooded scene. There are exits at right and left.

Lighting: No special effects.

A GIFT FROM JOHNNY APPLESEED

Characters: 4 male; 5 female; 1 male voice (offstage).

Playing Time: 20 minutes.

Costumes: Women and girls wear long, old-fashioned calico dresses, and Mitty and Rose change into long nightgowns at end of play. The men and the boy wear overalls and brightly colored shirts. Instead of a shirt, Johnny wears a burlap sack, with holes cut for his head and arms, over his overalls. He wears an old tin cooking pot for a hat, and he carries a burlap sack containing hair ribbons and Bible.

Properties: Several small paper packets tied with string, large handkerchief, tray with pitcher of cider and glasses.

Setting: The yard of the Trevis farmhouse in Licking Creek, Ohio. The porch of the house, with a few steps leading to ground level, is at left. A door leads from the porch into the house, and four chairs are on the porch. At right is a lilac bush, and an exit is at right.

Lighting: No special effects.

BARON BARNABY'S BOX

Characters: 5 male; 4 female.

Playing Time: 15 minutes.

Costumes: Old-fashioned dress. The women wear long, brightly-colored skirts and peasant blouses. Bess Goodwin wears a cape with a hood over her skirt and blouse. The men wear dark-colored knee breeches and white shirts open at the throat. Will Goodwin wears a cape over his clothes. Baron Barnaby is dressed in elaborate knee breeches and wears a vest over his shirt. He also wears a hat.

Properties: Two pennies, a wooden box filled with gold-paper coins (the box is tied shut), knife.

Setting: A village green. If a backdrop is used, it could show a few small houses and some distant hills. A row of small bushes stands in front of backdrop. At right and left are cardboard trees. A log lies at an angle upstage left.

Lighting: No special effects.